Augustus Lindley

Ti-ping tien-kwoh

The history of the Ti-ping revolution

Augustus Lindley

Ti-ping tien-kwoh
The history of the Ti-ping revolution

ISBN/EAN: 9783337238285

Printed in Europe, USA, Canada, Australia, Japan

Cover: Foto ©ninafisch / pixelio.de

More available books at **www.hansebooks.com**

太平天囯

TI-PING TIEN-KWOH;

THE HISTORY OF

THE TI-PING REVOLUTION,

INCLUDING

A Narrative of the Author's Personal Adventures.

BY

 LIN-LE.

FORMERLY HONORARY OFFICER, CHUNG-WANG'S GUARDS; SPECIAL AGENT OF THE TI-PING GENERAL-IN-CHIEF; AND LATE COMMANDER OF THE "LOYAL AND FAITHFUL AUXILIARY LEGION."

VOLUME II.

LONDON:
DAY & SON (LIMITED), LITHOGRAPHERS & PUBLISHERS,
GATE STREET, LINCOLN'S INN FIELDS.
1866.

COX AND WYMAN,
ORIENTAL, CLASSICAL, AND GENERAL PRINTERS,
GREAT QUEEN STREET, LONDON, W.C.

CONTENTS OF VOL. II.

CHAPTER XV.

Chinese Custom-houses.—Attempts at Extortion.—An Adventure.—Ruse de Guerre.—Its Success.—Peace Negotiations.—Their abrupt Termination.—The Plot thickens.—A Companion in Misfortune.—Negotiations renewed.—Their Failure.—Hostilities.—Critical Position.—Danger increases.—Attempted Rescue.—The Mud Fort Mandarin.—His Fate.—The Civil Mandarin.—Rescued at last.—The *Williamette* 425

CHAPTER XVI.

Hang-chow.—Ti-pings approach Shanghae.—Their Reception.—The *Casus Belli*.—The First Blow.—Filibuster Ward.—Admiral Hope's Exploits.—Captures Hsiun-tang.—The Consequences.—Hope's Policy condemned.—The real *Casus Belli*.—Defence of Shanghae justified.—Inducements to oppose the Ti-pings.—Official Reports.—Mr. Consul Meadows.—Recognition of the Ti-pings.—The *Shanghae Times*.—Mr. John's Report.—Edict of Religious Toleration.—Report continued.—Mr. Muirhead's Report 445

CHAPTER XVII.

On Board the *Williamette*.—Blockade running.—Arrival at Nankin.—Solemn Thanksgiving.—Domestic Arrangements.—Phillip's Wife.—The Wooing.—The Dowry.—The Wedding.—Trade established.—Imperialist Corruption.—Preparations for leaving.—An Elopement.—The Journey.—The Surprise.—The Repulse.—Arrival at Hang-chow.—Its capture.—The Particulars.—Cum ho.—The Chung-wang.—His mistaken Policy 475

CHAPTER XVIII.

Earl Russell's Despatch.—Its Effect.—"Taking the Offensive."—Official Reports.—General Staveley.—Attacks the Ti-pings.—General Ward.—Hope and Ward repulsed.—Che-poo attacked.—Its Capture.— Loot Regulations.—Kah-ding attacked.—Its Capture. — Ti-ping Loss. — Newspaper Comments. — Tsing-poo besieged.—Inside the City.—Ti-ping Losses.—Na-jaor besieged.—Cho-lin besieged.—Ti-ping Bravery.—Cho-lin captured.—The Chung-wang.— Kah-ding evacuated.—Consul Harvey's Despatch.—Despatch reviewed.— Ning-po threatened.—Captain Dew at Ning-po.—His Despatch.—The Reply.—Captain Dew's Rejoinder.—Preparation to attack Ning-po.—Captain Dew's Inconsistency.—His Ultimatum.—Official Despatches.—Ning-po attacked.—Ning-po evacuated.—Newspaper Reports ... 498

CHAPTER XIX.

A Double Wedding.—Its Celebration.—The Honeymoon.—Its Interruption. — Warlike Preparations. — Soong-kong invested. — General Ching's Despatch. — Tsing-poo recaptured. — Ti-ping Severity excused.—England's Responsibility.—Curious Chinese Custom.—The Chung-wang's Policy.—His Explanation.—The Ti-ping Court of Justice.—How conducted.—Opium Smoking.—Its Effects.—Evidence thereof.—Forbidden by Ti-ping Law.—Opium Trade 539

CHAPTER XX.

Ti-ping Disasters.—The Vampyre Fleet.—Important Letters.—Mr. Roberts's Case. — Mr. Consul Harvey. — Letters continued. — Misrepresentations. — Anti-Ti-ping Meeting. — The Sherrard Osborne Theory.—The Fleet Afloat.—The "Lay" and "Osborne" Agreement.—The Fleet repudiated.—Pecuniary Loss to England.—A Resumé.—General Burgevine.—Lieutenant Ridge.—Act of Piracy.—A Tartar caught.—Exit of the Anglo-Chinese Flotilla.—General Ward's Proceedings.—Progress of the War.—Death of General Ward.—Captain Dew's Disgrace.—How caused.—His Mode of Proceeding.—Its Effect upon Trade.—Operations before Kah-ding.—"Wong-e-poo."—General Burgevine dismissed from his Command.—Major Gordon takes Command.—Sir F. Bruce's Despatches.—His Objections to Gordon's Appointment.—Also to General Brown's Interference 562

CONTENTS.

CHAPTER XXI.

Personal Narrative continued.—Mr. Lobschied.—His Reception at Nankin.—Press Publications.—Mr. Lobschied leaves Nankin.—Operations before Tait-san.—The Assault.—Act of Bravery.—Rout of the Imperialists.—Gordon's Art of War.—Tait-san reinvested.—Siege of Tait-san.—Its Capture.—Manchoo Atrocities.—Treatment of Ti-ping Prisoners.—Mr. Sillar's Statement.—Quin-san captured.—Gordon's Report.—Gordon reinforced.—The Chung-wang recalled.—Critical Position of the Ti-pings.—The Chung-wang's Retreat.—Difficulties encountered.—Reinforcements.—The Scene of Battle.—Its Horrors.—Arrival at Nankin.—The Chung-wang's Army.—General Attack.—The Repulse.—The Surprise.—The Night Attack.—The Flight and Pursuit.—Death of Marie ... 598

CHAPTER XXII.

On the Wong-poo River.—Ningpo Sam.—The *China*.—Her Passengers.—The Ta-hoo Lake.—Its Scenery.—The Canals of Central China.—General Burgevine.—Soo-chow.—Deserters.—Burgevine suspected.—The Americo-Ti-ping Legions.—Burgevine's Policy.—Colonel Morton.—The Mo-wang.—Arrival of the Chung-wang.—The Loyal and Faithful Auxiliary Legion.—How regulated.—Affair at Wo-kong.—Recruiting.—Plan of Operations.—A *coup de main*.—Arrangement.—Interruptions.—Postponed ... 632

CHAPTER XXIII.

Renewed Attempt.—Its Success.—Narrow Escape.—British Interference.—How explained.—Its Failure.—The *coup de main* succeeds.—Groundless Alarm.—Route to Soo-chow.—Its Difficulties.—Generous Conduct.—Arrival at Wu-see.—Prize-Money.—Treachery.—Preparations for an Attack.—Manœuvring.—The Attack.—Warm Reception.—The Enemy repulsed.—The Result.—Wu-see evacuated.—Return to Shanghae.—Last Interview with the Chung-wang.—Manchoo Cruelty.—Result of British Interference.—Evidence thereof.—Newspaper Extracts.—Further Extracts.—England's Policy.—Its Consequences.—Its Inconsistency.—Her Policy in Japan.—Religious Character of the Ti-pings.—Their Christianity 658

CHAPTER XXIV.

Kar-sing-foo.—Christmas in Ti-pingdom.—Works of Art.—Dangerous Companions.—Narrow Escape.—Retribution.—Adieu to Ti-pingdom.—Mr. White's Case.—The Neutrality Ordnance.—Order of July 9th, 1864.—Intended Return to England.—Particulars of the Siege of Soo-chow.—Strength of the Garrison.—The Assault described.—The Nar-wang's Treachery.—Its Cause.—Major Gordon's Report.—The *Friend of China*.—Gordon's Report continued.—Narrative by an Eye-Witness. The Soo-chow Tragedy.—Major Gordon.—His Conduct.—Gordon's Letter to Sir F. Bruce.—Analysis thereof.—Newspaper Extract.—Gordon's "Reasons" refuted.—Analysis Continued.—Gordon's "Personal Considerations."—His Motives explained.—Newspaper Extracts.—Sir F. Bruce's Despatch.—Its Analysis.—Falsity of Gordon's Statements.—How proved.—Extract from the *Times*.—Deductions 694

CHAPTER XXV.

Operations Resumed.—Attack on Kin-tang—The Battle of the Brickbats.—Ti-ping Success.—Active Operations.—Manœuvring.—Hang-chow invested.—Fall of Kar-sing-foo.—Gordon's Proceedings.—Chang-chow-foo.—Narrative of the Siege.—Fall of Chang-chow.—The Foo-wang.—Manchoo Cruelty.—Debate on the Chinese War.—Lord Palmerston's Policy.—Its Errors.—Mr. Cobden's Policy.—Mr. Layard.—His Inaccuracy.—Extracts from the Debate.—Result of Lord Palmerston's Policy.—Fall of Nankin.—"Imperialist" Account.—The Chung-wang's Capture.—Other Reports.—Digest of Events.—The Chung-wang.—His Position in Nankin.—Events in the City.—Newspaper Reports.—Doubts as to the Chung-wang's Fate.—The Retreat from Nankin.—Newspaper Extracts.—The Shi-wang's Proclamations.—Lee Shai-Yin's Address ... 713

CHAPTER XXVI.

Results of British Policy.—Its Effect on Trade.—The Inspectorate System.—The Tien-tsin Treaty.—Present State of China.—Rebellion in the Ascendant.—Proposed Remedy.—The Mandarin Policy.—The Extradition Treaty.—The Mo-wang's Case.—Its Injustice.—Its Illegality.—Burgevine's Case.—Our Treatment by the Manchoos.—Russia's Policy in China.—Contrasted with that of England.—Russian Progress.—Statistics.—Acquisition

CHAPTER XXVI—(Continued).

of Territory by Russia.—Her Approach to British India.—Russia's Advantages.—Her Future Policy.—"Peking and the Pekingese."—Its Author's Misstatements.—Misquotations.—Examples thereof.—"Chinese Miscellanies."—Ti-ping Movements.—The Future of the Ti-pings Doubtful.—Latest Movements.—The Kan-wang.—Nieu-fie Victories.—Future Prospects.—Finis ... 788

APPENDIX A.

Decalogue	823
The Trimetrical Classic	827
Ode for Youth	832

APPENDIX B.

Export of Tea and Silk from China ...	838

APPENDIX C.

Memorandum of Ti-pings killed during the British Hostilities against them	840

LIST OF ILLUSTRATIONS.

CHROMOLITHOGRAPHS.

Brought to Bay at the Mud Fort	to face page	440
A view in the inner apartments of the Chung-wang's Palace—Miss Cum-ho and her two governesses..	,,	479
Interior of an Opium Smoking Saloon	,,	559
Imperialist attack on the River Forts at Nankin	,,	629
View from the Summit of a Mountain in the Western Tung-shan district on the Northern shore of the Ta-hoo Lake, province of Keang-su ...	,,	637
Naval Engagement and Capture of Imperialist Gunboats at Wu-see	,,	675
Map, Present state of China	,,	794

WOOD ENGRAVINGS.

The Mud Fort Mandarin	page	140
A View on the Journey to Soo-chow of a portion of country near the City of Wu-se lately desolated by Imperialists.	,,	657

CHAPTER XV.

Chinese Custom-houses.—Attempts at Extortion.—An Adventure.—Ruse de Guerre.—Its Success.—Peace Negotiations.—Their abrupt Termination.—The Plot thickens.—A Companion in Misfortune.—Negotiations renewed.—Their Failure.—Hostilities.—Critical Position.—Danger increases.—Attempted Rescue.—The Mud Fort Mandarin.—His Fate.—The Civil Mandarin.—Rescued at last.—The *Williamette*.

THE route by which I returned to the broad expanse of "The Son of the Sea" was, if possible, more infested with so-called custom-houses than that by which I had reached Sin-ya-meu. Every two or three *le* some wretched little bamboo-hut would make its appearance round a bend of the creek, with a long pole and a dirty white rag on the end, containing huge red and black characters, setting forth the official nature of the den. Then sundry opium-stupified, villanous-looking mandarin soldiers would rush from their pipes and gambling, catch up their rusty gingalls and long bamboo spears, and loudly call upon my Chinese captain to "soong mow" (let go the anchor), and pay a duty, or squeeze, into their dirty hands. Upon such occasions P—— and myself would be compelled to get on deck with our fowling-pieces, and drive the harpies off, when they would sullenly retire to their opium and cards, muttering curses upon the *Yang-quitzo*, and trusting for better prey next time.

This sort of thing may seem very like smuggling, but it was really far from being so. The duty upon my cargo was levied at Sin-ya-meu, previous to embarkation, and was paid to the customs officials; and from that town to

Kwa-chow the fifteen to twenty custom stations were every one of them charging in excess of the legal duty. Chinese have frequently informed me that the governor of a province lets these squeeze stations out to subordinate mandarins, who then farm them at discretion. The mandarins have *braves* enough to enforce their extortion; all passing junks are stopped until payment is made; and if the aggrieved people should complain, their petition goes before the governor who thrives upon the system. This is one of the many forms of Government corruption throughout China; to many the extortionate *régime* of the Manchoo must appear incredible, though it is a fact pretty widely known, even by those who are striving to uphold it.

Although during our dinner a couple of *braves* succeeded in getting on board from a squeeze barrier, which led to their tailor becoming acquainted with our shoemaker during the process of summary ejectment, myself and friend reached the great river without further mishap than an occasional exposure to the ill-aimed gingall balls of some of the baffled plunderers. At Kwa-chow, the entrance to the Grand Canal on the northern bank of the Yang-tze, we passed through a large fleet of Imperialist *Ti-mungs*, row-gunboats, and a big customs station; the officials evidently wished to squeeze us, but, I imagine, the vicinity of the treaty port Chin-kiang deterred them. Shooting into the yellow waters once more, a fair wind carried us bravely over the strong adverse current.

Winter having now set in, and the north-east monsoon commenced to blow up the whole length of the Yang-tze-kiang, thus enabling vessels to sail against the tide very well, we made considerable progress on our way to Nankin before anchoring for the night. At daylight we were under-weigh and sailing merrily along, myself and P—— keeping regular watch and watch—a course rendered necessary by the danger apprehended from the numerous Imperialist gunboats and fortified positions in the neighbourhood of Ti-pingdom.

Till noon we carried the breeze, but the day becoming hot the wind fell, and so we were obliged to run close to the bank, land our crew with a mast-head rope, and slowly track up stream. Just before dusk a light breeze sprang up again, and getting the men on board we made sail to round the "Mud Fort," situated on the extreme point of the elbow formed by the river at Nin-gan-shan. This fort, upon my passage down from Nankin, was held by the Ti-pings; upon this occasion, to my sorrow, I found the Imperialists in possession; its former garrison having betrayed their charge, and sold it to the enemy.

We had barely rounded the point, making almost imperceptible headway, when the wind failed, and the tide, at this point very strong, began to carry us down stream. At this moment, five gunboats put off from the shore and pulled directly towards my vessel. Upon nearing her, they hailed and ordered us to anchor. I now perceived that they were Imperialists, and, from the flags displayed, that they were of the squeezing, or custom-house genus. P—— and myself immediately armed ourselves, and ordered the *lowder* to hold on his course. The tide was fast drifting our vessel in to the bank, right under the guns of the fort, and directly the men in the gunboats perceived this, and saw only two foreigners on board, and that we mounted no guns, they surrounded us and opened fire.

Our position was now decidedly unpleasant. We had drifted to within a few yards of the bank, the guns in the fort were manned, several more boats were putting off, filled with men, and the shore was lined with soldiers, placing their gingalls and matchlocks, and making ready to fire upon us. I well knew the unscrupulous nature of these plundering Imperialists, that our duty-receipts from Sin-ya-men would not be regarded, and that they would most willingly cut our throats for the value of five dollars. With the force opposed to us, and no chance to make even a running fight, it would have been madness to have returned the gunboats' fire with our rifles and fowling-pieces; we therefore took it like lambs, and devoutly wished for a sudden puff of wind to waft us from our perilous situation. Not a breath, not the very gentlest zephyr came, excepting the wind caused by the shots that were flying all around, some of which, better aimed than the majority, were smashing into our poor old vessel, quite regardless of the consequences. The men on shore and the guns of the fort now opened fire; while the gunboats, finding we did not seem inclined to fight, appeared to be getting ready to board.

At this critical juncture a fortunate thought came into my head. I had my old uniform on board, and the idea formed was to use it to personate a foreign official, and so endeavour to save our heads by giving the imps an impression as to our importance, and a dread of the consequences in case of molestation. Jumping into the cabin, I quickly reappeared with uniform and sword. My friend P—— also had some uniform he had worn in the Indian navy, so following my example, he dived into his chest and then rushed on deck gorgeous in brass-bound array. We were not a moment too soon with our device, for P—— had just got on deck when one of our Chinese sailors was knocked over by a shot, and the rest, taking fright, suddenly let go the anchor, and casting adrift the halyards of the sails, let them go by the run; after which they ran and hid themselves down below. I now hailed the nearest gunboat to come alongside, telling my interpreter to state that we were foreign officers, or mandarins, that we were followed by a man-of-war, and that we were sailing about in the junk for pleasure.

When the *braves* observed our uniform, and were invited to board, their hitherto noisy courage seemed to vanish, and they would not come. However, they ceased blazing their confounded guns at us, much to our satisfaction, for although Chinese shot, with a tremendous whistling by reason of its uneven casting, makes much more noise than effect, and generally performs parabolas of singular eccentricity, *some* strike the object, especially when fired at a distance of only a few yards.

Our vessel was anchored within 30 feet of the bank, we were therefore completely in the power of the imps, who mustered at least 600 strong at that place. I again hailed the gunboat containing the man I imagined to be the principal officer, to come alongside, and let me know what they wanted; but the fellows seemed suspicious of some trap, and continued to lay on their oars, all talking and yelling together at the top of their individual voices, each trying to make himself heard above every one else, in approved Chinese style.

At last the mandarin in charge of the fort made his appearance on the bank, and after his attendants had shouted themselves hoarse, trying to make his orders heard above the din, the jabbering in the gunboats ceased, and the one I had hailed proceeded very slowly and cautiously to come alongside. She contained a couple of officers, whom we got on board, showing them our revolvers, and politely informing them, in pure mandarin dialect, that if their men followed them, we should be under the painful necessity of depositing a bullet or two in their yellow carcasses. This had the desired effect, and the fierce-looking *braves* were ordered to remain in their boats, much to their disgust, for their fingers, no doubt, were itching to handle the valuables of the "foreign devils."

When we had seated the two officials in our cabin, an old number of the *Hong-Kong Daily Press* was produced as our commission in the service of His Majesty the Emperor of America, while a Manchester rug, of the stars and stripes pattern, was displayed as our banner. To all this the Chinamen "chin-chin'd" with the greatest respect, but they still referred to the fact that our vessel carried a cargo, and declared their chief's intention to squeeze a certain amount of dollars out of us. The duty-passes we had received at Sin-ya-meu were then produced and the officers took them ashore to their superior. They soon returned, and requested me to accompany them to an interview with the head mandarin, stating that he was determined to have some money, which he chose to term "duty," for conscience' sake, I suppose, although it was certainly a most unmitigated attempt at robbery.

Before landing, I made my conductors fully understand that, upon the slightest attempt at treachery I should shoot *them*. I took my revolver with me, and proceeded to the mandarin's presence, leaving P—— on board, to preserve our effects from the plundering propensities of the villanous mob into whose clutches we had fallen.

My interpreter A-ling, our cook, Ganymede, and the *lowder*, accompanied me on shore as a retinue of state, somewhat suitable for the dignity of representatives of our supposed emperor. The *Daily Press* was carefully carried in an old glove-box by A-ling, while the cook was deputed to carry our cards (in the shape of two labels from bottles of Bass's pale ale) to the mandarin; the boy carried presents, consisting of a couple of empty eau-de-cologne bottles, an *Illustrated London News*, and a box of damaged percussion caps; the *lowder* brought up the rear with our (Manchester) banner streaming from a tall bamboo. Although the soldiers crowded round us they did not offer much annoyance; probably they were awed by our stately bearing and procession. We reached the Yamun (official residence), the pale-ale labels were duly delivered, and then we were ushered into the august presence of the cruel, sensual, dirty-looking mandarin, my followers imposingly taking up their position behind me. The *Daily Press* was displayed by A-ling, who, clever fellow that he was, to show its importance, bent on one knee while presenting it.

The display of the newspaper, the presents, and our uniform, seemed to make a decided impression upon the mandarin, and we should probably have been set free but for a *mal-à-propos* circumstance that now occurred. I had sent the *lowder* down to the beach, loudly ordering him to look out for the imaginary man-of-war steamer I gave our captors to understand was following me, and to report her approach whenever she came in sight. This had considerably subdued the mandarin's arrogant tone, for he was evidently not well up in foreign affairs, and provincial Chinese have a wonderful idea of the "fiery dragon ships" of the "foreign devils." He was just commencing a set apology for the mistake committed by his "ignorant *braves*," when in came our pig-headed *lowder*, or rather, into the apartment he was kicked by a couple of soldiers holding on to his tail, and most unmercifully thumping, kicking, and bumping him along from behind.

It appeared that the wretch had got into conversation with some of the *braves* on the beach; they had asked him where our vessel was bound, and he naïvely told them to Nankin, *the rebel capital!* They instantly seized and dragged him before the mandarin. The long-winded apology came to an abrupt termination, and the orator turned his attention to examining the miserable *lowder* as to our connection with the Ti-pings. The stupid captain of our sailors now declared that he only *thought* we were going to touch at Nankin *en route*, to make some demand upon the rebels with regard to the seizure of some foreign-owned junks. The mandarin at last ordered him to be taken into the fort, and dismissed us with an intimation that we must wait till the next morning to have a duty levied upon our cargo, and to adjust the whole affair.

The *Daily Press* was ceremoniously returned to the glove-box, the stars and stripes were rolled up, and we were escorted back to our vessel by the two officers. Upon getting on board, I found P—— all safe, and promenading the deck like a moving armory, with a rifle over his shoulder, a revolver and brace of horse-pistols in his belt, and a sword by his side; while four gunboats were chained fast alongside, the crews of which, with their heads poked over our bulwarks, were viciously eyeing the Cerberus who prevented them from indulging their natural propensities.

I found our vessel thoroughly secured by the imps, who had taken every precaution to guard against a *coup-de-main* upon our part. Chains were rove through each ring-bolt on our deck and fastened on board the gunboats, two of them being lashed on each side, full of armed men watchful and on the alert. A long chain was passed from our bows to the shore, and a number of matchlock men were encamped for the night right abreast. Even had it been possible to strike a sudden blow and release ourselves, as it was a dead calm they could have pulled after our vessel and blown her to pieces, if they could not have mustered courage to board us. There was nothing to do but to trust to the chapter of accidents for a way out of the difficulty, and, if necessary, to sell our lives dearly.

It was a matter of considerable surprise to myself and friend that the Imperialists did not behave worse to us, for they neither yelled "Yang-quitzo," threw stones, nor seemed so anxious to attack us as the generality of Manchoo troops would have been. This we afterwards accounted for by the fact that they had formerly been Ti-pings, and had not quite forgotten that they had once been worshippers of Yesu, and had looked upon strangers from the West as "foreign brethren." Their chief had turned traitor to the Ti-ping cause, and betrayed the "Mud Fort" to the Manchoo, in consideration of retaining his own followers, receiving *carte blanche* to squeeze all passing vessels, and being decorated with a mandarin button and feathers. They were a savage-looking set, these "Mud Fort" banditti, yet, bad as they seemed to be, were much better than the usual style of Imperialists; had we fallen into the hands of the latter we should have been treated with much indignity and violence, if not killed.

We were aroused in the middle of the night by a

tremendous hubbub, and, running on deck, found it was the Mud Fort people engaged seizing another unfortunate European vessel. Getting into our boat, I went on board, and found she was a *Ningpo Boat*, from Shanghae to Hankow, and that the only foreigner on board was an Englishman, to whom she belonged. The soldiers hauled his vessel close in to the bank a little below mine, and there made her fast in a similar manner. After talking over our mutual misfortune, we agreed that in the morning I should land, and endeavour to obtain our release; failing which, I was to get on board his craft with P——; we were then to man her guns (she carried two six-pounders), try to force both vessels adrift, and make a fight to escape.

After a not particularly refreshing sleep, I again went on board the *Ningpo Boat*, to settle our plan for the last time, preparatory to putting it into execution. Upon returning to my own vessel, we carefully loaded all our firearms; I then concealed my own revolver and a long bowie knife under my uniform, took A-ling and our cook with me; the one carrying the *Daily Press*, and the other two more pale-ale labels; and proceeded on shore.

The imps had at daylight cast off the chains wherewith they secured our vessel for the night; leaving, however, a couple of thick ropes fastening her to the bank by head and stern; these P—— had prepared an axe to cut in case of emergency. Our cabin was formed by a half-raised deck-house aft, on the top of this a few bags of charcoal were placed, so as to form a sort of fortlet, inside which the arms, with a good supply of ammunition, were hidden; the ropes were laid ready, fore and aft, to make sail, and the *Ningpo Boat* was hauled quite close to the bank, so as to enable me to get on board her in event of hostilities, while P—— could pull to her in our boat.

As I walked away from the bank, and observed P—— ensconce himself among the bags of charcoal, my feelings were not of the most pleasant description. However, there was no choice of conduct; so, making the best of a bad affair, I proceeded straight for the den of the bandit chief, assuming a stolid, immovable sort of Dogberry officiality, peculiarly effective with the Chinese. Upon sending in our extemporized cards, and being admitted to the mandarin's state hall (a dirty apartment in a dirty house within the dirty fort), I was kept waiting till noon for the appearance, from among his many wives and opium pipes, of the owner.

Meanwhile, a breeze had sprung up, and was gradually increasing; so that, although the delay proved rather discreditable as to my veracity about the expected man-of-war, a chance of escape was apparent. If we could not obtain our release by fair means, we might be able to get our vessels clear, make sail, and keep up a running fight.

At length, half-stupified with opium, the mandarin made his appearance, the remaining part of his senses seemingly concentrated into a dull cunning sort of ferocity. His first act was to summon quite a number of armed soldiers to his Yamun, who stationed themselves in and about the building. Our wretched *lowder* was then dragged forth, and presented a pitiable sight. He had been tortured by having his ankle joints crushed between logs of wood, and by placing smaller pieces between his fingers, which were then pressed together by several men, causing intense agony, and severely injuring the finger-bones. The torture had compelled him to divulge all he knew of our proceedings at Nankin, besides a great deal more which he did not know, but simply stated to anticipate the wish of his interrogators and another squeeze of the wooden bars, failing a satisfactory reply. He was now examined before me, and confessed that we had left Nankin, and were returning thither. The mandarin then declared that he must have 2,000 dollars, or else he would keep our vessel, and send us into the interior *as Ti-ping prisoners for execution.*

For some time I argued against either proceeding,

displaying the *Daily Press*, the duty-passes I had received at Sin-ya-meu, and endeavouring to convince the mandarin as to the serious consequences of exciting the anger of the Emperor of America by molesting either myself and friend, or the vessel seized during the night. At last, after the robber had lowered his demand to 1,000 dollars, and while the discussion was becoming very warm, a soldier brought a report to the mandarin, who instantly issued some order to an attendant officer. What the tenor of this might be I heard not, but my cook did, and it evidently alarmed him, for, exclaiming, " More bettah, go just now," he rushed out of the room and disappeared. A-ling immediately told the mandarin that he would pay his so-called custom-house authorities a sum of 500 dollars, and then, telling me not to stay any longer, left the Yamun, begging me to accompany him. Making a bow to the angered official plunderer, I leisurely walked forth, and, upon reaching the rear of the fort, quickly passed through the gate, just as he appeared in his doorway, and gave a sharp command to some of the attendant soldiers.

Before I had turned the angle of the fort and got within sight of my vessel, half-a-dozen officers with drawn swords came running after me, calling upon me to stop and return with them to the mandarin. A-ling, stating he would run to the pseudo custom-house, a few hundred yards distant, and bring with him the officials to receive the squeeze of 500 dollars that we had offered to pay, advised me to get on board as quickly as possible.

I waited until my pursuers had reached to within a a few feet, and then, suddenly drawing my revolver, jumped towards them with it levelled to the foremost. They instantly turned tail and rushed back to the fort, while I ran down towards the beach, holding the revolver above my head to signalize P—— and the master of the *Ningpo Boat* that danger was at hand.

Ere I had reached more than half-way between the

fort and the river, a tremendous outcry arose from the former, accompanied by the blowing of horns, the beating of gongs, and the noise of the Chinese drum. As I ran, I turned my head in the direction of the uproar and observed the mandarin, followed by a crowd of soldiery, rushing after me. Before I could gain the beach, to my surprise, I saw the *Ningpo Boat* land some of her crew, cast off from the bank, and proceed to track up stream, thus breaking the terms of the agreement upon which I had landed, and cutting off my only chance of escape from the pursuing imps. When I did reach the river bank, every boat had been warned away by the shouts and gestures of the mob behind me, and the *Ningpo Boat* was some distance off the shore, and fast tracking away.

For a moment I gazed around, and found myself completely at the mercy of my pursuers; in front ran the swift current of the Yang-tze—behind came the savage yelling crowd of armed men.

I had just time to notice P—— on the top of our cabin deck, rifle in hand, and hear him shout, while pointing to the receding *Ningpo Boat:* "The coward has made terms with them and deserted us—jump up in the boat on the beach; I will open fire on the imps if they attempt to seize you, and I'll get you off with our boat if I have a chance; the imps have stolen the oars, and our crew have stowed themselves away below!"

The boat my friend referred to was a large one hauled up slantingly on the beach, one side touching the water of the river, and the other turned towards my pursuers. She stood some four or five feet off the ground; and climbing into her highest part, which was about level with the edge of the river bank before it shelved down into the narrow beach upon which she rested, I turned to face the enemy, after answering P——, and telling him not to fire until I gave him the signal to do so by commencing with my revolver.

By this time the horde of banditti were within a few yards, armed in every fashion, and neither dressed as Imperialists nor Ti-pings, but clad in a multitude of colours. The whole garrison of the place seemed to be turned out, and with much gesticulation, and the usual terrifying yelling of Chinese soldiery, rushed along after their leader. Bamboo spears, gingalls, matchlocks, scythe-headed halberts, broad three-pronged pikes, and large knives, were waving all about, and beyond all I distinguished *the apparatus to which a prisoner is fastened when barbarously put to death by "cutting into a thousand pieces."*

On they came, with their fiendish cry, "Tah! tah!" until right down to the edge of the bank, where they formed a tumultuous crowd, brandishing their arms, some opening their clothing and beating their breasts in defiance, but all arrested by my levelled revolver. The mandarin used his utmost exertions to urge them on, but one and all seemed disinclined to become the *first* to draw a bullet from the six-shooter. The men who carried firearms in the front rank I sharply observed, and instantly took aim at any one who attempted to handle his weapon offensively. Meanwhile, upon either side, the men above and below my position got down on the beach, and gradually advanced towards me, while those not immediately covered by my revolver began firing their matchlocks.

I now, for the first time in my life, *really* experienced fear. In front and flank I saw nothing but a dense array of savage men thirsting to slay me; beyond them were a corps of executioners erecting their triangles in anticipation of having the cruel delight to slowly cut me into pieces; and when I gave a sidelong glance behind (I dared not attempt more, or the imps would have taken advantage and rushed forward) the deep and turbid river met my view.

For a moment or two, during which the enemy might have cut down or seized me without my being able to pull trigger, I became quite nerveless, while an icy chill came over my heart and made me feel both sick and helpless. Fortunately, I soon rallied. It is unpleasant to mention such a fear as I had felt, much less to dwell upon it. Just as the events of my life seemed striving together in a confused jumble for the first place in a rapid mental panorama, my presence of mind returned. I felt a sudden glow of enthusiasm for the Ti-ping cause, through which I had got into the danger, and a determination to die, if death it was to be, in a manner worthy of an Englishman before a mob of Chinese.

To this day I am surprised at the sudden revulsion of feeling I experienced. One moment I was powerless, trembling, and terrified; the next, I was keenly alive to every incident in the scene, collectedly watching each movement of my individual assailants, and confidently prepared for any result.

At this moment P—— hailed me: "I have covered the mandarin; shall I shoot him? I can cut her" (our vessel) "adrift. Jump into the river and swim off, I will pick you up."

A little sooner I should have done this, but now I was prepared to take advantage of the slightest chance of escape; the soldiers were still to be kept back by my revolver; a peaceful termination of the difficulty *might* be obtained; but if I were to take to the water I should almost certainly be shot like a dog in it, even if I were not swept away and drowned by the swift current.

I shouted to P——, "Hold on yet. I think I can keep them at bay myself." He had hitherto been supporting me with his rifle levelled at the mandarin. "Try and take me off with the boat."

Although our vessel was lying some little distance above me and some 30 feet from the bank, and although the oars had been stolen from our boat, P—— was a thorough sailor, and I trusted that he would find some means of dropping it down to me with a line. I did not think so without reason, for he replied to me:—

"Look out, then! I am going to put down my rifle. I will drop the boat down to you; stand by to jump into her!"

Meanwhile, the imps seemed striving to work themselves into a frenzy, when they would probably rush forward, receive my few shots, and overpower me by numbers. The mandarin kept running to his men and trying to make them point their matchlocks at me, but directly any one attempted to do so, my revolver barrel stared him full in the face.

At last, I had the satisfaction to hear P——'s voice again :—

"Stand by, old fellow," he hailed; "I am just going to shove the boat off from our inshore quarter with a line fast to her."

Without daring to turn my head for a moment, I replied : "All right, shove her off, and hail me directly she comes close enough for a jump."

The suspense of the next minute or two was very great, then I heard my friend shout: "Now, jump now if you can; I am covering the imps with my rifle."

I gave a half glance over my shoulder, but, alas! the boat was too distant. The rope had tautened too soon, and she had been swept into a parallel line with our vessel, without reaching within twenty feet of my position. Hauling her alongside, P—— and As-sam, our boy, got into her, and shoving well off with a boat-hook, drifted down, endeavouring to grapple the boat I stood in. Again she fell short, and was swept out by the tide, amid a storm of bullets splashing all around her, from the men behind, from whose fire I was sheltered by the front rank, but who were easily able to shoot at the boat, and who managed to wound As-sam in the arm.

P——, finding that without oars it was impossible to reach me with the boat, reluctantly returned on board to his former position behind the bags of charcoal, and there resumed his rifle. Just at the same time the mandarin, finding his soldiers afraid to break the ominous pause by attacking me and exposing their leaders to certain death, began to set the example himself. He was certainly a far braver man than any of his followers, for dashing forward, sword in hand, he got to the lowest end of the boat and clambered into her, although I could easily have shot him at any instant. Steadying himself, he began to advance towards me, along the gunnel of the boat, which was open amidships and had a decked bow and stern.

THE MUD FORT MANDARIN.

It was now a most trying moment for me. The mandarin was already within nine or ten feet, and another second would bring him to striking distance. His life was entirely in my power; I could have shot him; but the *first* blow was only wanted to break the treacherous calm, and cause the immediate slaughter of myself. I felt that my last chance of life depended upon delay; two more seconds would decide it one way or the other. The suspense of that smallest passage of time was indescribable; many days of intense excitement and danger seemed crowded into one moment. The short though terrible hesitation in my mind, whether to shoot the mandarin, fire the remaining barrels of the revolver at his followers, and then jump into the river and swim off, or to delay another second, so as to lose not the merest chance of

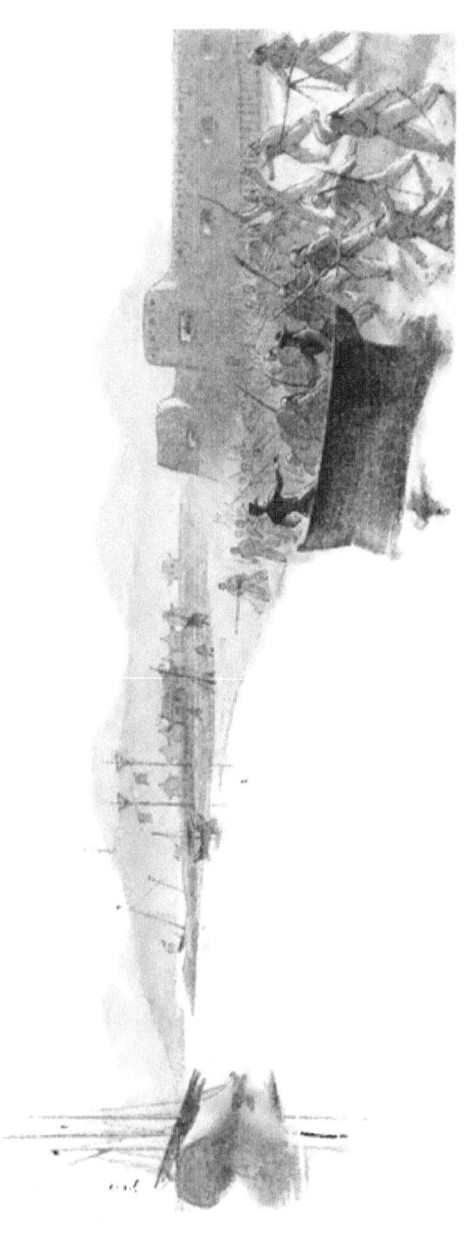

saving my life, seemed to occupy an age of anxious and momentous thought. At this crisis P—— spoke to me again :

"Shoot the mandarin," he shouted. "I will cut the vessel adrift, sheer her in, and try to pick you up. If I cannot quite reach you, take to the water; you can easily get on board, and I'll protect you by opening fire on the imps."

Rapidly glancing, as I fully expected for the last time, upon the clear blue sky above, the bright sun shining upon and making the earth *so* beautiful and attractive, and vividly recalling a far distant home and a loved mother for my latest earthly thought, I took steady aim at the mandarin's heart and pulled the trigger, shouting to P——, "Cut her adrift, and be sharp about it!"

I naturally expected to hear the report of my pistol, and to see the mandarin fall, while the soldiers would rush forward to avenge his death. Although I am certain I gave the trigger a sufficient pull, the hammer never fell and the mandarin at the moment, when another step towards me would have brought his uplifted sword upon my head, suddenly lost his balance and fell from the narrow gunnel of the boat to the beach. I instantly hailed P—— to "hold on," and he returned to his former position to watch the progress of events.

When the mandarin rolled on the beach, several of his officers seized him and dragged him up the bank, regardless of the struggles he made to return and attack me. Fortunately A-ling arrived upon the scene at this moment, and going to the mandarin, told him that he would go on board and bring the money required. While the leader of the robbers was being brought to his fort, A-ling was taken on board our vessel, after receiving my assent to procure the dollars from P——. Meanwhile the soldiers remained in the same position around myself, while I endeavoured to show them my indifference by producing a cigar and lighting it.

After A-ling had paid the money into the coffers of the banditti, he came to me with two inferior officers, and getting the soldiers to fall back, induced me to descend from my position of vantage, believing all danger was over. Although at first they seemed quiet enough and retired from the boat, I had no sooner reached some little distance from it than they crowded round me. Suddenly, and before I could use my revolver, I was seized from behind by many hands, and while every incident of my life rushed with supernatural rapidity and minuteness of detail through my mind, I was forced upon my knees, when one of the soldiers raised a long and heavy sword to behead me.

The steel flashed as it was raised above me, and commending myself to God, I shivered while for a fearful moment awaiting the blow. Again, however, I was saved from the very jaws of death. My would-be executioner was thrust aside, and I believe that I fainted for a second or two. I then found myself surrounded by a strange mandarin and his attendants, A-ling, my cook, and a few of the more kindly disposed among the robber band. A-ling informed me that the stranger was a "civil" mandarin who had just arrived from a neighbouring city; that he had happened to notice my gold band, and had opportunely rushed forward and rescued me. Thus for the first time the uniform had done me good.

At first, after expressing my gratitude, I felt perfectly safe under the protection of the fresh arrival, for I knew that the rank and authority of a civil mandarin was far superior to that of a military one like the commandant of the Mud Fort. However, upon the people around me moving a little away, I saw three soldiers on the ground, two dead and one severely wounded; for it appeared that P——, upon observing my seizure, had opened fire on the crowd. It was now evening and the dusk was fast approaching, and it was evident that not a moment should be lost in getting away from the place. Two men had been killed, and their chief would undoubtedly endeavour to avenge their death. After giving the watch I wore as a memento to the mandarin who had so kindly saved me, and being supplied with a boat by him, I at last got safely on board with A-ling and the cook.

My friend P—— had barely griped me by the hand and congratulated me upon my escape, when we were startled by the blowing of the war-horns on shore, and the clang of gongs. While we were hard at work getting our vessel underweigh, the soldiers came rushing down to the beach again, waving their flags and arms about, planting their gingalls, and swearing vengeance for the death of their comrades. In a few minutes they opened a heavy fire upon us, while a number of them ran along the bank in the direction of a creek where their gunboats were moored.

The wind had fallen comparatively light, and we would not have been able to escape from the smaller vessels of the enemy, when, to our great joy, a steamer rounded the bend of the river below, and came into full view. At this moment the gunboats were just shoving off from the shore, but directly they observed the steamship only a few miles distant they pulled up the creek again, while the men along the beach ceased firing and ran into the fort, doubtless believing that the approaching vessel was the man-of-war I had told them about.

When the steamer had arrived pretty near, I signalized her, and saw that she was one of the American river boats. To my horror, when close alongside she hoisted the Imperialist flag, and I then knew her to be the *Williamette*, a vessel belonging to the Manchoo Government. When right abeam she stopped and sent a boat to my vessel. Fortunately she was manned with an American crew, and in consideration of the sum of 300 dollars, her captain, whose name, singularly enough, happened to be Friend, Imperialist though he was, agreed to tow my vessel up to the Nankin forts.

Before dark we had the satisfaction to bid adieu to the Mud Fort, as we ploughed up the fast rolling yellow waters astern of the *Williamette*. To our sorrow, however, we were just able to discern on the beach the execution of our *lowder*, who was dragged down and decapitated there before our eyes, while we were powerless to save the poor fellow.

CHAPTER XVI.

Hang-chow.—Ti-pings approach Shanghae.—Their Reception.—The *Casus Belli*.—The First Blow.—Fillibuster Ward.—Admiral Hope's Exploits.—Captures Hsiun-tang.—The Consequences.—Hope's Policy condemned.—The real *Casus Belli*.—Defence of Shanghae justified.—Inducements to oppose the Ti-pings.—Official Reports.—Mr. Consul Meadows.—Recognition of the Ti-pings.—The *Shanghae Times*.—Mr. John's Report.—Edict of Religious Toleration.—Report continued.—Mr. Muirhead's Report.

HANG-CHOW, the provincial capital, was carried by assault upon the 29th of December. The Chinese part of the garrison, unable to endure the horrors of the close siege, after everything in the shape of food had been consumed, and even human flesh exposed for sale in the market-place, opened the gates of the outer city and surrendered to the Ti-pings. The Manchoo troops defended themselves to the last, neither giving nor accepting quarter, and when the walls of the inner city were carried by the victorious insurgents, the Tartar general, Luy, and a number of his men, sprang a mine and blew themselves up with their citadel.

The capture of this important city and of the treaty-port Ningpo having placed the Ti-pings in possession of the whole Che-kiang province, with the exception of Shanghae and a few miles around it, they resolved, upon the termination of the year, as previously agreed to, to follow up the enemy to this last stronghold.

Although, before his unsuccessful trip to Nankin, Admiral Hope had seemed willing to treat with the Ti-pings, when he returned to Shanghae, after finding it impossible to again deceive them, his conduct underwent a marked change, as evinced by the eager way in which he sought the opportunity to indulge his warlike propensities. This opportunity was soon afforded him.

Immediately upon the expiration of the year, Chung-wang, the Ti-ping Commander-in-Chief, moved an army towards Shanghae. No attack was made upon the city, but this force gradually occupied every position in the neighbourhood, till at length not an Imperialist soldier remained beyond gunshot range of its walls. The Ti-pings again manifested their extraordinary friendliness towards foreigners by not attacking the city, and with similar forbearance and moderation to that evinced upon their approach in 1860, endeavouring to open peaceable negotiation with the foreign authorities. The leaders of the different *corps d'armée* sent in the usual nobly worded proclamations, relating to the oppression of the Manchoo and their own mission to free and Christianize China; the success hitherto vouchsafed to their cause by the "Heavenly Father"; the earnest desire to enter into friendly relations with the "foreign brethren"; their wish to continue all present trade and to open the whole country up, &c.

Now, at this time the political position of England with regard to the rebellion was as follows. By the written guarantee of Sir George Bonham, by that of Admiral Hope, by that from the British representative at Ningpo, and by many other acts, her national honour was pledged to maintain a strict neutrality. The last orders to her officials in China were, as already quoted:—

"Her Majesty's Government desire to maintain . . . neutrality between the two contending parties;" save British subjects from punishment, "but otherwise you should abstain from all interference in the civil war."

[Dated, Foreign Office, August 8, 1861.]

This was the standing order; the only later direction being Lord Russell's suggestion: "But it *might* be expedient to defend the treaty ports *if* the Chinese would consent not to use those ports for purposes of aggression."

The way the British Consul, Admiral, and General, at Shanghae, abstained from all interference was by converting that city into the grand rendezvous of the Imperialist forces, and then helping them to defend the Chinese city by garrisoning it with British troops; by conveying Manchoo soldiery down the Yang-tze to Shanghae in English steamers; by supplying the Imperialists with artillery, &c., while strictly prohibiting any trade in the same articles with the other of the two "contending parties"; and by attacking the Ti-pings when they found that the Ti-pings would not attack them. That useful triumvirate —the sailor, the soldier, and the diplomatist—placed the following construction upon Lord Russell's ambiguous *ifs* and *ands*. "It *might* be expedient," they singularly understood to mean, it was expedient; and "*if* the Chinese, &c.," they converted into assisting and joining the Chinese "*to use* those ports for purposes of aggression." Consequently, in direct violation of their public orders, but in conformity with the conduct I have just stated, they issued the following reply to the friendly overtures of the Ti-ping chiefs:—

"Whereas we, the Commanders of the French and British forces now occupying the city and environs of Shanghae, have received letters from Lion and Ho, persons styling themselves . . . , informing us that said Lion and Ho are intending to attack and occupy Shanghae; and whereas we have no means of communicating with the said Lion and Ho, or any of their people:—Therefore, this is to give notice to whomsoever it may concern, that Shanghae city and its environs, Woo-sung included, are at present in the possession of the troops under our respective commands, and that if Lion or Ho, or any persons claiming fraternity with them, attempt to attack these places they will do so at their peril."

Even this was insufficient to effect the desired object, namely, to drive the Ti-pings to defiance, and force them to acts of retaliation. When, therefore, it became apparent that, notwithstanding all the aid afforded to the Imperialists, they could not succeed, and that eventually Shanghae must be given up to the revolutionists, or become annexed to France or England, the British Government threw off the mask, and prepared for open hostilities.

Consul Medhurst, in a despatch to Admiral Hope, dated "Shanghae, February 19, 1862," states the grounds upon which the good faith and honour of England were to be openly violated.

"Granting, of course, that a *strictly neutral policy* is at present the only correct one, and that whatever is done in the protection of this city and settlement must be undertaken with *careful regard* to that important axiom, it follows, I think, that there are two points to be considered as bearing materially on the present crisis. The first is, what resources we have in the way of supplies for the city and settlement; and the second, how far the present action of the Taepings so endangers those supplies as to make it necessary for us to interfere with them in our own defence."

The falsity of this shallow pretence for war becomes at once apparent. In the first place, it was simply necessary to allow the Chinese city to revert peaceably to the Ti-pings, when the inhabitants as well as they would have had ample supplies. In the second place, the vast river and sea communication of Shanghae was entirely open (excepting the Wong-poo branch), while a fleet of some two hundred European steamers and ships and several thousand large native junks crowded the anchorage, and could easily have furnished a line of communication for any amount of supplies. Evidence is abundant to prove what a mere pretence this *casus belli* was, but two reasons will be sufficient justification for so designating it. First. If the Ti-pings, by surrounding Shanghae, endangered its supplies, when they came with the most friendly feeling for Europeans, they would certainly, if driven to become enemies and to use the justifiable retaliation of enemies, have it in their power to utterly destroy those supplies by devastating the whole neighbouring country; therefore, in all human probability, an attack upon them would render imminent the very crisis to avoid which it was thought justifiable to violate a nation's pledges. Secondly. The following extract from Admiral Hope's despatch shows that he conceived that Consul Medhurst had not made a sufficient case. Upon the 21st of February, 1862, the Admiral struck the first blow. Upon the evening of the same day, in his despatch to the Admiralty, he gave this reason for his open violation of his own and his Government's faith :—

"These proceedings" (movements of the Ti-pings) "have been conducted at a distance much too close to be consistent with the *respect due to the occupation of the town* by French and English forces, or to leave its supplies of provisions and native trade *unaffected.*"

Is it to be supposed that any city could be captured or placed in a state of siege without native trade or supplies being affected, or is it to be argued that the Ti-pings should be crushed in consequence of the natural results of their patriotic struggle?

The presence of the Ti-pings only "*affected*" the trade and supplies it seems; when, had they been so disposed, they might have stopped the entire, excepting what could have been obtained by water.

The only thing that affected the supplies of Shanghae so far as Europeans and citizens were concerned, was the increase in the price, which was quickly raised by the provision-dealers, who are always ready to seize the smallest opportunity to make a little extra profit. Probably Admiral Hope saw this, and its damaging bearing upon his alleged *casus belli;* at all events, he thought fit to add another, though equally flimsy.

"The tract of country enclosed within the line BC, which this village, with others in their" (Ti-pings) "possession, entirely commanded, is that from which the supplies of Shanghae are chiefly drawn, and its proximity to the Woo-sung river was such as to afford the PROSPECT of the Chinese traffic, also material to the support of the town, being seriously impeded, if not altogether stopped; and for these reasons I considered the case to be one calling for my interference."

On these pretences war was made upon the Ti-pings. It will be noticed that nothing material has ever been *proved* against the revolutionists, or urged as an established fact, sufficient to justify hostilities, or even a remonstrance. The British officials in China and the Government at home attempt to justify their course of action by mere conjecture as to what they might do, but never do we find a plain or straightforward accusation made against them for anything they *had done*.

Admiral Hope, in his attack upon the Ti-pings, associated himself with one Ward, an American filibuster, in the service of the Manchoos. Previous to this, and to the Admiral's unsuccessful attempt to juggle the Ti-ping authorities into another agreement not to approach Shanghae, the said Ward was persecuted and reviled very fiercely; but no sooner did the Admiral and his colleagues think it necessary to pull in the same boat, than the Yankee filibuster became their pattern and ally. The whilom *rowdie* companion of *ci-devant* General Walker, of Nicaraguan memory, mercenary leader of a band of Anglo-Saxon freebooters in Manchoo pay, and sometime fugitive from English marines sent to weed his ruffians of their countrymen, suddenly became the friend and ally of the British and French Admirals, Generals, and Consuls. The surprise of Ward can only have been equalled by his gratification upon finding his very questionable presence, and still more doubtful pursuits, patronized and imitated. No doubt, at first, he felt considerably elated and vastly astonished at the idea of filibustering having become an honourable and recognised profession; but soon, poor fellow! a black, or rather green, shadow came across his uncertain dream of happiness and respectability—he became jealous of his friend Admiral Hope, whose talent and zeal for making war without declaring it or being authorized so to do by any Government, he found surpassed even his own.

The village of Kao-kiau was garrisoned by a few

hundred Ti-pings, and several thousand country people, who had just joined them, the whole mostly armed with bamboo spears. The force led against them by Admiral Hope comprised 350 British seamen with a six-pound rocket-tube, and about 600 disciplined Chinese, under Ward, besides which, the French Admiral, Protêt, commanded 160 Frenchmen, with a couple of field-pieces. Of course, the ill-armed Ti-pings were unable to resist the European artillery and arms of precision, and were consequently driven from the village, with a loss of more than 100 men killed. This gallant exploit was safely performed by the Anglo-Franco contingent, who, completely out of range of the few wretched matchlocks of the Ti-pings, shot them down at their ease with rifles and artillery, with a loss to themselves of *only one* French sailor, killed by a stray shot.

This murderous and cowardly deed was quickly followed up by the gallant Admiral, who seemed unable to refrain from action, especially when it could be indulged with comparative safety.

We have already noticed that one excuse Admiral Hope made to justify his broken faith was the probability that the Ti-pings might injure the supply of provisions. Strange to say, the Admiral did the very things he pretended the rebels might have done. At the capture of Kao-kiau all hands dispersed to loot whatever the Ti-pings had left behind; and, quoting from the official report of the affair, "Large stores of grain were discovered about the place, *the greater part of which were burned.*"

After the exploit of Kao-kiau, Admiral Hope, with a small party of seamen and Ward's filibusters, went roving about the country for a week in search of some one to fight. His warlike spirit was gratified at a place named Hsiau-tang, in the vicinity of Ming-hong (nearly twenty miles away from Shanghae), a fortified village occupied by several thousand Ti-pings. Directly he found this place in the way, an order was sent to Shanghae for reinforcements to attack it with. These having arrived, upon the 1st of March, 1862, the whole force, consisting of 750 of Ward's disciplined Chinese, 350 British sailors and marines, and 35 artillerymen, with four light howitzers, one field-piece, and some rocket-tubes, and 200 French, with two brass howitzers, moved forward to the attack. Again, as at Kao-kiau, the murderous work was executed, and the poorly-armed Ti-pings slaughtered with impunity. For more than an hour they bravely held their mud and brick entrenchments, but at last the crushing fire from the foreign artillery, and the sharp practice of the Enfield rifles, carried the day. After standing to their few gingalls to the last, amid a storm of shot and shell (all fresh from British arsenals and paid for by British tax-payers), they were driven from the lines of defence and through the village with immense slaughter. As they retreated from the rear, the shell from the irresistible foreign artillery "were thrown rapidly amongst them, committing fearful havoc. Numbers also fell under the fire from the rifles of the French and English sailors." In the centre of the village the rear guard made a gallant effort to repulse their pursuers, but they could not withstand the deadly volleys and bayonet charge of the marines; and although their bravest men fell in heaps, while many hand-to-hand conflicts took place, they were ultimately driven out with a loss of 1,000 killed and 300 taken prisoners, the English and French *not losing a single man*. A great massacre of the unfortunate non-combatants was perpetrated by the Imperialist soldiery, who actually forced very many of the living wounded into the flames of the burning village. In one official report it is stated:—

"The streets and houses presented an awful spectacle, the bodies in some places lying in heaps; and the plain beyond the village was strewed with those shot down in the flight."

Another report states:—

"The rebels ran from the fortifications and came to a stand in the main street. . . . Upon this, the field-piece from the *Impérieuse*, in charge of Lieutenants Stuart and Richardson, swept them down with grape and canister shot; after this their retreat became a flight, when the party of marines and Chinese detached to cut them off did considerable execution, some 900 or 1,000 having been killed and wounded."

The same report concludes with this sentence:—

"After all was over, *the village was set on fire,** and the foreign troops embarked for Shanghae."

What will those who falsely accuse the Ti-pings of devastating and destroying say to this? They have declared that the Christian patriots' "success in any locality is attended with its total destruction," &c.; but it appears that these totally destroyed places were reserved for Admiral Hope to burn down.

As this history progresses we shall find that although the Admiral made the damaging effect which the presence of the Ti-pings *might* have upon supplies one element of his *casus belli*, *he* actually destroyed the very supply of grain which he dreaded might be affected by the rebels!

There is a more serious matter to be deplored with regard to the numerous raids commenced and followed up by Admiral Hope, namely, the cruel slaughter of so many hundreds of his fellow-men. We have reviewed the unmeaning pretences invented by the Admiral and his coadjutors, but even should it be admitted they were valid, is it possible any Englishman can be found willing to justify the massacre of thousands of human beings, because, although ever friendly to them, they affected the mercenary speculations of a few merchants? If, in order to maintain the immediate profit of their mercantile adventurers, any Englishman can attempt to justify or palliate these summary proceedings against the unfortunate Ti-pings,

---

* *Vide* p. 6, "Further Papers relating to the Rebellion in China, 1862."

then I say, far better should that unholy traffic perish, cursed as it is by the slaughter of thousands of our fellow-creatures, whose blood has cried aloud to Heaven for vengeance upon their assailants.

Even the pretence that the revolutionists would have injured our "commercial interests" falls to the ground by the testimony of the very merchants themselves, for the leading mercantile house in China, Messrs. Jardine, Matheson, & Co., in their business circular, dated "Kong-kong, 27th February, 1862," referring to Admiral Hope's first massacre of Ti-pings, state:—

"During the interval that has elapsed since the date of our last circular there is no particular change to notice in the state of matters about Shanghae; but the policy the Allied Commanders are adopting will, it is feared, lead to disastrous consequences. . . . *Our interests call for a strict neutrality*, but so far from this course being pursued, our last advices report a combined expedition of English and French marines and sailors in conjunction with a force of Imperialists, commanded in person by their respective Admirals, against a body of some 6,000 rebels, which of course they defeated with great slaughter. . . . The whole country being in the hands of the Taepings, should this *suicidal* policy be persisted in, must in the end materially interfere with, if not ruin, all trade, as it cannot do otherwise than exasperate a foe by no means to be despised."

What stronger condemnation of the policy pursued against the Ti-pings can be made, coming, as it does, from the principal representative of the very class whose interests it was pretended necessary to protect? That this opinion of Messrs. Jardine, Matheson, & Co. was correct has at the present time been pretty well ascertained, for it did "in the end materially interfere with" trade, as the fall off of silk *after* the expulsion of the Ti-pings from the producing district proves. This, however, was not occasioned, as that firm expected, by the exasperation of "a foe by no means to be despised," for the Ti-pings (with a Christian humanity far excelling that possessed by their *civilized* enemies) never retaliated either upon the trade (entirely in their power) or the lives

of Europeans. The decrease of silk was caused entirely
by the ruthless nature of the war carried by British
officers and Imperialists into the once happy districts of
Ti-ping-tien-kwo. The Ti-ping patriots were either fools
or saints, for by their mad forbearance they suffered
themselves to be driven from their former possessions
with incalculable loss of life; whereas, a system of retaliation on their part would have endangered the entire trade
of the district, and consequently have forced the enemy
to relinquish hostilities which so conclusively endangered
the prospect of our " commercial interests."

As the first mercantile house in China considered the
policy of the British Government "suicidal," we may
safely pronounce the affected anxiety for commercial
interests a shallow pretext. What then remains to constitute the real *casus belli*, unless it be "the temporary
interest arising out of the indemnities," and the great
revenue arising out of the vile opium traffic, the loss of
which would have caused a deficit of many millions in
the British treasury?

The seeming inconsistency of allowing the Ti-pings to
take Ningpo and yet defending Shanghae against them is
easily explained. At the capture of the former city no
British force was present, and although the seven days'
grace so cunningly obtained from the Ti-ping leaders
seems to have been employed in endeavouring to raise a
sufficient force to oppose their entrance, this, in the
shape of H.M.S. *Scout* and several other vessels, arrived
too late, having reached Ningpo some hours after its fall.
Then, as Admiral Hope very wisely observed with regard
to the policy of exasperating the Ti-pings, "We cannot
afford to quarrel with them, as at any moment they *might*
stop the whole trade of Shanghae." Their wonderful
forbearance had not at that time become assured; directly
it was, hostilities were commenced. Before taking up the
sword for good, it became necessary to try the temper of
the Ti-pings. This Admiral Hope effectually did by his

arrogance at Nankin; his "every obstruction" plan at Ningpo; his raids around Shanghae; an example followed by the British and French authorities by their unwarrantable notifications and defence of Shanghae Chinese city.

There are, in fact, very many reasons by which the defence of Shanghae may be accounted for; but five of the most important will sufficiently illustrate the principle of the whole.

Firstly. The British Government and its officials interfered in order to save the indemnity and opium trade, which the capture of Shanghae by the Ti-pings would have annihilated, and they were strongly supported by the opium merchants, who, by this vile traffic, made their largest profits.

Secondly. A large number of the Shanghae foreign landholders approved of the defence of the city, because it enabled them to obtain fresh lots at their own prices from the Chinese proprietors. From the "minutes of a meeting of land-renters, held at the British Consulate, Shanghae, January 12, 1862," it appears that during a council of war with the Manchoo authorities of the Chinese city (all in accordance with the pledges of "strict neutrality," of course?)—

"The Taoutae undertook to do this also" (open a road to facilitate military operations) "*by obliging the Chinese renters interested to part with their land to the foreign applicants whose names stood recorded first for purchase.*"

Thirdly. A certain proportion of traders having taken advantage of the Ti-ping movement to circulate unfounded reports as to its brigandage, in order to monopolize the trade by frightening outsiders away, naturally sanctioned the defence of Shanghae, as the capture of the city would have exposed the trick by proving the Ti-pings were not brigands and robbers.

Fourthly. Many land and house speculators opposed

the success of the insurgents for this reason. The foreign settlements in the vicinity of the Chinese city had become crowded with fugitives awaiting the firm establishment of Ti-ping jurisdiction in the interior; by numerous lawless Chinamen attracted by the shadow of foreign protection and the opportunity of establishing gambling hells and bagnios, *ad libitum*; and by the manifold parasites and hangers-on of the Imperial authority in its last stronghold. Therefore, while this state of affairs lasted, the land speculators made prodigious wealth by the letting of their poperty to the natives at almost fabulous rents, but the capture of the city by the Ti-pings would have altered all this. The vile manner in which many colossal fortunes have thus been obtained is lost sight of in England by the glitter of the ingots.

Fifthly. A large proportion of partners in mercantile houses *upon the spot*, expected to make their fortunes and retire to their home in three years; but the occupation of Shanghae by the Ti-pings, and the natural effect of the civil war, must have interfered with the import trade and injured their immediate profits.

Upon these grounds British faith was dishonoured and a murderous war waged against the unfortunate Ti-pings. Admiral Hope continued the work of destruction with his artillery and rifles from a safe distance, until his recall to England. Violation of good faith, misrepresentation, and partial aggression, became superseded by regular hostilities, carried on without any previous declaration of war, or even statement of grievance. What would such manner of warfare be denominated in Europe?

Having reviewed the policy of the British Government, and the conduct of its officials in China, it may be well to notice a few reports upon the Ti-ping rebellion, well worthy of attention, even though ignored by the British Ministry. These testimonies prove that the Ti-pings have not been decimated because they were misunderstood by the British Government, but that the latter were as well acquainted with their Christianity, friendliness, political object, superiority to the Manchoos, and generally improved character, as the writer of this history, or the authors of the statements he quotes. Therefore, when the evil policy of those who authorized the unnecessary and unjustifiable hostilities upon the part of England shall become more generally admitted, they cannot palliate their wickedness by pleading ignorance of the true merits of the people. It is difficult to speak of this British interference in any but the most forcible and unmeasured terms of condemnation. Not a solitary excuse can be truly made for it; and when the selfishness of that policy is thoroughly appreciated (which is rapidly becoming the case), the atrocities committed by its sanction, and their consequences, will be looked back upon with grief and sadness by every loyal Englishman.

The first and most important of the above-mentioned reports was made by Mr. Consul Meadows to Lord Russell. Mr. Meadows was better acquainted with the Ti-pings than any other English official in existence. He was the most talented in China, the most honourable and disinterested; therefore, it may be that his statements were not regarded, and that his presence at Shanghae became an inconvenience. This difficulty was soon surmounted by the removal of Mr. Meadows from Shanghae to New-chwang, very soon after his truthful and independent exposition of the Ti-ping rebellion, and by naming as his successor a Consul who was more pliable.

The following despatch of Mr. Meadows bears date "February 19, 1861," and is worthy of most attentive perusal:—

"CONSUL MEADOWS TO LORD J. RUSSELL.—(Received April 12.)

"Shanghae, February 19, 1861.

"British trade and British-India trade with this country, and the revenues derived from the one and the other, are among the most important of British interests abroad. A necessary condition to the flourishing of these is the existence of order—of security to life and property—in this country; and the existence of this order and security, again, requires the existence of a strong national government. These propositions are so well established that I merely state them.

"But the hitherto existing Imperial Government, that of the Manchoo or Ta-tsing dynasty, which was already becoming weak from internal causes, has received its death-blows from the external action, first of British arms alone, and now of British and French combined. No strong national government now exists anywhere; and in large, and to us very important, portions of the country, anarchy and insecurity prevail.

"It becomes, therefore, of the utmost importance to look around us for some other power in the nation to take its place. If we find any such other power, we must not only not attack it, but must earnestly desire its speedy growth. An adherence, not less wise than just, to the principle of non-intervention, together with the due observance of the treaties with the Ta-tsing Government, should prevent our taking direct positive steps to aid that growth; but assuredly it would be a most suicidal course, as regards those large interests to which I have pointed, first to achieve the destruction of the government we find existing, and then to proceed to prevent any other from coming into existence.

"Now we have such another power in the Taepings, and such another government in the government which they have established at Nanking.

"It has been, and by many is still, denied that the Taepings have any regular government, or can be considered a political power.

"For one moment I will grant this, but only in order to point out that after maintaining themselves for eleven years in arms in China, and for eight in the centre of the empire, the Taepings are manifestly a power of some sort, and to ask—Are we, because this power does not come up to all that is expected of it, are we, therefore, gratuitously to attack it, and either greatly lessen or altogether destroy its chances of ever realizing those expectations? What else have we got to look to for the re-establishment of a government having power to preserve order?

"But I entirely deny that the Taepings have no regular government, and have no claim to be considered a political power.

"Ten years ago, almost immediately after they rose in arms, they threw off the characteristics of local insurgents, and proclaimed themselves the irreconcilable enemies of the Ta-tsing dynasty. From that time to this they have never left us in doubt of their object. It has always been the great one of making themselves the heads of the first state in Asia, and the governors of the largest people in the world. So much has been established, not only by their own published manifestoes, but by the official documents of their enemies.

"As to their manner of pursuing that object, whether it is such as befits a power assuming to be political, it would too much prolong even this letter to meet in detail all the objections of those foreigners who declaim against them.

"Speaking generally, these objections may be classed under two heads. First, those which are based on the application to this region and its peoples, of arguments drawn from the state of society and modes of political action of Western Europe, in defiance of the fact that these arguments are wholly inapplicable to a state of civilization and a polity so different; and secondly, those which are applied in entire disregard of the parallel transactions in Western Europe itself, a disregard of obvious analogies, which can only be the result of great ignorance or of wilful prejudice.

"Among the former, are nearly all the objections to their military discipline, tactics, and strategy, and to their administrative forms, whether of a civil or a military nature.

"Among the latter, are objections such as that they do not fix themselves in the places they take; that they take them and then leave them again, &c.

"The obvious rejoinder, drawn from the history of Western Europe is, how often, during the great rebellion in England, were important cities and strong places taken and evacuated or retaken? Did that prove that the English noblemen and gentlemen who first headed that rebellion were unfit to establish a government? Did it prove that Cromwell was neither a general nor an administrator? And when, ten years ago, the Italians left Milan to be reoccupied by its former oppressors, after these had been once expelled, and also allowed the foreign dynasties to reinstate themselves in their principalities, did that prove that the Italian party which aimed at expelling all these foreigners was not a political power?

"A stock argument against the Taepings was drawn from their destruction of the suburbs of the cities they occupied. This, however, was finally silenced when, on the approach of the Taepings to Shanghae a few months ago, the British and French garrison in that city fired all its suburbs, not excepting the densely peopled and commercially important suburb between the city and the river.

"Then, again, ruthless and wanton slaughter, not only of the foreign Manchoos, but of their Chinese countrymen, has been urged against the Taepings as a proof that they were a mere gang of robbers and murderers. But was there during the revolutionary struggle in France no mutual killing of the opposing parties of Frenchmen? I mention only the Reign of Terror, and the 'Noyades,' and, leaving it to your Lordship's memory to add further illustrative transactions, I ask, do such well-established historical facts prove that the revolutionary party were merely a large gang of robbers and murderers, and not a political power?

"While, however, considering it an established fact in the history of the Taepings that they, on taking Nanking, put the whole of the Manchoos to death, not sparing even the women and children; and while thinking it highly probable that they will treat in the same way any other of the military colonies of the Tartar conquerors of their country that may fall into their power, I have long ago arrived at the full conviction that the tales of the slaughter committed by them on their own countrymen are not only exaggerated, but very grossly exaggerated.

"My own experience has furnished me with an instructive example of gross exaggeration of the kind. In the beginning of September, 1853, when, not the Taepings, but the Triad Society rebels, suddenly rose and seized the city of Shanghae, I was travelling alone from Ningpo to Shanghae, *viâ* Chapoo. It was on reaching this latter place, about sixty miles from Shanghae, that I first got the news from the crew of my own river-craft, which had come there to meet me. The insurrection having broken out just as they had left, they themselves could give no particulars about it. But from other vessels, and from the local merchants and officials, I learnt that there had been a fearful slaughter in the city of Shanghae; that the streets were covered with dead bodies and blood; that the foreigners and the rebels had been fighting; and that the whole of the foreign community had retired in the shipping outside of Woo-sung. So uniform and consistent were these reports, and so certain did it appear that I should be unable to pass Shanghae out to Woo-sung, that I set about studying the Chinese maps, with a view of finding a succession of river-passages by which I might, keeping some twenty or thirty miles distant, make my way through the country inside of it, and so out into the Great River, and down that to the reported position of the foreign shipping. But before undertaking so serious a circuit I, of course, determined to approach nearer to Shanghae city. As I did so, I found the prevalent reports less and less alarming; and at length, when about twelve miles distant, ascertained the fact—one well known here at the time—that there had been no fighting whatever with the foreigners, and that, in the whole city the slaughter and bloodshed was limited to the killing of one man. Yet the current and fully-believed reports only sixty miles off were exactly like those we have so often heard of the slaughter committed by the Taepings. We know, from the experience of British troops during the last twenty years, that much loss of life usually ensues on the forcible occupation of Chinese cities from men destroying their families, and then themselves; from women, young and old, committing suicide; and from an unreasoning terror, that drives people into deep canals or rivers, in vain attempts to cross them. In these very ways several lives were nearly lost, a few months back, in the Chinese portion of this settlement before an alarm subsided which was caused by a sudden outcry that the Taepings were entering it, none being at the time within twenty miles' distance.

"From these habits of the Chinese, we may infer that there has been, in the many populous cities occupied by the Taepings in this province, much loss of life among women and children, as well as grown men—non-combatants; and the inference is supported by the fact of foreigners who having visited such cities seeing in the canals many unwounded bodies. But that the Taeping troops have directly put to death a greater proportion of their non-combatant countrymen, or have even refused quarter to the armed, to a greater extent than have done revolutionary parties in the civil wars of England and France, is, I am fully satisfied, a prejudiced repetition on the part of inimical foreigners of the interested calumnies of the Ta-tsing party.

"Some time back it had become a good conclusion that in the tracts of country occupied by the Taepings there must be greater security for life and property than in those occupied by the Ta-tsings. We knew that the Taepings had long given up that system of universal conscription on which they acted in 1853, and which then made their approach a source of peculiar terror. We knew that they depended on voluntary enrolment for the support of their fighting force, and that they were earnestly endeavouring to get the inhabitants generally of hamlets and open towns to remain at their usual occupations. This being the case, it was plain that the Taepings could preserve the public peace better than the Ta-tsings. For the bulk of the leading officials among the former were themselves not only fighting men, but about the best fighting men that they had; men who owed their position to their military qualities. To them there could, among their own party, be no open defiance. There might be nothing of that military drill and tactics which characterize European armies, but that discipline, which consists in strict obedience to orders could not fail to be there. On the other hand, the bulk of the leading Ta-tsing officials, the mandarins, were about the most inactive and timid, the most unwarlike of their party, and were, we knew, compelled to employ, as their chief fighting men, the ex-pirates of the south-eastern coast-land, who, with their followers, would not content themselves with their official pay, but would also, in defiance of the wishes of their weak employers, exact money from, or plunder outright, the peaceable populations whom they were hired to protect.

"These inferences have been amply confirmed by recent unquestionable experiences. Mr. John, an English missionary of education and intelligence, went two or three months ago from Shanghae to Soo-chow, and thence to Nanking, where he stayed for seven days. Mr. John put the question to the Taeping officials why it was that the walled cities held by them were so entirely deserted by their former populations of tradesmen, artificers, &c. He received answers to the effect that those cities had been transformed into fortresses, necessary to be held for the reconquest of the country from the Manchoos; that having been once deserted, no population was readmitted, as, under the guise of tradesmen, &c., they might gradually be filled with hostile forces; but that, as soon as their own progress advanced their frontier to other points, they themselves would be anxious to see these places repeopled by a peaceful population. In the mean time they were doing their best to protect, in the hamlets, villages, and open towns, all who choose to remain in them, in quiet submission to the Taeping rule.

"Now these explanations and statements were fully supported by the nature of the circumstances and by what Mr. John saw himself. He was altogether about a month in the country held by the Taepings. He traversed a tract of that country of about 120 miles in extent (Tsing-poo to Nanking), and travelled by night as well as by day, quite unarmed, and never molested. He found the country people quietly pursuing their usual occupations; and—a proof of the understanding between them and their Taeping rulers—saw the soldiers of the latter moving from place to place in large bodies without inspiring terror, and in parties of three or two without being assailed. At Soo-chow, both Mr. John and a well-educated and observant Chinese who accompanied him, and whom I questioned closely, saw the veritable landed gentry coming in parties to give in to the civil governor their adhesion to the Taeping dynasty.

"What, on the other hand, is the state of the country on this side of the Ta-tsing lines? Not only do the exactions of the mandarins for military objects equal any similar demands that can be made by the Taepings, but piracy and robbery are well known to be everywhere rife. During an excursion, in the end of October, of some ninety miles up the Yang-tze, I had myself full opportunity of observing the prevalence of piracy and the alarm of the country people; and reports came constantly in, on all sides, showing that the reign of lawless violence is rather increasing than diminishing.

"It is impossible to say how much of China proper the Taepings hold altogether, clear of Ta-tsing authorities or troops. But in proof of their right to be considered a political power, we have the fact that their armies are operating successfully up into Shang-tung in the North, down into Kwang-tung and Kwang-se in the South, and in Sze-chuen in the West, while nothing prevents their penetrating to the sea in the East but the presence of the foreign forces at Shanghae.

"On the religion of the Taepings little need here be said. Viewed as a piece of contemporary history, the fact of the rise and progress, in this old seat of Confucianism and Buddhism, of the Bible-spreading Taeping Christianity—be its exact character what it may—is one of the most interesting spectacles that the annals of the human race present; and if the Taepings succeed in becoming the rulers of the Chinese people, it will prove one of the most momentous. A foreign official agent, whose nature or the limited extent of whose information permits of his viewing that spectacle with indifference, must surely be adjudged mentally unfitted for the career he has chosen. But except as a deeply interesting piece of contemporary history, we have nothing to do with it. If we aid the Taepings on account of their professed creed, we propagate religion by the sword; if we attack them on account of it, we engage in a religious persecution.

"One circumstance, which does not directly interest us, remains to be considered; the disposition of the Taepings towards us. On this point, the testimony is continuous, always consistent, and remarkably satisfactory. On three or four occasions, on which foreign war-vessels have, without any previous communication, steamed right up to the river batteries of the Taeping fortified places, they have exercised the right—a right inherent in every belligerent power—of endeavouring to keep off a suspicious and, for their means of defence, formidable force. But so soon as they have been told that it was not the hired foreign steamers of their Ta-tsing enemies, but the Government vessels of neutral foreigners that were before them, they have in every instance at once ceased firing. Their superior officers have fully explained that if foreign neutral vessels would send small unarmed boats in advance, they would not be fired at; and whenever this has been done, they have kept faith. As for the white flag of truce, it is simply absurd to suppose that that purely conventional signal of the Western world can be known to the commander of every Taeping battery. But the Taepings have a complete justification for disregarding it, even if they knew it; they are fighting with an enemy who would not hesitate an instant about sending in his own foreign steamers to open fire or effect a hostile landing, with a white flag or a British ensign flying at each masthead. In no one of the numerous cases of one or more unarmed foreigners advancing to the Taeping outposts, since I first landed at Nanking in April, 1853, up till the most recent visits of Shanghae traders to Soo-chow, have they been received otherwise than peacefully; while in several cases those who have visited them as prejudiced unfriends have been converted into well-wishers by the friendliness of their reception.

"They appeared in force before Shanghae six months ago, but I have good reasons for feeling satisfied that they were deluded into so doing by certain foreigners who wished to bring on an irremediable hostility between them and us, and who had held out to them the hope that we should give up the place to them. They fired a few ineffectual shots at the Chinese troops who were mingled with the British on the walls, and who kept discharging their matchlocks. But they did not fire at all where there were only British in front of them, and not one of the foreign soldiers received a wound, though a number of the Taepings were killed by our fire. Lastly, during the half-year that has elapsed since they retired, foreigners have been received at their places, if not with the same hopeful cordiality, as peacefully and as civilly as before.

"We have a long succession of irrefragable proofs that the Taepings do earnestly desire friendly commercial relations with us. The fact is so well known that inimical foreigners have been constrained to endeavour, with a curiously blind ingenuity, to turn it against them. 'All that is mere pretence,' it has been argued; 'if they felt sure they were strong enough to attack us with advantage, they would do it.' In reply, I ask if it be so, in how far do the Taepings differ in that respect from the Russians, French, and Americans? Is the peaceful and civil reception the English get from these nations the result of pure friendliness or of policy? Would they attack us if they felt sure they could do so with advantage? What are our Channel fleets, our fortifications, and our 150,000 volunteers for?

"A few years back the aid of a small British army and naval squadron, operating along a portion of the Great River, could perhaps have enabled the Manchoos to suppress this particular Chinese rising against their rule; but now it would require a large fleet of steamers, operating throughout some 1,500 to 2,000 miles of the Great River and its larger branches, and some 20,000 troops, operating in three or four complete small armies in different parts of the tract of country mentioned above as being more or less in the occupation of Taeping forces, and which extends about 800 to 900 miles from north to south, and 1,000 to 1,100 from east to west. It would prove one of the most troublesome and costly wars that England ever engaged in; costly as regarded the direct outlay, and still more costly as regarded the consequences to our trade; for the region in question is that which, practically speaking, produces the whole of our tea and silk exports, and which consumes the larger portion of our manufactured imports; and the effect of our hostilities in it would be to overspread it with anarchy and desolation."

From this despatch it will be seen that every point upon which the British Government has based its hostilities against the Ti-pings is plainly disproved. The last paragraph may be regarded by some few bigoted pro-Imperialists as an exaggeration; but when they glance at the present state of China (1865), and see the Ti-pings still victoriously disputing the supremacy of the Manchoo, when they look upon the very diminished export of silk, and upon the rebellion rampant in every province of China, they can hardly dispute that a "large fleet of steamers" and 20,000 troops was correctly considered by Mr. Meadows necessary to suppress the revolution.

As for the justice of the British intervention, it is hardly necessary to speak any further. The belligerent character of the Ti-ping rebellion was recognised immediately after its origin, simply because the British remained neutral towards a Power carrying on war, and moreover, from the fact that English representatives sought out and made guarantees of neutrality with the Ti-ping authorities. But, while openly recognising the belligerent rights of the revolutionists, the British Government has invariably evaded a strict interpretation of its professions, and given a tacit support to the Manchoos, thereby making themselves a party to the war, and constituting themselves the allies of the latter Power.

The Ti-pings were fully entitled to equal rights with the Imperialists, whether upon the high seas, neutral waters, at the treaty ports, or elsewhere. They possessed a settled Government at Nankin, a vast territory, and *several* ports; and such being the case, should, and had the British authorities acted honourably would, have enjoyed any and every privilege given or allowed to the other party in the civil war. When the Spanish colonies cast off their allegiance to Spain, when Brazil revolted against Portugal, when Texas seceded from Mexico, when Greece rebelled against its Turkish rulers, when the Southern States of America seceded from the Union, when Santo Domingo rose against Spain, when the Neapolitans revolted against their Government, in every one of these, and countless other cases, each belligerent as a matter of right received equal privileges from neutral Powers.

Had England and other neutral Powers acted according to their own laws, they would have been bound to recognise the independence of the Ti-pings, for the utter inability of the ousted Manchoo Government to recover its authority within a reasonable time was apparent. More than this, it was universally admitted that the Tartars, if unassisted by foreigners, would be overthrown, and when such contingency became certain, England was dragged in to assist them. The excuse about danger to British lives and property from the occupation of the treaty ports by the insurgents is proved false by the capture of Shanghae in 1853, and the capture of Ningpo in

1861. The only other excuse of any moment is the "*might* injure trade" one; but is that to be considered a sufficient justification? In all the cases of rebellion just cited, England remained neutral; why then has she been made to assume to herself, in China *only*, the right to interfere in internecine strife? Why not interfere in America for the sake of trade and to prevent so-called rebels from collecting duties? As principle has nothing to do with the policy pursued in China, why should it elsewhere? Or why may it not be boasted that England feared to interfere in America, and therefore refrained; but acted differently in China, having no fear.

The *Shanghae Times*, a paper giving its general support to the Government, in its issue of March 15, 1862, thus describes the initiation of hostilities against the Ti-pings:—

"We believe that Admiral Hope is the first English officer of the present century who has adopted the unsoldierly practice of making war without having declared war. Having recognised the Taepings as a Power, according to the usage of civilized nations, he ought to have given them the alternative of retreat, submission, or butchery, before commencing the latter. This he did not. But as the Imperialists served him at Taku, he served the Taepings at Ming-hong. Honourable men condemned the conduct of the Imperial general at the Taku, and if the code of honour has not changed since then, it has been *grossly* violated in the two recent attacks on the Taepings."

We have in a former chapter noticed the false assertion of the British minister in China with regard to "all classes of observers" condemning the religion of the revolutionists, and his equally unfounded statement that the Revds. J. Edkins and Griffith John met with an "ungracious reception." The following reports by the Rev. G. John (of the London Missionary Society) will not only expose the truthlessness of Mr. Bruce, but also multiply proofs as to the Christianity of the Ti-pings, the evil policy of the British Government, and the astounding apathy of the missionary body at large.

The Rev. Griffith John, in a report to the secretary of his society, dated "Shanghae, December 6, 1860," states:—

"They" (the Ti-pings) "have created a vacuum, not only in the temples, but also in the hearts of the people, which remains to be filled. This is the missionary's work—*a work that might be done immediately, were it not for the unaccountable policy of the representatives of foreign Powers at this port.* My principal object in going has been fully realized.

"My object was to obtain from the chief an edict of religious toleration. This I have obtained. It gives full permission to missionaries of every persuasion to enter into and live in the insurgents' territory, for the purpose of carrying on missionary work. The phraseology, in some parts, is bombastic, and therefore objectionable; but the simple meaning is full toleration to all Christians, whether Protestant or Catholic. 'I see that the missionaries are sincere and faithful men, and that they do not count suffering with Christ anything; and because of this I esteem them very highly.' Such are the words of the edict. Then comes a command to the chief officers to issue orders to all the (insurgent) brethren to treat the missionaries well. I showed the edict at Su-chen, and asked the chiefs if they would help me to get a house, a chapel, &c. 'Yes,' said they, 'you come, and it will be all right.' I send you the original of this edict, written by the young prince himself, and bearing the seal of his father, and I intend to furnish you with a translation by the first opportunity. *I firmly believe that God is uprooting idolatry in the land, through the insurgents, and that He will by means of them,* in connection with the foreign missionary, plant Christianity in its stead. Let the prayers of our brethren in England be more fervent than ever in behalf of China. If these men succeed, the days of idolatry are numbered in the land. I am fully convinced that, should they succeed to establish order within the boundary of the Keang-sú province, it would be *nominally* a Christian province before the expiration of twenty years. The same observation will hold good of all the other provinces."

This is the edict referred to by Mr. John:—

"'EDICT OF RELIGIOUS TOLERATION,' BY THE CHIEF OF THE CHINESE INSURGENTS.*

"'Having received the decree of my Heavenly Father (God), of my Heavenly adopted Father (Christ), and of my Father (the Celestial King), I command all the King's officers, both civil and military, and all the

---

* "The original is written by the young prince, in the name of his father, on satin, with the vermilion pencil, and stamped with the seal of the Taeping-wang, the Celestial king."

Brethren, to be acquainted with it. The true doctrine of my Father (God), and of my adopted Father (Christ), is the religion of Heaven. The religion of Christ (Protestant religion), and the religion of the Lord of Heaven (Roman Catholic religion), are included in it. The whole world, together with my father and myself, are one family. Those who lovingly and harmoniously observe the regulations of the heavenly religion are permitted to come and visit (us). Now, from the *memorial* presented to us by my uncles, Kan, Tsan, Chung, and others, I learn that the foreign teacher G. John and his friends, esteeming the Kingdom of Heaven, and reverencing and believing in my Father (God), and my adopted Father (Christ), to whom be thanks for the bestowment upon us of authority, power, and wonders, of which those who are far and near have reverentially heard—have come for the express purpose of seeing the light, of beholding God and Christ, and of requesting permission to spread abroad the true doctrine. Seeing, however, that the present time is a time of war, and that the soldiers are scattered abroad in every direction, I am truly afraid that the missionaries might be injured by following the rabble soldiery, and that thus serious consequence might ensue. Still, I truly perceive that these (missionaries) are sincere and faithful men, and that they count it nothing to suffer with Christ; and because of this I esteem them very highly.

" ' Let the kings inform all the officers and others, that they must all act lovingly and harmoniously towards these men, and by no means engender contention and strife. Let all know, that the Father (God), my adopted Father (Christ), my father and myself, are one family; and let these men (missionaries) be treated exceedingly well.

" ' Respect this.'

" NOTE.—The Kan-wang told us that the chief is anxious that his son should feel an interest in the propagation of the Gospel, and therefore directed him to write it. . . .

" The expressions ' to the light,' and 'behold Christ and God,' are explained in the fact that Nanking is the Jerusalem of the Celestial dynasty. I asked the Kan-wang if the above edict opens up the whole of the insurgents' territory—Nanking not excepted—to missionary operations. He replied that it does. . . .

"Thus, then, the above throws open the whole of the insurgents' territory to missionary work, so far as the insurgents themselves are concerned. Here and there the phraseology is objectionable; still, this point is quite clear: they have done this not in ignorance, but with their eyes quite open to the difference which exists between them and ourselves."

In a letter, dated twelve days later than that already quoted from, Mr. John gives this reason for not going to live among the Ti-pings :—

"When I returned from Nankin I fully intended to go to live in that city, if practicable; but after much thought, *and some consultation with those who are in authority*, I have come to the conclusion that it would be premature to do so just now. . . . The river, I am told on good authority, is to be opened at once, and the ports of Han-kow and Kin-kiang are to become consular ports. Another expedition is about to go up the river, and then it will be determined what is to be done with the insurgents. They may be treated as friends, or, on the other hand, as foes. If not as friends, I AM CONVINCED THAT IT WILL BE OUR FAULT, because they cherish the kindliest feeling towards us, in spite of our conduct towards them when they visited Shanghae."

We will conclude Mr. John's reports with three short extracts; the first of which clearly shows what good might have been effected by the British missionaries had they performed their duty; the second goes far to establish the superiority of the Ti-pings over the Manchoos.

1. "The insurgents are making rapid strides, and are determined, as you will learn from my journal, to uproot idolatry in the land, *and to plant Christianity in its room*. The former they will do with a strong hand, and the latter will not be left undone, *if the Churches and missionaries are alive to their duty in reference to this great movement.*"

2. "They have doubtless gross defects; but in every respect—religious, political, social, &c.—they are centuries ahead of the Imperialists, and I cannot but wish them God speed."

The third and last extract from Mr. John's reports is taken from one dated "February 2, 1861," and fully shadows forth what England has *now* been compelled to understand, and what every sensible person fully comprehended long since. Mr. John states:—

"It is fortunate for us that the Tartars have their hands full just now, *as the value of the recent treaty rests solely on the weakness of the existing dynasty*. The Tartars hate us with an insatiable hatred, and would, in spite of the treaty, recommence warlike operations to-morrow had they the power. To break faith with the *barbarian* is not crime but virtue, according to their creed, if his humiliation and expulsion might thereby be effected. From the Manchoos we have nothing to hope, but everything to fear. They are sworn enemies to Christianity and civilization, and they have set their iron faces determinedly against both. They *can* do but little at present. The wonderful progress of the insurrection in the South, during the last year, and the repeated defeats and the complete discomfiture of the Tartar hosts in the North, have thoroughly undermined the Manchoo power. It must fall. There is no power in China to uphold it. The Kwang-si insurrection, on the other hand, must triumph, *if foreign Powers do not interfere.* The Manchoos might as well attempt to blow the sun out of the heavens as to quench this flame which their folly and tyranny have kindled. . . .

"The insurgents themselves are still determinately opposed to idolatry in all its features. At their approach the idols vanish, and the priests of Buddh and Tau disappear. The downfall of idolatry in the land seems to be bound up with their success. Never did China present such a spectacle to the Christian world. Will the Church, *unfaithful to her Head and false to herself,* as the depository of the blessings of light and life for the world, look on with indifference? Shall the four hundred millions of China remain in their state of darkness and death, *because of the worldliness and deadness* of the people of God?"

To these questions the British Government appears to have returned an affirmative answer.

A few extracts from a report of the Rev. W. Muirhead, in harmony with the testimonies of other missionaries, both as to the death-blow idolatry had received from the victorious arms of the Ti-pings, and the general knowledge of Christianity possessed by them, shall close our quoted evidence for the present. In the spring of 1861, Mr. Muirhead spent a month among the Ti-pings at Nankin, and while there was constantly engaged in preaching about the city, and thus describes his experience:—

"Going about sometimes for several hours a day, I have been abundantly encouraged by the number and attention of the audiences. It seems as if there were a foundation to go upon, from the amount of religious knowledge diffused among the people. There is a response, if not in their hearts, at least in their thoughts, to the tidings of mercy. They are made familiar at every step with the name and compassion of the Heavenly Father, *by the unprecedented practice of recording the fact over every door.* When, therefore, the same truths are announced in their hearing by a foreign missionary, *they give a ready assent, and express their cordial approval.* How different is all this from our experience in Shanghae and elsewhere! There we have a hard and strong ground to work upon; ignorance and *opposition* prevail in abundant measure. Here, on the part both of the military and civilians, there *is* knowledge, and there *is* appreciation of the truth to a certain extent, which renders the spiritual enforcement of it a more easy and pleasant duty."

These extracts must naturally make one believe that the "all classes of observers," so cunningly invented by Mr. Bruce and his ministerial friends, consist of Mr. American Baptist Missionary Holmes.

The Kan-wang, the missionaries' friend, having left the city while Mr. Muirhead was there, that event was mentioned in the following language:—

"In prospect of his going out, I had occasion some time ago to allude to his constant dependence on God, and to urge upon him the duty of earnest prayer. But in this I was anticipated by a previous request of his own, when, after describing the trials and difficulties of his situation, he said to me: '*Mr. Muirhead, pray for me!*' He has need of our prayers, and I trust his request will be attended to by many friends at home."

Poor Kan-wang! The only prayers have been those devoutly entertained by opium traders and "indemnity" interested people for the destruction of him and his confederates.

Of the Ti-ping women Mr. Muirhead states:—

"While walking along the streets, the number of females that are seen on the way is rather a novelty. They are in general well dressed, and of very respectable appearance. Many are riding on horseback, others are walking, and most of them have large feet. Not a few stop to hear our preaching, and always conduct themselves with perfect propriety. *This is new, as compared with the former course of things, and the whole reminds one partly of home life.* It will be a blessing if the revolution should tend to break up the system of female exclusion, hitherto practised."

We will conclude our extracts from Mr. Muirhead's report with the following interesting account of a conversation between himself a young Ti-ping soldier:—

"And now a word or two, with regard to the character and prospects of the movement. Those engaged in it speak not boastfully, but calmly and confidently, of its success. They acknowledge the difficulties in the way, yet believe in the Lord God that they shall be established. They do not apprehend it will be an easy thing to overcome their enemies; but fighting, as they think, under the banners of the 'Heavenly Father' and 'Heavenly Brother,' they contemplate a happy issue as a matter of course.

"As Kan-wang's followers were assembling in front of his palace, a young man came upstairs. I asked him if he was going out to join the army. He said yes. 'Was he not afraid of being wounded or killed?' 'Oh, no,' he replied, 'the Heavenly Father will befriend me.' 'Well, but suppose you should be killed, what then?' 'Why, my soul will go to heaven.' 'How can you expect to go to heaven? What merit have you to get there?' 'None, none in myself. It is entirely through the merits of the Heavenly Brother that this is to be done.' 'Who is the Heavenly Brother?' 'I am not very learned,' he said, 'and request instruction.' I then began to tell him that He was the Son of the Heavenly Father; but before I had finished the sentence, he replied correctly. 'What great work did Christ do?' I asked. The young man gave an explicit statement of the Saviour's work for sinners, of his coming into the world, suffering and dying in the room of sinful man, in order to redeem us from sin and misery. I inquired if he believed all this. 'Assuredly,' was his reply. 'When did you join the dynasty?' 'Last year.' 'Can you read?' 'No.' 'Who instructed you in these things?' 'The Tsan-wang.' 'What does he in the way of instructing his people?' 'He has daily service in his palace, and often preaches to them alike at home and when engaged in the field.' 'What book does he use?' 'He has a number belonging to the dynasty.' 'Do you know the New Testament?' 'Yes, but cannot read it.' 'Can you repeat the doxology of the Heavenly Father?' He went over it correctly. It contains in simple language the fundamental tenets of Christianity. 'Are there any special laws or commands connected with the dynasty?' 'There are the ten commandments.' 'Repeat them.' He went over a number of them, till he came to the sixth. 'Now,' I said, 'how is this command observed by you, seeing that so much cruelty and wickedness are practised by your brethren all around?' 'Oh,' he replied, 'in so far as fighting in the open field is concerned, that is all fair play and cannot be helped. It is not intended in the command.' 'No,' I remarked, 'that is not my meaning; but look at your brethren going privately into the country and robbing and killing the innocent people; what of that?' 'It is very bad, and such will only go to hell.' 'What, notwithstanding their adherence to the dynasty, and fighting under the same banners as yourself?' 'Yes, that is no matter; when the laws of Christ and the Heavenly Father are not attended to, these guilty individuals ought to die and go to hell.' 'But is not this the case with a great number of your adherents?' 'Alas! it is especially among our new recruits, whose hearts are not impressed with the true doctrine.' 'In all the public offices is care taken to instruct the soldiers and civilians connected with them?' 'Yes, every man, woman, and child of reasonable age in the capital, can repeat the doxology of the Heavenly Father.' 'And what about those in the country?' 'Those who have short hair are not yet sufficiently taught, but books are being distributed amongst them, in order that they may learn those things."

Can this be called a "blasphemous and immoral" basis of religion? If those who so designated it possessed but a tithe of the temporal practice and spiritual faith of this illiterate young Ti-ping, they would be happier men; but it must be admitted that their sentiments and actions hardly induce such a belief.

CHAPTER XVII.

On board the *Williamette*.—Blockade running.—Arrival at Nankin.—Solemn Thanksgiving.—Domestic Arrangements.—Phillip's Wife.—The Wooing.—The Dowry.—The Wedding.—Trade established.—Imperialist Corruption.—Preparations for leaving.—An Elopement.—The Journey.—The Surprise.—The Repulse.—Arrival at Hang-chow.—Its capture.—The particulars.—Cum-ho.—The Chung-wang.—His mistaken Policy.

THANKS to the impish steamer *Williamette*, we escaped any further annoyance at the hands of her friends, for, according to agreement, she towed us past all the Imperialist positions. Although I had paid rather dear for this favour, the danger we had escaped at that atrocious Mud Fort, and those troubles we avoided by towing past the unscrupulous batteries and piratical squadrons of the enemy, made it well worth more. Had we sailed to Nankin, our nights would have been far from pleasant, sleep being rendered impossible from the unceasing watching for some hostile demonstration, and the excitement attendant on the several skirmishes which we must have had with the Manchoos.

The worry and excitement of running the Nankin blockade can only be thoroughly appreciated by those who have experienced its perils. The Ti-ping adherents certainly found few pleasures to reward them, and their lot was very far indeed from being cast in pleasant places. Such dangers as myself and many others have endured while assisting the cause of these patriots have left an impression which even time cannot efface.

Perchance, we are sailing peacefully and slowly along the broad Yang-tze, dreaming of home or philosophizing upon the spread of liberty and Christianity by our Ti-ping friends, when crash comes a discharge of artillery from some Manchoo fort, as the first intimation that we were within the meshes of those who would destroy all hope of improving China or of realizing our own dreams, with equal indifference. This danger passes over, and the wearied have sought for slumber, when those on their anxious watch suddenly discover a squadron of the some-time pirate *Ti-mungs* hired to fight the battles of the Manchoo; and at the same instant those below are startled by the broadsides fired at their devoted vessel. After running the gauntlet of these heavily-armed vessels, the sleepers, with rifles by their side and revolvers under pillow, are subject to incessant disturbance from the attack of the centipede gunboats, as the latter pull from sly corners and creeks, in twos, tens, or twenties, and chase the passing ship, eager for the blood of those on board, or the pleasure of looting their effects.

Many of the few Europeans who were engaged assisting the Ti-pings were captured and barbarously killed by the Imperialists; yet, in spite of these dangers, and the certain prospect of a cruel death if unfortunate enough to fall into their hands, every man willingly incurred them, with a full conviction that the cause was worthy of any risk or sacrifice.

Some have been found daring enough to allege that personal profit was the motive which induced so many to incur suffering and danger in support of the Ti-pings. The absurdity of such a statement is made clear by the fact, that from 1860 to 1863 the principal supply of silk and tea was derived by the merchants of China from the Ti-pings, and that it was possible to carry on trade with the Imperialists with perfect safety, and with as large, if not larger, profit.

The true reason why those engaged in assisting the Ti-pings prefered that course, with all its troubles and dangers, is that, having once met the revolutionists, the immense superiority of the latter to the Manchoos had enlisted their sympathies and active support. Money, of course, in many cases had a great deal to do with the transactions of those who *traded* among the Ti-pings; but others, I am certain, were solely actuated by disinterested motives. He must, indeed, be a singular specimen of a man who could really know and experience the society of the Ti-pings, and not become a warm friend to them.

The *Williamette* was a powerful steamer, and on the evening of the day after she had taken us in tow, we had the satisfaction to be cast off right in the mouth of the Nankin creek, while the good ship continued on her way to Ngan-kin, whither she was bound with munitions of war freshly obtained from the British arsenals in China, to be expended in the slaughter of those who held England's pledge of strict neutrality.

Upon bringing up in the creek, I landed and paid my friend the Sz-wang a visit. He gave me a hearty welcome, and immediately set his servants to prepare a regular feast for myself and friend. I could not refuse the kind hospitality of my worthy host, even impatient as I was to get into the city and see Marie, who, he assured me, was in perfect health and happiness, and a vast favourite among the ladies at the Ti-ping capital, at the same time astonishing me by saying that Phillip had been married since my departure from Nankin.

At last, while the dinner was progressing, and the Sz-wang had for a moment been called away by a courier from the city, I left the table, and, assisted by his eldest nephew, who was a great friend of mine, I mounted one of his best horses and set off for Nankin, leaving my friend P. to excuse me and relate our adventures and the intentions of the so-called "foreign brethren" at Shanghae towards the Ti-pings; a point upon which the Sz-wang always felt the deepest anxiety.

Upon reaching the Chung-wang's palace, I found a large number of chiefs assembled in the "Heavenly Hall," and all greatly elated by despatches just received from the Commander-in-Chief detailing the capture of the seaport Ningpo. Anxious as I naturally felt to meet my betrothed, I was yet obliged to join the chiefs in the solemn thanksgiving they were about offering to the Great Giver of all victory. Upon this occasion, as usual, whether after triumph or defeat, the Ti-pings attributed their important success entirely to the will of "The Heavenly Father." Their absorbing reliance upon God, because of their belief in the righteousness and Christianity of their cause has often startled me by its singular devotedness and simplicity. It was not only those who had been of the original "Society of the Worshippers of God" in Kwang-si, that were so fervent and hopeful, but all *bonâ fide* Ti-pings, and even many among the latest recruits were equally inspired. It is a well-known fact that young boys, of twelve to fifteen years of age, are commonly the bravest soldiers and most daring spirits in the ranks of the Ti-ping soldiery. Formerly the very women fought by the side of their male relatives; at the present time they still undergo the hard dangers of the camp. Thus, upon consideration of all the facts bearing upon the motive and practice of the Ti-pings, it cannot be difficult to understand that some mighty inspiration has affected a large portion of the Chinese in a remarkably striking manner. Some term the cause and effect evil; others, not so self-conceited and hypercritical, say " it is good." By some the great Ti-ping revolution has been considered a religious fanaticism, an extensive leaguing together of banditti for the sake of plunder; the fact being that the only religious enthusiasm is to establish our Bible throughout China, and the only physical action an endeavour to liberate that vast empire from what even their worst opponents declare a hopelessly corrupt and oppressive Government!

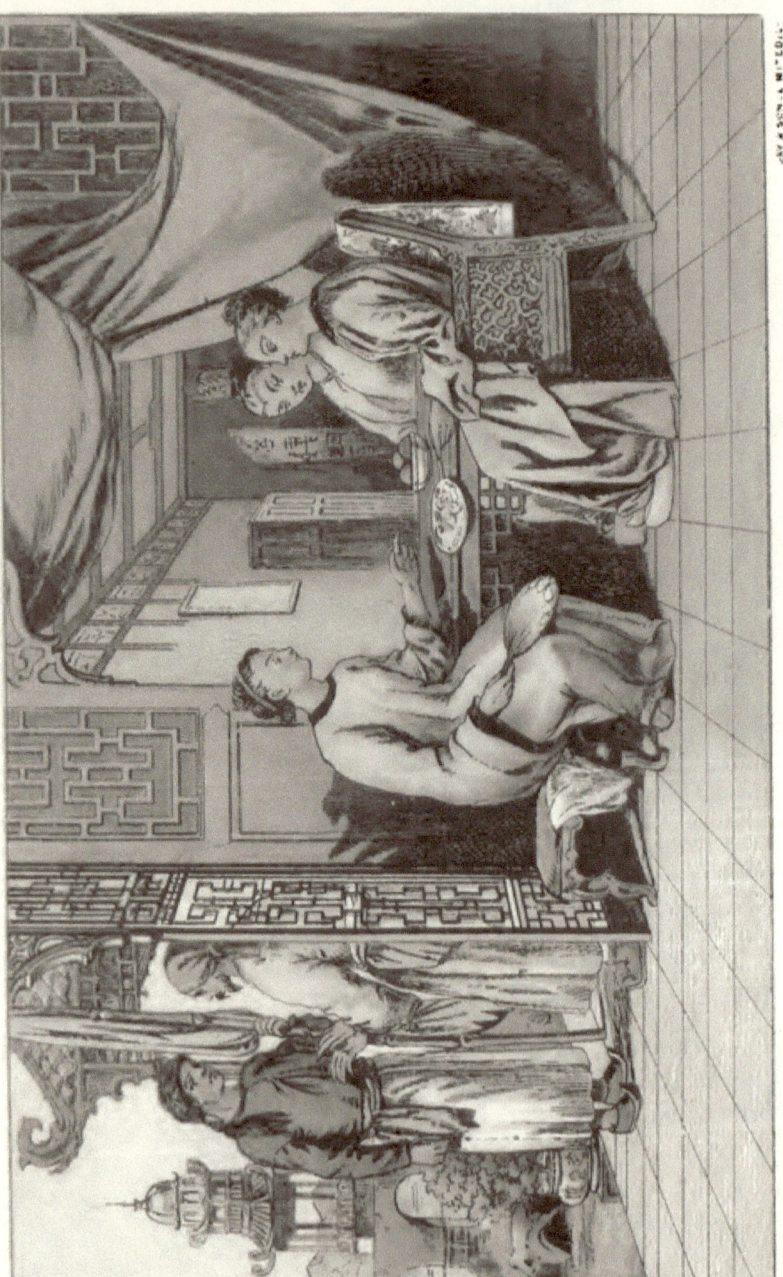

When the thanksgiving prayers in the "Heavenly Hall" were brought to a conclusion, I soon found my way to the inner apartments, and had the happiness to find Marie looking, if possible, better and more handsome than ever. She was delighted with the kindness of the Ti-ping ladies, and particularly noticed their sincere piety and continual study of the Holy Scriptures. Before long her inseparable companion, Miss Cum-ho, appeared, and considerably amused us by her round-about inquiries after my friend L., who, much to her satisfaction, I stated might be shortly expected.

While taking a stroll in the garden, Marie informed me that during my absence she had been much annoyed by the importunate attentions of a young chief, the son of the Tsan-wang, one of the principal members of the Ti-ping Government. In fact, to so unpleasant an extent had his sudden passion carried him that, upon two occasions, his emissaries had attempted her abduction, the last attempt having taken place only a few evenings before my return, and while she was walking in the palace grounds alone. The young chief I knew by reputation as a wild and unscrupulous character, but his father was a most influential personage; therefore, though I might readily have avoided further trouble by representing the affair to the authorities, I decided to take Marie with me and join the Chung-wang at Hang-chow, rather than excite any bad feeling by making a public case when it could be avoided. Ti-ping justice was remarkably prompt and severe, and conviction of the chief would very likely have led to decapitation. Before putting my plan into execution, it was necessary to await the arrival of L. with our lorcha.

In the evening I found Phillip with his wife waiting to see me in the old rooms at the back of the Chung-wang's palace. I had ample occasion to congratulate him upon his choice, for the lady was by no means wanting in personal beauty. She was a really fine girl, taller than the generality of Chinese women, with very pretty and regular features, light-complexioned and rosy-cheeked, and was quite black-eyed and long-haired enough to please the greatest brunette admirer; besides which she was fortunate enough to possess nice little feet, not deformed according to Imperialist Chinese taste. How Phillip met her, and how she became his wife, took place, as he informed me, in the following way :—

A week or two after my departure from Nankin, intelligence was received of the capture of the city of Ngan-kin by the Imperialists, and the defeat of the Ying-wang, who had been prevented effecting its relief through the delay caused by his communication with the British expedition up the Yang-tze. Reinforcements having been ordered from Nankin to the north bank of the river, so as to co-operate in the Ying-wang's retreat, Phillip accompanied them, taking charge of the few pieces of artillery they carried.

One day, while with the foremost of the advanced guard, he became engaged in an attack upon a fortified hamlet, which was obstinately defended by some Manchoo troops, who were assisted by the inhabitants. In such cases, of course, the Ti-pings treat the villagers as enemies, making prisoners of those who escape the battle, and seizing their effects.

While driving the Imperialists out of the palace, Phillip received a slight though painful spear-wound in one of his hands, and, upon entering a house to obtain some water, he saw his future wife for the first time. The house was, apparently, one of the poorest in the village, and the young woman, with her aged father and a little servant-girl, constituted its only occupants. They were naturally much alarmed by the conflict raging about them, and while the timid daughter supplied him with a draught of water, her father threw himself at his knees, *ketowing* and imploring protection.

Phillip was considerably impressed by the charms

of the celestial damsel, and with his brave though tender heart sincerely pitied her unprotected state, so he waited until the arrival of the main body of the forces; and then, after obtaining from the chief in command a protection *chop*, or paper, to affix to the door of the house, and thereby make it inviolate, he continued on the march, leaving father and daughter showering Chinese blessings upon his foreign head.

My friend had not proceeded very far when he reflected that a great proportion of the rear guard (which in this case was a position of no moment) was composed of quite new levies, many of whom had been Imperialist *braves*, and had only lately been enlisted as Ti-pings, and who, probably, still retained the old propensities to excess and plunder strong within them. Thinking thus, and, I dare say, with a lively remembrance of the daughter's pretty face—her equal not being seen every day in China—he determined to ride back and protect the old man's house, if necessary, till the last of the force had passed through the village. During his return he had met a number of the recruits as prisoners for looting houses and robbing country people, the punishment for which would almost certainly be decapitation, and upon reaching the place he found many were plundering and destroying all they could lay hands on.

Phillip had scarcely noticed this when the little girl he had seen at the house came running up to him, screaming and holding out her hands, and with the blood pouring from a large gash across her cheek.

Fearing the worst, and blaming himself for not having made greater haste, he left one of his men to attend to the poor child, and galloped up to the house with the rest.

The building was beginning to smoke where some of the marauders had just applied the torch, while, right across the threshold of his once happy home, the apparently lifeless body of the old man lay before my friend.

Hearing the noise of voices inside the house, Phillip expecting at each step to come across the daughter's corpse, drew his revolver and entered. He arrived not a moment too soon, for, upon reaching the inner chamber, he found the poor girl struggling in the hands of several soldiers. The next instant and his pistol had effectually released her, when she rushed fainting and dishevelled to his arms. Carrying her to the outer apartment, he laid her on a couch, and then turned his attention to the father. The latter still lived, but death was evidently fast approaching as his life ebbed away from several ghastly wounds inflicted by the heavy knives of the ruthless murderers.

The fire being extinguished by some of his men, Phillip got the poor old man moved into the house, and, assisted by the sorrow-stricken daughter, did all that was possible to save him. It was, however, soon apparent that his end was drawing near; he seemed quite sensible, though for some time unable to speak. At last, with a flickering revival before the total eclipse of life's lamp, he pointed with one nerveless hand to the wainscot, and ejaculated, "Tseen!—che-mo!" (Money!—take away the wood!) Upon going to the spot indicated, Phillip found a crevice in the panelling, and, using the blade of his sword, he managed to wrench away a large piece, exposing a hollow containing a small bundle tied up in blue Chinese cloth. While lifting this up he knew by its weight that it must contain gold, and when he placed it by the side of the dying man, the latter with difficulty managed to say "Gno—show—ne!" (I—give—you). Then, calling his daughter, he with a last effort stretched forth his arms, and, grasping her hand and that of the stranger from the far West, and feebly endeavouring to place them together, fell back, and in a little while expired.

After a distressing scene with the bereaved girl, Phillip was compelled to order the interment, under a few inches of earth, of her father's body. Immediately afterwards it was necessary to set out for the now distant army, and when Phillip overtook it his future wife was with him, as her fate would have been certain had she remained alone at the desolated village, defenceless, with her gold and beauty, before the incursions of Imperialist or Ti-ping marauders. There were many Ti-ping women accompanying their husbands with the army, so the poor girl had some of her own sex to comfort her. The expedition was not long away from Nankin, and upon its return to the city, Phillip and the orphan were married in the Ti-ping church, thus accomplishing not only what they supposed to have been the wish of the dead father, but also what accorded with their mutual inclination.

And so it was that my friend Phillip obtained a wife and a fortune with her, for that heavy little bundle contained more than sixty gold bars, each worth about 300 dollars. Phillip Bosse, or Boze, declared himself so satisfied with his wife, his present affairs, and the Ti-pings, that he vowed he would never leave them. He kept his word, for he died amongst the patriots, and as his relatives in Greece may never otherwise hear of his death, I give his name as I knew it; so that should this book ever fall into their hands, they may at least have the melancholy satisfaction to know where his body rests, and that he died like a gallant and noble-hearted man, serving a righteous and a great cause.

A few days after my arrival at Nankin, my friend L. brought our lorcha safely into the creek, accompanied by three other vessels of the same class, the owners of which had availed themselves of the passes I had given them from the Chang-wang. Each craft was deeply laden with rice and other provisions. My own junk and lorcha, containing rice belonging to the Ti-ping Government, we left in charge of certain officials, and my friends all joined me in the city. Soon after the arrival of L., several vessels came in from Shanghae to trade; these were succeeded by others, and a regular commerce sprang up and was continued for a year or two. In a few months the trade had become so great that it was quite common for more than thirty vessels (both foreign and Chinese-owned) to arrive in one day. The large supplies received by this line of communication were stored in the extensive Nankin granaries, and while these were always kept full, the residue was distributed through the town and villages of the district, the neighbouring country being much impoverished by the continual warfare raging around the Ti-ping capital.

The fraudulent and corrupt revenue institutions of the Manchoo Government have long been notorious. The enormous extortion practised upon foreign trade until the wars with Great Britian compelled a more regular tariff, and the plundering squeeze stations scattered over every half-mile of Imperialist territory, each of which pilfer a sum from the unfortunate owner of all passing merchandise, be he a foreigner who ought to pass clear by virtue of the transit duty clauses of the treaty, or a Chinaman who is legitimate prey, have made China a vast system of independent official violence and rapacity.

No wonder the naturally astute Chinese appear so particularly cunning and deceitful to Europeans! The possession of money is a sure attraction for the mandarin vultures; so that beyond the pale of the foreign settlements at the treaty ports, throughout the country, every native merchant and civilian is bred up to habits of mendacity, and particularly to conceal his real income and condition.

The endless ramifications of the Manchoo administrative extend from each remote corner of China to the central power; and although every one of the myriad feelers sucking away at the substance of the nation (in the shape of mandarins, all appointed with merely nominal salary, but given *carte blanche* to obtain emolument after sending an annual stipulated sum to the emperor), crams its individual self with spoil, the squeezing and contracting of the Manchoo canker feeds the insatiable core at Pekin. It is useless to think of curing or mitigating the evil, though some have vainly advocated doing so. The only remedy must necessarily be a change of dynasty, such as the Ti-pings would certainly have effected had they not been wickedly opposed by foreigners. Every branch of civil, military, social, political and religious organization has become so hopelessly corrupted since the Manchoo era, that any attempt to change or improve the deplorable results of their evil rule might be carried on *ad infinitum*, only to result in certain failure. But one course affords a prospect of cure and a consequent chance of happiness for China : that is, a radical change of Government.

Let foreigners be righteous, and permit the native to expel the Tartar; and the Chinese, when ruled by Chinese, will become benefited by western civilization, and (if the Ti-ping should not become exterminated by British intervention) in all probability Christianized.

In striking contrast to the excessively corrupt Imperialist customs, the Ti-ping revenue organization was just, regular, and simple. Throughout every part of Ti-ping-tien-kwoh but one custom-house was established at each town or village where trade was carried on. The rate of tariff has always been moderate, and the great advantage of the system consisted in being able to clear goods by one payment, upon which a pass would be given to take them free of further charge or hindrance to their destination. The Ti-ping Government deserved no little credit for the simplicity and effectiveness of their Board of Revenue, and it is mainly due to that branch of their administration that the valuable silk trade *increased* and continued progressing so favourably during their possession of the producing districts.

Not only can all who have traded at Nankin testify to the entire superiority of the Ti-ping custom-house, but many silk and tea merchants now revelling in England have to thank the admirable regulations and forbearance of the revolutionists for their well-lined pockets. Every customs establishment in the late Ti-ping territory was composed of a superintendent, several deputies, and a very efficient staff of surveyors, clerks, and weighers, and at places frequented by Europeans, one or more interpreters were always found. Rice and other grain were quite free of duty, and that upon dried and preserved provisions was very low. All other produce and general merchandise were moderately taxed, either by tariff or *ad valorem*. Such were the regulations, which were not (like the Imperialist maritime customs) simply binding upon foreign goods, but were applicable in an equal degree to the property of natives.

Before putting into execution the design I had formed to depart suddenly from Nankin, D., an old friend of mine, arrived from Hankow, where he was established as the principal partner of a large mercantile firm. He brought several vessels to trade with the city, and he came to an arrangement by which he was to sail with Captain P., and another European as mate, in our lorcha *Anglo Ti-ping*, the latter to convoy his junks and our old one. D. was a perfect Chinese linguist, and to him I am indebted for much valuable information.

I waited until P., in charge of the lorcha and her consorts, had sailed up the river to obtain cargoes of rice, edible oil, bacon, salt fish, and other articles of consumption, and then prepared to leave the city.

During a few days I sent Phillip and L. into the country to buy some horses, and at last, together with our own, managed to muster fourteen strong animals, which were then stabled at a remote part of the city, close to the north-east gate. Since the return of my friend and companion L., we had successfully concealed his presence from the female part of the Chung-wang's household, with one exception, and by this *ruse* he had obtained several interviews with the lady of his affections, the (according to his idea) incomparable Cum-ho. The result of these meetings soon transpired.

At length the day came, the close of which was settled for our exit from Nankin. Six picked men, belonging to an artillery corps we had formed of some of the Chung-wang's troops, were selected to accompany myself and comrades. The horses were particularly attended to, and our weapons were well cleaned and then carefully loaded, for danger had warned us against the risk of rusty locks and carelessly charged fire-arms. When all had been arranged, L. informed me that he had determined to carry Cum-ho, who had agreed to elope with him, to Hang-chow, and so induce her father to sanction their marriage. I found it impossible to dissuade him from doing so, and he assured me that the lady's mind was equally decided; therefore, much as I feared the affair would injure our satisfactory and friendly relations with the Chung-wang, I had no choice but to accede. Cum-ho, in order to find an opportunity to join us, had paid a visit to the Ying-wang's ladies, and as their dwelling was close by, she was only accompanied by her own female attendant.

Just when the shadows of evening were cast in long dark lines from the tall battlements and high pagodas of the city, we prepared to assemble at the appointed rendezvous. Phillip, with the six Ti-ping soldiers, I sent on to the stables, while L., with our boy As-sam, waited outside the Ying-wang's palace for Miss Cum-ho; and I, taking A-ling, my trusty interpreter, joined Marie in the Chung-wang's gardens. As the hour fixed upon for a general meet drew near, myself and party, each carrying a small quantity of baggage, left the gardens by a small door and proceeded to the somewhat distant stables. Upon reaching the rendezvous, I found Phillip had brought his wife with him, and also another horse for her use. We had not long to wait for L., who, with his fair runaway and her maid, arrived soon after myself.

The horses were now led forth, and we, numbering fifteen persons, having mounted, the word was given to spur and away.

Upon reaching the city gate we were detaind for a long while by the warder, in consequence of the late hour, although I had taken care to provide myself with the requisite pass from the proper authority to permit my egress or ingress at any time. At last the surly guardians of the portal turned out, shuffling their clothes about their backs with a style peculiar to the Chinese, who generally sleep quite naked, and have a curious way of drawing their arms from the sleeves of their clothing when dressed, and shrugging them up next their body. After the shuffling, stocking-pulling, and preliminary spitting (a great and indispensable habit with Chinamen), had partially subsided, the sleepy guards managed to draw back sundry huge wooden bars, to undo any amount of rusty locks and bolts, and then the massive doors creaked slowly open. While the gates of the city clanged together, we set off at a gallop for the road leading south, to reach which we turned westward and skirted a considerable part of the walls.

Chinese horses, though small, are wonderfully strong and enduring, and it was not till the close of the day after our start that we came to a regular halt, and only then because our fair companions were fatigued. My literally fair readers need not take umbrage at this appellation, for yellow-tinted celestial and dusky Portuguese as they were, their beauty was undeniable, and their figures such that many a European dame might justly envy. The rough riding through the mountain-passes on the southern road from Nankin affected our hardy animals but very little; and when our camp was pitched for the night under the shelter of the wall of a ruined Buddhist temple, and they were picketed in a semi-circle around, they set to work cropping the short grass as leisurely as though they had just left the stable. We carried three tents with our baggage, and these were pitched; one for the women; one for my comrades, A-ling, and our boy; and the other for our six men.

A large fire was lighted, and we had nearly finished the supper served up by As-sam, when crash came a volley of musketry among us, directed from the crest of a small hill directly fronting and overlooking our camp at a distance of some eighty or ninety yards. I had stupidly neglected to choose the other side of the wall for our resting-place. Of course, we instantly started to our feet and snatched up the arms at hand, and while the Ti-pings shortened in the tether of our horses, forming a close array of the well-trained, docile animals, fastened together head and tail, the rest of our party placed the women directly under the shelter of the living rampart. These measures were barely effected when a body of more than fifty horsemen dashed round the hill and charged upon our position. We had no difficulty in discovering them to be Ti-pings, and when they came closer we saw the Tsan-wang's son was at their head. Their first volley had fortunately been aimed far too high; it may be that, fearing to injure the woman he pursued, the chief had done this, trusting to cause an alarm, during which he might dash forward and carry off the prize. Our reply to the advancing party was not so bloodless as the commencement of their attack. My own comrades, and even A-ling and As-sam, were capital marksmen, while the six men had been selected for their approved courage and the well-known skill so peculiar to Chinese when properly instructed.

Every man of our party was armed with either an Enfield or some other rifle (two being Sharp's breech-loaders), and all were able to use them with deadly accuracy; therefore, the number of the approaching foe gave us but little dread, especially as we saw they were armed only with short European-made double-barrelled guns and Chinese matchlocks. We waited until they had galloped to within twenty yards, but receiving only the war cry, "Tah! Tah!" in reply to our challenge, we then took steady aim, and commenced firing upon them by successive volleys from each half of our number. The affair was settled in a moment almost. The leader and half a dozen of his men, with twice that number of horses, were quickly rolling on the turf, for at that short distance the difficulty would have been to miss them with our rifles. When their charge was entirely repulsed we ceased firing, a dozen men came forward on foot and carried off their fallen comrades and chief, and then they all slowly disappeared in the direction of Nankin. During their advance they had kept up an irregular fire, which, with the exception of grazing the other arm of our boy, As-sam (one had been wounded at the Mud Fort), and shooting away the ear of one of our horses, did no damage.

Upon the fortunate termination of the skirmish we dispatched the remainder of our supper, turned in for the night upon the opposite side of the wall, and kept three men on sentry till morning. Upon resuming our journey, we soon came to a rich and thickly-populated country, and during the next few days, while traversing the silk districts from end to end, along the eastern shore of the Ta-hoo lake, *viâ* the city of Soo-chow, Kia-shing-foo, and the Grand Canal, I particularly noticed the vast improvement that had taken place since my first visit to Soo-chow some eight months ago. Everywhere around the traces of war (always excepting the demolished Buddhist temples) had disappeared before the progress of peace and plenty; and although I may be accused of exaggeration, I do not hesitate to affirm that the establishment of Ti-ping supremacy and administration over these, the most valuable districts of China, had restored them to prosperity and happiness in a shortness of time hitherto unparalleled in the case of either Chinese or any other civil war desolation.

Although during my previous visit I had seen amply sufficient to undeceive me as to the wickedly false allegations of Ti-ping devastations, &c., still I was hardly prepared for the flourishing state in which I found the *settled* territory of the revolutionists. I knew that the export of silk within the current year (1861) had already increased to upwards of 20,000 bales more than during the corresponding period of last year (when till May the districts were under Imperialist rule); but then I imagined the great increase might be due to the wish of holders to realize. I found, upon the contrary, that the improvement was entirely due to the Ti-ping occupation. In less than two years the districts under Ti-ping jurisdiction had produced silk representing a sum of not less than £3,000,000 per annum more than previously! At each of the many villages and at every peasant's cot, the happy-looking people were engaged tending their silkworms for winter, reeling the last cocoons, or tilling their fields.

Great as the prosperity of the country seemed, there was something even more gratifying and interesting in the changed appearance and disposition of the people. All the unfavourable characteristics of the Manchoo-oppressed Chinese had vanished, and their natural character was manifested in a way which illustrated their candour, hospitality to foreigners, and native good temper.

After a twelve days' journey, the later part of the time in large canal boats, we arrived within a day's march of Hang-chow. Leaving the water route, we disembarked our horses and set forward in the direction of the provincial capital, guided by the continual booming of heavy guns. Upon reaching the crest of some high ground, the city lay before us in the clear frosty air of a fine December morning. But, as we find the case every day, the beauty of nature was marred by the passions and strife of mankind. The extensive city was in flames in several quarters, and the dense columns of smoke shrouded as with a pall the slaughter taking place beneath. As we rode forward through the beautiful neighbouring country, we were enabled gradually to discern dark masses of troops rushing forward against the city amid the constant roar of artillery and the rattling crash of smaller arms. It was evident that we had arrived at the moment of a grand assault by the Ti-ping forces.

As our soldiers each declared that the Chung-wang's head-quarters were to the west of the city, we made a considerable detour in that direction. We had not proceeded far when a disorderly crowd came in sight, hurrying away from the city. Directly they observed my party, the greater number turned off and precipitately fled in another line of retreat. As those who stood their ground were making ready with spears and gingalls to give us a warm reception, and as we were not out like a parcel of knights errant seeking adventure and fighting from pure love, we wisely followed those who ran away, and succeeded in catching one of the hindermost, to question as to the state of affairs in the city. At first the man was terribly frightened, and we could make nothing of him; then he became still more alarmed, and we found out all we wished. His fear was the usual one accompanying the flight of disorganized *undisciplined* troops, which with Chinese becomes a wild panic; not because the men fear death, for no people can meet it with the stolidity and callousness with which they will suffer execution and torture, but from the simple fact that they are not sufficiently disciplined to know how to be killed in an orderly manner on the field of battle. They see a chance of escape, and on one taking it the whole follow like a flock of sheep.

Having ascertained from our prisoner, who with his friends were all Imperialist soldiery from the garrison of Hang-chow, that the Ti-pings had just captured the city, we set him at liberty, and then galloped for the west gate. On the way we passed many fugitives fleeing in every direction. Upon reaching the rear of the Ti-ping lines of circumvallation, we found them almost denuded of troops, the few remaining being fully occupied in guarding prisoners. We soon found the Commander-in-Chief's head-quarters, but no Chung-wang was there. The scanty number of soldiers on guard were in a great state of excitement about the success of the siege, and we managed to elicit from them that the Chung-wang had entered the city with his whole force, and was now engaged attacking the Tartar quarter, an *imperium in imperio*, city within city, being protected by its own walls, and with a central citadel towering above all. Leaving the women in a house protected by the main guard, with the remainder of my party I rode towards the city. Upon entering by the nearest gate, we found the streets unoccupied, except by the bodies of the slain; but the noise of battle guided us to the spot where living men were busily engaged increasing the number of the dead and dying.

Hang-chow, cut off from all communication with the outside world, every line of supply severed by the besiegers, and famine raging among the unfortunate garrison and inhabitants, fell to the investing army upon the 29th of December, 1861. Early on that day the Chung-wang had commenced a grand assault, conducted upon each gate of the city. After a fiercely contested fight, the assaulting columns having gained some advantages at the south and east gates, the Chinese portion of the defenders at those points surrendered, probably induced to take that step by the very short rations to which they had been reduced. When the gates had been given up, the Ti-ping troops poured into the city with such ardour that the Tartar bannermen were quickly driven within their inner defence. Hundreds of the miserable citizens of the provincial capital were starved to death during the siege, hundreds more, with their families, committed suicide. The nature of war in China has usually been so merciless, and the conduct of victorious troops at the capture of a city so outrageous, that in many cases during the civil war, and the wars with Great Britian, the people, probably imbued with a dread of these consequences, have committed wholesale suicide when they were not in the slightest danger of being molested.

I managed to find the Chung-wang just in time to join the last attack upon the inner or Tartar city. The Commander-in-Chief, surrounded by his officers, received myself and friends with evident signs of satisfaction. His men had just been repulsed by the Manchoo troops, who were fighting with the greatest bravery and determination. The Ti-pings had eight or nine pieces of artillery turned against the wall of the inner city; but these were established in one position, firing point blank upon the rampart, so that when the assaulting parties moved forward the guns became useless. I instantly advised the Chung-wang to move two or three guns away upon each flank, so as to enfilade the parapet and protect the advance of his stormers. This was quickly done, and upon joining the leaders of the next assault, we had the satisfaction to find it successful. The Tartar bannermen retreated to the citadel in the centre of their city, fighting to the very last, assisted by their women, who fought with them like men, and one of whom inflicted a severe spear-wound upon Ling-ho, a Ti-ping general, when he would have saved her life. The greater portion of the Chinese troops garrisoning Hang-chow were captured, but the Manchoos fell almost to the last man. Their loss during the capture of the city was very great, and when at length they were driven into their citadel, Luy, their general, blew the remnant into the air, the entire Tartar force, men, women, and children, perishing in the ruins.

After the capture of Hang-chow, the anti-Ti-pings, who were in the habit of howling over Ti-ping atrocities, though oblivious to those of the Manchoo, indulged their distorted though vivid imaginations by inveighing against such indiscriminate slaughter. It is true that a great loss of life occurred, but not a man fell except in battle, neither were any non-combatants killed except by starvation or their own hands. It is a singular fact that those who have been loudest to exclaim against Ti-ping cruelty, have always delighted in Imperialist barbarities and success, the words being synonymous.

When the last note of conflict had died away, and the Chung-wang had fixed his head-quarters within the city, I broached the subject of his daughter's presence and her attachment to my friend. The time was propitious, for it was the moment of a great triumph, and I suppose it had put the Ti-ping generalissimo into an immensely good and benevolent frame of mind, for he simply expressed his intention to take her back to Nankin, and settle the affair upon our return to that city. In the evening Cum-ho waited upon her father, having taken up her quarters with the rest of our feminine fellow travellers in a house close to the large building occupied by himself and staff.

On the morning of the first day of the new year, a large body of the army was dispatched in the direction of Shanghae, under the command of the Shi-wang, with orders to occupy every town and village up to the walls of that port, and then to open negotiations with the British and other authorities, who had so unjustly assumed to themselves the right of holding a Chinese city for the Manchoo against the Chinese patriots. During the next few weeks the Chung-wang busied himself establishing the different offices of Ti-ping Government in Hang-chow, and completing his plans for the occupation and retention of the remainder of the provinces of Kiang-su and Che-kiang. At length the Commander-in-Chief, seldom more than a month in any city (during his remarkably energetic and rapid conduct of the Ti-ping operations), took his departure for Nankin, there to mature further tactics as to the mode of prosecuting the war against the Manchoo, and also to consult with his king the Tien-wang, and receive further commands.

I had ample opportunity to notice the exceeding popularity the Chung-wang had attained among the country people, for everywhere we passed they turned out to welcome his arrival, and all I questioned declared him to be a good and just man, who respected and protected the rights of the meanest peasant of the land. Many of the Ti-ping chiefs were popular with the civilians, some were disliked, all were considered better than the Manchoo, but none were so beloved as the Chung-wang. Before the troops had been marched towards Shanghae, a day of thanksgiving was held at Hang-chow; and although the motive of the Ti-ping is that of justice and Christianity, I could not help thinking of the similar practice among Europeans, who never fail to return thanks to God for triumph over their weaker brethren, whether their cause be righteous or quite the reverse.

On our march to Nankin, the Chung-wang took a route which embraced all the principal cities captured during the last year, including Hoo-chow, Kar-shing-foo, Soo-chow, Wo-kong, Quin-san, Tat-san, &c., and at each thanksgivings were offered up for the late important success. About this time the Commander-in-Chief committed his first great error. His mistake consisted in breaking up a large proportion of his forces into garrisons for the numerous walled cities in Ti-ping possession, and in moving the rest of his troops to other quarters.* It is true, he had nothing to fear from the enemy, all their armies in the field (with the exception of those operating against the Ying-wang, on the line of the Yang-tze river, above Nankin) having been utterly dispersed; but no preparation whatever was made to resist the probable hostility of England and France,

---

* This was, however, in accordance with the Tien-wang's orders.

beyond such defence as the widely separated fortified towns might be able to make. This neglect, when the British scheme of intervention came into full play, proved fatal to the welfare of Ti-pingdom. City after city was captured in detail by British *artillery* and troops; when, had the patriots only concentrated their numerous but greatly scattered forces, the result might have proved very different. I wearied myself, the Chung-wang, and many other chiefs, by continually representing the danger in case of foreign hostility (which I felt certain would be the result of Lord Elgin's policy in China), but the poor Ti-pings seemed infatuated, and resolutely refused to believe that the unbrotherly so-called "foreign brethren" entertained such perfectly unprovoked and cruel intentions. Fatally have they been undeceived! Deeply responsible have England and France become for the consequences!

CHAPTER XVIII.

Earl Russell's Despatch.—Its Effect.—"Taking the Offensive."—Official Reports.—General Staveley.—Attacks the Ti-pings.—General Ward.—Hope and Ward repulsed.—Che-poo attacked.—Its Capture.—Loot Regulations.—Kah-ding attacked.—Its Capture.—Ti-ping Loss.—Newspaper Comments.—Tsing-poo besieged.—Inside the City.—Ti-ping Losses.—Na-jaor besieged.—Cho-lin besieged.—Ti-ping Bravery.—Cho-lin captured.—The Chung-wang.—Kah-ding evacuated.—Consul Harvey's Despatch.—Despatch reviewed.—Ning-po threatened.—Captain Dew at Ning-po.—His Despatch.—The Reply.—Captain Dew's Rejoinder.—Preparation to attack Ning-po.—Captain Dew's Inconsistency.—His Ultimatum.—Official Despatches.—Ning-po attacked.—Ning-po evacuated.—Newspaper Reports.

AFTER hostilities had been commenced by Admiral Hope, and upon hearing of the capture of Ningpo by the Ti-pings, Earl Russell endorsed the violation of British faith by approving the hostile maintenance of Shanghae and the other treaty ports against the Ti-ping belligerents, in the following despatch to the Admiralty, dated, "Foreign Office, March 11, 1862":—

"I have, therefore, to signify to your Lordships the Queen's commands that Vice-Admiral Hope should be instructed to defend Shanghae, and to protect the other treaty ports not in the hands of the rebels, so far as it is in the power of Her Majesty's *naval forces* to do so."

Before, however, these instructions were received (they bearing date March 11, and occupying at least three months in reaching Mr. Bruce at Pekin, and being by him communicated to Admiral Hope at Shanghae), the war was carried far into the interior and thoroughly established, although, in the first instance, it had been pretended that the operations were only undertaken in defence of Shanghae.

Mr. Bruce having stated his opinion by the following passage in a despatch, dated March 4, 1862:—"Shanghae is threatened, and its supplies cut off, and the insurgents will be emboldened by our passiveness and their success at Ningpo to press us still closer. I have stated to Sir J. Hope that, in my opinion, we are perfectly justified in taking the offensive against the insurgents;"—Lord Russell again approves of the disobedience of his former orders, by stating in a despatch, dated "Foreign Office, June 2, 1862:—"I have to convey to you my approval of the views expressed in your despatch of the 4th of March, with regard to the course to be pursued towards the Taepings." This sanction for the British authorities in China to take "the offensive" was, of course, tantamount to a declaration of war against the revolutionists; yet Earl Russell and his co-adjutors preferred working in secrecy, the approval of Parliament was not sought, neither did Her Majesty's Ministers ever deign to trouble themselves by announcing their policy. This, however, can hardly be a matter of surprise, considering that they had no *casus belli* to set forward as a justification—the multitude of excuses sent home by those who violated solemn pledges in China no more constituting one than a number of petty faults would justify hanging a man in England.

Admiral Hope having reported his breach of faith and neutrality by the murderous raid upon Kao-kiau, which he termed "certain *moral* support;" and having requested the shadow of the Ministers' countenance and support in these words, "I therefore strongly recommend that the French and English commanders should be required by yourself and M. Bourboulon to free the country from the rebels within a line commencing at Kading on the Yang-tze above Woo-sung, through Tsing-poo to Sung-kong on the Woo-sung river, and thence across to a walled town opposite on the Yang-tze;" he received full approval from Mr. Bruce to continue as he had commenced, at his own goodwill and pleasure.

In his despatch, authorizing the very course he had previously stated would be more calculated than any other "to lower our national reputation," Mr. Bruce, with his usual bad memory and inconsistent policy, states of Ti-pingdom and the people "that its sources are exhausted; that neither money nor supplies are to be drawn from the *deserts* to which the provinces overrun by them are reduced;" completely oblivious of the "85,000 bales" of silk he had declared, only a few months previous, were drawn from the producing districts—the *deserts* of his vivid though forgetful imagination.

The report of the Admiral and the reply of the Minister each discuss the radius project shortly established against the Ti-ping belligerent only, and the further increase and support of Ward's and fresh legions of mercenaries. This is the first official mention of those now notorious schemes.

When the Kao-kiau massacre, the radius plan, and the organization of foreign-disciplined filibustering corps, *à la* Ward, were reported to him, Earl Russell again followed the path already laid out by his subordinates in China—a system of policy that could not be defended on principle, and still worse in execution.* The officials in China always acted directly against the spirit and letter of their *public* instructions; then reported what they had done, and obtained the sanction of the British Government.

Admiral Hope, immediately upon receiving the support of Mr. Bruce, gathered together his well-armed sailors and marines, his big guns and his little guns, and, assisted by the French Admiral, Protet, and Brigadier-general Staveley in command of the British troops, eagerly continued "taking the offensive" against the badly-armed

---

* Lord Palmerston's Government had one great quality—it manfully supported its subordinate officials whether right or wrong; it is at least doubtful whether his successors will have courage to pursue the same policy.

Ti-pings. The war upon those to whom England was pledged to observe neutrality—a war never stated to the British Parliament—and, moreover, a war never even declared to the Ti-pings themselves, was rapidly prosecuted. General Staveley having assumed chief command of the allied Anglo-Franco-Manchoo filibuster operations, did so entirely against the spirit of the orders of his Government, for not until some months later did the approval of Admiral Hope's conduct (bearing date, "Foreign Office, June 12, 1862") reach China, and even these instructions only referred to the *naval expeditions*, already authorized by the despatch of March 11, 1862.

Mr. Bruce admits this in a despatch to General Staveley, dated "Pekin, April 23, 1862," although at the same time he prompts him to join the Admiral's raids. He thus states :—

"It is clear that, at that date, Her Majesty's Government had not resolved on doing more than aiding in the defence of the treaty ports by means of the naval forces on the station."

Now, it is utterly impossible that Mr. Bruce can have received the instructions to *employ* the naval force so soon as the 23rd of April. The first despatch of Lord Russell, authorizing Admiral Hope to defend the treaty ports against the Ti-pings bears date March 11, and has already been noticed; but even supposing it left England on the same day, it could not have reached Pekin when Admiral Hope and General Staveley had taken the offensive, and made incessant attacks upon every Ti-ping position within some thirty miles of Shanghae. The last instructions from Earl Russell were those suppositional ones, dated 7th September, 1861 :—

"It *might* be expedient to defend the treaty ports, *if* the Chinese Government would consent not to use them."

Referring back to the only definite order of Her Majesty's Government at the time of the unparalleled breaches of neutrality, we find it to be that bearing date August 8, 1861:—

"Her Majesty's Government desire to maintain, as they have done hitherto, *neutrality* between the two contending parties in China."

Thus, it cannot fail to be seen that hostilities were established against the Ti-pings, not only in violation of the pledged faith of England, but also in direct opposition to the *public* orders of her Government. Eventually the Government sanctioned and authorized a continuance of these raids, although they carefully avoided making any straightforward announcement of their policy. Their plan was always to approve the aggressive action of the officials in China, but never to order them publicly. The despatches approving General Staveley's unjustifiable attack upon innocent men respectively bear date — "Foreign Office, July 7, 1862," and "War Office, July 23." These documents, however, which take the odium and responsibility of the massacres from the active agents, and place them upon the British nation, could not have reached Pekin, and been communicated to the naval and military commanders at Shanghae, until late in September. We shall see what unauthorized and unnecessary hostilities were perpetrated previous to their arrival.

General Staveley, having assumed the principal command of the raiding expeditions, finding that the friendly Ti-pings would not come and fight him, went to fight them. Upon the 3rd of April a strong force of 2,207 British and French troops, with naval detachments under command of Admirals Hope and Protet, and thirteen pieces of artillery, moved out from Shanghae to continue "taking the offensive." The place doomed to destruction was a large, and for Chinese warfare, strong, entrenched Ti-ping camp at Wong-ka-dza, garrisoned by about 4,000 men. After a hot day's march, the whole force, including some hundreds of Imperialists dragging the guns, carrying portable bridges, extra loads of ammunition, and every requisite appliance of modern warfare, arrived at a deserted village within twelve miles from Shanghae, and about two from the Ti-ping camp. Here they encamped for the night. Early on the following morning the combined forces,* taking advantage of the cover afforded by a thick mist, moved on the position of the Ti-pings, establishing themselves within a few hundred yards of the defences just as the fog cleared away. The entrenched camp consisted of some ten or twelve stockades, each surrounded by a ditch, yet communicating with the others. The Ti-pings, as usual, waited for those they invariably looked upon as "foreign brethren" to take the offensive. They had not long to wait. Having taken up a position fairly within range of their Enfield rifles and artillery, but safely out of range of the useless gingalls and matchlocks of the Ti-pings, the "foreign brethren" opened a murderous fire upon the line of entrenchments. The devoted defenders replied as well they could, without artillery or effective fire-arms, and bravely held their stockades for nearly an hour, amid the storm of shrapnel-

---

* The forces consisted of :—
French, under Rear-Admiral Protet :—
    Small-arm men and Marines; field-piece party and 4 guns 410
English, under Brigadier General Staveley :—
    Royal Artillery, 6 guns . . . 78
    5th Bombay N. I. 440
    H.M. 99th Regiment . . . 56
    22nd Punjaub N. I. . . . 519
  Under Captain Borlase, R.N. :—
    Field-piece party, 3 guns . 45
    H.M.S. *Pearl* small-arm company 60
    Axe party 16
  Under Captain Willes, R.N. :—
    H.M.S. *Impérieuse* small-arm company 189
    Marines of Squadron . . 94
                                               1,497
Disciplined Chinese of General Ward's legion . . 300
          Total 2,207

shell, rifle-balls, &c., poured in upon them with terrible effect. At length the irresistible foreign artillery drove them from the stockades with heavy loss, and played upon their retreating columns with deadly accuracy. During the attack and retreat the Ti-pings lost upwards of 600 killed and wounded (the wounded falling into the hands of the Imperialists were all put to death), while the allies had *one* man killed and another wounded.

Admiral Hope, who grounded his precious *casus belli* upon the *possible* destruction of supplies *by the Ti-pings*, states in his report of this and the following actions:—

"All these camps, which contained large quantities of rice collected from the surrounding country, were burnt, AND THE GRAIN DESTROYED."

A few days before the attack upon Wong-ka-dza, H.M. gunboat *Flamer* attacked and destroyed a fleet of 300 Ti-ping boats, "*deeply laden with rice and live stock.*" Who, then, proved to be the devastator and marauder; the uncivilized Chinese, or the civilized Christian? Yet the principal pretence given for attacking the Ti-pings was that they *might* do what Admiral Hope and his colleagues so effectually *did*.

After chasing the fugitives so long as the Enfield would reach them, the allied force gave up the pursuit, and retired to the village of Che-poo, where they had rested the previous night. Meanwhile, those who escaped from this slaughter met with another enemy, in the shape of a strong contingent of the filibuster Ward's disciplined Chinese. This ally of Admiral Hope, chagrined at having lost this opportunity, determined to attack another fortified camp with his own men. The position assigned to this respectable person during the first engagement was to cut off and kill the Ti-pings as they fled from the fire of the British and French artillery. Fortunately for those unoffending people he arrived too late. When he did honour his worthy friends with his presence, history telleth not whether they were tired, or engaged looting, or making merry; but certain it is that they let him make his attack unassisted, except by Admiral Hope.

This PAR NOBILE, on valorous deeds intent, heedless alike of mud, heat, and fatigue, marched for several miles by intricate pathways, through creeks, ditches, and swampy paddy-fields, to the rebel camp near the village of Lu-ka-kong; and elated, doubtless, by the Admiral's narration of his chivalrous deeds at Wong-ka-dza, and assured by his loss of only one man, halted in front of the Ti-ping stockade.

Drawing his mercenary sword, and brushing back the Yankee locks, General Ward gave the word to assault in a tone of assured victory. The disciplined Chinamen, led by their foreign officers, rushed forward bravely enough; but the Ti-pings had not been half destroyed by shot and shell; neither at that time had they lost their best troops in conflict with the British and French, nor the moral effect of their former triumphs. Consequently, after three attempts to storm the stockade, when five officers and seventy men were placed *hors de combat*, Admiral Hope advanced to call off the men, and was rewarded with a Ti-ping bullet lodged in the calf of his leg. Ward, having none of the resistless artillery to mow down the patriotic Ti-pings, found them more than a match for his men—disciplined, led by foreigners, and well armed as they were. A retreat was therefore sounded, and the British Admiral was ignominiously carried away upon a litter borne by sundry cursing Celestials.

To avenge the glaring insult and audacity of those rebels who had dared to deposit a bullet in the calf of a leg of a British Admiral, who was doing his utmost to kill them, the next morning the allied forces brought their artillery to bear, and without a single casualty succeeded in driving the Ti-pings from this and several neighbouring entrenchments, killing some 300, and burning and destroying the large quantities of grain, as stated by Admiral Hope. Not only in this instance, but very many others, the allies acted with far more wanton destructiveness than ever the Ti-pings did.

The next attack upon the Ti-pings by the gallant allies came off on the 17th of April. Upon this occasion the redoubtable Admiral was unable to act, in consequence of his injured limb. The place at which the combined English, French, and mercenaries gathered fresh (Chinese) laurels, was the village of Che-poo, with its defences, situated about 18 miles S.E. of Shanghae. The attacking force mustered some 2,500 strong, with 14 pieces of artillery, the whole commanded by General Staveley and Admiral Protet, assisted by Captain Borlase, R.N., and the filibuster Ward.* These troops were embarked in a flotilla of British and French gunboats, and carried up the Shanghae river, to cause as much devastation and bloodshed as they had already created elsewhere.

It was a splendid morning, and the landscape seemed beautiful, as the troops, after landing in the neighbourhood of Che-poo, marched forward on their mission. Through fields rich with the ungathered crops, which it was pretended the Ti-pings might devastate, over seven or eight miles of smiling and profusely-cultivated country they wound their way. Upon arriving within a mile of the village, they halted for their guns to come up, and rested preparatory to the coming attack.

The guns having arrived, at 2 P.M. were in position,

---

* The force consisted of :—

British Naval Division, with 3 howitzers	350
Royal Artillery, with 4 howitzers	90
H.M. 99th Regiment	80
22nd Punjaub N. I.	400
5th Bombay N. I.	400
French Contingent, with 5 rifled guns and 2 field-pieces	700
Disciplined Chinese of Ward's legion	400
Total	2,420

and opened a most destructive fire at 500 yards, and in half an hour the rebels were in full retreat. The poor fellows endeavoured to face the overwhelming hail of shot and shell; and, as one official report states, "returned a desultory fire, *but without doing any mischief,* while the allies made dreadful havoc amongst them." Driven from their works by the irresistible artillery, the Ti-pings retreated in three columns in the direction of the walled city, Chan-za, when, as the official report states, "the Royal artillery and naval guns were brought to bear upon the retreating mass with terrible effect." The loss of the Ti-pings, out of a total strength of less than 4,000, amounted to more than 600 killed and 300 taken prisoners, who were, of course, cruelly executed by the Manchoo mandarins; the allied loss was *nil!*

The Ti-pings had not expected any attack upon that day, and when the camp was entered, their dinners were found smoking in the cups, while half-finished letters were lying on the chiefs' table.

The report published in the *Shanghae Daily Shipping List* states:—

"As the houses were *ransacked,* great quantities of valuable jewels, gold, silver, dollars, and costly dresses were found, which was fair (?) *loot* to the officers and men. One blue-jacket found 1,600 dollars, and several soldiers upwards of 500 each, while many picked up gold bangles, earrings, and other ornaments and pearls set with precious stones. *It was a glorious day of looting for everybody,* and we hear that one party, who discovered the Ti-ping treasury chest with several thousand dollars in it, after loading himself to his heart's content, was obliged to give some of them away to lighten his pockets, which were heavier than he could well bear—a marked case of *l'embarras des richesses.* The rebel stud of ponies was well supplied also, and many of the soldiers rode back with their booty."

All this *looting* and butchery of unresisting men (it would be absurd to term the defence of the Ti-pings, resulting in one Englishman wounded, but hundreds of themselves killed—a resistance according to military *parlance*) was executed, we must particularly remember, because their cause, which had for its sole object expulsion of the foreign Manchoo and establishment of Christianity, *might* interfere with British commercial interests, and that "temporary one arising out of the indemnities!"

The *Shanghae Daily Shipping List*, just quoted from, was the paid official organ of the British Government, and when it stated the above, it may easily be imagined what the disgraceful scene really was. This journal, under a variety of style and title, has been repeatedly quoted in the Blue Books upon China, issued by Her Majesty's Government, as the opinion of the press in China. Its truthfulness may fairly be estimated from the following comparison of a statement which appeared in its columns upon the massacre at Wong-ka-dza, and another upon the one at Che-poo. Both places are situated in the same tract of country, and only a few miles apart. In its detail of the first affair, the official organ, speaking of the slaughter of the Ti-pings, terms it :—

"A just retaliation on those wretches who had made their smiling land *a scene of misery and desolation.*"

Reporting the second affair, it states :—

"*The aspect of the country looked charming*, as the expedition threaded its way among *cultivated fields covered with the green crops* sown by the industrious inhabitants."

Like all other unscrupulous sources of opposition to the revolutionists, the *Shanghae Daily Shipping List* is sufficiently condemned by its own words. It needeth not a partizan to advocate Ti-pingdom; any person not blinded by prejudice or dollars, and who will take the trouble to study both sides of the question with proverbial English fair-play, cannot fail to become favourably interested in the insurgents, simply through the rabid diatribes which prove the bigotry of opponents and the inadvertant contradictions which prove their falseness.

In order to avoid quarrelling about the plunder, General Staveley and the Admirals entered into the following agreement with regard to the future freebooting exploits. Immediately after the heavily laden heroes, sailors, soldiers, marines, and all had deposited their *loot* in safe quarters, the triumviri, in solemn conclave, assembled upon the 22nd of April, and made the following formal regulations:—

"Previous to the capture of Kah-ding and the other towns from the rebels, proper arrangements shall be made . . . to collect whatever may be of value, in order to its fair distribution amongst the troops, to whom the same is to be made known before the commencement of the operations."

Eager to try the merit of their regulated loot hunting, on the 27th of April, the allies again set forth to attack the Ti-pings. Upon this occasion their looting propensities were indulged in at the town of Kah-ding, situate about 30 miles to the N.W. of Shanghae. The allied force consisted of nearly 4,000 men, with 30 pieces of artillery,* assisted by an army of Imperialist *braves*, under the command of Le, a Chinese general.

The advance guard of the allies having been arrested by two small stockades, defending the water approach to Kah-ding, upon the morning of the 29th, the artillery was

---

* The allied force consisted of:—

British troops, under General Staveley:—
- Royal Engineers 22
- Royal Artillery, with 7 guns and 6 mortars . 100
- H.M. 31st Regiment 552
- H.M. 99th and 67th Regiments . 280
- 5th Bombay N.I. . . . 350
- 22nd Punjaub N.I. . . . 350

French force, under Admiral Protet:—
- Algerian Infantry, Chasseurs, Marines, and Seamen, with 8 guns 900

British Naval Division, under Captain Borlase, R.N.:
- Seamen and Marines, with 9 guns . 330

Ward's disciplined Chinese . . . 1,000

Total 3,884

Assisted by Imperialist troops under Manchoo General Le . 5,000

brought into play and the defenders of the out-work driven back upon the city, losing some 50 men during their resistance and retreat, the European enemy following in rapid pursuit up to the walls of Kah-ding without a single casualty.

The last day of April was spent by the allies in reconnoitering the city and landing the heavy guns, which had been brought in boats from Shanghae. Before dawn on the morning of May the 1st, the whole of the guns were in position, and the troops safely under cover in the ruined suburbs, ready to pick off the defenceless Ti-pings with their far-reaching rifles. The country traversed during the preceding days is thus spoken of in the *China Mail*, a paper bitterly hostile to the insurgents:—

"After marching along a good road, and through *a beautiful country with fine thriving crops*, the troops reached the southern suburb of Kah-ding."

Daylight of the 1st of charming May was ushered in by the roar of a large park of foreign artillery. Kah-ding, although a walled town, was undefended with cannon, and its garrison of some 5,000 or 6,000 men were, for the most part, armed with bamboo spears. The European troops having invested three of the city gates, the fourth, the only way of retreat for the besieged, was watched by the Imperialist *braves*, commissioned to cut up the Ti-pings as they fled from the British and French artillery. To the concentrated and terrific fire of thirty pieces of large ordnance, the defenders of the city replied with a brisk though totally ineffective discharge of gingalls. The storm of iron poured upon them soon silenced their fire and drove them from the walls, and with a loss of several hundred, they fled from the town, cutting their way through the Imperialist troops, who watched their only line of retreat. In order to delay the storming of the city, and so afford time for its evacuation, a small body of the Ti-ping soldiery nobly remained and sacrificed themselves for their comrades. This devoted band, numbering about 130, held their post at the south gate, the principal point of attack, until the European stormers were on the walls, three little 2-pound Chinese guns on the gate tower having been worked till the parapet, overthrown by the crushing fire of the siege train, fell upon and buried the gunners beneath the *débris*.

Driven back by the overwhelming advance of the storming party, the heroic few retired to the north gate, through which the garrison had made their escape; here to a man they fell, while courageously placing themselves between the foe and their retreating comrades. The greater number of them were mere boys, and from the richness of their dress, evidently of good position among their friends. Three little fellows, each armed with a small matchlock, were seen by a friend of mine to rush forward directly a large shell would knock down a portion of the parapet and fire off their puny weapons at the foe. They were too small to reach the loop-holes, and so waited till the 32-pound shot of the besiegers made a hole for them to use. To avoid the deadly rifles they never used the same hole twice, but nevertheless were all killed, for my friend, when passing round the walls, found their bodies lying close together and crushed by a mass of fallen stonework.

The *China Mail*, in its account of the assault, states:—

" The scene was now most picturesque. A shell had set fire to part of the city close at hand; the early morning sun was shining pleasantly upon the fields, *rich with ungathered crops*, and the French band played as the troops scaled the walls."

The loss of the Ti-pings at the capture of Kah-ding was nearly 500 killed in the city; 2,000 slaughtered while escaping from the murderous artillery, by the Manchoo troops under Le, who had the bodies mutilated, and offered to produce their ears to General Staveley; and about 1,000 taken prisoners, who, although captured by the assistance of British soldiers, perished in the Manchoo execution shambles.

The stolen property agreement proved very useful at the capture of Kan-ding, nearly 200,000 dollars' worth having been seized in that city without the loss of a single life to the brave allies.

The *China Mail*, in its issue, "15th May, 1862," although mistakenly considering the Ti-ping revenue (obtained from taxation, silk, &c.) as "the poor people's property," very rightly condemns the wholesale system of brigandage practised by the allies. After referring to the "mercenary" and "sordid" nature of the intervention, it states:—

"There is another matter of regret, and that is, that while we are stigmatizing the rebels as robbers and bandits, we should take their treasures and divide it among ourselves."

Again it continues:—

"It would be difficult to say which are the more shameless robbers of the two, the Taepings who spoil the people, or the English forces who retake the spoil and share it among themselves, while those originally robbed are famishing in Shanghae. It may well be questioned whether the whole history of warfare can record a parallel example of forgetfulness, utter forgetfulness, of all propriety to this loot-hunting game which Admiral Hope is now engaged in. An expedition against the rebels is now shown to be so harmless to those engaged in it that we may expect to hear of gentlemen giving their wives and sisters a pic-nic in front of the next town that is besieged, when we have no doubt that much amusement could be had among the engineers and artillery by allowing the girls to point the guns. And this is the sort of warfare in which the heart of the jaded and harassed soldier is to be cheered with *loot!* . . . There is every reason to believe that England's chivalry is likely to be kept a profound secret from the people of China so long as her affairs are under the present guidance."

Such is the opinion of a journal always hostile to the Ti-pings.

Having loaded their boats with plunder, and placed a garrison of some 500 European troops in Kah-ding, the British and French warriors returned to Shanghae and vain-gloriously displayed their evilly acquired riches about the rum-shops of that model settlement, while their worthy allies, the *braves*, made a gallant and triumphant entry, with trophies of Ti-ping heads, cruelly hacked from the men vanquished by British and French artillery. When these heads became unpleasant to parade about the foreign settlement, and the *loot* became exhausted, or the allied commanders eager for more, the combined forces were mustered together for another desolating raid into a a country that would have been happy and peaceful but for their wicked interference.

The city of Tsing-poo, situated close upon 32 miles to the west of Shanghae, although falsely represented by officialdom as " in the neighbourhood," was next selected for sack and pillage.

Starting from Shanghae in British gun-boats (which, by the by, always returned towing long tiers of loot laden boats) upon the 7th of May, the expedition, after being placed in country boats about twenty miles up the river, arrived before Tsing-poo on the evening of the second day.

General Staveley was Commander-in-chief, assisted by the French Admiral, while the English Admiral, in spite of his wound, was present as an admiring non-effective.

The combined force comprised 2,613 British and French troops, with nearly forty pieces of artillery ; about 1,800 of Ward's filibusters ; and an Imperialist army of 5,000 to 7,000 men, under their general, Le.* Tsing-poo was garrisoned by some 4,000 Ti-pings, very few of whom escaped.

Before daylight on the 12th of May, the besieging forces, with guns and ladders, covering and storming parties, were in position. They moved up silently in the dead of night and early morning, and were in their places by 4 a.m. Then came a short half-hour of the peculiar suspense before battle, while all those valiant British and French well-armed troops lay flat on their faces, safely under cover, and breathing not a word, for

* *See Note*, p. 509.

fear the doomed Ti-pings *might* by a singular piece of good fortune manage to hurt some of them. By this time, however, the warm summer day was dawning, and the beleaguered garrison, discovering the formidable array against them, opened fire with the few small guns they possessed, sending their uneven roundshot whizzing over the heads of the crouching enemy.

Almost at the same moment the besiegers opened fire from their numerous and overwhelming artillery. Armstrong guns, naval 32-pounders, French rifled guns and mortars (with one French 68-pounder, rifled piece, mounted on board a light draught gunboat) in breaching and enfilading batteries, commenced a terrific bombardment of the south gate and wall.

The city, during the night, had been surrounded by the Chinese *braves;* no hope of escape presented itself, and the besieged fought as desperate men will fight for their lives. Amid the torrent of shells, shrapnel, Moorsom, conical, diaphragm, Armstrong, and other scientific engines of destruction crashing and continuously exploding among them, they bravely stood to their four or five 2-pounders, and resolutely manned their walls under the fearful and murderous fire. The poor Ti-pings, in order to protect themselves from the irresistible foreign shell, or "twice eye shot," as the Cantonese in their *pidgeon* English term it, had built a sort of stockade all round the city wall; this, with the parapet, formed a passage, which was covered in with a beamed and tiled roof. Instead of affording safety to them, however, this work added to the destructiveness of the enemy's fire, though it would have been better for the doomed men to have been killed outright by British shot than be captured and tortured to death in the execution grounds of the Manchoos. A battery of four Armstrong guns enfilading the wall sent almost every shell through the roof, to burst between the parapet and stockade, thereby inflicting fearful havoc among the crowded defenders.

After about an hour's bombardment, two practicable breaches were effected by the besiegers; the English and French storming parties then advanced, protected by strong covering parties, who kept up a deadly rifle fire on the besieged, while the field-pieces being dragged forward enfiladed the parapet and breaches, mowing them down by dozens as they courageously crowded behind their broken wall to repel the stormers. The two snake flags of the Chief were planted on the summit of the breach, while his bravest men surrounding him did their utmost to drive the assaulting column back. The carnage at this point was immense; the defenders no sooner rushed into view than withering volleys of musketry and a storm of grape and canister destroyed them. The principal Ti-ping chiefs were killed at the head of their men; still, a smart fire from jingalls was kept up till the stormers gained the top of the breach and effected a lodgement; and then, it is sufficient to say, the defenders were attacked with the British bayonet. Even when driven from the wall, several hundred of the Ti-ping soldiery rallied at its foot, and fruitlessly sacrificed themselves in attempting to expel the successful enemy.

The Ti-pings lost upwards of 1,000 men in their obstinate defence, the Allies 2 killed and 10 wounded! About 2,000 were taken prisoners, the greater part of whom supplied the Shanghae execution ground, while the remnant of the garrison succeeded in cutting their way through the hostile lines. Not more than half of the prisoners were fighting men.

Whether the most Christian and civilized allies had not obtained sufficient loot, or killed enough fellow-creatures to satisfy them, I am unable safely to state, but I opine that in neither particular were they satiated. At all events, after sacking Tsing-poo and delivering up their unfortunate captives to the tender mercies of the merciless Imperialists, General Staveley and his coadjutors started off in quest of further glory, dollars, and

Ti-pings. These noble crusaders at length came to the fortified village of Na-jaor, where one of the *triumviri* met with his death.

Na-jaor was simply a village, but a wall having been built around it, a small outwork erected, and the whole surrounded by dykes and dry ditches, with *chevaux de frize* and pallisades between them, it would have been a difficult place to capture without artillery. The outwork mounted three small guns, and a few others were divided between the usual square flanking defences of a Chinese wall. The garrison of this place can scarcely have numbered 1,000, all told.

The Armstrong guns and other artillery of the British and French opened fire and shelled the defenders out of the small redoubt, upon the afternoon of the 17th of May. While this was going on the garrison of the village made a spirited sortie, but, with only an armament of bamboo spears and rusty jingalls, were of course driven back with great loss. At last the fire of the besieged seemed silenced, while their wall was breached and crumbling in every direction. The stormers now rushed forward with their usual bravery, sword in hand and bayonet to the charge, to assault a Ti-ping post that had been thoroughly shelled for a couple of hours, and in which nought but a few frightened fugitives and the bodies of the slain were likely to be found. In the case of Na-jaor, however, there was more courage required than the attacking force imagined, for, instead of finding the walls deserted except by the killed and wounded, and the garrison in flight, they were suddenly faced by an ambuscade which had been concealed under comparative protection at the interior slope of the wall during the bombardment. The British and French were rushing forward at the double, their leading files had already reached the ditch at the foot of the rampart, when the Ti-pings, starting from their cover, re-manned the walls and opened a sharp fire with jingalls, matchlocks, and the few European-made fire-arms which they possessed. Cheering vigorously, or rather yelling, the defenders maintained a well-directed fire for some little time, killing the French Admiral with a ball through his heart, and wounding about a dozen other of the assailants. The allies experienced a momentary check, but the whole resistless array of artillery having swept the walls with their iron tempest, the storming parties again rushed forward and succeeded in establishing themselves upon the walls before the defenders were able to re-man them. Then the work of slaughter was continued with the rifle, the unwieldy bamboos, with iron spikes at the ends, proving a worse than useless defence.

Mercy seems never to have entered into the minds of those Christian warriors, who loudly inveighed against the Ti-pings as "bloodthirsty monsters," &c., &c.; for when victory crowned their unparalleled feats of arms, no effort to save the defenceless and unresisting fugitives was ever made, but while those who had thrown down their arms were vainly trying to hide or flee from the deadly rifle, or stood blocked in a gateway of the tower, the valorous conquerors calmly and easily continued to shoot them down so long as they remained within range.

The total loss of the Allies at the capture of Na-jaor was, the French Admiral killed, and sixteen men wounded. The Ti-pings left dead at their posts, which they had *really* bravely though fruitlessly striven to defend, upwards of 500 men, more than half their whole force. Directly the place was fairly in their possession the respectable victors dispersed in search of plunder; as one report has it, "looting parties were formed, the French looting one half and the English the other."

The ill-gained spoil having been stowed away in the boats, the Allies marched on for the next Ti-ping position devoted to destruction, leaving a strong detachment in charge of Na-jaor. The place which had now attracted the cupidity, love of military *glory*, or some unknown sentiment of the Allies, was a small town named Cho-lin, situated about six miles from Na-jaor, 26 miles to the S.S.W. of Shanghae, and within two miles of the sea.

Having arrived before Cho-lin during the night of May 18, the Allies began to establish their powerful batteries, and on the morning of the 19th opened fire upon the town. The Ti-pings in garrison, some 2,000 or 3,000 strong, replied to the best of their resources with a few pieces of immoveable Chinese artillery, jingalls, and matchlocks. At noon the besiegers ceased firing and refreshed themselves with *chow-chow* and brandy. Meanwhile, a Ti-ping chief performed an act of the most daring courage with remarkable coolness and audacity. Having observed the occupation of the besiegers, this chief, leaving the town by the opposite side, made a circuit, and coming upon the rear of the enemy's position, calmly rode right through it with a few followers, satisfying himself as to their composition and numbers. "Everyone took him for an Imperialist and allowed him to pass on. When he got near the town he rode for his life, and got to his friends inside the city." So reported one of the officers engaged in the attack. Undaunted by the powerful artillery and formidable array of the European troops, the Ti-ping chief determined to hold and defend his trust against them, even although he must have been convinced that he had no effectual means by which he could repel or reply to their attack. The day passed on and with it the last hope of the beleaguered garrison, who scorned to take advantage of the opportunity to evacuate the town and save their lives.

At daylight on the 20th all the Allies' guns, being in position, opened fire again, the Armstrong guns and field pieces sweeping the defenders from the walls, and the hoarsely-roaring 32's steadily firing to effect a breach. Storming, covering, and sharpshooting parties waited around the devoted place until the murderous shelling should subdue all opposition to their heroic advance. At length, two practicable breaches were effected, the enfilading batteries, established on either flank, poured their crushing *mitraille* along the parapet, sweeping away every man who dared to show himself, and the assaulting column pushed forward to the breaches. The Ti-pings had in this case been able to maintain a small number of troops on the wall by means of some ingeniously contrived bomb-proofs. A few narrow pits were dug behind the parapet and covered in with planks overlaid with earth, under which some hundred or two found shelter. When the artillery ceased its fire as the stormers mounted the breach, these men made a desperate defence, while the rest of the garrison, emerging from their places of concealment, rushed to man the walls and assist them. But what could these miserably armed men effect against the hundreds of perfectly equipped Europeans pouring over their shattered walls? They fell bravely, disputing every inch of ground.

The defenders driven from the ramparts or killed, the gallant Allies rushed through the small town, *indiscriminately massacring every man, woman, and child within its walls*. The Ti-pings had so earnestly endeavoured to shut out the besiegers that they had most effectually blocked themselves in, and were consequently butchered almost to a man. After the massacre was over, an officer of the force, writing to the *North China Herald*, stated, "Almost every house we entered contained dead and dying men."

The *China Mail*, in its report of the affair, terms it: "A most indiscriminate carnage on the part of our Allies at the taking of Cho-lin." The *Overland Trade Report*, in its issue of June 10, states :—

"Since the death of Admiral Protet the French troops have been behaving like fiends, killing indiscriminately men, women, and children. Truth demands the confession that British sailors have likewise been guilty of the commission of similar revolting barbarities—not only on the Taepings, but upon the inoffensive helpless country people. It is a most singular circumstance, but no less strange than true, that the Taepings *have never yet committed an act of retaliation* upon any European who may have fallen into their hands."

Cho-lin captured and the *loot* safely packed up, the conquerors, who only lost *one* killed and four slightly wounded, proceeded to destroy the town itself.

The correspondent of the *North China Herald*, in his report, says:—

"At two o'clock the order was given to set the city on fire, which was executed with such rapidity that the Sikhs had hardly time to get the ponies out of the town, and most of the loot collected had to be abandoned."

The poor horses were admittedly roasted alive; but, when the writer goes on to state "a great many dead bodies" were left in the fired city, he forgets the wounded and "dying men" whom he found in "almost every house," and who no doubt perished in the flames.

With the destruction of Cho-lin the murderous and desolating track of the British and French was for a time arrested. Hitherto, without exception, they had, in Mohawk Indian style, surprised and captured isolated towns and villages. Nothing but the garrisons of these places had opposed them. Upon the day of their last exploit, however, intelligence reached General Staveley that the Chung-wang, with a large army, had taken the field against him, and that Kah-ding was already invested, Tsing-poo threatened, and the Imperialist troops everywhere flying like chaff before the stormy wind. Hastily returning to Shanghae, the authenticity of these reports was at once confirmed by the abject state of terror in which the Manchoo authorities were plunged. It appeared that, during General Staveley's laurel-gathering exploits, nearly the whole available force of Imperialist troops had been concentrated upon Kah-ding, and, having moved upon the next Ti-ping city, Tat-scang, had been there totally defeated; the fugitives, a few hundred out of an army nearly 20,000 strong, having been chased about thirty miles, and into the village of Woo-sung under the protection of the Allies' artillery.

In consequence of this, and the inability of the Manchoo authorities to even garrison the places captured from the patriots by the allied forces, General Staveley proceeded to the relief of Kah-ding with a strong force of British troops. Upon reaching the village of Na-zain, a few miles from the city, they were continually attacked by the Ti-ping force investing it. In all these attacks, however, the assailants were driven back by rifle and artillery fire with heavy loss, the English losing but *one* Sepoy killed and four wounded. It now appearing that the Ti-pings were in the field in force, that the communications of Kah-ding were in their hands, and that the towns of Tsing-poo and Soon-kong were also infested, General Staveley decided upon evacuating Kah-ding; and, pending the arrival of reinforcements, discontinuing his raids upon the Ti-ping strongholds.

We must now for a while turn to other quarters, and record the performance of another act of the Ti-ping drama. While the allied forces were violating their pledges, their orders, and the ordinary laws and usages of civilized or Christian men, the Ti-pings at Ningpo, as everywhere else, were scrupulously observing all their promises, and striving to enter into friendly and commercial relations with foreigners.

It will be remembered that the withdrawal of British missionaries from Ningpo, upon the capture of that city by the Ti-pings, has already been noticed; also Mr. Consul Harvey's sinister reason: "This step will tend to simplify considerably our future relations with the Taepings at Ningpo." We will now proceed to notice what those "future relations" were.

Mr. Consul Harvey having been requested by Mr. Bruce to report upon the character of the Ti-pings, and having been prompted even in the *public* despatches, forthwith indulged his feelings of hostility against those people. It is desirable to notice some of the more salient and characteristic features of the despatch of Mr. Harvey as briefly as possible.

The despatch containing Mr. Harvey's exposition bears date March 20th, 1862, some three months after the occupation of Ningpo by the Ti-pings, and *after* hostilities had been established against them by Admiral Hope and his friends.

Mr. Harvey states:—

"*Not one single step** in the direction of a 'good government' has been taken by the Taepings; *not any attempt* made to organize a political body or commercial institutions; *not a vestige, not a trace of anything* approaching to order, or regularity of action, or consistency of purpose, can be found in any one of their public acts."

In a despatch dated "Ningpo, December 31, 1861," he had stated as follows:—

"They *have* even established a native custom-house, wherein duties will be levied on the Chinese after ten days' grace. . . . It has been reported to me that the insurgents propose establishing a foreign custom-house at this port, such being, it is said, one of their favourite ideas, and forming part of their programme in the capture of Ningpo."

And again—

"The Taepings possess a regular embodied force, a draft from which forms the nucleus of the body of men sent upon any special service."

Mr. Harvey, with an extraordinary self-complacent assumption of impartiality, proceeds to declare that he "judged of Taepingdom in sober sense and dispassionately," yet he concludes the same paragraph by stating that at Ningpo "the last three months had produced ruin, desolation, and the annihilation of *every* vital principle in *all* that surrounds the presence, or lies under the bane, of the Taepings." Again, only a few lines further on, he says:—

"It is palpable that a party which, after ten years' full trial, is found to produce *nothing*, and to destroy *everything*, cannot pretend to last, or be admitted, even indirectly, into the comity of nations."

---

* Italics are by the Author.

Now, as Mr. Bruce himself reports that "85,000 bales of silk" were obtained from people who "destroy everything," and as the Ti-pings did "pretend to last"—so much so, indeed, that British and French assistance to the Manchoos was necessary to save them from total destruction, Mr. Harvey's "sober sense," to say the least, seems very doubtful.

The despatch under review is one of the most extraordinary series of contradictory terms ever produced, and really deserves a place in the British Museum or some old curiosity shop, as the "sober" creation of a person who takes remarkable care to assure his readers that he is perfectly "unbiassed." Within half a dozen lines of the last quoted passage Mr. Harvey audaciously protests:—
"I repeat I have no bias one way or the other. . . ."
He then proceeds to state:—

"I have found in official dealings with them" (the Ti-ping chiefs) "*a rough and blunt sort of honesty quite unexpected and surprising*, after years of public intercourse with the Imperial mandarins."

Now, in the very next paragraph he speaks of them as—

"The naturally suspicious Taepings, who, amongst other peculiarities, *possess a power of concealment and general secresy quite wonderful* to meet in China."

Mr. Harvey attempts to prove the plundering propensities of the Ti-ping soldiery by the following invention:—

"On questioning decently-dressed Taeping soldiers as to how they liked their profession, the reply has ever been the following:—

"'Why should I not like it? I help myself to everything I choose to lay hands upon; and if interfered with, I just cut the man's head off who so interferes.'"

By the side of this we will just place Mr. Hewlett's report to Consul Harvey of his embassy to the Ti-pings at Yu-yaou, upon their advance to Ningpo:—

"We saw but few dead bodies about, and of those some were their own men *who had been caught plundering and burning.*"

Endeavouring to vilify the social *régime* of the Christian patriots, Mr. Harvey trusts to his inventive genius again, and writes :—

"Your Excellency is doubtless aware that marriage is strictly forbidden amongst the Taepings, and forms, with opium-smoking, a capital offence."

Now, Mr. Harvey makes this false assertion in face of the " Proclamation by Tien-wang, establishing a scale according to which the number of wives are to be regulated in all ranks," as published in 1862, at page 45, Blue Book upon "The Rebellion in China," and which commences—

"Formerly I made a decree as to the canon of marriages. . . ."

This unbiassed official winds up his sober and dispassionate effusion with a few equally temperate conclusions. For example—

"I now, therefore, take the liberty of declaring, once for all (*and for ten years I have firmly adhered to, and been consistent in, this opinion*), that the Taeping rebellion is the greatest delusion as a political or popular movement, and the Taeping doctrines the most gigantic and blasphemous imposition as a creed, or ethics, that the world ever witnessed. . . . There is nothing in past records so dark or so bad ; such abominations committed under the name of religion ; such mock-heroic buffoonery ; such horrors accompanied by pantaloonery ; and so much flimsy web worked in the midst of blood and high tragical events."

If the "ten years" of obstinate adhesion to an opinion formed before anything was known of the Ti-pings, is Mr. Harvey's idea of "sober sense" and "no bias" (and he declares it is), we can easily believe that the "dispassionate" ruminations of so long a period destroyed what little reason and religion he may at one time have possessed. His partizanship even lays him open to the charge with which he has so falsely accused the Ti-pings when stating that their doctrines were "the most gigantic and blasphemous imposition," &c. ; inasmuch as the Ti-ping doctrines are taken from our Bible, are in all essential particulars precisely similar to our own, and alone constitute their " creed, or ethics."

Mr. Harvey terms himself "a sensible and reasoning Englishman," and proceeds to declare the revolution—

"A sanguinary raid, and an extended brigandage over the country, burning, destroying, *and killing* EVERYTHING *that has life in it.*"

In a surprising manner, after a few sentences, he brings the dead to life:—

"They come, and the helpless inhabitants crouch down and submit. They (the Taepings) go, and the people breathe again and rejoice."

"Tel maitre, tel valet," it is said, and Mr. Harvey seems to have likened into Mr. Bruce amazingly. Mr. Bruce has stated, "every locality is totally destroyed by the Ti-pings." Mr. Harvey chimes in with the above, "killing everything," and "not a vestige" diatribes. Mr. Bruce, in a despatch dated "Pekin, April 10, 1862," inclosing Mr. Harvey's precious production to Earl Russell, states with regard to the Ti-pings:—

"No commerce can co-exist with their presence, and no specific relations are possible with a horde of pirates and brigands, who are allowed to commit every excess, while professing a nominal allegiance to an ignorant and ferocious fanatic."

Again, in a despatch dated "Pekin, April 18, 1862," Mr. Bruce states that their presence in any district is "accompanied by the *utter* destruction of the materials of trade."

Singularly enough, General Staveley, although chief leader of the massacres of Ti-pings, in a despatch to the Secretary of State for War, dated "Shanghae, July 3, 1862," entirely and absolutely contradicts the imaginary devastations of Mr. Bruce and his Consul by the following statement:—

"Europeans continue to visit the rebel country *for purposes of trade*, and are treated with civility; *large quantities of silk* have been brought into Shanghae during the last fortnight, *and trade seems in a thriving state.*"*

* *Vide* "Further Papers relating to the Rebellion in China," 1863, p. 43; Inclosure in No. 27; Brigadier-General Staveley to Sir C. Lewis.

Mr. Harvey concludes his judgment passed in "sober sense and dispassionately" by the following words:—

> "Your Excellency may rest assured that we shall only arrive at a correct appreciation of this movement, and do it thorough justice, when it is treated by us as land piracy on an extensive scale—piracy odious in the eyes of *all* men—and, as such, to be swept off the face of the earth by *every means* within the power of the Christian and civilized nations trading with this vast empire."

Such are the avowed sentiments of the man who protests that he has "no bias" or prejudice.

Although the occupation of Ningpo by the Ti-pings actually increased the export trade, and although even Mr. Consul Harvey admitted that it was captured and held with "wonderful moderation;" still, when hostilities had become established by Admiral Hope and General Staveley, it was impossible either their designs could succeed while Ningpo was in Ti-ping possession, or the anomalous policy of holding Shanghae, and not Ningpo, be continued. Consequently, both to stop the supplies and munitions the Ti-pings obtained at the port, and to follow out the hostile policy settled upon, the British authorities determined upon driving them out of Ningpo on the first opportunity. As the scrupulous good conduct and friendliness of the revolutionists afforded no cause of hostility, it became necessary to invent one. How this was effected the following account will show.

One day (the 22nd April, 1862), while giving a salute upon the return of the General Fang from Nankin, several shots appear to have been fired by some Ti-pings in the direction of the foreign settlement. It was thereupon *reported* that these shots had killed a Chinaman or two in that location. This, however, seems very doubtful. At all events, the affair was immediately taken up by Captain Cragie, of H.M.S. *Ringdove*, who wrote to the Chiefs upon the subject, and received a completely satisfactory answer, stating—

"I beg to assure you that, as soon as I have discovered the offenders, I will punish them very severely. I hope, then, that you will think no more about the matter."*

Upon the 26th of April Captain R. Dew, with H.M.S. *Encounter*, arrived at Ningpo from Shanghae, having been ordered there by Admiral Hope. Judging by the conduct of the Admiral at that time, and by the whole circumstances of the war upon the Ti-pings, it becomes morally certain that Captain Dew was dispatched with the reinforcement to Ningpo on purpose to drive them out. The day after his arrival (27th April, dates are important), Captain Dew wrote as follows to the Ti-ping generals in command of the city:—

"*Encounter*, Ningpo, April 27, 1862.

"Sir,—We have received from Commander Cragie your communication regarding the *accidental* discharge of bullets whilst firing a salute . . . as well as the communication from General Hwang. Both these are *so satisfactory*, and tend so much to impress on us your wish to maintain friendly relations with the English and French, that we beg to inform you that *we shall not insist on the demolition of the battery at the point*,† but we still do that you remove the guns. . . .

"We again inform you that it is the earnest wish of our Chiefs to remain neutral‡ and on good terms with you at Ningpo. Till the late acts, they had every reason to be satisfied with your conduct, and you may rest assured that no breach of friendly relations shall emanate from our side. . . .

"(Signed)   R. DEW."

As Colonel Sykes, M.P., has very justly observed in his work, "The Ti-ping Rebellion in China," "incredible as it may appear, the very day after the above letter was sent, which condoned all previous offences, and which expressed the most earnest wish to remain on friendly

---

* This and all following extracts are taken from the Official Correspondence presented to both Houses of Parliament in Blue Book form.

† Compare this with the next despatch of Captain Dew's.

‡ These Chiefs were at the time conducting the murderous raids from Shanghae, already described.

terms, Captain Dew, in oblivion of his promises, addressed the following letter to the Generals:—

"*Encounter*, Ningpo, April 28, 1862.

"Sir,—" (After mentioning the firing of musket balls during the salute, he continues) "I have been sent here *with a considerable force to demand apology*. . . . Having consulted with the officers here in command, I have come to the conclusion that the foreign settlement is now being seriously menaced by a large battery in course of construction at a point outside the city wall . . . *so I have to request that you will cause it to be immediately pulled down*, and that all guns now mounted on the walls opposite our settlement, be removed as well. I am requested by my Admiral to inform you that it would grieve him much* to be obliged, by the hostile acts of your people, to come into collision with them. He will be very sorry to resort to force (!), as he has not the intention or wish to interfere with the Imperialists and yourself at Ningpo, and if the former should attack the city, *we should be entirely neutral, and will not even allow the foreign settlement to harbour the Imperialists*." (After threatening to destroy the battery and capture Ningpo if the guns and fortifications were not removed in "twenty-four hours," Captain Dew concludes with the following passage:)

"When these, my *reasonable* (!) demands, have been carried into effect, I beg you will report them. . . ."

"I have, &c.,
"(Signed)   R. DEW."

It is to be remembered that Captain Dew had received and accepted the "apology" on the 27th, and had replied by stating, "we shall *not* insist on the demolition of the battery." The renewal of the demands which had been formally abandoned on the previous day convinced the Ti-ping generals that Captain Dew was determined to quarrel with them. That officer knew perfectly well, as Colonel Sykes has forcibly expressed it, "that no human being with an ounce of militant blood in his veins would comply with such insulting demands."

The Ti-ping generals, ever forbearing, and always truly earnest in their efforts to obtain the goodwill and friendship of the "foreign brethren," made the following

* Did it grieve the philanthropic Admiral "much," I wonder, to massacre them in his raids from Shanghae?

admirable reply to Captain Dew's grossly offensive despatch, and its readers will find every word truth and sound reason:—

(Précis.)

"Hwang, General, &c., Pang, General, &c., in official communication with Captain R. Dew, R.N., H.M.S. *Encounter*:— In reply to your letter requesting the removal of the battery and guns, we would remark that ever since the capture of Ningpo, both parties have been on most friendly and intimate terms. No suspicions or dislikes; *we have done everything in our power to protect your trade, and kept good faith in every respect;* have always inquired into complaints made to us of our soldiers, and even beheaded some men who broke into a foreign hong; *have wished to keep a lasting peace with you,* and have done all in our power to that end.

"The discharge of bullets in firing the salute the other day was *quite accidental;*—have already taken steps towards punishing offenders. With regard to the erection of a fort at the point, *it is a precautionary measure that a proper regard for the lives of our soldiers renders indispensable, and has nothing whatever to do with foreigners,* as has been already stated to Captain Montgomerie. It is now completed, and we cannot assent to its removal; so also we cannot agree to the removal of the guns from the walls. We have continually esteemed good faith and right. . . .

"With good faith and right feeling as the alpha and omega of one's conduct, each party can afford to put up with one or two trifling matters. With regard to that part of your letter having reference to a probable outbreak of hostilities (we would inform you) that we are not in the least concerned thereat [*lit.,* we are not apprehensive, nor do we take offence thereat]; *we could not bear to break the oaths of friendship we have sworn.* We cannot remove the fort or the guns; should you proceed yourselves to move the same, then it is evident that you have the intention of quarrelling with us. You can, if you please, lead on your soldiers against this city; you can, if you please, attack us; *we shall stand quietly on the defensive* [*lit.,* we shall await the battle with hand in the cuff, *i.e.,* we shall not strike the first blow]. . . . You still wish to be on friendly terms with us; let, then, these dislikes and suspicions be committed to the deep. . . . In any large army good or bad are to be found; do not, therefore, let a small matter like this occasion a breach of such a grand principle as amity. Good fellowship would request you to give our argument your very best consideration."

The remainder of the despatch is irrelevant to the subject of the correspondence. It was received 29th April, 1862. If the Ti-pings had acted rather as angels than men, their rights would not have been respected.

Captain Dew, neither satisfied by their arguments nor conciliated by their tone, addressed to them the following cartel :—

"*Encounter*, Ningpo, May 2, 1862.

"SIR,—We have the honour to inform you that your letter of the 29th ult., in reply to my demands for the insults offered to the French and English flags, and in which you refuse to comply with those very moderate demands,* have been forwarded to our admirals. In the mean time, pending the decision of our chiefs, I have moored the foreign ships two miles down the river, and cut off communication with the city, and am, moreover, ordered by our chiefs, in the event of the following demands not being complied with, to prepare to blockade Ching-hae, and prevent all foreign ships entering the river :—1. *An ample apology.* 2. Removal of all guns from battery and walls opposite our ships. 3. That an officer shall be specially appointed, and that proper measures, by means of guards, shall be taken to prevent anybody whatever coming on the wall opposite the ships or into the battery.—I have, &c.,

"(Signed)   R. DEW."

This repeated attempt of Captain Dew to make the Ti-pings disarm themselves, and his attempt to ignore the apology he had already accepted in his letter to the chief dated 27th April, must afford convincing proof that a premeditated and organized arrangement to quarrel with the Ti-pings existed. The generals in command at Ningpo gave the following reply to Captain Dew. They declared the battery and guns necessary to defend the city against an attack by a fleet from the coast, which in fact appeared, commanded by the notorious pirate Apak, on the 7th May. They promised to remove all ammunition from the guns and to prevent armed men going on the ramparts, but, as Colonel Sykes says in his review of the affair, "Had the generals chucked the guns into the river there would have been some new demand." In their reply the generals state :—

"In reply to letter of 2nd inst., submitting three demands, we beg to inform you that we have carefully examined its contents, and that we will

---

* We may safely presume that Captain Dew was gibing the chiefs.

agree to those demands as far as we are able. In reference to the first, our previous letter *has afforded full explanations on that head*, how that it was the result of an accidental discharge of bullets during the salute . . . In reference to the second point, demanding removal of guns, &c., *our former despatch has already explained that those guns are meant as a precaution against an attack from Ting-hae*, that the multitude of lives in the city that have to be taken care of urgently demands . . . We shall on no account fire the guns, unless the imps attack us. Under the circumstances stated by you, we agree to stop up the port-holes of all the guns bearing on Keang-pih-gan, and to remove all the shot and powder from thence, *so as to manifest to you our desire for lasting amity*. Infer from the third point in your letter that you are afraid that, if people are allowed on the wall, there will be some lawless persons who will fire the guns by mistake. Far from allowing anybody whatever to come on the walls, there are most strict orders against allowing any one to go on the walls, not only on those opposite to Keang-pih, but also all round the city. . . . *We are inordinately desirous of remaining on good terms with you*, and this is our reason for this distinct statement." (Dated 3rd May, 1862.)

Affairs remained in this position till the 7th of May, when Captain Dew wrote to Admiral Hope, stating that on the evening of the 5th, Consul Harvey received a communication from the late Manchoo Governor of Ningpo, to the effect that he was about to attack the city with a strong force, and requesting support from the English and French admirals. The same evening Captain Dew proceeded down the river, found the Imperialist fleet (consisting of the pirate Apak's vessels), and visited the Governor; again, on the following morning, Captain Dew visited that functionary, and the latter, accompanied by his pirate-admiral Apak, returned the visit. While closeted with Captain Dew, they made their arrangements for the forthcoming attack on Ningpo, and the former wrote to his senior officer:—

"So I told them that in consequence of the rebels refusing certain demands we had made, I should have no objection to their passing up, *but that they were not to open fire till well clear of our men-of-war*."

Now Captain Dew may flatter himself that this statement has hoodwinked the people of England, but unfortunately for his reputation, people judge a man by his actions.

Instead of these piratical vessels keeping "well clear" of his ships, they proceeded to execute their part of the programme of attack by keeping *well foul* of his men-of-war, according to previous arrangement.

On May 9th, Consul Harvey reported to Mr. Bruce the movements of the Imperialist, or rather pirate fleet, under the notorious Apak, as follows:—

"Their fleet of junks is at the present moment *lying in front of our settlement*, making preparations for an assault on Ningpo."

He then adds:—

"The Taoutae* Chang, with Commander-in Chief Chin, came to see me this morning (9th) at the Consulate, *in a private manner*, and he informed Captain Dew and myself, that if no unforeseen event happened, the Imperialist attack on Ningpo would take place to-morrow morning at *daylight*."

Now Captain Dew (as the representative of Great Britain) having made the following formal declaration in his despatch to the Ti-ping chiefs, dated April 28th,

"That he has not the intention or wish to interfere with the Imperialists and yourself at Ningpo; and if the former should attack the city, *we should be entirely neutral, and will not even allow the foreign settlement to harbour the Imperialists*."

And again, in his despatch dated April 27th:—

"You may rest assured that no breach of friendly relations shall emanate from our side"—

He was bound to fulfil his pledges of neutrality. He was perfectly well aware that the city could not possibly reply to the fire of the Imperial fleet without endangering the men-of-war and foreign settlement. It was therefore his duty, as he himself expressed, "not to allow the foreign settlement to harbour the Imperialists," or, to have withdrawn the ships of war from the line of fire, as Admiral Hope had no "wish to interfere."

* Governor of a city.

Yet we find Consul Harvey stating that the pirate lorchas are "lying in front of our settlement, making preparations for an assault on Ningpo," and Captain Dew not only authorized this proceeding but declared it a *casus belli* should the Ti-pings venture to return their fire! There are, in fact, ample grounds for the statements in some of the China newspapers, and in many private letters, that the whole affair was arranged between the ex-Governor, the pirate Apak, Captain Dew, and Mr. Consul Harvey: and the idea seems strengthened by the fact that Mr. Harvey, in his letter to Mr. Bruce, dated May 9, terms the arrival of the piratical fleet "an extraordinary but fortunate coincidence, and that it was far too good an opportunity to be lost."

Immediately *after* his second interview with the ex-Governor and the pirate, Captain Dew and the French senior officer sent the following crafty and equivocal ultimatum to the Ti-ping chiefs, dated May 8th:—

"This is to inform you, on the part of the English and French senior naval officers, that had you agreed to their demands, and removed your guns from the walls, they should have felt bound in honour to have acted up to their promise, and have prevented an attack on you on the settlement side by Imperial forces, which in countless numbers and heavily-armed ships advance to attack you. We now inform you *that we maintain a perfect neutrality*, BUT IF YOU FIRE THE GUNS OR MUSKETS FROM THE BATTERY OR WALLS OPPOSITE THE SETTLEMENT ON THE ADVANCING IMPERIALISTS (thereby endangering the lives of our men and people in the foreign settlement), WE SHALL THEN FEEL IT OUR DUTY TO RETURN THE FIRE AND BOMBARD THE CITY."

This was equivalent to saying, "If you defend yourselves against the Imperialists we shall kill you;" for in firing upon the pirate vessels as they advanced from the foreign settlement and amongst the British men-of-war, these latter must inevitably have been endangered.

The following extracts from official despatches and other memoranda will show how the British squadron joined the fleet of pirates in driving the Ti-pings out of Ningpo.

On the 10th of May, Captain Dew wrote to Admiral Hope:—

"SIR,—I found it necessary to capture the city of Ningpo, and drive the rebels out, under the following circumstances:—

"You are aware, Sir, that the rebel chiefs had been informed that if they again fired, either on our ships or in the *direction* of the settlement, we should deem it a *casus belli*. This morning at 10 a.m., the *Kestrel*, and French vessels *Etoile* and *Confucius* were fired on by the Point battery. I cleared for action in this ship, when a volley of musketry was fired on us from the bastion abreast. The undermentioned vessels, viz., *Encounter*, *Ringdove*, *Kestrel*, and *Hardy*, with the *Etoile* and *Confucius*, French gunboats, now opened fire, with shell, on the walls and batteries, which was replied to with much spirit from guns and small arms."

The despatch continues to this effect:—At noon the Ti-ping guns were silenced and practicable breaches effected. At two o'clock the city was stormed, and at five o'clock, all opposition having ceased, the ex-governor and his troops landed from their junks. Captain Dew gave them charge of the city, and re-embarked his men. We must now find out what had become of the ex-governor, his troops, and Apak's fleet during this time. Captain Dew carefully avoids stating whether they had made the attack *at daylight*, according to arrangement, or left him to play the bravo alone, for he does not mention *one word* about his allies, until he hands over the city to them. Consul Harvey, however, in a despatch to Mr. Bruce, dated May the 16th, throws some light upon the subject; he states:—

"Shot and shell were poured into this large city with very little intermission for a period of five hours *by the combined fleet*, at the end of which time the walls were scaled, and the Taeping forces were at once completely routed and dispersed."

The only fleet was *eighty* lorchas of the pirate Apak, the English and French aiding by six vessels only, a fact suppressed by Captain Dew.

The final expulsion of the Ti-pings from Ningpo was thus effected:—

Early on the morning of the 10th, the piratical fleet

commenced the attack upon Ningpo, advancing from the foreign settlement and then manœuvring round and round the British and French gunboats, firing at the Ti-pings when *between* their line of fire and the foreign vessels. Captain Dew never attempted to enforce his pretended order for them to keep " well clear " of his vessels. For some time the Ti-pings bore this attack silently and without reply, doubtless trusting that Captain Dew would either move his vessels or make the pirates give them a clear berth. This, however, was not done, the intention being to compel the Ti-pings to open fire on the attacking fleet, when, as the latter were placed directly between the British and French men-of-war and the guns of the town, any shot must necessarily pass in the " direction " of those vessels, and thereby constitute the false *casus belli* required, and eagerly watched for by Captain Dew with his vessels quite prepared and his guns loaded and ready.

At last human nature could bear no more, and the Ti-pings opened a musketry fire upon the pirate lorchas, yet still with extraordinary forbearance, and such a desire to avoid endangering the foreign ships or settlement, that they did not make use of their artillery. It is perfectly certain that the Manchoo piratical fleet dared not have ventured to make their attack unless fully assured of foreign co-operation. That such assistance *was* guaranteed and arranged has scarcely ever been doubted.

Many of the Ti-ping soldiers had been killed by the fire of the pirate fleet before they replied with musketry. The very instant they did so, the British and French vessels came to the aid of their allies, and commenced bombarding the town. It is said that a couple of bullets from the volley fired upon a lorcha, which having just delivered her broadside was tacking under the stern of the *Kestrel*, struck the quarter of the latter vessel. This may have accidentally occurred; but it is, however, perfectly certain that the Ti-pings did not fire upon the foreign men-of-war, as stated by Captain Dew.

The Ti-pings fought their battery against the overwhelming fire from the heavy pivot guns of the smaller vessels and the broadsides from the *Encounter* until every gun was dismounted and the work knocked to pieces. When the British and French storming parties carried the walls of Ningpo, the defenders offered a determined resistance; but shell and Enfield rifles at last overcame it; though not until both the generals Hwang and Fang were severely wounded did they evacuate the city, leaving about 100 dead within and around the walls. The British loss was only 3 killed and 23 wounded.

Even Consul Harvey termed the conduct of the Ti-pings when they captured Ningpo "wonderfully moderate." What will the British public think of the following account of the behaviour of Captain Dew's allies when re-established in the city? Contrasting the events which followed the Ti-ping seizure of the city with those which occurred on its subsequent capture by the British and French, can any question arise as to which was the most civilized and merciful? The correspondent of the *China Mail*, under date the 22nd May, 1862, states:—

"The rebels retreated through the west gate—the pirates then entered the city and began the work of destruction, and in a few hours did more damage than the rebels did in the whole of the five months that they had possession. . . . On *Sunday* the reinstated Taoutae was busy chopping off the heads of the unlucky rebels that he caught, and otherwise torturing them. I saw some fearful sights; such as a boy with his entrails cut right out, from a great gash across the stomach, carried round the back—a man with all the flesh torn off his ribs, leaving them quite bare—a man whose heart had been torn out and his head cut off; together with others equally revolting. . . . On Monday the same scenes were enacting. . . One of the principal murderers and torturers of the poor fellows found in the city was one A-fook, the *British Consul's* boy or personal attendant, who was dressed up in silks, and who, stuck upon a pony, paraded the city with attendants, ordering them to execute unfortunates, and issuing orders (which were actually obeyed) to the English soldiers."

Now it can safely be declared that the Ti-pings have *never* committed similar atrocities to the above. They have, it is true, often killed large numbers at the capture of obstinately defended towns, but their prisoners were never tortured to death as their comrades, captured by British troops and then delivered up to the cruel Tartar mandarins, have been under the shadow of the Union Jack.

The *China Overland Trade Report* of October 14, 1862, states :—

"So much mystery and double-dealing has been practised by the allies to wrest this port from the Taipings, and so little regard for veracity pervades the official despatches regarding their doings, that the truth is most difficult to arrive at, and has certainly never yet been published. . . The possession of Ningpo by the Taipings was peculiarly adapted to thwart those schemes for aiding and abetting the Imperial cause, which have so peculiarly characterized the British minister. The Taipings held the province, and it is evident that the possession of a seaport would have enabled them not only to have deprived Shanghae of the greater proportion of the customs duties,* but to have diverted the same into their own exchequer. Now Mr. Lay was acting Chinese ambassador in London, and the absorption of these duties would have entirely frustrated the object of his errand † and indeed have destroyed the main stay of the Imperial cause. Besides, the possession of Ningpo would have enabled the Taipings to have obtained all the munitions of war which they stood so much in need of. It would have dispelled the *illusion* of their being inimical to foreign trade. . . . Admiral Hope . . . from some such cogent reasons as are above named, fell into the British minister's views, and clearly resolved on the recapture of the place by fair means or foul. The mode of accomplishing this design reflects *indelible disgrace* on British prestige. . .

"Admiral Hope detached a portion of his fleet to Ningpo under command of Captain Dew, of H.M.S. *Encounter*, clearly to act in concert with this piratical squadron, with which daily communications were established. The day before the Taoutae arrived at Ningpo, the British ships had taken up their stations, and had cleared for action. Captain Dew had opened a correspondence with the Taiping chiefs, the drift of which was a demand that they should remove a certain battery on some absurd pretext, which they refused to do. The night prior to the attack, a council of war was held on board the *Encounter*, and a private note was seen by several Europeans at Ningpo, written by a certain British official, which stated that the city would be attacked the following morning. The pirate fleet arrived

---

* From these duties the indemnity for the war was being extracted.

† The errand was to obtain the notorious Anglo-Chinese flotilla.

accordingly, and proceeding in driblets *between* the British men-of-war and the city, opened fire. This could not possibly be returned without directing the guns towards the men-of-war. The result is known and need not be repeated."

The *Hong-kong Daily Press*, in a long article upon the capture of Ningpo by the Anglo-Franco-Manchoo-piratical fleet, makes precisely similar statements to those quoted from the *Overland Trade Report*, and commences with the following paragraph:—

"There never was a falser, more unprovoked, or more unjustifiable act than the taking of Ningpo by the allies from the Taipings. It should, in fairness, be recorded *to the eternal disgrace of Captain* RODERIC DEW, *of H.M.S. Encounter.*"

CHAPTER XIX.

A Double Wedding.—Its Celebration.—The Honeymoon.—Its Interruption.—Warlike Preparations.—Soong-kong Invested.—General Ching's Despatch.—Tsing-poo Recaptured.—Ti-ping Seventy Excused.—England's Responsibility.—Curious Chinese Custom.—The Chung-wang's Policy.—His Explanation.—The Ti-ping Court of Justice.—How Conducted.—Opium Smoking.—Its Effects.—Evidence thereof.—Forbidden by Ti-ping Law.—Opium Trade.

SOON after our return to Nankin, the Chung-wang, having left the Shi, Mo, Ting, and other Wangs, in charge of the lately captured Shanghae and Hang-chow districts, despatched considerable reinforcements to the Ying-wang, on the northern side of the Yang-tze river, and to the Ti-ping positions along the southern bank. These troops quickly dispersed the Imperialist force supposed to be investing Nankin from the hills on the opposite side of the river, and recaptured many towns on the southern side.

Meanwhile, at the Ti-ping capital, Marie became my wife, while my friend L. received the Chung-wang's youngest daughter in marriage. When Cum-ho's father ascertained the state of that young lady's affections, he sanctioned her union with L., although his better half made no little opposition at first, her ambitious mind being directed to the Mo-wang as a suitable son-in-law. This, however, she eventually accomplished by giving the chief her next eldest daughter as a wife. We were married according to the ritual of the Ti-ping church, but with the addition of using a ring, in conformity with the usage of our own. The Kan-wang's own chaplain, who was an ordained teacher of the London Missionary Society at Hong-kong, performed the ceremony.

Since the arrival of the Kan-wang at Nankin, he had altered the Ti-ping marriage service so as to closely resemble that of the English church, to which he had been used when principal native instructor and catechist of the London Mission. Although by the laws of the state polygamy was allowed, the improvements introduced by the Prime Minister, in fact we may term them regulations, had almost abolished the custom, so that few among the people married more than one wife.

Although L. and myself were married on the same day, and nearly at the same time, there was a vast difference between the style of the two ceremonies. Marie agreed with me in preferring a quiet solemnization, with only a few friends present; but L., taking to wife a chief's daughter, was obliged to undergo the usual pomp and festivity.

After my own marriage had been concluded, preparations for that of my friend were made in the "Heavenly Hall" of the Chung-wang's palace. The Hall was decorated with flowers and a profusion of silken flags and streamers. Several large tables in a side chamber were loaded with bridal presents from friends, who, with all the household, were assembled to witness the ceremony. The Chung, Kan, Foo, and all the other Wangs present, wore their state robes and coronets, while the dresses of many of the ladies were still more beautiful and dazzling. Besides the Kan-wang's chaplain, the principal ecclesiastic in Nankin officiated, dressed in a splendid black silk garment broidered with gold and silver crosses, both of whom, attended by several priests, took up their position before the altar, which was decorated with large garlands of flowers.

At last, when everything was ready, the bride, completely enveloped in a long white veil, was escorted to the

Hall by nine young girls dressed in scarlet, and with red flowers in their hair. At the same time L., in the full costume of a Ti-ping chief of the "Woo" rank (to which he had been raised by the Chung-wang's wish), came to the right side of the altar attended by nine young chiefs. After the bridegroom and bride were united, the ceremony was concluded by a short service, nearly approaching to that of the Sabbath, and then, entering two magnificent sedans, they were conveyed to their new home (a house given them by the Chung-wang) by a vast and gorgeous cavalcade. The newly-married couple now entertained a number of guests to a festive meal in the principal hall of their house. Meanwhile, with my wife, I removed from the Chung-wang's palace and took up my abode with L., the house being divided between us.

During several months, as it is, I presume, with nearly all newly-married people, we paid but little attention to the outside world, and, with the exception of the periodical arrival and departure of our friends D. and Captain P. with the vessels, and the addition of three Frenchmen, who had served in the French artillery at Shanghae, to our corps of the Chung-wang's army, but little occurred to divert us from our honeymoon. In the mean time the Commander-in-Chief was occupied making his plans for further operations against the Manchoo, with the intention of recapturing the towns and territory that had lately fallen into their possession, and making a movement against their capital, Pekin. Before, however, these tactics could be put into execution, news came from the Shanghae district of the hostilities commenced by the British and French, and of the consequent defeat of the Ti-ping local forces, and the capture of their cities and villages. Immediately, orders were sent recalling the reinforcements despatched to the Ying-wang, and the force operating along the southern bank of the Yang-tze, while from the garrisons of Nankin and other cities troops were concentrated upon Soo-chow.

With natural reluctance I prepared to accompany the Chung-wang on his march to the threatened districts, accompanied by my friend, who felt how difficult it was to part with his youthful Ti-ping bride. Our feelings were not indeed to be envied when, upon a misty, heavily raining, and more than usually disagreeable Chinese morning in May, between the chilly hours of three and four, we set out on the march for Soo-chow. Even Phillip, although his honeymoon had terminated long before ours began, appeared to feel as gloomy as myself and L. upon parting with our wives.

As we slowly rode through the high city portal, dimly lighted by the glare of lanterns and torches, the rain poured down in continuous streams, as though it never intended to cease again. Fortunately we had the promise of the rainbow, and I imagine the Chinese must have known it also, or the whole force might have become panic-stricken with the dread of another deluge. Splash, splash went our horses, and tramp, tramp came the soldiery, through the mud, the former drooping and the latter dripping. The tenacity, consistency, and otherwise sticky properties of Chinese mud, are really wonderful, and in wet weather cause the pedestrians' feet, to sound like a huge sucker suddenly torn from some sympathetic substance. The rain beating in our faces every now and then compelled us to close our eyes and risk their being picked out by the iron spikes on the ends of the bamboos carried by the surrounding spearmen. Every thing and animal presented a miserable and draggled appearance. The few trees in the neighbourhood of the city, dimly seen in the hazy grey of morning as we passed under their shadows, looked more like huge spectres outlined against the foggy background. The very houses presented a weird and desolate aspect as they became faintly visible through the heavy rain and dense atmosphere.

A march of five days brought our forces to the city of

Soo-chow, when preparations were immediately made to move the troops to the defence of the Ti-ping territory in the vicinity of Shanghae and Ningpo. The Tow-wang, with the principal part of his forces, had been recalled from the northern side of the Yang-tze, leaving the Ying-wang in command of the different positions still held. This contingent, with those from Nankin and Soo-chow, the Chung-wang's immediate command, and other detachments, composed an army of some 50,000 men. The Commander-in-Chief, a few days after his arrival at Soo-chow, moved forward in three columns to the threatened quarter. With my company of partly disciplined men and a few light pieces of artillery, I accompanied the division attached to the Chung-wang himself. Each of the other *corps d'armée* were respectively commanded by the Mo and Tow Wangs.

Marching rapidly upon the places lately captured by the allied Anglo-Franco-Manchoo forces, those garrisoned only by Imperialists were very quickly retaken. On Kah-ding and other cities held by the foreigners with their irresistible artillery, no direct assault was at first made. The Chung-wang's tactics were, circulating exaggerated rumours that with an immense force he was marching for Shanghae, and by continual mock attacks upon Kah-ding, Na-ziang, &c., with men carrying numberless flags, to harass the garrisons so as to compel them to abandon their positions. These tactics were entirely successful. General Staveley, and the other commanders, fearing for the safety of Shanghae and the fate of their detachments guarding the lately captured towns, evacuated all excepting Soong-kong, which was held in conjunction with the filibuster General Ward's disciplined Chinese.

Having recaptured Kah-ding, the Chung-wang established his head-quarters at the city of Chang-za, some forty miles north-west of Shanghae, while his subordinate generals successively occupied the places evacuated by the allies. The brave Ling-ho, with his regiment of Honan guards, made a dashing attempt to carry Soong-kong by storm. Just at daylight on the morning of May the 30th, this gallant chief, with less than 1,500 men, made a desperate attack upon the north-east side of the city. So suddenly was the attempt made, that when the garrison had manned the walls, the scaling-ladders were actually planted against them. These ladders consisted simply of two long bamboos secured together at either end about two feet apart, the man to ascend being pushed up by men from below with another bamboo, while he assisted himself with the uprights. Soong-kong would certainly have been captured but for the circumstance of its being held by a strong detachment of the seamen and marines of Ward's dear and invaluable friend Admiral Hope, who, at the expense of the British tax-payers, instead of attending to his ships, chose to scour Chinese territory, hunting for Ti-pings wherever they were to be found. The first to man the walls of Soong-kong were the men of H.B.M.S. *Centaur*, who opened a heavy fire upon the assaulting column at a few yards' distance. In spite of this, Ling-ho led his men up their scaling-ladders, and was himself the first upon the wall, the second being the French commander of his regiment. Their gallantry, however, was unavailing, the deadly Enfield rifles and the showers of grape and canister crashing among the Ti-pings within half pistol-range proved irresistible. Ling-ho fell mortally wounded while striving with his usual surpassing courage to animate his men to follow him, and his brave French officer was killed by his side. This settled the action, and sorrowfully carrying off their wounded leader, the Ti-pings retired from the attack.

During the next few days a part of the Chung-wang's division having arrived before the place, Soong-kong was closely invested. On the 2nd of June a large Imperialist force was driven out of some strong stockades they had erected close to the city, while one of the *Centaur's* gigs and a dozen Chinese gunboats loaded with arms and ammunition were captured in a neighbouring creek. Seeing this, the whole British force, accompanied by a body of Ward's Chinese, made a powerful sortie, and succeeded in recapturing the gig and two or three of the gunboats, the rest being carried off by the Ti-pings. During the 3rd, 4th, and 5th of June, each day an attempt was made to storm the city, and outside the west gate a battery was erected, from which the besiegers opened fire in the morning, but upon every occasion it was effectually silenced by the superior fire of the British guns on the walls.

The gig's crew and some other Europeans captured in the gunboats were not harmed by the Ti-pings, although, had the latter simply followed the law of retaliation, they would have met with the fate of the unfortunates who were delivered over to the Manchoo execution-grounds, after having fallen into the hands of British soldiers during the late freebooting raids of Admirals Hope and Protet, and General Staveley.

I cannot do better than give a few extracts from the summons to surrender sent into Soong-kong by Ching, the chief in command of the besiegers. General Ching, after a preamble setting forth the object of the Ti-ping revolution, stated:—

"Now, having received our king's commands to hold the city of Soochow, we had intended to remain there, and give the Heavenly * soldiers rest, and not to take your place, not imagining you would league with the foreigners and attack my cities, forcing me to rise up and retake them. *For this causeless misfortune, for this injury to the people, who then is to blame?* Had you not invaded my territories, I should not have troubled you; *the people would have remained undisturbed.* Would not this have been better for both sides?

"Again, all the officers, both military and civil, all the soldiers, too,

---

* The title (Tien-ping) of the Ti-ping soldiery.

and the people, are without exception Chinese; and you eat the bread of the Tsing[*] dynasty, serving a stranger. . . .

"As for you, O foreign troops, you had best return to your native country, as quickly as may be; *for, being a distinct race,* AND SEEKING TRADE ONLY, *why should you contend with me, or why should I be compelled to overcome you?* . . If you are resolved and will fight with me, I fear, indeed, your trade will suffer."

Upon the 10th of June the Mo-wang succeeded in recapturing Tsing-poo, the garrison of Ward's Chinese, a British force 600 strong, with six guns, evacuating the city *after almost completely destroying it by fire!* The filibuster officer (Colonel Forrester) in command of Ward's force having, in his hurry, forgotten to carry off some of his loot (gathered during the late successful campaign against the Ti-ping cities), ran back for it, and was captured by the Mo-wang's men just as he was rushing away loaded with sycee and dollars. This man, whom the Europeans captured at Soong-kong, as also eleven British seamen taken prisoners at the evacuation of Kah-ding by the allies, were all liberated by the Ti-pings. In vain I represented to the Chung-wang the policy of retaining them as hostages for any of his own chiefs who might fall into the hands of the enemy, and most probably be delivered over to the reeking execution-shambles at Shanghae and elsewhere. He would not retain them, but had them released, so as to exhibit his unalterable friendship for Europeans.

I would not willingly screen a single fault upon the part of my Ti-ping friends; but, after viewing all events calmly, when many thousand miles away from aught that could bias or warp the judgment, I must confess that I can scarcely find the slightest grounds for censure upon any point.

I had certainly intended to blame the Tow and Mo-wangs for the severity of their measures towards the people of those villages, which, upon the successful raids of the allied forces, had proved renegade, and had given in

[*] The Manchoo.

their allegiance to the Manchoo. But, consideration of the primary cause of the destruction of many Ti-ping cities and villages, and the subsequent devastation of some that had been left whole by the allies, conclusively fixes the guilty responsibility upon the latter, by reason of their wanton attack upon the Ti-ping territory. After the recapture of some places, people who had been well known as subjects of the Tien-wang were found with the shaved head (the badge of the Manchoo) and other strong and irrefragable proof of their traitorous conduct; many of these were decapitated, and their property confiscated. In like manner, some of the villages that had, with Chinese apathy, at once gone over to the Imperialists, were burned down, and the people compelled to labour as coolies. These measures may appear harsh; but, if events had occurred otherwise, and the Imperialists had occupied the position of the Ti-pings, fresh evidence would be given that there were prototypes of the notorious Yeh in every Manchoo official!

The Shanghae district had been captured by the revolutionists; after that event, the people were gradually settling down to the new state of affairs, while those who had naturally fled from the shock of war were fast returning to their homes and giving in allegiance to the dominant power. In fact, so well were the lately disturbed departments recovering from the effect of the civil war, that in a short time they would certainly have attained the high state of prosperity enjoyed by the silk districts, then thoroughly settled under Ti-ping rule. The question as to the relative right of each belligerent has nothing to do with the present argument. Each party to the civil war had their own causes and reasons, and these certainly concerned no one but themselves. The simple question is this:—After the Ti-pings had proved their power to successfully dispute the Manchoo authority, and had wrested large tracts of land from their foreign yoke, who became responsible for again carrying the horrors of war, with its attendant misery and desolation, into a country which would otherwise have remained happy in its freedom, peaceful and nominally Christian? Who other than England?

Upon the suppositional " mights" elsewhere described, Admiral Hope and his colleagues captured the cities and villages within a radius of thirty miles from Shanghae, burning and destroying (as proved in this work by the words of the Admiral himself) everywhere. These places were then captured a second time by the Ti-pings, and subsequently recaptured by the allies. Now, for the cruelties and devastations inflicted four times over by the sword of Asiatic warfare, in the words of the Ti-ping general long since in the presence of his God, I ask, "For this causeless misfortune, for this injury to the people, who then is to blame?"

Plain it is to all who will judge fairly and honourably, that England is heavily responsible for the effects of the unprovoked hostilities carried by her soldiers and sailors into the Ti-ping dominions. Besides the more direct evil consequences of that most evil policy, there were others not so well known though closely connected with it. In the first place, few people are aware, or trouble themselves to reflect, that the wholesale destruction of grain and rice by the allies (as per Admiral Hope's despatches) led to the starvation of many thousands of the unfortunate country people. The Ti-ping system of Government is one of a paternal form (so favourite with the Chinese, but so seldom obtained), involving a community of interests upon the part of every subject. Consequent upon this, all rice crops and other descriptions of grain were gathered regularly into the state granaries, and from thence supplied to every person and family in the respective departments of the "Land divisions of the Ti-ping dynasty." Consequently, when the whole stores of food were destroyed in the districts ravaged by Admiral Hope and others, the miserable people had literally nothing to eat; so that, although the Ti-ping soldiery were killed in hundreds by the irresistible foreign artillery, the non-combatants perished by tens of thousands from famine.

Then again: the only means of support for the large Ti-ping armies, the Government and administratve machinery, were precisely similar to those of other nations; that is to say, from direct and indirect taxation. Naturally, therefore, when England maintained the treaty ports against the Ti-pings, and when Admiral Hope invaded their territory, many valuable sources of revenue were cut off. If a nation, or organized body of people, possess neither settled territory nor regular revenue, they must plunder their neighbours in order to exist, and by this mode of reasoning it is evident that England is responsible for all plundering or brigandage committed by the Ti-pings when driven from their dominions, and defrauded of their just dues by her intervention. At the time, however, to which we have now arrived (summer of 1862), the revolutionists had not been expelled from the valuable silk, and a great proportion of the tea, districts, the revenue upon the productions of which exceeded £2,500,000 sterling per annum. Previous to their expulsion from these districts, the Ti-pings only acted as marauders when literally compelled to do so in order to save their own lives, and when any people in the world would have acted in the same manner. When driven back by the raids of Admiral Hope and General Staveley, the troops and people, rendered destitute, fell upon the nearest places to forage and subsist. Otherwise, the only plundering ever indulged in by Ti-ping soldiery was upon the *public* property of the enemy. Private property, except in dire cases of necessity, was always respected: most especially were the troops careful to avoid injuring the standing crops of grain—a course of conduct which forcibly contrasts with the destruction of the cultivated fields of the unfortunate New Zealanders by English soldiers, and with the outrages committed by the forces of the Emperor of the French in Algeria! Most unjustly the Ti-pings have been represented as "hordes of banditti," "ruthless marauders," &c.; but these statements may invariably be traced to interested quarters. If a few examples of sack and pillage have been selected to blacken the character of the Ti-pings, are we to forget the names of Magdeburg, Badajos, and Ciudad Rodrigo? Are we not to remember the progress of the Federal General, Sheridan, through the Shenandoah Valley, as recorded in the columns of the *Times* of the 30th March, 1865? "Burning houses and barns, he passed through the valley, and may boast of a destruction such as *no* Asiatic chief ever surpassed!"

When Admiral Hope ascertained that Soong-kong, the only remaining Manchoo place outside the walls of Shanghae, was seriously threatened by the Ti-ping forces, he sent up strong reinforcements to it, commanded by Captain Borlase, R.N. Upon this, the Chung-wang gave orders to abandon the siege; and, after placing strong garrisons in all the recaptured cities, returned with the rest of his forces to Nankin. During the march from Soo-chow to the capital, I became acquainted with a singular custom of the Chinese. We had just passed through a village, when we came upon a party of country people carrying a coffin to the burial-place. To the great surprise of myself and European comrades, instead of interring the corpse or building a grave over it, according to the usual Chinese customs, two forked wooden stakes were fixed in the ground, and the coffin placed upon them at either end. Upon inquiry, we were informed that the dead man had been killed by lightning, and that the common practice throughout the country was to dispose of the bodies of those who perished in such a manner by placing their coffin on stakes which would support them above the ground.

Soon after reaching Nankin, the Chung-wang seriously turned his attention towards operating against the

Manchoo forces further up the Yang-tze, whose successes, though unimportant when compared with the great Ti-ping victories in Che-kiang and Kiang-su, were yet becoming dangerous to the supremacy of the revolutionists in that part of China. When the Commander-in-Chief drew off all his troops from the Shanghae district, after having retaken all the places previously captured by the allies, he did so under the impression that neither England nor France would again make war upon the re-established Ti-ping territories. A man so noble-hearted, large-minded, and honourable, could not realize the determined hostility entertained against his cause, or credit the intention of Admiral Hope and General Staveley to resume active warfare upon the arrival of reinforcements from Tien-tsin and India; he therefore left garrisons amply sufficient to repel any effort of his natural enemies, but neglected the precaution of leaving in the district even a single *corps d'armée*, which would have frustrated the future triumphs of his unexpected foemen. It was certainly necessary that large additions should be made to the Ti-ping forces opposing the progress of the Imperialists from the upper waters of the Yang-tze towards the city of Nankin; still, this could have been thoroughly accomplished, and a field force of at least 50,000 men left in the neighbourhood of Shanghae at the same time. Had any such disposition been made, the easy success of the allies, during their next campaign, would have been exceedingly different; the disasters that subsequently befell the Ti-ping cause would never have taken place; while the standard of liberty and Christianity would now wave erect and triumphant.

During the interval between our return to Nankin and the commencement of further military operations, I was frequently closeted with the Chung, Kan, and other chiefs, upon the discussion of political matters. On one occasion, at an interview with the Commander-in-Chief, my friend D—— was present, and translated a certain speech, which was subsequently published in some of the Shanghae papers. He asked the Chung-wang "why he had ventured within the limits of Consular Ports;" and received this reply:—

"Why? Because foreigners have broken faith with us! The English and Americans stipulated with us to remain strictly neutral in regard to our war with the Manchoos. This agreement was kept on their part by assisting, in every way they could, in the collection of the very 'sinews of war' for the Imperialists; allowing their subjects to enter the Manchoo employ, and at the same time sending a man-of-war to force, at the cannon's mouth, the return, and even punishment of the few foreigners who had joined us! Was *this* neutrality?

"This was not all: they actually, with their own Government troops, *invaded* our territory, and violated the most sacred usages of war, by permitting, or not preventing, the Chinese troops from committing the most atrocious barbarities. It has been told us that, among foreigners, the proof of courage is clemency towards the vanquished. But the torture inflicted lately upon some of your helpless prisoners proves to us the quality of your *neutrality!* Neutrality! Every few days we see several Manchoo steam vessels, laden with munitions of war, all to be expended to our destruction, passing under the very walls of our capital, but flying the American flag! They are called by foreigners the *Koong-foo-tze* (Confucius), *Kee-me-et* (Williamette), *An-te-lok* (Antelope), etc. But for that flag we would have sunk them hundreds of times. Is *this* neutrality? Is it not a most shameful perversion of the American nationality? Is it not a vile trading —a base jobbery in the dignity and honour of a noble people, who have never permitted their officers to *openly* violate our rights? Would not these great foreign sovereigns blush to see the degradation of their flags, perverted to such ends as private aggrandisement and infamous prostitution?

"Moreover, as lords of our immense territory, we have a perfect right to levy taxes on goods of natives passing through our dominions; but by acts of gigantic fraud,* the foreign consuls have given to native craft papers, and their national flag, simply for a fee- thus robbing us of our revenues, in as far as they *could!* Would any *other* nation have borne these outrages for years, as we have done, without making reprisal? And we have been accused of relentless barbarity; of burning towns, slaughtering the people, &c. Well, granted. It is the hard necessity of war, which we would avoid if we could; but knowing, as we do, the conduct of Napoleon in Europe, of the British in India, &c., and the Americans in their own country, we think such accusations come with a bad grace from

---

* Perfectly true.

foreigners. The Ming dynasty was founded by a revolution such as is now in progress; and we have never heard of a people who expelled tyrants from their country who did not suffer both offensively and defensively.

"That the foreign Powers are playing a game to suit their own profit in China, is to us perfectly clear. When, some time ago, we addressed their authorities on this subject (at the Consular Ports), our communications were returned *unopened*. This contemptible insult taught us that you foreigners" [the translation of this part cannot be literally given, by reason of the Chung-wang's use of idiomatic and figurative language, but may best be expressed as follows :] "thought our cause a sinking one, or intended to make it so; and, like rats on shipboard, you would desert—*not us, but your own professions towards us*. Not long after, our capital was called, in a public print, the 'City of Coolie Kings.' This title, which was meant for a sneer, we thought the highest compliment possible: we are indifferent as to what the Duke of Pa-le-chiau * thought of the remark, or the Americans, whose capital might be called by the same name with equal justice. It was easy to judge, from these circumstances, and many others, at what value we could esteem the lofty sentiments of honour, justice, and equity, which foreigners professed towards the Chinese people. 1st. They struck a nearly fatal blow to the Manchoo power; then, in pretence of seeking the real good of the nation, they bolster up the tottering *simulocrum*, and actively carry on operations against us. They reform not one abuse of the Tartar Government, and send for Captain Osborne's fleet! † Will the most noble Empress of England, the mother of her people, permit her brave soldiers, and noble-minded naval officers, to serve under the most cruel and corrupt Government officials in the world, and furnish them with means to come to the Middle Kingdom, to crush out at the cannon's mouth the last vestige of liberty, and freedom of being governed, while professing our religion, as seems to us most conformable to the sacred book (Bible)? We cannot think so, though her officers have refused to receive our communications!

"Will not one of you here present make it known to the sovereigns of England and America, that by this conduct we can only judge of them, and that it seems that they desire to exterminate us. Of the French we have nothing to hope; *they* have never professed any friendship for us! They (the French Jesuits) materially assisted the Manchoos in getting possession of the throne, for the sake of propagating a religion which English missionaries have taught us to condemn. But, at least, they have never deceived us by false professions!"

---

* The French General in command during the Pekin campaign, who received this title from his emperor.

† The proceedings to raise the "Vampyre" fleet in England were then nearly concluded, and were known to the Ti-pings.

Within two months after our return to Nankin, I became utterly prostrated by one of the forms of low fever prevalent in China. My illness was long in duration and slow in disappearing, even when recovery commenced. During many months I was confined to a sick-bed, from whence, but for the tender and unremitting attentions of my wife, I should never have risen again. In the meanwhile my comrades had all left the city, having proceeded with another expedition against the Manchoo.

Shih-ta-kae, the I-wang and brother of the Ti-ping king, had been recalled to the capital, and in the month of September, 1862, marched forth in command of an army destined to operate along the south bank of the Yang-tze. The Chung-wang, with a still larger army, crossed the river, and commenced a campaign having for its principal objects the recapture of Ngan-king and the capture of Pekin.

While these armies are marching along their several routes, we will digress for a little and notice two subjects particularly favourable to the moral aspect of the Ti-ping revolution, though one of them has excited no little hostility to the great movement.

The justice courts of Ti-pingdom form the theme of our first eulogy. These are invariably conducted with the strictest and most simple equity. The disgusting scenes, the inseparable concomitants of the Manchoo magisterial dwelling, or *yamun*,—such as the torture of litigants, criminals, and prisoners,—are entirely abolished. Defendant, plaintiff, and witness, are fairly confronted; but under the sway of the Tartar despotism either the one or the other is tortured if any party chooses to bribe the presiding mandarin; or, if none have the sense and means to sooth the majesty of justice with lumps of virgin sycee, the *whole* are tortured by that impartial functionary. The infamous system of bribery is entirely unknown in a Ti-ping court of justice; *not one* form of torture is permitted by law,* and prisoners or litigants are afforded every facility to defend themselves consistent with justice. In no way can a rich and superior adversary obtain any unfair advantage over a poor man, none being convicted or punished but upon the clearest and most decisive proof of guilt.

Ti-pingdom is one of the last places in the world likely to please a lawyer; plaintiff, defendant, and prisoner having to plead their own cases, which are then decided upon according to their respective merits by the presiding chief and his assistant officers. All trials are conducted more by the dictates of right and justice than the trammels of law, so that the glaring injustice frequently caused by European legal technicalities and quibbles is seldom committed.

The Ti-pings have one very singular custom in connection with their "Judgment Halls." Two large drums are always kept hanging just inside the porch of the outer gate, and are at the use of any person who may consider himself aggrieved, or may wish to present a complaint, when he is at liberty to strike upon the drums and demand justice from the chief. A Ti-ping court of justice is generally a very imposing affair. The gorgeous dress of the chiefs, their numerous attendants and body guard, the many beautiful silken banners around the walls, and especially the brilliancy of colour, strongly impress the observer's imagination with an idea of what Europe must have been during its earlier career, when it delighted in the same barbaric splendour and feudal display.

The second subject of our digression is the abolition of opium-smoking by the Ti-pings, which is almost the principal cause of the hostility the British Government and nearly all merchants who trade in the drug have hitherto entertained against the revolutionists. Although the arguments to prove the utterly health-destroying and

---

* The different methods of legal torture are numerated in the Imperialist code by hundreds.

mind-pervading effect of opium are many and incontrovertible, we may dispense with them and give a few facts to establish the value of the prohibition by the Ti-pings. In India, as well as in China, the unfortunate natives are thereby utterly destroyed. In a communication forwarded by General Alexander to Earl Shaftesbury (then Lord Ashley), from Mr. A. Sym, dated the 13th of March, 1840, the following passages occur:—

"The health and morals of the people suffer from the production of opium. We are demoralizing our own subjects in India; one half of the crime in the opium districts—murders, rapes, and affrays—have their origin in opium-eating. . . . One opium cultivator demoralizes a whole village. Thus thousands of our fellow-subjects in India are oppressed, and their health and morals destroyed, for the sake of this infernal opium trade. So completely is the production of opium in the hands of the East India Company* that not a single poppy can be grown in the extent of their vast territories without either the permission of the Government or an infraction of its laws. The grower of the poppy derives only a bare subsistence for its cultivation, and the difference between 250 rupees and 1,200 to 1,600 rupees a chest goes to the Government, which exchanges the drug for silver at the auction mart."

This sort of thing has been continually on the increase since the above statements were written, and the opium trade has now reached an enormous extent, being fully equal to if not greater in value than either the silk or tea trade. While the price of opium has been steadily maintained or increased, that of western manufactures has gradually fallen off to one-third the former rates, although the latter trade has not largely increased, and that in opium has been more than doubled. The vast amount of specie drawn from China in payment of this deleterious drug is diverted from a more beneficial and righteous trade in British manufactures, or in the cultivation of cotton, which the East Indian districts now devoted to the poppy are so well adapted to produce. If Lancashire would only look abroad it might see a

* The power has, of course, reverted to the Home Government since the Sepoy revolt.

mode of easily increasing the British exports to China, till the eight or nine millions annually paid in cash for the produce of China were replaced by them, and the abolition of the opium trade had enabled the Chinese to barter for English manufactures to a greater extent. The amount of clear profit realized by the Indian Government upon the sale of opium is considerably upwards of £5,000,000 per annum,* being the difference between £25 a chest they give for it, and £115 they sell it at. The opium, upon reaching China, extracts from that country the vast amount of specie above mentioned, which would otherwise be expended on British produce.

Only a few years ago the following evidence was adduced before the Select Committee of the House of Commons, on our commercial relations with China, by Mr. Montgomery Martin, who was Her Majesty's treasurer in India:—

"I inquired of the Taou-tae of Shanghae what would be the best means of increasing our commerce with China, and his first answer, in the presence of Captain Balfour, was:—'Cease to send us so much opium, and we shall be able to take your manufactures.' . . . The true remedy for our deficient trade with China is not to be found in the reduction of £1,000,000 to £2,000,000 sterling of tea duties, but in perfect freedom of intercourse with China; in facilities of access to the interior of that vast country; and in the abolition of the pernicious opium traffic, which absorbs £4,000,000 per annum, which would be devoted to the purchase of British manufactures."

Proofs of the immense injury the opium traffic inflicts upon British export trade to China might be multiplied *ad infinitum*. The drug not only destroys the moral and physical principles of those who connect themselves with it in any way, but it has been the direct cause of every war England has had with China. The following statement by Mr. Martin is so identical with what I would

* By the last official return (1863-4) the export of opium from India to China is given as 42,621 chests, and the gross revenue derived therefrom, Rupees, 5,20,72,358.

say myself that I cannot do better than quote it with the appreciation it so well deserves. It was adduced before the Committee of the House of Commons already referred to:—

"Minute 3491. In what respect do you think the trade injurious to us in our relations with China?

"3492. Politically, with reference to our position with the Government of China, had France, or America, or Russia, granted us an island on their coast as a commercial station,* had they prohibited the use of opium, believing it to be injurious, we dare not, in that case, have made it a smoking-shop for the empire; and I would not act to the Chinese Government in a different manner than I would act to a Government in Europe. Then, socially speaking, I believe it is the duty of this Government to uphold moral principles and to disseminate religious truth, and she cannot do that with one hand, while on the other she is introducing into China an amount of opium which furnishes 17 grains a day to each of 3,000,000 of people, and which, in the language of Mr. Lay, Her Majesty's late consul at Amoy, 'is ham-stringing the nation.' I think it is desolating China, corrupting its Government, and bringing the fabric of that extraordinary empire to a state of rapid dissolution. Commercially speaking, it is injurious to us, because it prevents the extension of our manufactures in China. Four or five mercantile houses are engaged in the traffic, and derive a large amount of revenue from it; *but the trade of England is materially cramped by the extension of its consumption in China to the extent of at least four million sterling a year.*"

Now, this truthful statement was made in the year 1857, since when the evils mentioned have increased to more than double their extent at that period. We will also examine the opinion of the Chinese themselves with regard to the introduction of opium into their country. Kinshan, one of the most celebrated of the *literati* of China, has written on the subject, and how correctly all can affirm who know anything of opium-smoking in that empire. The following is his statement:—

"Opium is a poisonous drug brought from foreign countries. At first the smokers of it merely strive to follow the fashion of the day, but in the sequel the poison takes effect, and the habit becomes fixed. The sleeping

---

* Alluding to Hong-Kong.

smokers are like corpses—lean and haggard as demons; such are the injuries it does to life; it throws whole families into ruin, dissipates every kind of property, and destroys man himself. There cannot be a greater evil than this. 1st. It exhausts the animal spirits; hence the youth who smoke will hasten the termination of their years. 2nd. It wastes the flesh and blood; the faces of the weak who smoke become black and cadaverous. 3rd. It dissipates every kind of property. 4th. It renders the person ill-favoured—mucus flows from his nostrils, and tears from his eyes. 5th. It promotes obscenity. 6th. It discovers secrets. 7th. It violates laws. 8th. It attacks the vitals. 9th. It destroys life. When the smoker has pawned everything in his possession, he will pawn his wife and sell his daughters; such are the inevitable consequences."

To every word of the above statement, from my own personal experience, I can give the most unqualified assent. The following extract from a manifesto addressed by the distinguished Imperial Commissioner Lin to the Queen of England, with regard to the *forcible* introduction of opium by British subjects, places the wrongly despised China-man in pleasing contrast with the opium trafficking European. Commissioner Lin said:—

"That in the ways of Heaven no partiality exists, and no sanction is allowed to the injury of others for the advantage of one's self—that there is not any great diversity (for where is he who does not abhor death and seek life?), these are acknowledged principles. Though not using opium one's self, to venture, nevertheless, on the manufacture and sale of it, and with it to seduce the simple folk of this land, is to seek one's own livelihood by the exposure of others to death—to seek one's own advantage by other men's injury; and such acts are utterly abhorrent to the nature of men, and are utterly opposed to the ways of Heaven."

No wonder the Rev. Dr. Medhurst, one of the most experienced missionaries in China, has said: "Opium is demoralizing China, and become the greatest barrier to the introduction of Christianity which can be conceived of." And to prove this he states that almost the first reply of a native, when urged to believe in Christ, is, "Why do Christians bring us opium, and bring it directly in defiance of our laws? The evil drug has poisoned my son, has ruined my brother, and well nigh led me to barter my wife and children. Surely those who import such a deleterious substance, and injure me for the sake of gain, cannot wish me well or be in possession of a religion better than my own. Go first and persuade your own countrymen to relinquish this nefarious traffic, *and give me a prescription to correct this vile habit,** and then I will listen to your exhortations on the subject of Christianity."

Never has there been a viler or more utterly debasing institution upon earth than that of the opium-smoking dens in China. "Truly," as the Rev. E. B. Squire, formerly a missionary to that empire, once said, "it is an engine in Satan's hands, and a powerful one." It is necessary to remember that this same engine of wickedness and abomination has been systematically, and by the medium of several wars, forced upon China by the English nation and the produce of her Indian possessions.

The very day that the monopoly of the China trade by the East India Company ceased, the British Government commenced forcing the opium traffic, by which means they brought about the first opium war. Although the drug destroyed by Commissioner Lin was surrendered up *according to agreement* by H. B. Majesty's representative, Captain Elliot, yet its destruction was afterwards perverted into a *casus belli*. From that event may be dated a course of policy that all posterity will assuredly condemn, terminating as it did in the Chinese Government being compelled to legalize this nefarious trade.

Opium has ever been made contraband by the Ti-ping law, its use being forbidden under penalty of death, and all cases of infraction being strictly visited with the punishment of decapitation. As opium has in every case been the primary cause of each war with China, and as it was universally known that the success of the Ti-pings would have utterly abolished the trade, it is by no means

---

* These very words have frequently been addressed to myself by Chinese opium-smokers, and I fancy scarcely any European has been in China without having experienced the same.

unfair or unreasonable to ascribe a great proportion of the hostility the revolutionists have experienced (from those bound by every other motive to be their warmest friends) to the same cause. It is indisputable that nearly all who became acquainted with the Ti-pings during the early part of their career, and even many who did not, entertained for them the most friendly feelings; but no sooner was it thoroughly understood that they were determined not to submit to the introduction of opium, when, in spite of their Christianity, &c., a strong party arose against them.

In China it is quite notorious that one of the principal mercantile houses (Dent & Co.), after vainly endeavouring to establish an opium trade with the Ti-pings at Wuhu (a city some fifty miles above Nankin, on the Yang-tze River), by the means of their opium-ship *Nimrod*, which was stationed there for six months, and where I have myself seen her, did, after the failure of the attempt, become their most signal revilers, and use all the interest they possessed against them.

Too many merchants, and, unfortunately, their national representatives interested in maintaining the great opium revenue, have, in China, by the blind pursuit of profit, sacrificed principle to lucre, heedless of the grievous consequences. It is no less unfortunate that many of those who are now designated " merchant princes" some years before made their capital by opium smuggling; equally deplorable is it that still their largest profits result from what by fire and sword has become the legalized trade. Such, however, is the case, and principally for this reason has it become popular to stifle the birth of freedom and Christianity in the opium-ruined Chinese nation.

CHAPTER XX.

Ti-ping Disasters. — The Vampyre Fleet. — Important Letters." — Mr. Roberts's Case. — Mr. Consul Harvey. — Letters continued. — Misrepresentations. — Anti-Ti-ping Meeting. — The Sherrard Osborne Theory. — The Fleet Afloat. — The "Lay" and "Osborne" Agreement. — The Fleet repudiated. — Pecuniary Loss to England. — A Resumé. — General Burgevine. — Lieutenant Ridge. — Act of Piracy. — A Tartar caught. — Exit of the Anglo-Chinese Flotilla. — General Ward's Proceedings. — Progress of the War. — Death of General Ward. — Captain Dew's Disgrace. — How caused. — His Mode of Proceeding. — Its Effect upon Trade. — Operations before Kah-ding. — "Wong-e-poo." — General Burgevine dismissed from his Command. — Major Gordon takes Command. — Sir F. Bruce's Despatches. — His Objections to Gordon's Appointment. — Also to General Brown's Interference.

DURING the absence of the Chung-wang on his campaign to the north, and while I was still confined by illness in Nankin, important events disastrous to the Ti-ping cause were occurring elsewhere. These events, which must be described before continuing my personal narrative, consisted of the organization of that extraordinary flotilla known in England as the *Anglo-Chinese*, but principally as the *Vampyre* fleet in China; the resumption of hostilities against the Ti-pings by General Staveley and his colleagues; and the conversion of Ward's old mercenaries into a British contingent, besides the formation of several other similar legions both at Shanghae and Ningpo.

The origin of the *Vampyre* scheme to regenerate China by exterminating the Ti-pings, is as yet uncertain, although Mr. Lay (late Inspector General of Chinese Customs) in his pamphlet intituled "Our Interests in China," thus describes its first practical adoption:—"Threatened by Sir F. Bruce, 'that Her Majesty's Government will not go on protecting Shanghae for ever,' . . . [Blue Book, 1863, pp. 13 and 67], and alarmed by the news of the loss of Ningpo, and of the advance of the Ti-pings upon Shanghae . . . they (the Manchoo Government) saw that they must comply,* or perish. . . . The Prince Regent (Kung) accordingly declared himself ready to adopt any measure that Sir F. Bruce might advise. What was his bidding? 'Get foreign ships and engage foreign officers.'† 'Procure us the ships and the officers,' was the rejoinder."

Accordingly some one whom Mr. Lay terms "my *locum tenens*, Mr. Hart," received from the Manchoo Government "a certain sum of money for transmission to England for the purchase of a steam fleet." Meanwhile arrangements were made between Mr. Lay and Captain Sherrard Osborne, R.N., by which that officer agreed to receive the *elevation* to a Manchoo Admiralship. The British Government suspended the Foreign Enlistment Act, ignored the pledges of neutrality, and "at the Court at Windsor, the 30th day of August, 1862," passed an "Order in Council authorising the enlistment of officers and men, and the equipment and fitting-out of vessels of war for the service of the Emperor of China."

Although fearing I may tire my readers, I cannot resist quoting from a small book of official letters under my hand in order to prove by most conclusive authoritative testimony the *false pretences* upon which the raising of the flotilla and the enlistment of British subjects in the service of the barbarous Manchoo despotism was permitted in England. The letters have been lent to me

---

* With the schemes of the Bruce, Wade, Lay, &c., politicians.

† This is a startling contrast to what Mr. Bruce declared would be the "*worst*" course to pursue.

by a distinguished Member of Parliament, and are written by one of the first Shanghae merchants to his brother, a member of the present Government. These letters have, I am informed, been submitted to various ministers; therefore, it may be concluded that in addition to the despatches of Consul Meadows, &c., the Government had ample means of becoming acquainted with the favourable characteristics of the unfortunate Ti-pings they have devoted to destruction.

The letter I now propose quoting is written in reference to Earl Russell's speech in the debate upon China in the House of Lords on the 2nd of July, 1862, and commences by stating "Earl Grey's view is far sounder than that of the Government." Passing over Earl Russell's preamble the letter states:—

"II. Earl Russell next propounds two questions:—

"*First.*—Will the Ti-pings give us the same advantages which the Government of China is bound to give us?

"*Second.*—Can the Ti-pings form a Government with which foreign Powers can treat?

"He argues a negative answer to these questions, and I take issue with him on his argument as follows:—

"*First.*—He alludes to the agreement made with the Ti-pings at Nankin by Admiral Hope, restricting them to a limited distance of thirty miles from Shanghae. The arrangement was made about the end of 1860, and was generally understood at the time to be limited to the space of one year. *The agreement was faithfully kept for that time.* When Admiral Hope and Mr. Parkes went to Nankin at the close of 1861,* they found the Ti-pings

---

* To completely prove the error of Lord Russell's assumption, and the slightness of its foundation, we will read the following extract from "A Memorandum, dated October 15, 1862, addressed to Rear-Admiral Kuper, by Vice-Admiral Sir J. Hope, on resigning the Command of the Station." [Blue Book, June, 1862, to February, 1863, p. 111.]

"*The only question of real importance on which we are at variance with the rebels,* arose from their desire to possess themselves of Shanghae, and their capture of Ningpo, since retaken.

"On my first visit to Nanking, . . . I effected an agreement with them, *but limited to the year,* that they should not approach it within 100 *li* (thirty miles), *on the whole tolerably* WELL KEPT *during that time,* but which they refused to renew on the occasion of my last visit."

stubborn, and, I believe, the latter would give no further pledge, while Shanghae, under our protection, was made the arsenal, mint, and storehouse of their opponents! . . . I believe that the Ti-pings acted in good faith, as far as they knew, and that *the accusation is fallacious.*

"Earl Russell, on the assumption of their want of faith, proceeds to say :—' They approached very near to Shanghae. Junks belonging to British owners were seized, the crews were imprisoned, *one* European was murdered, and every determination was shown to interfere with the British *trade* at that port.'

"This is a very sweeping sentence, and to a great extent fallacious.

"' A. The Ti-pings certainly, early *this* year, came in strong force close to Shanghae. Their leaders sent in a note immediately to the British and French authorities. . . . *All negotiation was repudiated by our authorities.*'

"Seeing that Shanghae was the centre, from which, under cover of our flags, safe from harm, the Imperialists organized all their plans, provided all the necessaries of war, and found a ready treasury in the customs' revenue, it is not to be wondered at that the Ti-pings were most anxious to get possession of a place so important to the success of their cause; and it is scarcely reasonable, in this view, to suppose that they ever intended to pledge themselves in perpetuity, to allow such a state of matters to continue.

"' D. Junks belonging to British owners were seized, and their crews imprisoned.'

"This is so vague, that it is difficult to know what instances are alluded to. Some boats, British owned, were, during last season, stopped at the passes from the silk districts, in possession of the rebels, *from their attempting to run the pass without paying the usual toll.* I have never heard of any boat being molested which stopped and paid the moderate duty exacted by the *de facto* power. . . .

"' C. One European was murdered.'

"To what case does this allude? Several Europeans have been murdered. A Frenchman, named Salabelle, having imprudently gone up the Yang-tze in a China boat with a lot of dollars, was murdered by pirates in collusion with the boatmen. The Ti-pings had nothing to do with that.

"Another man, in charge of a silk-boat, was attacked on his way to Shanghae by a band of robbers. He was killed, but the robbers turned out to be Imperial soldiers—not Ti-pings. I have not heard of any European being so murdered by the Ti-pings. On the contrary, both last year and this season, numbers of Europeans have been engaged in the silk and green tea districts in pursuance of their business, and have been perfectly welcome, on paying the duty on their produce. . . .

"' D. And every determination was shown to interfere with the British trade at that port.'

"*This, to a person on the spot, is a most extraordinary statement.* Both last year and this season the Ti-pings have had possession of the entire silk district, and a great part of the green tea district. Yet, for the year ending the 30th of June last, we exported 75,000 bales of silk, and fully 50,000 bales have come to market already of the new crop. What sterling money do these 125,000 bales of silk represent? Take them at £80 per bale, you have £10,000,000 sterling, or one-third of the £30,000,000, which Earl Russell correctly states as about the present annual value of the Shanghae trade. The Ti-pings might have cut off nearly all this, had they been so inclined, but they have allowed it all to come to market on payment of a moderate duty. I have not the figures of the green teas by me at this moment, but a very full supply was exported up to 30th June last, a great part of which came from districts in possession of the Ti-pings.

"Are these facts consistent with Earl Russell's assertions?

"I think they confute them altogether. . . . You are trying to patch up a rotten Government, which will only get weaker for all your efforts to mend it. Finally on this head, the Ti-pings have all along professed anxiety to keep on friendly terms with us, till our decided hostility, and harbouring of the Imperialists at Shanghae, has made their wish impracticable. They are not inimical to trade, as the facts above prove. They are not the savages who would murder every European who goes among them on peaceable pursuits, as many who have been among them could prove; and I believe that if we could only give up the unfortunate Imperialism we have espoused, we should find them quite ready to give every facility of trade we have now, and to restore this unlucky province to peace.

"*Second.* Earl Russell asks:—

"'Is there any chance, supposing the Ti-pings consented not to annoy us any longer, and we made peace with them, that they could form a regular government?—and upon this point we have most convincing testimony.'

"Convincing testimony, indeed! Mr. Roberts* is the first. . . .

---

* Mr. Roberts, an American Baptist missionary already referred to in this work, joined the Ti-pings at Nankin about the end of October, 1860. Of all missionaries in China he was the least qualified for such a position. Intolerant and bigoted to the Baptist dogmas, irritable, peevish, inconsistent, and vacillating—a man singularly illiterate, without stability of character or pleasantness of manner—his presence at Nankin did far more harm than good. His objections to every other Church, and to every other denomination of dissent except his own, went far to give the Ti-pings a dread of that diversity of doctrine among the British and Americans which they had always looked upon with surprise, thinking, as they did, that God

Some time back Mr. Roberts went to join his former pupil at Nankin. Whatever faults the chief might have, he was always most kind to his

---

could not be well served by those who were always quarrelling about it. The circumstances attending the advent and career of Mr. Roberts among the Ti-pings I have avoided as a worthless episode, but, as the facts of his indecorous flight from Nankin have been misrepresented, I think it necessary to notice the subject. Mr. Roberts accepted temporal rank under the Ti-pings, and by his unwise dogmatical obstinacy frequently provoked unpleasant discussion. During a dispute with the Kan-wang, who had entertained him since his arrival, that chief had particular occasion to chastise a boy of the household. Mr. Roberts was so blinded by passion, the idea that Europeans would never know the reverse of his statement, or some other reason, that, in a paroxysm of rage, he fled from the city, and sought refuge on board H.M. gunboat *Renard*, which happened to be lying in the port. By some obliquity of vision best known to himself, Mr. Roberts mistook the stick used by the Kan-wang for a sword, and declared that his boy *had been* brutally murdered. Not satisfied with this, although on the previous night he had retired to rest fully believing the surrounding people saints, the very next day, after his quarrel with the Kan-wang, he awoke to find them howling sinners. The many years that he had praised the Ti-pings as holy men were, by a moment of passion, forgotten, and within one day Mr. Roberts not only declared himself to have been deceived so long, but, for the act of one man, gave up the hundreds of thousands in the Ti-ping cause to fire and sword. We will just contrast the different statements of Mr. Roberts, one with the other, and then dismiss the subject.

This is an extract from the first, made on board the *Renard* :—

"Kan-wang, moved by his coolie elder brother—literally a coolie at Hong-kong—and the devil, without fear of God before his eyes, did on Monday, the 13th instant (January, 1862), come into the house in which I was living, *and with malice aforethought murder one of my servants with a large sword in his own hand, in my presence*, without a moment's warning or any just cause. *And after having slain my poor, harmless, helpless boy, he jumped on his head most fiend-like, and stamped it with his foot.*"

Now, at Canton, on the 3rd of April, 1862, when it was generally known that the above charge of murder was incorrect, Mr. Roberts retracted these words [Blue Book, 1862, p. 5], having reference to the Kan-wang's form of baptism :—

"A miserable apostate, (?) polygamist, *and murderer, too,* to wish to administer an ordinance held sacred by those who practise it. What a sacrilege! But as to that boy, *I have since been told that he evinced indications of life after he was dragged out,* by one who saw him. But I think it would have been less cruel in Kan-wang to have smoothly cut off his former teacher. The reverend gentleman, however, was alarmed one day, and left the place precipitately, and therefore wrote a recantation of his former belief in Ti-pingdom. He could not have been quite in his senses at the time, for the boy whom he said was murdered before his eyes, was seen alive and well afterwards. . . .

"His opinion is not worth much.

"The next authority is Mr. Consul HARVEY of Ningpo."

The writer of the letter deprecates the idea of using this gentleman's testimony in a grave debate, especially because it was permitted to overrule the opposite evidence adduced by the talented and trustworthy Mr. Consul Meadows. It is unnecessary to say more upon this subject than notice the fact that Mr. Meadows is a man of honour, of noble mind, and possesses a thorough knowledge of Ti-ping and Manchoo; Mr. Harvey is—Mr. Harvey!

The letter continues :—

"On the strength of these valuable witnesses, Earl Russell proceeds to say, 'It must therefore be clear to your lordships that it is quite impossible anything like civil relations can be established with the Ti-pings, or that they can govern the Chinese empire, or conduct relations with foreign countries upon the footing of amity upon which alone peace can be preserved.'

"Well, if their lordships are content to come to this conclusion on this valuable evidence, they are very likely to find out their mistake in doing so."

After citing proof of the "very great system in their

---

head than to send him out even half killed, destitute, and naked, to freeze and starve to death. *Whether the boy was killed directly or not, I cannot esteem Kan-wang, and his elder brother, who prompted him to the wicked deed, less than murderers; and hence, in my judgment, they ought both to be treated as such.*"

In the pamphlet, "A Letter to the Bishop of Victoria, regarding the Religion of the Ti-ping Rebels," the author states, "Of course you now know that the story of that person's boy being murdered by the Kan-wang is a fabrication. 'The Kan-wang called on me,' said Mr. Roberts, when I asked him about the matter, 'and desired me to punish the boy. I told him I would first remonstrate with him; and then he, the Kan-wang's brother, dissatisfied with my answer, beat him, *as I thought,* to death.'"

military department," the writer of the letter goes on to state with regard to the Ti-pings:—

"If men can thus conduct the details of a military department, is it not probable that they have also the power of conducting the details of a civil department, when the military necessity is past? At Soo-chow, which the Ti-pings have now had for eighteen months, the country people round about are now living quietly enough, and carrying on their usual avocations. . . .

"With regard to the attack at Ningpo, Earl Russell asserts that the Ti-pings first fired on Captain Dew. The fact was, I believe, that the pirate, 'Apak,' anchored his boats near the English ships, so that in firing at 'Apak,' the shot from the rebel batteries came close to, or over, the foreign ships. An excuse for attack was wanted, this was enough, and the place was taken.

"The Earl goes on to say, 'It appeared clear from this that there was no chance of our being able to maintain any relations of amity with the Ti-pings; and as they seemed determined to destroy us, all that we could do was to protect our trade and the lives of our merchants.'

"It is not to be expected that we can be on terms of amity while we make Shanghae the arsenal of the Imperialists, and carry out our intervention on the principle by which it has hitherto been characterized.

"A most disgraceful affair took place the other day. Nine young gentlemen, members of the Shanghae Mounted Volunteer Corps, went out one afternoon with Captain BORLASE, of H.M. ship *Pearl*, and a party of men, to reconnoitre. They came on a number of Ti-pings, who on seeing the horses, immediately threw away their arms, and ran off half naked. Captain Borlase gave the order to pursue *and to give no quarter*.* These young gentlemen accordingly amused themselves that afternoon in cold-blooded murder, and their captain distinguished himself, it is said, by the chivalrous action of killing a man lying badly wounded on the ground. One of the number, a young friend of mine, I am glad to say, refused to obey the order he received. I say that if H.M.'s officers are to be permitted to give such brutal orders, the sooner we cease to talk of Ti-ping cruelties and the savageries of General Butler the better. . . . A cry has been *got up* about the cruelties of the Ti-pings, for want of a better war-cry, and our people are taught to illustrate Christianity by the perpetration of cruelties, considering our lights, infinitely more atrocious. The conduct of the Ti-pings, notwithstanding all the provocation they have received,

---

* This affair happened on the 25th of August, was reported to the Shanghae *Daily Shipping and Commercial News* of the next day, and was widely known in China. A certain Mr. CHALONER ALABASTER, of the British consular service, is mentioned in connection with it.

towards foreigners who have had to enter their lines on business, contrasts in their favour with our conduct to them.

"From Captain Osborne's appointment, I infer that my friend Lay has been entirely Imperialist in the advice he has given the Government.

"I regret that Osborne should have taken such an appointment, and that Government should have sanctioned it.

"I regret still more that Palmerston should be making what I consider such a grave mistake on this question, and that is one of the main reasons why I write these letters. Another is that I am convinced our present policy will be detrimental alike to British interests, and to the interests of the Chinese people."

We have seen that Messrs. Jardine and Matheson pronounced the policy of their Government "suicidal." We have now noticed the important evidence of another of the principal merchants, in whose interest it was alleged to be necessary to slaughter the Ti-pings. The British Parliament was persuaded by fallacies, and the "Vampyre" fleet was made ready and sent to China, while the British people were led into the belief that it was organized merely to act against Chinese pirates, the Government organs representing the Ti-pings as "attempting to force a way to the sea coast, where they hope to take to the amphibious life a Chinaman always loves, and prowl at sea or penetrate the inner waters as necessity or opportunity may tempt or dictate." This, and innumerable similar fabrications, are perfectly astounding by the depth of their untruth and the total absence of any foundation. The above-quoted statement is only surpassed by another in the same article of the same newspaper:—"It is, however, *the people of China* who have broken the force of the Ti-pings, and it is under the dread of their terrible reprisals that the Ti-pings are now attempting to force a way to the sea-coast"!!!

This article, so horribly wicked in purpose and so thoroughly false in substance, was one of those written upon the grand meeting held at the rooms of the Royal Geological Society upon the subject of the "Anglo-

Chinese flotilla." The leaders of the quasi-regenerating expedition here held forth to the scientific gentlemen of the Society, their friends, and sundry members of the Government. The speeches they made, their arguments, facts, and declared intentions, were equally reasonable and trustworthy as the statement in the newspaper article eulogising them, and which, by some most extraordinary perversity of knowledge, represented the bitter and ruthless warfare prosecuted by Admirals Hope and Protet, Generals Staveley and Brown, and others, against the Ti-pings, as "*the people of China* who have broken the force of the Ti-pings." Certes, had such been the case, it required an astonishing quantity of British shot, shell, artillery, and men, to enable the Manchoo Government to occupy any single village or foot of land held by the "broken force!" And one can hardly discover the object of the flotilla if the "people of China" had already done the only thing for which it was being organized; for which Prince Kung was paying, and Mr. Lay, Captain Sherrard Osborne, and his men, receiving a goodly share of that Manchoo mintage. Five months later, this "broken force" was found to be so well able to convert its opponents into a similarly unpleasant state, that upon the 9th day of January, 1863, another order in counsel was passed, making it "lawful for all military officers in Her Majesty's service to enter into the military service of the Emperor of China."

To resume the history of the "Vampyre" expedition. At the oratical display of the civil leader and the naval chief, the Chancellor of the Exchequer (with a keen eye to the guarantee the flotilla might afford for the payment of the indemnities by China) was present to see, to hear, to judge, and to wind up in most affecting and impressive style by giving the well-paid, and doubtless well-deserving, adventurers his blessing.

Mr. Lay, with a surprising theory for a questionable purpose, told the meeting that the great cause of the civil war in China was its crowded population, "which the productive power of the soil was not sufficient to maintain." Emigration of the Ti-pings (when he caught them) was his remedy. Now, how that clever, though it is just possible, mistaken gentleman, expected to forward the change of habitation with the Armstrong and Whitworth guns, and other deadly weapons of exceedingly killing power he was carefully providing, is by no means clear, unless, indeed, the emigration was to be eternal. Neither is it by any means easy to understand that if the production of the soil was not sufficient to maintain the natives, the distress could be alleviated by making it support, in addition, a large number of very expensive foreign officers and men, besides a costly fleet of steamers.

Captain Sherrard Osborne then succeeded the would-be Dictator General of China, and with no less extraordinary principles than his civilian superior, made the astounding declarations:—1. "That his first duty in China would be to bear in mind that he was a member of the Geographical Society." 2. "That he was going to China to spread peace, and not to shed blood" (with his Armstrongs and &c.s). 3. "That his object was to teach the Chinese rather the duty of sparing than the art of killing" (singular that such pains were taken to procure the most effective armament England could furnish). 4. "And that he hoped to report that Nankin was taken without the loss of one life after the assault was over."

1. As the *Daily News* wrote at the time, "Though this may be very advantageous for Burlington House, it affords an adequate explanation of the way China is to benefit by his vaunted advent. Perhaps, however, it may be accepted as a proof of his being a philanthropic adventurer; that his first care will be to look after, not the interests of the Chinese Government, which pays him 3,000*l.* a year, but those of a society to whose funds he is called on to contribute."

4. This naïve announcement is a startling one for the

"pirate" dodge of the gallant captain's friends, and proves that the only motive, which, in fact, is admitted by all save a few bigots, was suppression of the Ti-ping revolution.

Of Mr. Lay and his fighting-man, the *Daily News* well said, "As these gentlemen seem to have the power of carrying on their scheme for the present, they will doubtless do so, but it is a mistake for them to depart from the policy of reserve which they have hitherto followed."

In dire alarm and trouble, Prince Kung grasped at the offer of a fleet to save the Manchoo dynasty, as a drowning man will clutch at a straw. The British Government, wisely thinking that the fleet would guard the treaty ports against the Ti-pings, and thereby protect both the payment of the indemnity and the opium trade at the expense of the Chinese, quickly seized the opportunity it shadowed forth. The justice of their conduct is a very different matter, and it would be interesting indeed to know by what right the capture of Nankin was undertaken,—a city far in the interior of China, the owners of which only entreated the friendship of foreigners, while striving to throw off a foreign yoke and enjoy the blessing of the Christian faith and self-government.

The worst part of the tale has now to be related. Upon the individual authority of Mr. Lay, the flotilla (consisting principally of British men-of-war) having struck the English flag, hoisted a green and yellow rag, and without commission or any authority to constitute them national ships of war, proceeded to the high seas in true pirate fashion. The laws of England were unscrupulously violated, her navy indelibly disgraced, and all who took share in the expedition perfectly fooled, by the *unofficial* countenance of a Manchoo Prince, and the indecent haste of British ministers to comply with his ambiguous request for a fleet, in order to gratify their own ulterior motives.

Prince Kung simply authorized Mr. Lay to buy a number of vessels, but those ships were despatched from England fully manned and armed, as though they had been duly commissioned, which was not, and never became, the case. Mr. Lay and Captain Osborne, between them, prepared an agreement (that being the authority and regulation upon which the crews were engaged, and merely a private understanding, strangely resembled the bond of a piratical organization), which, had it been carried into execution, would virtually have consigned the destinies and executive of China into their hands. These were the salient features of the agreement :—

"4. Osborne undertakes to act upon all orders of the Emperor which may be conveyed direct to Lay; and Osborne engages not to attend to any orders conveyed through any other channel.

"5. Lay, upon his part, engages to refuse to be the medium of any orders of the reasonableness of which he is not satisfied."

No wonder the Manchoo Government repudiated this pretty arrangement, fleet and all, when it arrived in China. There is, however, another reason to account for the ignominious failure of the "Vampyres,"—ignominious because they had neither right nor justification to be placed in the position of mercenaries, or to be subjected to dismissal by a barbarous court. The Imperialists were willing enough to receive a fleet upon *any* terms when the success of the Ti-ping revolution was certain unless foreigners interfered; but when the "Vampyres" did arrive, the dread of the avenging Ti-ping no longer existed. By English troops and English officers in command of Chinese disciplined legions, the revolutionists had been driven back from Shanghae and Ningpo, and were still retreating before the shock of foreign arms. Mr. Lay and Captain Osborne came too late. They could not become the slaves of the Manchoo, neither could they constitute themselves his tyrants, and consequently Prince Kung repudiated all his obligations with characteristic treachery.

When the flotilla reached China the Imperial Government endeavoured to place it under the command of the provincial authorities, and by this determination they effected its dissolution. Captain Osborne refused to lower himself into the position occupied by British officers in the neighbourhood of Shanghae and Ningpo—that of filibusters, subordinate to the *local* authorities—but the Tartars had the best of the argument, for the precedent existed in the terms upon which the military had taken service with them; they were therefore justified in applying the same reasoning to make the navy of England subservient to their inferior officials. Prince Kung and his colleagues were decided upon this point and the repudiation of other guarantees; Captain Osborne remained equally firm; consequently Mr. Lay lost his lucrative appointment as Inspector General of Chinese customs, Captain Osborne did not become a Manchoo Admiral, and the naval force of no nationality was sold, while the officers and men had to go back to where they came from.

The Chancellor of the Exchequer's magniloquent benediction, in which he prophesied of "the day when its leaders would come back rich in professional fame, and bringing also with them fresh glory to their country," vanished and disappeared in thin air, thanks to the failure of the attempt to "spread peace" with rifled artillery. Mr. Lay, since his tardy appreciation of the Manchoo, in "Our Interests in China," thus describes the state of affairs which led to the failure of his regenerating scheme:—

"When I left China, the Emperor's Government, under the pressure of necessity,* and with the beneficial terror established by the allied foray to Pekin in 1860 fresh in their recollection, was in the best of moods, willing to be guided," &c. "What did I find on my return? The face of things was entirely changed. There was the old insolent demeanour, the nonsensical language of exclusion, the open mockery of all treaties, the

---

* From the success of the Ti-pings.

declared determination to yield nothing that could be evaded. In short, all the ground gained by the treaty of 1858 had been frittered away, and we were thrust back into the position we occupied before the war—one of helpless remonstrance and impotent menace."

A pretty state of affairs truly! Re-established, too, by British politicians, who, by supporting the Manchoos, have perpetuated a system which the Ti-pings would have altered for ever.

Time has already proved the truth of the above assertion by Mr. Lay; time will yet prove the bitter hatred the present dynasty of China entertains towards Great Britain, the nation which has frequently chastised them, forced them to break their own laws and receive the obnoxious opium, humbled them before their people and compelled them to eat the fruit of humility, and worse than all, originated the once irresistible Ti-ping revolution by the importation of Christianity. They would not be men did they forget the blows (not always justifiable) they have received; they would not be Manchoo did they forget to revenge themselves *when* able.

Financially considered, this Anglo-Manchoo expedition was rather a serious matter for the British Government. The only authentic estimate of the expenditure which is at present available shows that the portion consequent merely on the return of the flotilla when its services were rejected, amounted to 213,000 taels, or £71,000, which was advanced in the first instance from the Manchoo customs and subsequently refunded by England when receiving the quarterly payment of the Indemnity.

Here is what Captain Osborne says:—

"Dire necessity made Pekin accept our aid in a form likely to be beneficial to China and England. Reason or argument had nothing to do with it, so far as the mandarins were concerned. Most unexpectedly to them, our authorities repulsed the rebellion, without taking any guarantees from Pekin for future behaviour. The mandarins were at once rampant; they are not such fools as to spend their revenue in maintaining order, if we Englishmen will do it for nothing. The fear of rebellion is past. Lay, I, and the force may return to England."

With regard to the failure of the Osborne, Lay, and Gladstone theory, we can only say that it was deserved. Mr. Lay was dismissed from the service of the Manchoo, through the "Vampyre" embroglio. The many years that he had faithfully and energetically served them were lost sight of in the squabble arising from this unparalleled affair. He most likely was sincere in his efforts to regenerate Tartars; he has certainly been badly treated by them. Lay's motive in undertaking the notorious flotilla scheme seems to have been his philanthropical idea (brightened by the receipt of £5,000 a year), of regenerating China. Some people say he was a puppet in the hands of "taller men" behind, who worked the wires. Osborne's acceptance of the command without a commission may be ascribed to the erratic notions of that gallant officer, and *his* natural philanthropy.

The arrival of the "Vampyre" fleet was hailed with general disapprobation upon the part of the foreign community at Shanghae; its flight, without spreading peace, with no less satisfaction. During the short time the would-be mercenaries—the cream of the British navy, as they were loudly proclaimed to be, by ultra-philo-Imperialist papers and people—remained at that port, they managed to create no little ill feeling against themselves. Although they possessed neither warrant nor Imperial authority for their position and action, they nevertheless had the audacity to constitute themselves into a sort of police by *land* and water. No business could be transacted on shore, no vessel move upon the waters of the harbour, or work its cargo, unmolested by their inquisition. Vessels were seized, and their crews imprisoned in irons, upon the merest suspicion that they might be destined to assist the Ti-pings; houses were broken into and searched throughout the British and American settlements for supposed Ti-ping refugees, by parties armed to the teeth. They took, however, particular care not to venture upon the French settlement, as the Gallic authorities had given their own police orders to arrest them if they went there; and, if they resisted, to shoot them. The whole place was thrown into a regular ferment and uproar by their proceedings.

Just previous to the ignominious flight of the "cream of the British navy,"—which, by the way, possessed an extraordinary sympathy for another sort of cream peculiar to the Shanghae rum mills,—I happened to become personally acquainted with some of their piratical outrages, while visiting Shanghae for medical advice, and other reasons which will transpire by-and-by.

General Burgevine, successor to Ward in command of the disciplined Chinese contingent, having been badly treated and cashiered by his Manchoo masters, had joined the Ti-pings at Soo-chow. At the time of my visit to Shanghae, Burgevine was supposed to be there also; and, using this as their pretext, the "Vampyres" made a descent upon the house of my friend, Mr. Tarrantt (Editor of the *Friend of China*), where we were passing the evening with a social party. The dwelling was situated in a compound, also containing the house of the American Marshal; and, while walking round the grounds with my friend and another gentleman, we were suddenly pounced upon in the dark by a party of "the cream of the British navy," hitherto concealed in the shrubbery. At the same moment other detachments rushed into the adjoining houses with a zeal and alacrity tending to prove what capital burglars they were becoming, and, making prisoners of all the men they could find, marched them up to the position we had already been conducted to, in the broad colonnade extending along the front of the American Marshal's house. It was very fortunate neither myself nor any of our company were armed, otherwise, from the suspicious and sudden circumstances under which they had made their appearance, we might very naturally have mistaken the men who sprang upon us for the assassins, or robbers, whom they so strongly resembled. The "Vampyres" were commanded by a Lieutenant Ridge, the most ungentlemanly and discourteous British officer it has ever fallen to my lot to meet.

When our friends were all assembled under the guns of his men, he turned to the latter and distinctly gave them this order, at least in substance: "Now then, men, allow none of these gentlemen to leave this place; *if they attempt to do so, shoot them down!*" This spirited British officer then led off a party bristling with rifle, bayonet, cutlass, and revolver, himself with sword in hand and a huge "Deane and Adams" slung round his neck, and proceeded to tear up the flooring of Mr. Tarrantt's printing-office, in order to search for arms destined for the dreaded Ti-ping! Of course none were found. The man and his men then proceeded to the sanctum of the editor, and ransacked this and the adjoining rooms, emptying and breaking open boxes of letters, papers, and other editorial correspondence, leaving the whole scattered about the floor in a state of inextricable confusion, after their fruitless search for some trace of Burgevine or his doings.

When this gallant exploit had been brought to a termination by the fact that no private place under lock and key remained to be broken into, the leader of the outrage turned his attention to the neighbouring mansion. Having rummaged every nook and corner from top to bottom with a fruitless result, excepting indeed a spoil of two old muskets, a fowling-piece in good order, and another without any barrels, which they carried off in triumph, the "Vampyres" released us from the unpleasantness of their presence and took themselves off, visibly disappointed at their want of success.

Mrs. Pindar, the wife of the American Marshal, told us that Lieutenant Ridge had even penetrated into her bed-room and ransacked the drawers of her toilet table, &c. That Yankee lady accompanied him during his impertinent and unwarrantable intrusion, and assisted him by suggesting that he had better explore the chimney pots, have the carpets lifted to see whether Burgevine was hidden there, or perhaps he would like to search her pockets, &c. The "Vampyre" officer wore a uniform of unknown nationality, consisting of simple anchor buttons and a British naval badge with the crown cut off! When asked by Mr. Tarrantt for his authority, he produced an informal warrant from the British consul, which could only have been legally used by a consular constable. When this was explained to him, he agreed to the justice of the fact and pleaded orders from his commanding officer. He was thereupon asked for his commission, and he naïvely admitted he had none. He was next asked upon what authority his commanding officer was acting, and his reply was, upon Captain Sherard Osborne's commission from the Emperor of China (this in ludicrously pompous language and manner). He was then asked whether he was aware that Captain Osborne did *not* possess any such commission, and confessed that, although he believed the reverse, he thought the Commander-in-chief might have gone to Pekin to obtain it! The judicial proceedings that would have been instituted against the "Vampyres" but for their fortunate retreat from China, would almost certainly have found them guilty of unqualified piracy, not only in the case I have just described, but in several others equally outrageous.

About this time, and while it was fully expected that the flotilla would shortly proceed to attack Nankin, the following squib appeared as an advertisement in the *Friend of China*:—

"WANTED:

"Several first-class ships, to convey several thousand rebels from Nankin to Labuan.

"Apply to

"LAE, HORSEBORN, & CO."

Many foreign merchant vessels were in the habit of flying long pennants from the main truck, a practice indulged in by some of the shipping at Shanghae. This proved offensive to the "Vampyre" officers, who chose to consider that it was an infringement of their *quasi* right to the man-of-war emblem. They consequently amused themselves by boarding sundry easy-going Dutchmen, who, alarmed by their brass-bound appearance and peremptory orders to strike the obnoxious pennant, generally complied very quietly. Upon one occasion, however, while I was at Shanghae, the would-be Tartar martinets caught a Tartar of the implied characteristics, if not literal nationality.

An American vessel with a particularly extensive pennant, which it was afterwards rumoured had been rigged up on purpose, happened to attract the "fe fi fo fum" sense of a "Vampyre" commander. Instantly a cutter was despatched with a lieutenant to humble the offending parties. The officer proceeded on board and ordered the chief mate to haul down the pennant. Mr. Mate immediately sang out, "Cook, bring a bucket of hot water aft," but before this could be brought, the "Vampyre" was over the gangway "like a streak of greased lightning," as the Yankee mate afterwards related to an admiring audience on shore, and shouting with might and main to his boat's crew: "Give way, men!" in order to escape the warm reception preparing for him.

By such acts the "cream of the British navy" made few friends and many enemies, and the lament of few indeed accompanied their ignominious departure. During their stay some of the gallant tars deserted and went over to the enemy, and I cannot forget a very characteristic fact related by a friend of mine who was present. While passing a certain rum shop in the "model settlement" of Shanghae, my friend, with several companions, became mixed with a crowd of the tars, who were on leave, and had just issued from the shop. Willing to see a little of the sort of men represented as the *élite* of the finest navy in the world, my friend got into conversation with a warrant officer, although the man and his companions had evidently been indulging their creamy propensities. The result was that when questioned as to their feelings for the service they had engaged in, the leader of the party made this exposition of principle: "D'ye see, my hearty, so long as we gets the dollars and can make a haul, d—— my toplights if we cares who we fights for, the himperor of Chiny or his hinemies the t'other longshore Chinymen."

Organized upon principles of wrong and injustice, the Anglo-Chinese flotilla came to an unregretted, disreputable, and premature end. In the words of the same friend who communicated the above incident we will dismiss the subject: "Captain Sherard Osborne, like Cæsar, may exclaim, 'I came, I saw;' unlike Cæsar, 'I did *not* conquer.' The fleet was equipped, set sail, arrived, and—was not wanted."

We must now turn to survey events far more disastrous to the Ti-ping cause than the advent of the foreign vessels of war we have just finished with, although the fact of their arrival, connected with what we are about to notice, helped to produce the misfortunes.

Soon after the Chung-wang had re-captured all the places formerly taken by the allies, and had returned to Nankin with the greater proportion of his troops, General Staveley, having received the desirable reinforcements of British troops from Tien-tsin and Hong-kong, resumed hostilities.

Although Admiral Hope had respect enough for the usages of civilized nations to invent a *casus belli* for the raids he first initiated, General Staveley proved himself to be above such petty considerations when they could be ignored with impunity, and therefore, upon commencing a fresh war against the Ti-pings, did not trouble himself to pretend that they might, could, would, or should do anything inimical to British interests. However much scrupulous people may think that an English general should have paid *some* regard to the rules of civilized warfare, the gallant officer in question cannot at all events be charged with hypocrisy.

During the month of August, 1862, the filibuster, General Ward, assisted by detachments of British and French troops, succeeded in taking several fortified villages from the Ti-pings and re-capturing the city of Tsing-poo; the success of the operations being attributable to the large park of artillery always employed. After the fall of Tsing-poo, Ward moved off with the principal portion of his force into the Ningpo district, and joined a column already operating there. Since the atrocious expulsion of the Ti-pings from Ningpo by Captain R. Dew, R.N., and his pirate ally, Apak, the advance of filibustering and piracy had made wonderful progress. Several contingents of disciplined Chinese were raised, the most important being an officially-authorized British legion and a similar French one, both entirely officered by foreigners, including English, American, French, and representatives of other nations. At first, these organizations consisted of about 1,500 men each, besides artillerymen to work the numerous heavy guns they were supplied with. In addition to these, and other bodies of foreign disciplined and officered mercenaries, Captain Dew devoted the entire service of the squadron under his command to their assistance and support, perfectly oblivious of the fact that he was a British officer, and that the ships prostituted by him to an infamous alliance with pirates and freebooters were the property of British tax-payers, who maintained them solely for the protection of their own interests.

The British men-of-war, the Manchoo gunboats, the French vessels, the American, English, and French drilled filibusters, the Cantonese pirates, and Imperialist troops, all leagued themselves together in the war to exterminate the unfortunate Ti-pings, and *loot* their cities. In spite of their numbers, their boundless supplies of every munition of war, their irresistible shell and artillery, and the co-operation of the friendly legions swarming from the grand depôt, Shanghae, these heterogeneous marauders found the "broken force" able to give them many hard knocks and many a severe repulse, although the *Times* happened to think that "the people of China" had somehow converted the Ti-ping revolution into a crowd of fugitives running away from their mythical "terrible reprisals." This statement might do very well to excite the horror of pious people in England ready to believe anything dreadful; but the mercenaries banded together against the would-be freemen and Christians found that to break the force of the latter many a deadly encounter, and many a cunningly contrived Moorsom or shrapnel shell, was required. During a period of nearly twelve months, extending from August, 1862, to the middle of the summer, 1863, the horrors of Chinese warfare fluctuated backwards and forwards over what would otherwise have been one of the fairest parts of God's earth. The Ningpo and neighbouring districts possess a beauty and variety of scenery, added to a surpassing richness of production (tea, silk, cotton, &c.), second to none in the world. Yet a few experimental warriors and politicians have been permitted to create misery and ruin throughout this smiling land, and strew its plains with mouldering skeletons.

The war conducted by Captain Dew and his colleagues raged furiously for many months. The cities of Tse-kie, Yu-yaou, Fung-wha, Shou-shing, &c., were each taken, re-taken, lost, and won, several times over, by the Allies and by their Ti-ping enemies, and were at last finally held by the former.

To give any detailed account of the numerous actions

fought within the Ningpo province would be impossible. With one exception they resembled those in the first compaign of Admiral Hope and General Staveley. The same great slaughter of the Ti-pings with the deadly artillery, to which they could make no reply; the same gallant efforts to repel the stormers, who rushed forward after the defenders had been thoroughly shelled for many hours; the exception being that few of the cities were carried by assault. It is, I believe, due to the fact that a great proportion of the Ti-ping soldiery about the Ningpo districts were Cantonese, or Kwang-si men, that nearly every attempt to storm the cities they held was repulsed. They were ultimately driven out of the province, and the cities were, almost without exception, evacuated, although the besiegers had been severely repulsed, being rendered untenable by the severance of their lines of supply and communication.

There are two important episodes of Captain Dew's war which, from their influence upon future events, it is necessary to notice. The first is the death of General Ward; the second, the attack upon Shou-shing, in consequence of which Captain Dew was reprimanded by his superior officer and the British Government, and was thereby compelled to desist from actually participating in the further hostilities.

General Ward, whatever his failings might have been, was a brave and determined man. He served his Manchoo employers only too well, and at the last, by closing a career of peril and fidelity with the sacrifice of his life, he sealed all faults with his death, and left those who cherished his memory to regret that he had not fallen in a worthier cause. While directing the second attack upon the small town of Tse-kie, some ten miles inland from Ningpo, on the 21st of September, 1862, Ward, the American filibuster, and the first foreigner to take military service under the Manchoo, was mortally wounded by a Ti-ping musket ball. This adventurer originated the force that finally was the principal instrument in driving the Ti-pings from the dominions they had established as "Ti-ping tien kwoh." By such apparently insignificant means does the Great Ruler of the Universe overthrow the efforts and establish the destinies of man! The death of Ward placed *Colonel* Burgevine, his immediate subordinate, in command of the force. Burgevine could not agree with the mandarins, was badly treated by them, resented their treatment, was dismissed from the command, and the old Ward force became transformed from a rowdy, filibustering, hired legion, into a regular contingent of British mercenaries.

The disgrace of Dew, the Ti-ping slayer, came about in this wise:—The city of Shou-shing, distant more than *one hundred miles* from Ningpo, was attacked by an Imperialist army, to which the Anglo-Chinese and Franco-Chinese contingents were attached. These forces were defeated with severe loss, including their French general, Le Brethon, who was killed before the city. A French captain of artillery, by name Tardife, succeeded to the command; Captain Dew joined forces with him, and together they proceeded to besiege the place, and to avenge the disgrace of their former defeat.

Besides several field-pieces landed from the British men-of-war at Ningpo and a large park of howitzers and mortars belonging to the disciplined forces, Captain Dew provided them with a large 68-pounder lent to him for the occasion by General Staveley. Lieutenant Tinling, of the *Encounter*, with a party of seamen, had charge of this gun. On their march, the allies entered a large town, which the men thoroughly pillaged during two days; the consequence being, as it is written by one who was present, "that it was only after much trouble they could be got to move forward against Shou-shing. When they did so, at least 500 boats followed, each soldier having his own private *san-pan*, containing, and ready for more, *loot*. Many of the officers were almost as bad as the men, drinking and smoking, and taking hardly any care to maintain discipline." Here is a pretty description of the doings of those who were supposed to be protecting the country people from the "ruthless marauders!" The town referred to was not in Ti-ping possession, and all the looting was from the unfortunate inhabitants. Facts, that can be multiplied *ad infinitum*, exist to prove that the foreign intervention, and the manner and details thereof, seriously increased the anarchy, desolation, and loss of life, caused by the civil war previous to that event. The unavoidable devastations had passed away, peace had become established by the supremacy of the Ti-ping, when, alas! mercenary-minded Europeans wickedly deluged the peaceful districts with the blood of fresh victims, and causelessly maintained and prolonged the unmitigated ravages of war.

Upon reaching the devoted city of Shou-shing,—which, in expectation, General Tardife had promised his freebooter following the pleasure of "forty-eight hours" to loot,—Captain Dew placed his big gun in position, and proceeded to make a hole in the wall, by which the respectable allies might get at the prizes within. Now it so happened that the Ti-pings were determined neither to part with their city, nor their private valuables. A great breach was made, a battalion of European ruffians, and the nondescript disciplined and Imperialist troops, rushed forward to take possession; but the defenders—who, to use the language of an eye-witness, "fought with admirable pluck in the breach, and exposed themselves freely"— drove them back with a loss of half the European brigade of Shanghae *rowdies*, half the officers of the disciplined contingents, and many men *hors de combat*. Almost at the same moment General Tardife was killed, and Lieutenant Tinling mortally wounded.

The death of the last-mentioned gallant young officer, by drawing the attention of Admiral Kuper (on the station), and that of Parliament at home, to the subject, led to the disapproval of Captain Dew's disgraceful proceedings, and his removal from a part of China that he had contaminated by his presence. When brought to task for his participation in hostilities more than 100 miles from a treaty port, his shuffling excuse was "that I had gone to watch the proceedings, and prevent, if possible, any false step being taken by the Chinese disciplined force, which would at once have imperilled Ningpo." Well, it is an old saying that, if the blind lead the blind, both fall into the ditch; and this was undoubtedly realized by Captain Dew. The untrue statement about "any false step" being certain to imperil Ningpo, distant 100 miles, and protected by several strong cities directly on the way, is perfectly absurd; the crafty device was to avoid the censure he dreaded and deserved by frightening his superiors about the safety of Ningpo, which he pretended rested upon his exploits at Shoushing. Admiral Kuper, however, states in a despatch to the Admiralty, "I have informed Captain Dew that . . . . I consider he exceeded his instructions," and the Admiralty declares "that my Lords have desired the Rear-Admiral to inform Captain Dew that he exceeded his instructions." No wonder that the Chinese papers stated :—

"How Captain Dew, and all his crew, are allowed to do just what they have a mind to, is more than we can tell. Clearly all the people he slays he murders. He is violating every law, human and divine, to an extent which cannot be overlooked."*

It is a well-known fact that vast quantities of *loot*, and a money bonus from the Imperial authorities, almost invariably attended the capture of every Ti-ping city; and I have under my hand many apparently authentic statements in the press, accusing Captain Dew particularly, and others generally, of having been induced to carry on

* *China Overland Trade Report*, February 20, 1863.

hostilities against the Ti-pings for "private aggrandisement," and from "far less disinterested motives than 'the love of glory.'" As for the effect the Dew war had upon trade, the following extract from a communication dated "Ningpo, March 28, 1863," and forwarded to H.B.M. Consul by a number of influential firms, will show:—"So great a panic exists among the natives on account of the lawless proceedings, that our trade is in a worse condition than when the rebels were in the neighbourhood!"

Captain Dew attempted to shirk the responsibility of Lieutenant Tinling's death at a place where duty did not call him, although his commanding officer's orders did, by declaring that he (the Captain) was there as an "amateur!" Killing one's fellow man, even when conscience-bound by the plea of duty, is bad enough; but roving about, seeking whom to destroy, and slaughtering innocent men for pleasure, is somewhat different. We have seen that even the Government, which has approved every other proceeding, completely repudiated the unpardonable conduct of Captain Dew; we therefore say adieu to that officer, trusting there are few like him in the British service.

It is now necessary to notice the last of the events referred to at the beginning of this chapter. Since the death of the lamented filibuster, various members of General Staveley's staff and command had been in a perfect state of ferment, intriguing for the command of the Ward force, which it was determined should be converted into a British contingent. A battalion of Chinese, wearing shoulder-straps with the badge "67," drilled and officered by members of the British regiment of that number, and popularly known as Captain "Kingsley's force," was organized and raised to a strength of 1,000 men. Other corps, and some of Chinese artillery, were formed, while British officers were induced to accept various commands pertaining to the Ward force and its head quarters at the city of Soong-kong.

After a series of preliminary operations, General Staveley effected the re-capture of Kah-ding on the 24th of October, 1862. After a desperate defence, the Ti-pings were driven from the city with heavy loss. According to the safe *modus operandi* acquired by experience, General Staveley shelled the defenders for some hours from 40 pieces of heavy artillery and mortars. The besieging army consisted of 5,500 disciplined troops, including about 3,000 British and French, and a large co-operating force of Imperialist *braves* and soldiers. The Ti-pings, out of a garrison less than 5,000 strong, lost upwards of 1,500 men; while the allied loss amounted to 4 killed and 20 wounded. Soon after the capture of this city, the Ting-wang from Hang-chow, the Mo-wang from Soo-chow, and the Tow-wang from Hoo-chow, each commanding about 5,000 men, were ordered by the Shi-wang (chief in authority over their districts) to attempt its recovery, and also that of Tsing-poo. This army was attacked by *General* Burgevine's force, a column of 500 British troops, some 10,000 Imperialists, and an artillery detachment with 20 guns. The Ti-pings had just intrenched themselves by the light field works usual among the Chinese, when they were engaged by the enemy. Unable to reply to the murderous artillery of the British and disciplined troops, they still held the position, although the shot and shell committed fearful havoc in their close ranks. At last, when the enemy had become tired of their shell practice, and imagined the Ti-pings were sufficiently decimated, a general assault was given. An episode in this transaction is worthy of notice.

A division of the attacking army was led by one "Wong-e-poo," a young Chinese officer who had been promoted to a captaincy at the request of Admiral Hope, who had also presented him with a sword for conspicuous bravery during the raids he had lately conducted against the Ti-pings, and in which the officer had served as a sergeant of Ward's force. This gallant young Chinaman was the first to cross the line of intrenchments, and almost instantly fell mortally wounded; he then gave the sword to General Burgevine, whom he begged to keep it, and to give his young wife a few dollars to keep her from want—this was his last request. The Ti-pings, when driven from their slight defences, made a stand at a village just in the rear, and were three times brought back to the charge by a fine-spirited young chief, who was the Mo-wang's brother, and whose gallant bearing and handsome trappings attracted universal attention. At the last charge, Vincente, the late *General* Ward's *aide-de-camp*, spurred his horse into the Ti-ping ranks. Misled by the fact that he had separated himself from the enemy, and believing he came over as a friend, the chief unsuspiciously advanced towards him and held out his hand; the Manillaman replied to his friendly gesture by shooting him dead, and then, singular to relate, managed to gallop back to the enemy in safety.

After two hours' fighting, during which the artillery mowed them down by hundreds, the Ti-pings were driven out of the village, and, being then hemmed in against a wide creek, which they had only one small pontoon bridge to cross by, suffered terribly from the deadly fire of grape and canister shot during their retreat. Their loss in this disastrous action was 2,300 killed (600 bodies were counted in one portion of the intrenchments) and 700 prisoners, the latter being barbarously put to death by their captors.

The frightful atrocities perpetrated upon the unfortunate Ti-pings by those into whose power they had fallen, even excelled the cruelties of the cruel Chinese and still more cruel Tartars. "How the Ti-pings were driven out of the Provinces of Kiangnan and Chekiang," from notes kept by an officer under Ward, Burgevine, Holland, and Gordon, is a lengthy narrative published in the *Friend of China*. The portion contained in the columns of that journal of April 25, 1865, describing the engagement just noticed, states:—" General Burgevine darkened the victory with a foul deed. The poor rebels who had been captured *were cruelly blown away from the guns*, to the delight of a few we will not mention, but to the disgust of the greater part of the officers." Who, after this, shall talk of *Ti-ping* cruelties? The revolutionists had neither made war upon, injured, nor even insulted foreigners; yet the foreign officers, supported by the help of British troops, actually massacred their unoffending and helpless prisoners of war in cold blood! Perhaps *General Burgevine* thought he was paying a graceful compliment to his British allies by imitating their deeds in India. No doubt some war-Christians think these latter proceedings exceedingly worthy and proper; however, the Ti-pings have never yet reached such a state of Christian civilization as to copy them.

The allied loss was 5 killed and 15 wounded, including three Europeans! And this may be taken as a fair sample of all the succeeding battles with the British, French, and other disciplined and artillery-supplied forces. The Ti-pings have always done all that men of flesh and blood were capable of doing, but, without artillery to resist or reply to that overwhelming arm of the enemy (supplied freely from the British arsenals), their bravest and best fell to the iron storm, and the rest fled before it.

Very shortly after the above action, *General* Burgevine became the victim of the scheming carried on between the mandarins and those British officials who desired to establish the Ward force as an English contingent. Having taken a large amount of specie from the house of Ta-kee (the banker to the force, and in the service of the Imperial Government), which he had been compelled to seize, *nolens volens*, in order to satisfy his men, who were in an open state of mutiny for their arrears of pay—pay, too, that seems to have been purposely kept lying idle at Ta-kee's house, probably with the cunning idea it would act (as in reality it did) upon the force, and produce some outbreak that could be taken advantage of

to disgrace Burgevine and replace him by a British officer
—he was dismissed from his command and a reward
offered for his head by the Manchoo governor, or Fu-tai,
of the province. The excuse given by the Mandarins for
this transaction was that Burgevine had disobeyed orders,
resisted lawful authority, and seized the money. Some
measure of this is very probably true; but whatever offence
had been committed by him, the mandarins had themselves been the cause of it by their peculation, withhold-
ing the wages of the troops, and underhand intriguing.
Probably the fact that Captain Holland, R.M., was
installed as Burgevine's successor, may account for the
events leading to the latter's dismissal.

The Imperialist Mandarins were only too eager to fall
into the views of those who assisted them; the command
of the once despised filibustiers' force by Englishmen
meant taking all the danger and responsibility of repelling
the Ti-pings out of their own hands; consequently,
availing themselves of the subserviency of British officers
and authorities, they accepted Captain Holland as the
commander of their disciplined troops, and the services of
any others who were willing, and did not feel dishonoured
by hiring themselves out to support such a cruel and
corrupt cause. From this moment the active operations
by British troops ceased, but Ward's old legion became a
British contingent, and has continued one ever since.
Backed up in all their operations against the Ti-pings
by the presence of British troops to support them in case
of reverse, and supplied with every munition of war,
artillery, ships, &c. they required, the various mercenary legions infesting the neighbourhood of Shanghae
and Ningpo have managed (with the assistance of the
ordinary Chinese and Manchoo soldiers, who alone out-
numbered those of Ti-ping tien kwoh) to terminate the
allied operations by driving the revolutionists from their
once happy territory.

Soon after the command of the force had been

assumed by Captain Holland, it met with the most severe defeat the Ti-pings have ever given it, and he resigned the appointment in disgust. The Order in Council permitting British officers to take military service with the **Emperor** of China having just reached Shanghae, Major Gordon, R.E., took command of the disciplined Chinese, and many other officers joined in the questionable service. From this time forth the British Government became committed to the **success and** responsibilities of the force; and for every atrocity **perpetrated by** the Imperialists, and for every life destroyed, are equally as much accountable as they were for the previous conduct of their own troops. Under such auspices, and with boundless supplies of all the material of war, similar necessaries being successfully prevented from **reaching** their antagonists, it is easy to appreciate the consequent course of events—continued triumph of the Anglo-Franco-Manchoo mercenaries, **and repeated defeat of the** Ti-pings, already much weakened **by** the loss of **many of** their best troops, **and diminished in** their prestige **from the result of the raids headed by** Admiral Hope and **General** Staveley.

The worst **feature** attending the conversion of **the** mercenary **legions into British auxiliaries, is** the fact that **Sir F. Bruce, the** English **Minister at** Pekin, distinctly **repudiated any** such action; and yet his Government saw **fit to sanction the** arrangement when it was reported to **them** by Generals Staveley and Brown, who **seem** to have been foremost among **the** Shanghae local advocates of the system. *General* Burgevine having **proceeded** to the Manchoo **court at Pekin,** stated his case, and was by them reinstated **in his former command;** receiving, also, the full approval **of Sir F. Bruce.** Upon his return to Shanghae, with **an** Imperial Commissioner to place him **in** position, the British generals and their colleagues in **collusion** with the Imperial authorities, disregarding the **direct instructions of Sir F. Bruce,** successfully opposed **his reappointment, and managed to retain** Major Gordon in command; by what means being best known to themselves.

We will conclude our notice of the establishment of the Anglo-Manchoo contingent with a few facts proving the singular, if not sinister, circumstance, that Sir F. Bruce, although a virulent enemy of the Ti-pings, has always carefully avoided authorizing the employment of British officers against the insurgents; and, in fact, has invariably disapproved such measures, as well as the movement of British troops to support and succour the contingents when in difficulty.

In a despatch to General Staveley, dated "Pekin, March 12, 1863,"* Sir F. Bruce, referring to the liberty granted to officers to enter the Chinese Imperial service, states:—"I should prefer that the military men employed by the Chinese Government should *not* belong to the great treaty Powers;" and, with regard to British officers choosing to enter what the Press in China has termed "the disgusting service," he expresses the opinion that "they will then bear a Chinese, and not a British character." How *literally* this belief has been fulfilled, the torture of Ti-ping prisoners captured by the Imperialists, the treacherous massacre of the prisoners at Soochow, and the great loss of life which occurred, after cities were captured, sufficiently prove.

In a despatch dated "April 10,"† Sir F. Bruce expresses his wish to the same officer that Burgevine should be reinstated to the command of the Ward force, and, speaking "of the charges brought against him," states: "I took occasion to examine them at length, and I am perfectly satisfied that General Burgevine acted from a regard to the interests confided to him, that he was sacrificed to an intrigue of some Chinese subordinate officers, and to the jealousy entertained by the Governor towards the Chinese drilled force." If the Minister had added the names of a

---

* Blue Book, China, No. 3, 1864, p. 68.   † *Id.*, p. 80.

few foreigners as being privy to the "intrigue," he would have hit upon the whole truth. The Governor was jealous of the force as a Chinese one managed by foreigners, and successfully plotted, with no little ingenuity and shrewdness, to make it a foreign force officered by Englishmen, and countenanced by British authorities, who accepted all the responsibility entailed.

Upon the subject of Major Gordon's appointment to the coveted generalship of mercenaries, Sir F. Bruce, in a despatch to General Brown, dated "June 11," states:* "It is not expedient that British officers should command Chinese troops in the field against the insurgents, beyond the limits of the radius deemed necessary for the security of the ports where they are stationed. . . . I am further of opinion that, unless the force be properly constituted, and relieved from the necessity of obeying the orders of the local Government, it will do no real and permanent good; and that the officer who commands it will speedily find himself in a position which is neither compatible with his professional reputation, nor what is due to the character of a British officer. Under these circumstances, I must *decline* accepting the responsibility of authorizing the employment of British officers beyond Shanghae. . . . I have informed the Chinese Government of my objections to the employment of British officers in the field." Singularly enough, every word prophesied by Sir F. Bruce came to pass; the force became an instrument of evil in the hands of local Mandarins, to be used for their individual purposes, and then got rid of; the officers found their honour tarnished by complicity in deeds of blood and treachery; some were disgusted, but the Commander retained his position until he was *compelled* to break up the force by orders from his Government. In a despatch to Earl Russell, dated "October 13," Sir F. Bruce declares:† "It was reluctantly,

---

* Blue Book, No. 3, 1864, p. 96. † *Id.*, p. 162.

and in deference to the naval and military authorities, that I consented to our assuming the responsibility of defending the thirty-mile radius round Shanghae, and I spared no effort to bring about an arrangement of Burgevine's dispute, so as to avoid the necessity of having to place an English officer at the head of the force destined to operate beyond the radius." Yet members of Lord Palmerston's Government have had the hardihood to declare that the operations against the Ti-pings *were approved* by Sir F. Bruce.

When Major Gordon's force was in danger, General Brown moved detachments of British troops to support him, and to garrison the captured towns and hold them against the Ti-pings. Sir F. Bruce, in a despatch upon the subject, dated "October 6,"* clearly condemns his conduct in these words:—" If officers go into the Chinese service, we are not entitled to facilitate their operations by moving men, or placing garrisons in towns beyond the radius for their support, further than we should be if the corps assisted were commanded by a Chinese general. We are *not* entitled to lend them artillery, or men to work their guns *on any pretext!*" In the very teeth of these distinct instructions, General Brown persisted in every measure they condemn. It was the favourite *modus operandi* over again—the military or naval authorities acting in direct violation of orders, the disobedience being ultimately endorsed by the Government, and the apparently disobedient receiving praise and C.B.'s by way of punishment.

* Blue Book, No. 3, 1864, p. 163.

CHAPTER XXI.

Personal Narrative continued.—Mr. Lobschied.—His Reception at Nankin.
—Press Publications.—Mr. Lobschied leaves Nankin.—Operations
before Tait-san.—The Assault.—Act of Bravery.—Route of the Imperialists.—Gordon's Art of War.—Tait-san reinvested.—Siege of
Tait-san.—Its Capture.—Manchoo Atrocities.—Treatment of Ti-ping
Prisoners.—Mr. Sillar's Statement.—Quin-san captured.—Gordon's
Report.—Gordon reinforced.—The Chung-wang recalled.—Critical
Position of the Ti-pings.—The Chung-wang's Retreat.—Difficulties
encountered.—Reinforcements.—The Scene of Battle.—Its Horrors.
—Arrival at Nankin.—The Chung-wang's Army.—General attack.—
The Repulse.—The Surprise.—The Night Attack.—The Flight and
Pursuit.—Death of Marie.

WHEN at last I became convalescent and able to leave my house in Nankin, for several reasons I determined to take a trip to Shanghae. My wife wished to see her relations there; I was anxious to ascertain the political and practical position of affairs; and, besides, there were many things to be done toward assisting the Ti-ping cause. The principal inducement for the trip was, however, the fact that my friends, D. and Captain P., had, upon their last voyage, brought me some letters from Chin-kiang (to where they had been forwarded by my agent at Shanghae), stating that the Rev. W. Lobschied, a distinguished missionary, was anxious to visit the Ti-ping capital. I at once decided to proceed to Shanghae and afford him every assistance by placing one of our vessels at his service for the journey to and from Nankin.

During the last few months of my illness messengers had

continually arrived from the head-quarters of the I- and Chung-wang's armies, reporting the uninterrupted successes of both. But at the same time intelligence was received of the second capture of Kah-ding and Tsing-poo, the capture of Fu-shan by the allies, and the treachery of the chief in command at the city of Chang-zu, who had accepted the large bribes offered by the enemy, and surrendered the city. Orders were consequently despatched to the I-wang's victorious army, already beyond the Po-yang lake, and that chief detached a considerable portion of it to return and protect the threatened districts. This force, at the time I left Nankin (early spring of 1863), was already besieging Chang-zu, having closely invested the city upon every side.

Having embarked with my wife on board our lorcha, the *Anglo-Ti-ping*, we proceeded under sail to Chin-kiang, and then took passage in a steamer to Shanghae. A month after our arrival, every motive for the visit being accomplished, and the Rev. W. Lobschied having arranged to accompany me, we returned to Chin-kiang together, and then, getting on board the lorcha, made sail for Nankin. When halfway there I engaged a small steamer to tow us up to the forts, in order to oblige the missionary, who was averse to the delay the calm weather seemed likely to occasion.

In a couple of days we were cast off at our destination, and I proceeded on shore with Mr. Lobschied, introducing him to the Sz-wang, who received him very kindly, and immediately sent word of his arrival to the Government inside the city. The next morning horses and attendants were in waiting to escort us to the Kan-wang's presence. Upon reaching the palace, Mr. Lobschied met with so warm and friendly a reception from the Kan-wang and many other chiefs, that I am quite sure he can never cease to remember it with pleasure, and at the same time with regret that he has not been more energetic or useful to what he knew full well was the cause of Christianity and righteousness. Many of the Ti-pings had known him at Canton in former days, when they had studied the wondrous truths of Scripture, and some, I believe, had been his own converts and pupils. These men were most anxious that he should stay among them, and earnestly entreated him to do so; but the Rev. W. Lobschied, as he informed me, had to attend to some appointment at Canton, and the wishes or whims of a young wife. Thus the last opportunity for a teacher of the Gospel to support the cause of Christianity in China was thrown away; my trouble lost (not that I cared for ought but the fact that it was not used to advantage when every opportunity was offered); and the visit of the last missionary who came to the Ti-ping capital, rendered utterly fruitless. Something did result from the visit in the shape of the following letter :—

"THE TAEPINGS.

"*A Visit to Nanking, and an Interview with the Kan-Wong.*

"(To the Editor of the *Daily Press*, Hong Kong.)

"SIR,—The dreadful accounts given of the condition and character of the rebels had long made me anxious to visit their capital, and see for myself how far all that has been said of them be true. There is a brisk trade carried on outside the city of Nanking. The fields within the ancient wall were well cultivated, as well as the country around; and wheat, barley, and large beans, appeared to be there in abundance. The people within the city *were certainly looking better than in any town along the Yang-tse-kiang.* New shops and fine buildings were in course of erection, and the people were in general well dressed. The women moved about performing their daily work as they do here in the South; aged persons were playing with their grandchildren, and wheresoever I came I was treated with respect and kindness. The kings, and particularly Kan-Wong, received me with great kindness, and I felt that I was as safe in Nanking as in any Chinese town I have ever visited. They were anxious to know why England was so hostile against them. 'Have we ever broken faith with foreigners? Have we ever retaliated the enmity of England and France?' said Kan-Wong. 'If they force us to the conclusion that we are to be treated as outlaws, then the day of retribution will come! We are fighting in our own country, and to rid ourselves of a foreign power, and woe to the stranger who falls into our hands after the first shot has been fired against Nanking.* We need not then take cities and hold them, or allow foreigners to assist the Imperial inaps in surrounding us; we shall then move in one compact body, ravaging the country and destroying trade.† We have not as yet sent men into the foreign settlements to burn and destroy, but have strictly prohibited such acts. Who can prevent us from committing such acts, if we choose? And why should we not make the sojourn of foreigners here intolerable, if they come to destroy us who *would* and *have* opened to them every port we hold, and tried to be friends with them? We will spare neither Hankow nor any other place held by foreigners, who will then see the difference between forbearance and determined hostility.' They told me that they had *repeatedly* applied to the foreign consuls, in order to come to some arrangements, but all their communications had been returned *unopened*, and no reply given. I was present at their religious meetings, which are regularly held every morning and evening, but would not join them until I knew what they were doing. They sang a hymn; and having previously placed three cups of tea on the table,‡ they knelt down, one of them § reading or saying an appropriate prayer. There was *no worship of Taiping-Wong*. Whilst sitting in the palace, there came frequent orders for books on religious subjects, and, so far as the Chinese care for religion, *these men sang and prayed with a will and with apparent devotion*. As the Imperialists are going to *restrict* the development of trade on the Yang-tze-Kiang as soon as *Osborn's* fleet has come out, and as the rebels *are willing to open the whole country to foreigners*, if they will stretch out a friendly hand to them, everybody may judge for himself which party will serve him best. China was conquered by the help of Roman Catholic missionaries, and the Imperial House has for 150 years been under their influence. So long as the Emperors made use of them they prospered; and the moment they expelled them from Pekin, misrule and effeminacy became the order of the day. Sir Frederick Bruce will one day be recalled to give an account of the *ruinous course of policy he has advised his Government to adopt*, and foreign influence will at last prevail in the council of the rebels. But whether that will be upon the ruins of the silk and tea plantations, or upon the graveyards of thousands of British subjects, we shall soon have an

---

* Alluding to *Admiral* Sherard Osborne's 'Vampyre' fleet.

† Since the loss of Nankin, and all their former cities, through British hostility, this has resulted to a certain extent only; for still, with wonderful forbearance, the Ti-pings have not begun to ravage the country, their moderation in the neighbourhood of Amoy, where they now are in force, being well known.

‡ In honour of the Holy Trinity.

§ The officiating priest.

opportunity of witnessing. As almost all the officers now in the service of the Imperialists are on half-pay, *and receive besides an enormous salary from the Chinese*, nobody need feel any surprise at the *strange doings* of men worthy a more honourable death.* And if *General* Gordon does receive 1,200 taels per month from the Imperialists, and his half-pay as an officer of the British army, where then is British neutrality? The proclamation of the Queen is dust thrown into the eyes of Europe and America. But more on this subject for the second mail of this month.

"Yours respectfully,
"Hong Kong, 10th June, 1863." "W. L.

The Rev. W. Lobschied, by his departure from Nankin and return to the south of China, sacrificed a glorious opportunity of serving the cause of the Master whose word he came abroad to teach. Had he installed himself at the Ti-ping capital and proclaimed that fact, and then reported the favourable points of their sincere Christianity, friendliness to foreigners, desire for unrestricted commerce and intercourse with Europeans, and general moral and physical superiority, in *all* the particulars for which the Chinese are condemned, he would most likely have been the means of arresting the interference of England, and purifying the religious errors of the only voluntary native worshippers of Jesus in Asia.

Had Mr. Lobschied so acted, every mission society and ordained member of the Church of England would necessarily have supported him; this would simply have been their duty to God. Popular opinion, when fixed by the voice of a well-known divine, speaking the *truth* from Nankin, and with all the authority of his presence among the revolutionists, and undoubted personal knowledge of them, would almost certainly have compelled the British Government to remain neutral.

Unfortunately Mr. Lobschied had private business which possessed greater charms for him than this, although success was certain if the effort were made. The

---

* It is hardly to be understood how dishonourable men are "worthy a more honourable death."

Manchoo-Imperialists, unassisted by foreign mercenaries, would have fled before the progress of Ti-ping tien kwoh like fine chaff before a gale of wind. The ultimate results would have been the sure establishment of Christianity, freedom, and modern civilization, throughout the vast Chinese empire.

Private affairs overpowered all other considerations, and so, after a few days spent at Nankin, I placed the rev. gentleman on board a passing steamer and bid him adieu.

Soon after my return to Nankin, reports of disaster to the Ti-ping forces in the Shanghae district were received; but previous to noticing these I must describe the complete defeat the Anglo-Manchoo legion experienced before the city of Tait-san.

Shortly after being placed in command of the drilled force, Captain Holland was ordered by the Fu-tai, Le, Governor of the province, to advance upon Tait-san and wrest it from the Ti-pings. Burning to distinguish himself, and probably not averse to the *bonus* it is believed the Fu-tai offered for the capture of the city, besides the prospect of much *loot*, the newly-fledged *general* led forward his men.

This expedition was accompanied by British volunteers, and the British officers belonging to the force, besides which General Staveley lent several large howitzers, the property of the English nation, to the commanding officer. Attached to *General* Holland, as body-guard, was a motley brigade of European mercenaries, consisting of almost every nationality. The whole strength of the disciplined division inclusive was considerably over 3,000 men, with 22 pieces of heavy artillery, field-pieces, and mortars, supported by an army of 10,000 Imperialists. The legionaries, and a great proportion of the irregular troops, were well armed with English rifles and muskets, well equipped in every way, and supplied with abundance of ammunition.

After driving the Ti-pings from several small outworks and tearing from a neighbouring village all its "doors, windows, tables, &c.," as one account states, the Imperialist forces took up a position under the walls of Tait-san. Of course the Ti-ping maligners, who followed upon the track of the allies, raven-like croaked forth from the destroyed village about the "ruthless devastation" of those "bloodthirsty monsters." They should have seen the village, or rather those who have been misled by their howling should have done so, *before* the gallant Anglo-Manchoo forces stripped it of furniture and partially pulled down the houses. Undoubtedly many who have accused the Ti-pings of wanton devastation have unintentionally mistaken the ravages of their own friends for that of the people they condemned, though it is hard to believe that any one could credit such opinions, when, in every account of the Imperialist operations, the destruction of some Ti-ping city, village, or store of grain, is prominently set forth.

Rows of stakes had been driven into the creeks by the Ti-pings, and the boats carrying the siege train of the enemy were delayed in their advance upon Tait-san until they could be pulled up. In spite of obstructions and a strong sortie made by the garrison, which was not repulsed without a sharp fight, the guns were landed during the night of the 13th of February, 1863, and placed in position.

Early on the following morning the garrison received strong reinforcements from the Ti-ping army investing Chang-zu, distant less than twenty-five miles, which were welcomed with immense cheering. Shortly afterwards the besiegers opened fire from their numerous artillery.

In about five hours a large and practicable breach was made in the city wall, and Captain, or rather *General*, Holland ordered the assault. Now it so happened that the defenders had wisely sheltered themselves from the deadly artillery fire to which they had only one or two small 6-pounders to reply, and instead of recklessly exposing themselves in the usual Ti-ping style, had remained perfectly silent behind their defences.

Led by a party of the body-guard and their European officers, the trained troops rushed gallantly forward to storm the city. At this moment the defenders suddenly manned the breach, and although fearfully thinned by the enfilading artillery fire, kept up a fusilade which told with terrible effect upon the dense masses of the enemy. A few crossed the moat by their bridges, only however to be shot down, and the whole division of stormers wavered and hesitated on the brink. A sergeant-major of the disciplined rifle regiment here performed an act of bravery that no European could have outdone. Seizing the colours of the regiment, Ward's old flag, he rushed to the front with it, and calling on the men to advance, stood there alone, a mark for the fire of the besieged. It is remarkable that, though six bullets pierced his clothes, not one injured him, or even cut his skin.

Unable to advance against the shower of missiles directed from the breach and city walls, where even the little boys were stationed with heaps of bricks to throw upon them, the Imperialists fell back on their guns in confusion. *General* Holland then ordered the artillery to the rear, and a rapid retreat commenced. This, however, they were not allowed to effect so easily, for the Ti-pings dragged a 6-pounder into the breach, where it was worked by some Europeans, and directed upon the men endeavouring to remove the siege guns, with deadly effect. At the same time the garrison sallied forth from two gates, while others rushed through the breach and attacked the enemy with vigour.

For some time the rifles and 1st regiment of the British contingent, together with the European company, fought desperately to save the guns. Meanwhile the main Imperialist army was routed with much slaughter, and, with all the other regiments of disciplined troops, fled in every direction from the field. The troops who so gallantly protected the retreat of their comrades, managed also to save all the artillery, except two heavy 32-pounders and several light howitzers. Upon these guns the Ti-pings incessantly charged, and both sides lost heavily in killed and wounded. General Holland had left the field, and it was entirely due to Colonel Barclay and Major Cooke, who jointly conducted the retreat, and well animated and kept their men together, that only a few pieces of artillery, instead of the whole park, were captured by the Ti-pings.

Seeing that his men were falling thickly, and that they were in danger of being surrounded, Colonel Barclay abandoned the guns and made a pretty orderly retreat. The Ti-pings marked those guns for their especial prey, and concentrated on them such a hail of shot that no one could approach them from the hostile ranks and live. The enemy found that it would be impossible even to spike them without a terrible loss of life, and so left them uninjured as trophies for the victorious garrison of Tait-san.

The day following their defeat only 1,500 of the British contingent mustered at their head-quarters, but stragglers shortly came dropping in. The same force lost 5 officers killed and 16 wounded. The co-operating Imperialist army was totally dispersed, and lost more than 2,000 men *hors de combat*. The Ti-ping casualties were also very heavy, for the men had rushed gallantly into the breach under withering volleys from the disciplined and well-armed assailants, and at least 1,000 were killed and wounded during the defence and subsequent fighting.

General Holland, upon reaching Shanghae, resigned his command in disgust, and was superseded by one Major Gordon, of the Royal Engineers, a cold, calculating man, who possessed qualities far more conducive to successful operations against the Ti-pings than even brilliant and dashing generalship. His tactics were to destroy them from a distance by his long-range artillery, which was a thing to be done generally with perfect impunity, because the Ti-pings were almost entirely without cannon.

The aim of the revolutionists is to get at close quarters with the enemy, and wherever they have been able to accomplish this, even the disciplined and foreign-officered troops have been beaten. Unfortunately they have seldom been able to effect their favourite manœuvre against the latter, the overwhelming artillery and regular volleys of musketry sweeping away every attempted formation of the Ti-ping troops long before it could be completed.

General Gordon having assumed command of the once despised mercenaries, that is to say, despised before the despisers were able to handle the loaves and fishes, he very wisely spent several months in thoroughly reorganizing his troops and raising his artillery to a strength and state of efficiency perfectly irresistible by the Ti-pings. During this period, besides the officers of the force, numerous drill-instructors were supplied by the British general at Shanghae, so that Gordon's, Kingsley's, Cooke's, and other legions, soon became formidable both as to numbers, armament, and discipline, *à l'Anglais*.

The first operations directed by Gordon were against Fu-shan and the beleaguered city of Chang-zu, the former of which was captured and the latter relieved, the Ti-pings losing some 1,200 men; Gordon's force, 2 killed and 3 wounded! These relative casualties afford a fair sample of the usual result of nearly every engagement. The immense loss of life upon the Ti-ping side during the years 1862-3-4, and part of the present, may easily be imagined, and will be found stated in detail in the approximate table at the end of this volume,* which has been compiled principally from official sources. Gordon, in his own report of the operations above referred to,

---

* Table of Ti-ping loss of life.

states: "The number of guns was terrific, and although after every shot the rebels would fire from one or two loopholes, it was evident they had no chance." The position exposed to this "terrific" fire was simply a few open stockades, undefended by artillery.

At this time Gordon's force mustered, all told, about 5,000 men; Kingsley's, 1,000; Cooke's, 1,500; and the Franco-Manchoo contingents, commanded respectively by *Generals* D'Aguibelle, Giquel, and Bonnefoi, from 3,000 to 4,000. Subsequently other legions and artillery corps attached to the irregular Imperial troops, about 2,500 in all, were formed and commanded by *Colonels* Bailey, Howard, Rhode, &c., while the total force of trained Chinese generally maintained the relative strength here given, viz., 14,000.

The disaster to the Ti-pings in the vicinity of Shanghae, the report of which, as mentioned before their victory at Tait-san, reached Nankin shortly after my return, consisted in their loss of the former city, and the still more important one of Quin-san, after a desperate and gallant defence at each.

General Brown, Commander-in-Chief of H. B. Majesty's forces in China, having, by every description of help and assistance, placed Gordon's troops in a state of complete effectiveness, the latter once more moved upon the devoted city of Tait-san.

Upon this occasion Gordon was supplied with a heavy siege train, including 8-inch howitzers and large mortars, *all belonging to the British army;* while General Brown sent a force of 550 men (including detachments of Royal Artillery, H. M. 31st regiment, Belooches, and B. N. I.) to look after his guns and take care that his *protégé* should not suffer a similar defeat to that experienced by *General* Holland. In fact, General Brown maintained a large force at Shanghae for the express purpose of assisting the Imperialists, supplying them with artillery and men to garrison the cities they captured.

SIEGE OF TAIT-SAN.

The capture of Tait-san is one of the most desperate encounters on the records of the Anglo-Manchoo forces.

In addition to the trained troops, Sing, a Manchoo general, joined in the attack with 5,000 to 7,000 men. The strength of the garrison was not less than 4,000, including little boys, who, according to the usual custom, were stationed with heaps of stones to throw upon the assailants.

After shelling the Ti-pings from their outworks, Gordon arrived under the walls of Tait-san on the 2nd of May, 1863. In his report to *General Brown*, Gordon states:—" About noon fire was opened from two guns, and by degrees more guns were brought into action, till at 2 p.m. every gun and mortar was in action, *the troops being under cover*. As the defences got dilapidated the guns were advanced, and at 4.30 p.m. the boats were moved up and the assault commenced. The rebels swarmed to the breach, and for ten to twelve minutes a hand-to-hand contest took place, canister being fired into the breach from this side of the ditch, and a heavy musketry fire kept up."

From this statement we find that after crumbling the ancient city walls to dust, and pouring in the tremendous fire of his numerous artillery for four hours and a half, his own men being in perfect safety, while the unfortunate defenders were torn to pieces by the storm of shot and shell to which they could make no reply, *General* Gordon at last ordered the assault. This, however, was gallantly repulsed by the brave garrison, who, though almost decimated by the murderous artillery, despite the hail of " canister " from enfilading batteries and the " heavy musketry fire " poured upon them by the adverse covering parties, rushed into the wide-spread ruins of the breach and drove the assailants back in a desperate hand-to-hand encounter.

Rallied by their officers, the division of stormers again returned to the assault, only, however, to be met with equal determination by the Ti-pings, who again successfully repulsed them.

General Gordon now placed his men under cover, inflicting heavy loss upon the defenders of the breach by pouring continual discharges of grape and canister shot into their dense ranks. For some time this artillery practice was resumed; a fresh storming party was then told off, and the breach again attacked with much bravery, and again defended with equal courage. The trained troops wavered and were nearly driven back a third time, but being reinforced by fresh men, rallied, and finally carried the breach. This, however, was not effected until the commandant of the city had been severely wounded, and a great proportion of his officers killed or disabled. The Ti-pings then gave way and escaped, carrying off many of their wounded, with their wives and children, through the gates at the other side of the town. The snake flags of Tsah, the commandant, remained in the breach until the summit was in possession of the enemy, when they were carried off in safety.

The Imperialists were assisted by the steamer *Hyson* in their attack upon Tait-san, which vessel caused no little alarm to the garrison by steaming along the creeks encircling the city, and throwing heavy shell among them, besides seriously menacing their line of retreat. Another great help to the besiegers consisted in the presence of the British *corps de réserve*, stationed at the village of Wy-con-sin close by, and which the Ti-pings fully expected would attack them should the disciplined Chinese be defeated.

The loss of the Anglo-Manchoo force upon this occasion was about two hundred; the Ti-pings, soldiery and civilians, killed in action, or afterwards caught by the Imperialists and cruelly put to death, cannot have been less than two thousand.

At Tait-san, as at Kah-ding, Tsing-poo, and every other city wrested from the Ti-pings either before or subsequently, the capture was followed by the perpetration of most revolting barbarities by the Imperial troops and Mandarins, whenever the attention of the British officers who assisted them to capture the places was withdrawn. *General* Gordon and the commanding officers of other contingents saved some of the Ti-ping prisoners who had been captured; but for the destruction of many thousands of innocent men, including country people, non-combatant inhabitants of the cities, and women and children, they are criminally responsible.

Upon the first capture of Kah-ding by the British forces, when General Staveley's *humane* disposition led him to station the Imperialist troops so as to intercept the flight of the garrison from his artillery fire, the following scenes were enacted, as appears by a letter from the Rev. Mr. Lobschied, published in the *Hong Kong Daily Press* of June 28th:—

"A small gate being the only issue through which the women and children could escape from their *deliverers*, they rushed upon the wall, and threw themselves down a great height, rather than fall into the hands of the combined forces. Those that were immediately killed were lucky enough; for they were saved from the sufferings that awaited the survivors. Whilst looting and killing was going on within the walls, until darkness threw her veil over the scenes of horror, several hundreds of men, women, and children, whose only crime was that of being citizens of Kah-ding when taken by the rebels, were lying outside the city walls with broken limbs, helpless, and parched with thirst. When morning arrived, a few gentlemen passed outside the wall through the narrow gate, in order to take a retrospect of the field of action. What did they see? The Imperialists, having become aware of the large number of sufferers outside the wall, had resorted thither long before the rising of the sun, were just stripping the poor people, and cutting off their heads, which they would take with them as trophies of their victory, when the two gentlemen (one of whom was an officer) happened to disturb them."

The unfortunate people above referred to were a portion of those massacred by the troops of the Chinese general Le, the same worthy who, when reporting to General Staveley his execution of the duties assigned him, offered to produce the left ears of 1,300 rebels.

At Tait-san similar atrocities were committed by the forces of Sing, the Manchoo commander. Hundreds of civilians were killed for the sake of their heads, and some prisoners were actually taken to the camp of the British *corps de réserve,* formed in conjunction with an Imperialist one, and there cruelly tortured to death. The execution of seven victims in particular is fully attested by Dr. Murtagh,* 22nd B. N. I.; other "eye-witnesses," including the Bishop of Victoria, have personally assured me of their positive knowledge as to this and other atrocities more revolting, and upon a more extensive scale, that have been inflicted upon Ti-pings captured by means of the British alliance with the Manchoo. The following is an extract from a letter published in most of the Shanghae papers, and vouched for as being true by Dr. Murtagh :—

EXTRACT FROM THE "NORTH CHINA HERALD" OF JUNE 13, 1863.

Treatment of Ti-ping Prisoners.

(To the Editor of the *Daily Shipping and Commercial News.*)

" . . . About 11 o'clock a.m. on the day following the capture of Tait-san (*Sunday,* May 3rd), seven prisoners were brought into the Imperialist camp near Wy-con-sin; being stripped perfectly nude, they were each tied to a stake, and tortured with the most refined cruelty. Arrows appeared to have been forcibly driven into various parts of their bodies, from whence issued copious streams of blood. This mode of torture falling short of satiating the demoniacal spirit of their tormentors, recourse was had to other means. Strips of flesh were cut, or rather hacked (judging from the appearance presented, the instrument seemed too blunt to cut), from different parts of their bodies, which, hanging by a small portion of skin, presented an appearance truly horrible. . . .

"For hours these wretched beings writhed in agony. About sunset they were led forth more dead than alive by a brutal executioner, who, sword in hand, thirsting to imbrue his hand in blood, seemed the very incarnation of a fiend. Seizing his unfortunate victims, he exultingly dragged them forth, mocking and insulting them, and then, by hewing,

---

* *Vide* pp. 126 and 108, Blue Book on China, No. 3, 1864, for Dr. Murtagh's letter, and the attestation by Bishop Boone and the Bishop of Victoria of the statements of two other eye-witnesses.

hacking, and using a sawing motion, he succeeded eventually in putting an end to their sufferings by partially severing the head from the body. Such are the bare facts, which can, if necessary, be fully substantiated by other eye-witnesses. . . .

"(Signed) AN EYE-WITNESS."

As further evidence of the atrocities which were committed in these fearful times, the following letter will speak emphatically. It was written at the time, and addressed to the editor of the *Shanghae Recorder*, by Mr. J. C. Sillar, a merchant of high position, by whose permission it is now published:—

"NO MORE MURDERS.
"(To the Editor of the *Shanghae Recorder*.)

"SIR,—A gentleman who was present at the capture of Tsingpo informed me that he held the heads of fourteen women with his own hands while their throats, which had been cut by the English or French soldiers (perhaps both) were being sewn up. There were many more, but he held the heads of fourteen with his own hands.

"I trust that, in the event of the capture of Kading, steps may be taken to prevent such atrocities either by our own men or the 'disciplined Chinese.' "Your obedient servant,

"Shanghae, October 18, 1862. J. C. SILLAR."

"The women stated that their throats had been cut by the English soldiers; but, upon being asked to identify them, pointed to the French.
"J. C. S."

Placing the Manchoo, Sing, in charge of Tait-san, *General* Gordon moved forward to reconnoitre Quin-san, the next Ti-ping city in the direction of Soo-chow, the provincial capital. After establishing a large Imperialist army in a stockaded position close to its walls, he returned with his own force to Soong-kong, the head-quarters, for the purpose of obtaining from General Brown, at Shanghae, further supplies of H. B. Majesty's shot and shell, preparatory to bombarding the city. When all the necessary munitions of war had been received from the British arsenals, Gordon returned to his allies outside the east gate of Quin-san.

The garrison, upon the arrival of Gordon's troops, sallied forth upon them in strong force, but after a desperate attempt to come to close quarters were driven back by the artillery with much loss. Now, unfortunately for the Ti-pings, the scientific knowledge of their enemy led him to investigate the strategic and defensive position of Quin-san with unmistakable perception of its weak points. He quickly discovered that the place was so situated as to possess but one line of retreat or supply, in consequence of the numerous small lakes, Imperialist outposts, and broad creeks in every other direction. Consequently, instead of directly attacking the city, Gordon moved his army, supported by the steamer *Hyson* and a large fleet of well-armed gunboats, against its only line of communication, a road constructed along the bank of a wide creek leading to Soo-chow. This movement was no sooner perceived by the garrison of Quin-san, than, finding their position rendered perfectly untenable, they commenced to evacuate the city as fast as possible. Refugees from Tait-san and the surrounding country had increased the number of inhabitants considerably, and, as at many places their only line of retreat was but a few feet broad, with deep creeks on either side, and continual narrow bridges spanning the numerous canals intersecting the country with a perfect maze of water, their escape from the city occupied the entire day, and their long thin line stretched for miles along this narrow road. The rush of the panic-stricken people was so great that the Ti-ping troops became inextricably mingled with and confused among them.

A few miles from Quin-san the *Hyson* and the gunboats came upon the fugitives where their line of retreat was intersected by the creek, up which the vessels were advancing; their progress, however, was for some time arrested by a couple of stockades, into which a few soldiers managed to throw themselves, and by an obstruction presented by a strong row of stakes driven firmly across the creek. During the delay, the *Hyson's* European officers amused themselves by an incessant fire of grape and canister poured among the helpless people seeking to escape almost in front of the muzzle of her 32-pounder bow gun. Gordon, in his report to General Brown,* after noticing the "well-cultivated" appearance of the country, states that the *Hyson* continued this murderous work for "over three hours," at the expiration of which time he arrived with his troops and drove the defenders from their stockades. Immediately upon this, the *Hyson*, as Gordon states, "overhauled the rebels and followed them slowly up. The creek was positively jammed up with their boats, and at the bridge at Edin the crush was awful." Now, how those who directed the fire of shell and *mitraille* from the *Hyson* managed to avoid injuring the women and children, who constituted a great proportion of the people contained in the boats, does not appear.

When the unfortunates had been leisurely followed up and ceaselessly attacked until they reached the vicinity of Soo-chow, and the protection afforded by its garrison, the steamer turned about and slowly ran back. The report, continuing from this point, states:—

"All this time rebel stragglers had been dropping into the Soochow road from all parts, and the *Hyson* had to *continue her work* all the way back, sometimes being so close on masses of rebels that she had to resort to some measure to get clear of them, and so adopted the novel expedient of using her steam whistle, which, singular as it may appear, had the desired effect. . . . Mounted men would try and gallop by the steamer not six yards from her; others positively rode or tried to ride past when she was alongside the road. *The grape and canister must have told fearfully*, owing to their numbers. . . . We had not ceased shelling until 2.30 *a.m.*"

At least nine-tenths of the wretched people who thus perished under the orders of *General* Gordon—who, by the way, seems to have become very quickly imbued with the "Chinese character" prophesied by the British minister

* *Vide* Blue Book on China, No. 3, 1864 p. 111.

at Pekin—were non-combatants. The manner in which British officers dealt destruction to their victims during *twenty hours*, with absolute impunity to themselves, would be too revolting to be credible, but for its plain avowal by Major Gordon, R.E., himself. This almost unparalleled proceeding is merely the prototype of many other atrocities perpetrated by the Anglo-Manchoo legion and its Imperialist allies. During all the operations against the Ti-pings, and all the terrible consequences following the fall of their cities, can Major Gordon say how many were peaceful inhabitants, whose only fault was the fact that they were inmates of a town captured and held by the revolutionists? Fully nine-tenths of the Ti-ping killed and wounded, so vain-gloriously, were only guilty of submission to the *de facto* Power; the remainder were *bonâ fide* Ti-ping soldiers, whose only crime was their endeavour to expel the foreign and oppressive dynasty, and to establish the Christian faith, the persecution of the first converts to which caused their revolution.

Thousands of the people who fled before the ceaseless shelling from the *Hyson* had never seen a steamer before; even the few who had, like all Chinese, were greatly awed by the supposed qualities of the "fiery dragon ship;" thus, the shrieking of the steam whistle, the dashing noise of her paddles, the flaming appearance of her funnel, and the fearful effect of her artillery fire, must have thrown them into the wildest consternation. Other steam gunboats, similar to the *Hyson*, were shortly added to the flotilla attached to Gordon's force, and ever afterwards their appearance threw the Ti-pings into confusion, and proved more effective than a great army in the field. The dread inspired by the steamers was always fatal to every Ti-ping position they attacked, and not without cause. They were each protected by iron mantlets, proof against musketry fire, which was all they had to resist, and carried a heavy bow gun and another at the stern.

If the garrison of any stockade attempted to resist them, their artillery soon battered down the defences or shelled the defenders, and then came a massacre similar to that attending the evacuation of Quin-san. The whole country between Shanghae and Soo-chow is low, marshy, and cut up by innumerable creeks, canals, dykes, and lakes, the only roads being a few narrow causeways built along the sides of the principal creeks; therefore, whenever the garrison of a stockade was driven out, their only line of retreat was along the bank of a creek, up which a steamer could follow them for miles, and pour in deadly discharges of grape and canister at a distance of only a few feet.

It has been estimated that the Ti-ping loss during the evacuation of Quin-san and the subsequent route was not less than 3,000. Gordon's force lost 2 killed and 5 drowned!

Having noticed the particulars of the disastrous loss of Tait-san and Quin-san, we must now come to the still more unfortunate effect caused by the receipt of the intelligence at Nankin, and the further report that the ships of the Anglo-Chinese or "Vampyre" flotilla were arriving at Shanghae.

These events took place in the month of May, 1863, and immediately the Ti-ping Government heard of them, couriers were despatched in hot haste after the Chung-wang, recalling his army to the capital. At this time the Commander-in-Chief had advanced about four hundred miles in the direction of Pekin, having captured many cities from the enemy, and completely defeated several large Manchoo armies, one led by the Imperialist Prince Sung-wang, or Sau-ko-lin-sin, as he is known to Europeans. Upon receipt of the orders from Nankin, the Chung-wang was compelled to forsake all the important advantages he had gained, and derive no benefit from the series of victories he had achieved, by abandoning every captured position and precipitately returning to the capital.

The Ti-ping forces had quite lately reached a fertile part of the country, where they were recruiting and gradually recovering from the hardships endured throughout the previous march. From the edge of the river Yang-tze, in the vicinity where the army first crossed from Nankin, throughout a naturally sterile country, for a distance of more than three hundred miles, the retreating Imperialists had devastated everything far and near, so as to stay the advance of the Ti-pings by the deadly medium of famine. Every rice-field, farm, and plantation were destroyed and made a desert waste, so that not the smallest article of food could be obtained. Fortunately the Chung-wang's commissariat was well supplied, so his troops were able to traverse the desolated regions without very much suffering, and by quick movements to limit the devastation to an extent of three hundred miles.

At the time, however, when the Chung-wang received his orders to return to Nankin, the supplies of his army had become well nigh exhausted, and the urgent tone of the despatches made an immediate retreat so imperative, that no delay to gather in the standing crops or otherwise collect a sufficient quantity of provisions was possible.

Besides the fall of Tait-san, Quin-san, &c., and the presence of several "Vampyre" ships at Shanghae, where others were momentarily arriving, other dangers menaced the Ti-pings; namely, either the destruction of their best army by starvation, or the prevention of its retreat to Nankin, by the immense fleet of Imperialist gunboats threatening the city.

Since the fall of Ngan-king (towards the close of the year 1861), the Imperialists had gradually approached along both banks of the river, until at last they managed to capture every place up to the walls of Nankin. This result was accomplished entirely by the presence of the well-equipped and innumerable flotilla of row-galleys, just at the period the Ti-ping Government was alarmed by the loss of Tait-san and Quin-san. But though the revolutionists were unable to dispute the supremacy on the great river, simply because they were entirely destitute of war vessels, they held the country within five miles of the water for a considerable distance above Nankin on the south bank of the Yang-tze.

The army commanded by the Chung-wang consisted principally of veteran troops, natives of the south of China, who originally joined the movement, and was by far the best in the Ti-ping service. Its strength of fighting men was not less than 50,000, while numberless refugees, prisoners, coolies, and others, far more than doubled those figures.

From the intelligence conveyed in his despatches, the General knew at once that only one course—an instant retreat by forced marches—was possible, either to save his army from destruction, or succour the hardly-pressed garrisons of the cities of the silk district. Gathering all the rice at hand, though it was quite unripe, and foraging everything that could be used as food, though a full treasury could have supplied them with suitable provisions had such been available in sufficient quantity, the army broke ground and commenced its disastrous return to Nankin. The supplies soon proved inadequate to last one half the distance to be traversed; consequently, this retreat proved more terribly destructive to the army than a dozen bad defeats would have been. The latter part of the forced marches these starving men had to perform led through desert places and low marshy ground; and, to add to the horrors of their situation, the Yang-tze having considerably overflowed its banks, the low country for a great distance inland was completely flooded. Through this, and many a weary mile of bamboo swamp, had the exhausted and starving Ti-pings to force their way.

Whenever a piece of firmer ground was reached, it could only be passed after defeating the Manchoo troops in occupation, who, well supplied with food, clothing, and boats, swarmed around the perishing and retreating army in thousands, now that it could be done with impunity. As the unfortunate Ti-pings approached nearer and nearer to the bank of the river, their sufferings (if possible) became increased. Frequently they came to places totally impassable except by swimming, and at such they had to cross exposed to the attacks of numerous squadrons of Imperialist gunboats, stationed at every available position to cut off or harass their retreat. Can anything more dreadful than the state of these unhappy patriots be imagined? For nearly a month they had subsisted entirely upon the grass of the fields, the green tops of bamboo, and the bodies of the dead!—while their march lay through the mazes of dense bamboo jungle, and swamps of mud and water—frequently of a depth which prevented fording. During the whole of this fearful retreat, their rear, front, and flanks were incessantly harassed by the attacks of the cowardly and bloodthirsty enemy, who cruelly murdered hundreds of exhausted men, whom they were quite unable to withstand in fair fight. Thousands perished in this manner, and thousands more were horribly suffocated in the morasses, or drowned among the swamps. Who is responsible for all this misery and loss of life? It was *caused* entirely through British intervention, and the material aid given to the Manchoo. At last the leading division of the army made its appearance opposite Nankin, and then arose the difficulty of transporting it across the river.

During several days preceding the arrival of the remnant of the Chung-wang's troops, the enemy had maintained an incessant attack upon the batteries and forts commanding the passage of the river, and had particularly concentrated their efforts against a large fort on the opposite side, the capture of which would have placed the whole north bank in their hands, and would also have cut off all retreat. About a week previous, the *Anglo-Ti-ping*, with my old craft and three junks, had run the Imperial blockade and safely arrived at the

Nankin creek, each heavily laden with rice and other provisions. My friend D—— had caught a passing steamer, and proceeded on to Shanghae upon business. P—— remained with the lorcha, and I joined him on board, taking my wife with me, as the Sz-wang and principal chiefs in the city had requested me to assist in the defence of the river forts. Directly the Imperialists became aware of the near approach of the Chung-wang's army, they began their attacks upon the fort on the other side of the river. This work, Kew-fu-chew, as the Ti-pings named it, was directly opposite the batteries (at the entrance of the creek) which extended along the edge of the river, on the narrow strip of land forming the outer bank of the creek until it turned inland towards the city. These batteries mounted a number of heavy guns; though, as nearly all were of Chinese make—huge, unwieldy masses of iron, bigger than an English 68, but with the bore of only a 4 or 6-pounder—few were moveable or manageable. As a rule, until taught by Europeans, the Chinese are wretched artillerists, their guns being usually lashed firm in one position, from which they can neither be moved by the muzzle radius, nor breech-elevating principle; so that, be the object far or near, the guns are fired at the same range in every case. Among the many useless guns, the appearance of which had far more to do with frightening away the enemy than their effectiveness, I at last found five or six that were really serviceable— including an English naval 32-pounder, one 18-pounder, a large French cannon, and several fine brass Chinese guns. As there happened to be nearly thirty European and American trading vessels at the port, I managed to raise a corps of about twenty-five volunteers to work the artillery. My own lorcha carried two beautiful pivot-guns amidships, which proved of no little use during the different actions.

Regularly at daylight every morning the enemy would commence their attack upon Kew-fu-chew, and the smaller forts above the Sz-wang's position. Their plan of battle was well formed and very picturesque in appearance; successive squadrons of gunboats would sail down and engage the fort, delivering their fire; and then, filling away before a fair wind, returning to their position up the river. These vessels were assisted by others co-operating from below the Ti-ping lines; all being profusely decorated with gaudy flags, and propelled by numerous oars on either side.

The whole scene of battle formed a never-to-be-forgotten spectacle. The gallant appearance of the innumerable gunboats tacking down stream, and opening fire, one after the other, in regular order; some crossing in every direction, and others running back dead before the wind, with their broad and prettily-cut lateen sails stretching out on either side like a pair of snowy wings; the incessant roar of the cannonade; the flash of the guns; the curling smoke, at first dense and impenetrable, and then dissolving into thin wreaths, gracefully circling round the rigging and the white sails; the steady reply from the flag-covered forts, now enveloped in clouds of sulphurous vapour, anon standing forth clear and sharply defined against the dark background formed by the waving bamboo; the peaceful current of the noble Yang-tze river—here narrowed to a point less than 1,800 yards across, though stretching far and wide immediately beyond on either side; the grim embattled walls of Nankin, towering over the plain a few miles distant; mountains of fantastic shape on every side—some near, impending and majestic; others, cloud-capped and dimly visible in the distance; the cheer and cry of battle mingling with the echo of artillery—all combined, produced an effect truly grand and imposing.

At last the garrison of Kew-fu-chew reported that the leading columns of the Chung-wang's army were in sight; upon which further reinforcements were instantly thrown into all the forts, while every boat was made ready for the purpose of transporting the approaching troops across the river. Even when they had arrived within sight of their capital, the sufferings of the unfortunate people were not completed until they had endured much more loss by the assaults of the enemy. Upon the arrival of the famished and emaciated troops at the brink of the river, they were saluted with one continuous cannonade from the gunboats that now found ample opportunities of slaughtering them as they crowded the bank for a distance of nearly two miles. With incredible fortitude they maintained their position, and did not flinch backward by the least perceptible movement; and, in the face of the terrible fire poured into their dense masses at point-blank range (mostly from *English* guns), proceeded to the work of embarkation as steadily as their weakened condition would permit.

Directly the first detachment appeared on the beach, I sailed over to help them with all my vessels, and getting a dozen Europeans on board the lorcha, worked her against the enemy with considerable effect. The fearful sights that met my gaze upon every part of the shore I shall never forget. Very many of the weakest men, totally unable to assist themselves further, were left to die within sight of the goal for which they had striven so hard and suffered so greatly, their number being so large that their comrades were not sufficient to help, or get them over the river in the presence of the enemy. The horrible "thud" of the cannon shot crashing continuously among the living skeletons, so densely packed at places that they were swept off by the river, into which they were forced by the pressure from behind; the perfect immobility with which they confronted the death hurled upon them from more than a thousand gunboats; and the slow effort the exhausted survivors made to extricate themselves from the mangled bodies of their stricken comrades, were scenes awful to contemplate. It was dreadful to watch day after day during the time occupied in getting the remnant of that once splendid army across the river, with but little means to succour them, the lanes cut through the helpless multitude on the beach by the merciless fire of the enemy; all so passively endured. The gaunt, starved forms, and wild staring eyes of those who had laid themselves down to die, haunted me for many a future night.

Frequently during the passage of the river, some small boat, with its scarcely living freight, would be drifted away from the protection of the Nankin batteries by the strength of the tide, the overcrowded boat being too heavily laden to be moved quickly enough by the weakened arms of the rowers. Whenever such an event took place, the mandarin boats would dart upon their defenceless prey, and immediately chop off the heads of all on board in the most brutal manner, throwing the bodies of the victims into the river within sight of their comrades, who were totally unable to assist them. In these cases the poor fellows struggled and fought against their murderers with the energy of despair, as desperately as their enfeebled condition would permit; but this was of little avail, for nearly all their fire-arms were rendered useless, the powder being saturated with water, while they were far too weak to wield other weapons effectively.

I received the Chung-wang on board my vessel, and carried him to the Nankin side, when he had seen the greater part of his surviving troops safely across the river. My comrade, L——, was with him, also the Sardinian officer of the late Ling-ho's regiment; but I never saw my brave lieutenant, Phillip Bosse, again: he had fallen at the head of the Chung-wang's guards, while gallantly protecting the retreat of the main body.

Upon the twelfth day all who could be saved were across the Yang-tze, and under the friendly shadow of the Nankin walls, whilst, on the other side of the river, none remained but the garrison of the fort and the numerous bodies of those who had perished of hunger or had been slaughtered by the enemy. At last all seemed laid in the sleep of death, until some poor wretch would suddenly crawl to the brink of the desired water, and then fall into the swift current either to quench his burning thirst or terminate his agony.

Even now the bleached skeletons of many thousands of these unfortunate victims to British intervention may be seen in the positions in which they fell, waiting for the hand of decay to obliterate the last sad trace of their existence.

The Chung-wang's army had formed the best and bravest part of the whole Ti-ping forces; in fact, his troops were the *élite* of the whole military organization, being principally composed of veterans who had joined the cause from its infancy, and to whom defeat was really unknown. A great proportion of the original nucleus of the revolution was included in its ranks, consisting of the men from Kwang-tung, Kwang-si, and the Miau-tze, who, inspired with the religious enthusiasm so conducive to the wonderful success which attended the earlier stages of the Ti-ping movement, and imbued with that spirit of chivalry which defied all obstacles, dreaded no dangers, and endured cruel torture, became the true champions of the great religious and political Chinese revolution. Unless Christendom chooses to deny the theory that Asia is to be Christianized by a process similar to the manner in which it was itself converted from Heathenism, it is impossible to dispute the fact that Hung-sui-tshuen and his followers have commenced a work that shall never perish nor be forgotten. The very fact that the leaders of the Ti-ping movement, from the first day of its existence, forced their tenets upon the sage contempt of the literati, the general repugnance of the people, and the well-known hatred of the innumerable Manchoo employés, proves most convincingly that

2 s

it was a holy element which animated those chiefs and their followers, and which induced them to forsake the theories of their ancient and deeply venerated sages, to rely upon the help and attributes of an Eternal Judge.

Unfortunately, by the disastrous retreat to Nankin, the Ti-pings lost the greater proportion of those adherents whose religious fervour has induced me to compare them to the heroes and champions of the early Christian Church. There are doubtless those who, from their self-erected pinnacle of righteousness, will prove sceptics as to the reality of Ti-ping Christianity; but I trust all who have had the patience to accompany me through this history will consider that point effectually proved in favour of the revolutionists.

The remnant of the Chung-wang's army scarcely amounted to 15,000 effective men, and from this number reinforcements had to be thrown into Nankin, Soo-chow, Chang-chow, Wu-sie, and other cities menaced by the enemy; consequently, when the General-in-Chief proceeded to the districts invaded by the Anglo-Franco-Manchoo mercenaries in the neighbourhood of Soo-chow, he was not accompanied by more than 7,000 troops; yet with this small force he managed to keep the overwhelming numbers of the enemy for some time at bay, to control and reassure many garrisons wavering in loyalty, and to protect a great extent of frontier. Had his once splendid army been intact and serviceable, the Imperialists and their allies would have to tell a very different tale to that of the expulsion of the Ti-pings from their former territory.

On the day succeeding the passage of the last surviving troops across the river, the enemy seemed determined to vent his wrath at their escape by a general attack upon all the fortifications. From early morning the assailants had swarmed down in countless gunboats, covering the whole expanse of the Yang-tze, and completely hiding the fort of Kew-fu-chew from our view by the dense clouds of smoke proceeding from their ceaseless bombardment. The adverse flotilla in the neighbourhood of Nankin was closely estimated at a strength of 3,000 gunboats of all sizes, some carrying only one light gun in the bow, others mounting four or five rather heavy cannon.

The Imperialists maintained their attack with much vigour and determination until late at night. Throughout the day we were unable to do much harm to them, their vessels being nearly always perfectly concealed by smoke, so that our guns could only be pointed at chance range. The roar from nearly 2,000 pieces of artillery was terrific and deafening beyond description. As night closed in we were enabled to make much better practice from our batteries by noticing the flashes of the enemy's guns, and aiming in the direction indicated. At about 10 p.m. our fire proved so effective that the whole fleet relinquished the attack and retreated both up and down the river. Owing to the vast number of gunboats which were crowded together in the comparatively small space between the Nankin batteries and the fort opposite, our fire must have inflicted severe loss, yet they persisted in the engagement with a courage I have never before or afterwards seen equalled by troops of the Manchoo Government.

In spite of this resolute attack, the Ti-pings garrisoning the fortifications were singularly indifferent, and laughed to scorn the idea that the *Ya-mun-qui* (Mandarin-palace devils, as they delighted to call them) could ever capture any outwork of Nankin. When I remonstrated with the old Kung-wang about the negligent guard at night, he replied: "I have held these forts for twelve years, and, unless Tien-voo deserts me, shall hold them twelve years more, so far as the 'Imps' are concerned." That very night, or rather morning, he found occasion to regret his overweening confidence.

The lurid glare of battle during the early night, the thunder of artillery, the crashing of shot, the fiery track of the arrow-headed rockets, followed by the occasional explosion of a gunboat, the whole din and prospect of tumult, had died away, and been replaced by the deathlike calm of a beautiful summer's night. Dirty, begrimed with powder, and fatigued with labour and excitement, my party of European volunteers, L—— (who had remained on board our lorcha), Captain P——, and myself, took advantage of the quiet interval and retired to rest. Unfortunately for us, the deceitful calm proved doubly treacherous.

Tap, tap, went the bamboo signals of the solitary sentinels around the forts under whose shadow our vessel rode silently at anchor; tum, tum, sounded the drums of the guards ensconced in the little look-out houses perched along the walls; and at last these monotonous echoes, sharply distinguished from out the surrounding stillness, proved irresistibly somniferous; gradually they became fainter and less frequent, and then ceased altogether.

How long our sleep lasted I do not know, but suddenly I was aroused by the crashing roar of artillery seemingly right alongside our vessel. At the same moment I heard my friends start up in the adjoining cabin, and together we rushed on deck.

Daylight was just dawning, but it was not required to enlighten the scenes taking place around. The water, neighbouring shore, and forts, were illuminated by the red glare of war. Above and below on the river; outside the batteries; on the broad arm of the Yang-tze, running past the Nankin creek and forming Tasohea Island; everywhere, in fact, the gunboats of the enemy were upon us in countless numbers; while the vivid and repeated flashes of their artillery made the air alive with bright coruscations. Early on the morning of June 28, 1863, the Imperialists made their daring and partially successful *coup de main*. In dense lines, completely covering the broad expanse of the river, they had pulled rapidly down stream; running the gauntlet of the stronger forts held by the Sze and Kung Wangs, and making the weaker ones

just beyond the entrance of the Nankin creek the object of their attack. Each gunboat maintained a very quick fire of cannon, heavy gingals, rockets, fire-arrows, and every description of missile known in China, many of which took effect among the light-built houses inside the larger forts. On the other hand, the Ti-pings were entirely taken by surprise; the guns of the river forts were not loaded, and, being heavy, could not be quickly enough worked, or sufficiently depressed to obtain more than a couple of rounds before the last division of the enemy had swept past, the first having run by, and entered the channel between Tasohea Island and the mainland, almost before the alarm was given. The few shots that were delivered inflicted great havoc among the closely-packed gunboats right under the muzzles of the heavy artillery in the Kung-wang's fort; and the yellow waters of the mighty Yang-tze engulphed many a shattered man and vessel, while pieces of wreck were strewed upon the surface, and swiftly borne away to excite the wonder of distant villagers on the banks of the rapid river.

When off Theodolite Point, hundreds of the war-boats pulled inside the island, and made a dash upon the small forts on the mainland, and the foreign trading vessels anchored in the channel; while many soldiers, landing from others, captured the works on the end of the island, killing man, woman, and child, as the affrighted people rushed from their houses and attempted to escape. The small forts, being surrounded by overwhelming numbers, were quickly taken and then set on fire. Three large war-junks defending the mouth of the Nankin creek were also fired by the enemy, before their crews were fairly awake or had time to deliver a second broadside. At this moment I rushed on deck with my comrades. Our lorcha was lying close astern of the last *Ti-mung*, or war-junk, and many European craft were at anchor closer to Tasohea Island, and nearer to the main river;

some of these I saw boarded by the Imperialists, who instantly murdered the few Europeans, plundered the vessels, and then set them on fire.

I saw at a glance that nothing but instant flight could save our lives, if it were not already too late. The gunboats were everywhere around, firing away indiscriminately in all directions. Fortunately our old junk was fast alongside the lorcha, which was far too heavy to escape from smaller craft; so abandoning the latter, containing all our property and nearly everything we had in the world, with my wife and friends I went on board the lighter vessel. We then cut her adrift and tried to escape down the channel. The land on each side being occupied by hostile troops, and the upper part of the channel leading into the river being crowded with their war-boats, it was the only course open.

At the moment we shoved off and left the *Anglo-Ti-ping* to her fate, several gunboats boarded her from the opposite side, while others poured a terrible fire into our old junk, whose decks were covered with grape-shot, which had fallen harmless, from the hurried loading of our assailants.

While all around seemed a mass of fire and flame, the daylight obscured by the dense pall of smoke above, the earth shaken by the ceaseless cannonade below, and while the fiery track of rockets, accompanied by their hissing sound, and the "wheep" of the shot whistling everywhere about, kept up the jubilee of war and destruction, we had drifted with the tide a few cables' length away from the lorcha, and made sail to the light though freshening breeze that offered our only chance of escape.

A squall of wind was parting the heavy volume of smoke and fire, and coming towards us, when a number of gunboats appeared in full chase, keeping up a very heavy fire, the crew of the nearest throwing stink-pots, with which they managed to ignite our mainsail. I was just turning to my dear wife to hurry her below, when a volley of musketry was poured in by the troops on board the attacking vessels. I saw my faithful friend and companion, L——, fall to the deck, but almost at the same moment, struck by a spent ball, I became senseless.

I know not what period may have elapsed, but when at length I was restored to consciousness, it was but to realize the exquisite bitterness of my loss. Close to where my best and long-proved friend had fallen, lay the lifeless form of my well-loved wife, pierced by a flight of bullets.

CHAPTER XXII.

On the Wong-poo River.—Ningpo Sam.—The *China*.—Her passengers.—The Ta-hoo Lake.—Its Scenery.—The Canals of Central China.—General Burgevine.—Soo-chow.—Deserters.—Burgevine suspected.—The Americo-Ti-ping Legions.—Burgevine's policy.—Colonel Morton.—The Mo-wang.—Arrival of the Chung-wang.—The Loyal and Faithful Auxiliary Legion.—How regulated.—Affair at Wo-kong.—Recruiting.—Plan of Operations.—A *coup de main*.—Arrangement.—Interruptions.—Postponed.

TOWARDS the close of a fine October day in 1863, an ordinary Shanghae *san-pan*, or passage-boat, might have been seen slowly sculling up-stream against the ebbing tide of the Wong-poo river, and carefully hugging the bank opposite to the foreign settlements. Besides the hardy Chinese owner (working away with a big oar over the stern, and rejoicing in the euphonical cognomen "Ningpo Sam"), the boat was occupied by two foreigners, seated under the arched mat cover. One seemed to be of Anglo-Saxon race; the other, by his dusky skin, long moustache, and jet-black hair, a native of the East Indies.

To a close observer there was something suspicious in the management of the *san-pan* and the movements of the people on board. All passing craft were carefully avoided, and whenever a European ship on the river, or European dwelling on the shore, was approached, down came the outside mat from the cover, screening the front of the boat, and completely hiding the two passengers inside. If the observer had been near enough, he might have been farther edified by hearing sundry energetic expressions addressed by the irritable foreigners to "Ningpo Sam," whenever that stolid individual did not sheer his boat sufficiently far from strange vessels to preserve their incognito.

As the shades of evening fell upon the shipping on the river and the trees on the shore, the strength of the tide gradually relaxed, and the *san-pan* proceeded much more rapidly on her course. The see-saw rocking from side to side became less vigorous and unpleasant as the arms of the sculler were tired, and at last, when a point nearly three miles above Shanghae had been reached, "Ningpo Sam" ran his boat into the bank, threw down the heavy *yulo*, or oar, and emphatically declared his determination not to proceed any further until he had satisfied the cravings of his inner man with the *chow-chow* (to "che fan"—eat rice—as he said), bubbling over a little cooking stove in the sternsheets.

The Chinese are an obstinate people; some are essentially mulish, and "Ningpo Sam" seemed to be of the latter order; consequently his passengers very wisely produced a large hamper, and hauling bottles of beer, with a cold fowl, *et cæteras*, from its innermost depths, were soon busily engaged eating and drinking. By the time the hamper had been repacked night had closed in, but still the boatman's capacious jaws went "munch, munch." Meanwhile the dark-hued passenger, having lighted a cigar, was taking a fisherman's quarter-deck walk—that is to the extent of two steps and overboard—on the small fore-part of the *san-pan*. The second traveller reclined on the thwartship seat, and seemed absorbed with his own reflections, plainly not of the most happy tenor. He was far from being displeased when his companion aroused him by exclaiming:

"Jump up, sir; jump up; the steamer is coming!" and then shouting to the Chinaman, still feeding in the stern, "Yulo, yulo, Sam!"

Sam, however, did not seem at all inclined to obey the summons; upon the contrary, he jerked the rice into his mouth and handled his chopsticks more vigorously than ever, spluttering out at intervals "Hi-ya!—how can?—my—wantchee chow-chow—no can yulo—just—now; by-em-by—finish chow-chow—can—do."

Upon the termination of this cool reply, the European passenger passed to the after-part of the boat, and with the assistance of a stout cane, succeeded in making "Ningpo Sam" forsake gorging and resume his oar, much to that worthy's disgust, who, for some time, gave vent to his outraged feelings by a low-toned muttering of choice Ningpo "Billingsgate," which, however, excited not the smallest attention from the abused parties, who were intent upon the approaching steamer.

When the steamer had arrived quite near, the Indian produced a bright bull's-eye lantern and displayed it for a few moments. This was answered by a light shown over the vessel's side, and by the stoppage of her engines. The *san-pan* was then sculled alongside, and her passengers taken on board. Directly the baggage had been received, the ship went on ahead at full speed, while "Ningpo Sam" and his boat disappeared in the distance, his gratified expectations finding vent in the following adieu: "Chin-chin, ga-la! *Numbah one*, massa; mi too much thankee you."

Soon the loud protestations of gratitude died away in the distance, and the only sound which disturbed the stillness of the cool night air was the regular beat of the screw propeller, as the small steamer steadily proceeded on her course.

The little steamer was named the *China*, belonged to Messrs. H—— & Co., of Shanghae, and was employed in the silk trade. This valuable branch of commerce was wholly in the hands of the Ti-pings, and unrestricted until their expulsion from the producing districts, when the Imperial Manchoo mandarins closed the interior to foreigners, and the trading of steamers or other vessels was entirely prohibited.*

The passengers who so mysteriously embarked themselves were on their way to Soo-chow. One was *General* Burgevine's *aide-de-camp*, the other being myself. Burgevine had quite lately put into execution his plan to join the revolutionists, and was established at the large city of Soo-chow in command of ninety to one hundred Europeans, and a batallion of 1,000 Ti-pings, placed under his orders to be drilled according to foreign tactics, and officered by their instructors. Burgevine's *aide* was proceeding to join his master. I was anxious to ascertain the principles and practical worth of the newly-formed Americo-Ti-ping contingent, and also to rejoin the Chung-wang.

The voyage of the *China* terminated at the town of Nan-zing, situated almost in the centre of the silk district; and here she remained while the Chinese supercargo went into the country with many thousands of dollars to purchase silk; the regions under Ti-ping rule being so safe to travel, that all the vast amount of specie (from 8 to 10 millions sterling per annum) used during each season was carried about the country simply under the protection of the Chinese *shroff*, employed by the firm to whom the money belonged.

Having obtained a fine large boat from the Governor of Nan-zing—a most friendly and courteous chief—I proceeded with my companion on our way to Soo-chow. Although the direct distance was not much over fifty

---

* In the *Friend of China*, March 10, 1865, and subsequent numbers, the following advertisement appears:—

"The Steamer *Donnington*.—The undersigned" (H. Evans), "*in consequence of the determination of the provincial authorities not to permit the navigation of inner waters for trading purposes* by vessels of the above class, being thus disappointed in the purpose for which he had her constructed, is desirous of disposing of her."

This direct violation of the last treaty is one effect of the Manchoo restoration to power, by British means, in the Kiang-su province.

miles, in consequence of the capture of Quin-san, and another city named Wo-kong, by the enemy, the approaches to Soo-chow from the east and south were not available; so that we were obliged to cross the great Ta-hoo Lake, and reach the provincial capital by making a considerable *détour* to the west. The Ta-hoo, though so extensive that from its centre no land but the highest mountains can be seen, has nowhere more than an average depth of twelve feet; and in many parts its waters are so encumbered with floating weeds and interwoven stems of tough aquatic plants growing from the bottom, that navigation is impossible. The lake, similar to every piece of water in China, swarms with fish; thereby affording constant employment to numerous congregations of fishermen. These men, like their brethren of the sea-coast, clan together, and are by no means averse to a little piracy upon a favourable occasion; we were consequently compelled to keep a sharp look-out while passing through the lake; and, when at anchor during the second night, at least fifty miles from land, we were under the necessity of firing into a number of boats that bore right down upon us in a very suspicious manner. My Indian comrade had three cases of rifles, and one of revolvers, which he was taking to Soo-chow for his master's force, and of these we had loaded a sufficient number to repel any attack, unless made by overwhelming numbers; therefore, when the advancing boats were suddenly received by thirty or forty shots fired within as many seconds, they quickly "topped their booms" and sheered off.

The scenery of the Ta-hoo is inconceivably grand and varied. Mountains rise to a wondrous height; limestone rocks—worn into the most grotesque shapes—project into the clear waters of the lake; valleys of great beauty intersect the densely wooded hills and jagged sterile mountains; while murmuring rivulets sweep past secluded villages, on their journey to the broad, though shallow, waters of the lake. One of the most beautiful and

romantic regions in all China is that extent of country situated to the north-east, north, and north-west of the Ta-hoo. Being of a mountainous nature, it is termed by the Chinese "Tung-shan," or the Eastern Hills. After sailing past the three largest islands on the lake, famous for producing the finest silk in the empire, we reached the most easterly part of the Tung-ting district. This had long been celebrated for the splendour of its mandarin palaces and heathen temples; but, when I visited the once-admired locality, its glories had departed, for the grand edifices of Tartar magnate and Pagan god were alike levelled with the dust; the Ti-ping was the dominant power, and its iconoclasm and hatred of the Manchoo had been practically manifested by the destruction of the monumental buildings, alike degrading to the patriotism and the religion of the nation. The villages and isolated cottages which studded the picturesque valleys still remained; and, by their life and prosperity, offered a striking contrast to the desolation of palace and temple.

Passing on to the Western Tung-shan district, we reached the wildest and most imposing region I have seen, either in China or any other part of the world. Far removed from the noisy haunts of men, and peopled with but a few solitary hamlets, it reposed in its romantic beauty, undisturbed save by the voice of Nature, and undefiled by the hand of man. Drawing our boat on to a long sandy beach, I wandered through the wild and lonely region for some hours with my dark companion, who I found could appreciate Nature's beauties more truly than many with a whiter skin. I rambled through the silent valleys and almost impenetrable forests of the Tung-shan, impressed with the solemn feeling that I trod where mortal foot had not fallen before. The landscape was most varied in its nature: massive mountains, peaceful valleys; wild and desolate cliffs; foaming cataracts, and then the calm and shaded waters of the lake; while the waving of the thick forest, the verdant and feathery bamboos; the water-lilies stretching wide on the surface of the lake; the wild orange-trees, and sweetly-perfumed shrubs and flowers blooming around, completed an almost unrivalled picture. After leaving this exquisite scenery, and just before entering the creek by which we were to reach Soo-chow, we passed underneath a great natural arch of rock, projecting some 90 feet into the lake, with a height of nearly 150, and joined to a second small arch on the outside.

This singular formation of rock lies on the border of the Ta-hoo, about forty miles to the north-west of Soo-chow, and is an object particularly noticed in the legendary lore of the superstitious natives.

After leaving the lake, our journey lay through a complete network of those interminable creeks, lagoons, and canals intersecting the whole of south and central China. Some were broad and river-like, spanned by handsome, many-arched bridges, the banks covered with fine houses and regular pathways; others were narrow, tortuous, almost hidden by rank vegetation and long drooping osiers, and crossed by bridges composed of a rough slab of granite laid horizontally upon the ends of two upright blocks, and elevated scarcely six feet from the water. Wherever we passed, the country people complained bitterly of the foreign soldiers (meaning Gordon's, D'Aguibelle's, and other mercenary legions) coming to fight the Ti-pings; they were all long-haired and happy under the new *régime*; they were naturally averse to lose their heads because the British Government chose to support the oppressive and merciless Manchoo; and many of the finest grain-producing districts having been captured by the allied Anglo-Franco-Manchoo forces, together with a number of the principal Ti-ping granaries, a vast influx of destitute refugees added considerably to the daily increasing distress caused by the scarcity and exorbitant price of food.

When at last, after threading miles of creek and canal,

I reached Soo-chow, I found that I had arrived at the moment of an important crisis—no less an event, indeed, than the dissolution of the short-lived Americo-Ti-ping contingent. This, however, was a matter of no surprise to me, as I had never placed the slightest faith in the composition and motives of the force, nor felt the least hope from its formation. Burgevine, its originator and commander, like Gordon, the uncommissioned *General* of the Anglo-Manchoo force, was essentially a mercenary and filibuster; the only principle of either seems to have been an absorbing selfishness and care for personal interest, doubtless a very natural sentiment upon the part of the cosmopolitan adventurer, but not a trait to be admired in the character of the British officer. Such a principle, when supported by the material power of the British Government, succeeded very well with those who allied themselves with the Manchoo, simply because the latter were treacherous, thoroughly mercenary, hated foreigners with a bitter intensity, and would naturally enough have suspected any *apparently* disinterested assistance, as a means of rendering any of them liable to distasteful obligations. The British authorities took particular care to prevent any mistake, with regard to their motives, for they always stated that they were solely interfering in their own interest, so the Manchoo rejoicingly obtained a large revenue from the foreign merchants, and then handed back a portion to pay the British indemnity, which has proved the salvation of their dynasty, by in a great measure causing the alliance against the Ti-ping.

Upon reaching the west gate of Soo-chow, we were very kindly welcomed by the guard, and were furnished with an escort to the commandant's palace. The city I found to be strongly garrisoned by veteran troops; new flanking stone works were being built against the outer face of the high walls; handsome buildings were being erected inside; provisions were very plentiful; the soldiery and civilians seemed in high spirits, and quite ridiculed the idea of losing their city; in fact, excepting the distant report of artillery, Soo-chow had no more the aspect of a besieged place than London has at the present moment, neither did its capture by the enemy thundering at its defences seem even probable.

When we arrived at the commandant Mo-wang's palace, a number of wounded Europeans belonging to Burgevine's contingent were being carried inside. These men proved to be the survivors of a series of accidents that had occurred two days previously, when the whole force, accompanied by a division of Ti-pings under the Chung-wang, and the little steamer *Ka-joor*, which Burgevine had seized from the Imperialists and carried off to Soo-chow, had attacked a position of the enemy established about twenty miles to the east of the city. The expedition was at first successful, having turned the flank of the Imperialist stockades and captured a flotilla of twenty-six large gunboats; but, almost immediately afterwards, by the carelessness—some say drunkenness—of the Europeans working the *Ka-joor's* pivot-gun, her magazine was ignited, the explosion blowing the fore part of the vessel to pieces, and badly wounding several of the crew.

Soon after this catastrophe, *General* Burgevine landed a battery from the gunboats accompanying him (the principal way of communication being by water), and opened fire on the stockades, held by a force of disciplined Anglo-Manchoo mercenaries commanded by *Colonel* Rhode,* and a number of Imperialist *braves*. The enemy were just being driven out of their intrenchments, and a storming party advancing to take them, when the largest of the prizes—a gunboat, full of powder, shells, &c., and mounting six cannon, and in which the wounded from the steamer had been placed—blew up; the fire from her explosion communicating with four more of the captured vessels, they were also blown to pieces, killing outright twelve, and

---

* Now in the service of the Ti-pings.

dangerously wounding seventeen of the sixty or seventy Europeans present. These disasters were caused by the free use of the liquors taken from the wreck of the *Ka-joor*—officers and men alike indulging, and the whole affair forcibly illustrating the *rowdy*, disorderly nature of the Americo-Ti-ping legion. It is stated, and not without strong reason, that Burgevine himself was in a state of intoxication; still he has this excuse—the pain and debilitating effect produced by an old and terrible wound (received in the service of the ungrateful Manchoo), rendered the use of stimulants necessary.

After the accidents we have just noticed, the attack upon the Imperialist position was abandoned, and the force retired upon Soo-chow, carrying off the wounded and the remainder of the prizes.

As the Mo-wang was outside the city, and Burgevine had not returned with the wounded men, I proceeded to one of the gates with a party of the latter's officers, in order to go to the front of the Ti-ping outworks, where it was expected they would be found. When we had arrived at the gate, however, we were not allowed to pass by the soldiers on guard. This was the first intimation I received that affairs were going wrong with the auxiliary force, and that the Ti-pings were suspicious of their foreign allies. At night, it appeared, they were not without reason for their want of confidence, for, after Burgevine and the Mo-wang had returned, *Colonel* Morton, the second in command of the contingent, was reported absent against orders, with all the Europeans outside the city. When this fact was ascertained, Burgevine and the officers with him seemed certain that the absentees had gone over to the enemy; in fact, I soon understood that the intention for the whole force to desert had been on the *tapis* for some little time, only Morton and his companions had, however, taken the opportunity to get clear themselves and leave their co-adjutors in the lurch.

Previous to this report I had obtained an interview

2 T

with the Mo-wang, and then dined with him. He informed me that the Chung-wang was encamped with an army outside the city; he also gave me to understand the nature of his suspicions against Burgevine, in all of which I entirely agreed with him. After explaining the caution rendered necessary in all dealings with foreigners, because of the treachery and bad faith with which they had always acted towards the Ti-pings—as particularly exemplified by the English breaches of guaranteed neutrality, non-observance of the pledge to prevent Manchoo expeditions equipping at Shanghae, capture of Ningpo by the British, French, and piratical flotilla, &c.—he proceeded to specify his reasons for dissatisfaction with the foreign contingent.

In the first place, he spoke about the extraordinary conduct of Burgevine himself, who, he declared, had made numerous promises, none of which had been fulfilled. That officer had guaranteed to obtain men, arms, and co-operation from Shanghae; large sums of money had been supplied for the purpose, but the only return had been many cases of brandy, brought by him after several visits to that city, and with which both officers and men were made incapable. All the money had been squandered or mysteriously lost, and not a single musket had been shown for the large expenditure. Then it appeared that Burgevine and many of his officers continued to wear the uniform of the Ward force, which they had only left shortly before joining the Ti-pings; while, to place themselves in a still more suspicious position, they made a practice of visiting at night their old friends in the hostile lines occupied by Gordon's troops. This conduct made the chiefs distrust the loyalty of their auxiliaries and fear some organized treachery. Another ground of suspicion was the fact that Burgevine kept his men aloof and distinct from the people he came to serve, at the same time striving to induce the chiefs to sanction his formation of an independent force. This was certainly a bad way to gain the confidence of men so often deceived by foreigners, so accustomed to community of interests, and so much imbued with the religious and patriotic enthusiasm of their cause. Moreover, the Ti-ping leaders had quickly penetrated the selfish and mercenary motives of their unsatisfactory allies, and naturally felt but little faith in their services; neither were they mean enough to desire the support of such ignoble assistance, nor pander to it after the style of their more unscrupulous antagonists.

Regardless of all principles of honour and chivalry, directly the Americo-Ti-ping legionaries found that they could not reckon upon external support, large pay, and much booty, they were not a little disappointed; having no heart in the service they had suddenly adopted, they became discontented and anxious to desert a failing cause for some more congenial and *profitable* employment. They were certainly not Quixotic enough to fight for honour, glory, or the freedom and religious liberty of a vast empire without some substantial pecuniary recompense.

Out of a strength of 125 Europeans, not more than twenty were of any use to the revolutionists; these few comprised men who were able to drill and organize a disciplined force, and others who were good artillerists; the remainder being sailors and vagrants, totally unacquainted with the smell of powder, and not so useful in the field as the worst coolie spearmen of the Ti-ping army; these facts were also inimical to the existence of the force.

When, added to the circumstances just reviewed, the paroxysms of temporary insanity (during an attack of which he wounded one of his best officers), or the natural extravagance and obliquity of character of the commanding officer himself, and the dissensions among his subordinates, are considered, the failure of Burgevine's enterprise is fully accounted for.*

* In the mutual recriminations between the leaders of the force, upon their arrival at Shanghae, Captain Jones states (referring to Burgevine):—

In the evening, after Morton's absence had been reported, the Mo-wang, accompanied by several of his chiefs, proceeded to Burgevine's quarters and spent several hours in conversation with him. I was present during this interview, and was favourably impressed by the magnanimous and friendly temper of the commandant, who, despite the ample provocation he had received from the suspicious and unsatisfactory conduct of the auxiliaries, declared his intention to supply them with money on the succeeding day, and to make any arrangements which would tend to harmonize, gratify, or prosper the future welfare of the force. That these promises would have been faithfully executed by the Mo-wang, Burgevine has himself testified.

After the departure of the commandant, Burgevine, with some of his favourite officers, talked over their proposed desertion from the Ti-pings, as a long-arranged and premeditated affair, their motive for this determination being the fact that their present service did not seem likely to prove so easy and advantageous as they had expected. In the course of conversation the *General* personally informed me that his intention had been to raise a large body of disciplined and well-armed Ti-pings, and then to convert them into an independent force, acting upon his private account; that is to say, he joined the revolution with the intention of ultimately deserting it, and proceeding upon a career of filibusting through China. This wild scheme he also mentioned to *General* Gordon, of the Imperialist mercenaries, proposing that they should mutually desert their colours, join forces, and commence a system of independent conquest.

"He further accuses us of trying to make out a good case against him, thinking he would never return to Shanghae. To this I answer, that he and I were the instigators of the defection from the Ti-ping cause, for I confess I at once fell into his plans, glad of the opportunity to escape from what appeared likely to turn out *unprofitable*, and having, besides, for some time before lost confidence in his capacity to command."—*Vide* Blue Book on China, No. 3 (1864), p. 179.

Whether this and other equally extravagant notions were caused by mental derangement, consequent upon the effects of his wound and the stimulants he used, or may be attributed to his natural character, seems doubtful; but whatever may have been the cause of *General* Burgevine's reckless conduct, it is quite certain that he sacrificed a splendid opportunity to insure the success of the Ti-ping revolution. Had he at first heartily espoused the movement, and unreservedly amalgamated his men with its members, he would infallibly have obtained the confidence of the chiefs. He could then have organized a disciplined and foreign-officered force far superior in material to the Imperialist auxiliary legions, and these latter were the only forces of the enemy that the Ti-pings had the slightest occasion to dread.

On the morning of the day succeeding my arrival at Soo-chow, intelligence came into the city to the effect that, at about 4.30 a.m., *Colonel* Morton had deserted with the detachment of Europeans under his command, and gone over to the enemy, Morton shooting two soldiers of an outlying picket who came to warn him of his vicinity to the Imperialist lines. By this act of cowardly treachery, deserting his own colleagues and the wounded in the city, he placed them in much jeopardy, and caused the Mo-wang to feel very great exasperation, and strongly to suspect further treachery from the remainder of the contingent. However, he proved himself to be a more noble-minded and merciful man than any of the traitors left behind imagined, by offering free passes and boats to any and all who might wish to leave the city; at the same time he expressed great disgust and contempt at the mean, dastardly conduct of Morton and his followers, because he had always made the fact public, that any foreigner wishing to leave Soo-chow had simply to express the desire, when everything necessary in the way of boats, passes, &c., would be furnished to the confines of the Ti-ping territory.

When the fact of *Colonel* Morton's desertion became established, I must confess that, well as I thought I understood the noble character of the Ti-ping chiefs, I feared the remainder of the traitors might meet with condign punishment. In consequence, I at once sought an audience with the Mo-wang, and having obtained it, requested that he would not wreak any vengeance upon Burgevine and his companions. To my surprise, although the inferior chiefs and officers were greatly excited about the treachery of their foreign allies, the commandant instantly gave me to understand that my fear was groundless. "Puh pa! puh pa!" (do not fear, do not fear), he said. "These men joined me willingly and with clean faces" (*i.e.* honour); "they can leave if they wish to do so, in like manner; but if they sneak away to the Imps, they will lose face, and so shall I."

Just at this moment Burgevine's interpreter came into the hall and informed the Mo-wang that he was commissioned to ask liberty for the remainder of the force to depart from the city and return to Shanghae. The chief readily professed his compliance with this request, but said that he could not definitively settle anything until the arrival of his superior, the Chung-wang, whom he expected in the city towards evening to consult upon the affair.

Meanwhile, with the exception of a dozen who were old adherents of the Ti-ping king, the foreigners were in a great state of ferment, for they fully expected the momentary appearance of executioners to cut off their heads. Some were drinking *samshoo* to encourage themselves; others proposed fortifying their quarters; while a few of the boldest advocated sallying forth and attempting to force their way out of the city. The groans of more than twenty wounded men, some horribly burnt by the late explosion of the steamer and the gunboats, rendered pathetic an otherwise ridiculous scene.

Early in the evening the Chung-wang arrived, escorted

by 1,000 men of his body-guard, and at once proceeded to a council with the Mo-wang and other chiefs. When their deliberations were concluded, I presented myself to the Chung-wang, who, together with the Sze, Le, and Foo-wangs (they having accompanied him from Nankin), received me with great manifestations of pleasure, having all concluded that I had been killed at the disastrous loss of the outer Nankin forts. I have hitherto forgotten to mention that my faithful interpreter, A-ling, was still with me. He also met with a very kind reception from the chiefs, for they appreciated his services, and knew that he was warmly attached to their cause.

Immediately upon my arrival at Soo-chow, I had determined, if possible, to raise another body of Europeans, with whom to form a disciplined Ti-ping force, for I saw that the dissolution of Burgevine's legion was near at hand. Still, after the irritation the chiefs must have felt at the treachery of their present foreign auxiliaries, I could not think the time appropriate to submit the subject to them. I was pleasantly surprised when, during the course of the evening, the Chung-wang proposed that I should undertake the very work I was myself anxious to perform. He stated that his confidence had never been placed in Burgevine, and he expressed much satisfaction at the prospect of the early departure of that leader of mercenaries with his men.

About this period the small steamers attached to *General* Gordon's force were being used with great success in the daily attacks upon the Ti-ping stockades outside Soo-chow; consequently, the Chung-wang proposed that I should not only endeavour to raise a contingent of disciplined troops, but a flotilla of two or three steamers to operate with them. He also expressed a great desire to capture Gordon's vessels, upon which I told A-ling to obtain a separate commission to cut out any of them I might find an opportunity to seize. The Chung-wang made a practice never to sleep inside the walls of any beleaguered city, his tactics being to relieve them by an army of co-operation under his own command. It may be that he pursued such a plan as a safeguard against treachery; but whatever the cause, he was always to be found encamped outside. As the night advanced, he therefore made ready to leave Soo-chow, after passing an edict and signing a special commission written for me by his own secretary.* As I was well known to four or five of the Wangs present, they were much pleased when I accepted the authority to raise a new force; and before we separated, they became quite enthusiastic about the anticipated results.

The designation of the proposed contingent was decided by the Commander-in-Chief to be "the Loyal and Faithful Auxiliary Legion," a title closely assimilating to his own, Chung-sin-wang, which may be translated as the "Middle Heart Prince," *i.e.* the loyal or faithful prince. The terms of organization agreed upon were: the force to be commanded by myself, or any European I might see fit to appoint, and subject only to the orders of the Chung-wang. The Europeans engaged to be solely officers, two hundred in number, each captain of a company to receive 200 taels per mensem (nearly £70), others to be paid proportionately, and lodging found for all. Myself and principal officers to receive no pay, but serve as commissioned volunteers, a position which I had always maintained for myself. Two steam gunboats to be obtained, similar to the *Hyson*, in the service of the enemy; these to be attached to the land force, not to be used for any other purpose. The governorship of the first city recaptured from the enemy to be placed in my hands, while the revenue of the place would constitute a reserve fund for the legion (including pension to disabled men, expenses for sick and wounded, &c.), my own head to be pledged for the loyalty of the Europeans engaged, each of

* See Frontispiece.

whom were to become "Ti-ping brethren," and be entitled to every consideration as citizens.* The rules of European warfare to be strictly those of the legion, and, moreover, to be observed by any Ti-ping force acting in conjunction with it. Many other regulations were drawn up, but these are some of the principal.

Upon the conclusion of the agreement to raise the Loyal and Faithful Auxiliary Legion, the Chung-wang left Soo-chow and proceeded to his intrenched camp nine miles distant. On the following day passes and boats were provided for Burgevine and the remainder of his men. Among the Europeans were twelve who had served in the Ti-ping army some time previous to the advent of Burgevine, but had been placed under his orders upon his arrival at Soo-chow. These men, and fifteen others, who were not quite so mercenary as their fugitive comrades, and felt more attachment to the cause, refused to desert their colours, and volunteered to remain under command of one *Captain* Smith, formerly a brave non-commissioned officer of the British Marine Artillery. He was almost the only unwounded man on board Admiral Hope's flag-ship at the disastrous attack on the Peiho forts. The volunteers were all attached to the Mo-wang's command, but the Chung-wang promised that, upon the formation of the legion, they should, if required, become members, some of them being good artillery-men or drill-instructors.

All these arrangements were carefully concealed from every European except myself, few of those in Soo-chow being at all trustworthy, and the few exceptions not being particularly attractive as objects of confidential communication. In consequence of the daily increasing strength of the forces besieging Soo-chow, time was precious and not to be wasted in commencing my undertaking; I therefore departed from the city on

* The want of some such clause in Burgevine's arrangements originally excited the suspicion of the Ti-ping chiefs.

the third evening after my arrival, and proceeded to Shanghae as fast as possible, going part of the way in company with some of the late Americo-Ti-ping legion.

We were enabled to travel by a much shorter route than that by which I had reached the city, in consequence of a great victory achieved within the last few days by a Ti-ping army before the walled town Wokong, which freed from the presence of the enemy a more direct road. The battle was fought against Imperialists unassisted by foreign artillery and disciplined troops, who were, therefore, according to the almost infallible rule in such cases, utterly defeated, and Wokong would have been recaptured in a very short time had not Gordon moved from Soo-chow to its defence, when artillery decided the unfair fortune of war against the Ti-pings. The force engaged had been brought up from Kar-sing-foo by the Chung-wang's orders, and should have formed a junction with another body of troops advancing from the city of Hoo-chow-foo, the combined forces being destined to operate against the left flank of the Soo-chow besiegers, while the Chung-wang himself acted against their right. Unfortunately, the impetuosity of the leader of the first division (the Yoong-wang) led him to commence hostilities before effecting a junction with his allies from Hoo-chow, and, although at first eminently successful, his rashness led to his subsequent defeat by Gordon's disciplined troops and artillery, and also to the repulse of the second division, each corps being compelled to fall back upon the cities from which they had advanced, and of which they constituted the garrisons.

The heroic determination with which the Ti-pings disputed the irresistible odds the enemy possessed by their artillery may be seen by the following extract from "How the Taipings were driven out of the Provinces of Kiang-nan and Che-kiang. From Notes kept by an Officer under Ward, Burgevine, Holland, and Gordon."

"The rebels again attempted, from Kar-sing-foo and Ping-hong, to capture Wo-kong. Again, therefore, a detachment was sent down there, and they were driven back, while the artillery made terrible havoc amongst them. But we must give them their due. They fought this day like demons, advancing up to the muzzles of the guns, where they of course met with death."—*Friend of China*, June 27, 1863.

Immediately upon reaching Shanghae I commenced engaging men for my force, and within a few days obtained about a dozen. These were all of good character and particularly promising for drill-instructors. Among them were seven non-commissioned officers, formerly of the French army: Major Moreno, of the Sardinian army, who had seen much service in Asia, Italy, and the Crimea; a Frenchman named Lavery or Labourais (once first sergeant of the 3rd Chasseurs d'Afrique), who had served the Ti-pings for more than a year, but had been carried off against his will by the deserters under *Colonel* Morton; and my friend George White, who had lately been introduced to me as a Ti-ping well-wisher, though formerly a captain in the Franco-Chinese contingent at Ningpo, a service he had resigned in disgust. Besides these, I obtained the services of several men who had served their time in a British regiment and had received their discharges; while many others promised to join me as soon as they were able. This, for a beginning, was not so bad; and, to favour my object still more, Major Moreno obtained the guarantee of certain European ordnance officials to supply me with any quantity of war material. Their sudden desire to assist the Ti-pings was caused, I believe, entirely through jealousy of the British operations conducted by General Brown, *General* Gordon, &c.; at all events, their aid would have proved substantial, for a sample case of French rifles and bayonets was escorted through Shanghae by French soldiers, and safely deposited with my colleague.

Within two weeks I was enabled to send fourteen good men—all soldiers—under the command of Labourais, to

Soo-chow, one of the number being a bugler of the French regiment stationed at Shanghae. Unfortunately, the last seven recruits left just one day too soon, thereby causing me no little trouble during the execution of an enterprise within twenty-four hours after their departure, and for which I was obliged to engage half a dozen strangers, who subsequently proved to be of worthless and disreputable character.

Besides A-ling, who held a Ti-ping commission, I was accompanied from Soo-chow by two officers who had shaved their heads and assumed the Imperialist; their object being to assist me in capturing one of the enemy's steamers, if a chance offered, and to pilot us into the Ti-ping territory, while their presence would incontestably prove the belligerent nature of the act, should we be fortunate enough to cut out a vessel. These officers were provided with a special commission for the purpose.

On the morning of the day following the departure of the last batch of the Loyal and Faithful Auxiliary Legion, an Imperialist war-steamer arrived from before Soo-chow, and anchored abreast of a training camp some two miles above Shanghae. A-ling had engaged two Canton men, members of the Triad Association, one of whom was always kept on the watch for such an arrival; consequently the steamer was scarcely anchored before I received information to that effect. I at once decided to attempt her capture. Major Moreno was to remain at Shanghae, where he was acquainted with many French officers who were willing to serve the revolutionists, and, as he spoke Hindoostanee perfectly well, he had managed to ingratiate himself with native officers of the 22nd B. N. I. and Beloochee regiment, some of whom had promised to join him; it was, therefore, agreed that he should continue his present work, and await the result of the capture of the steamer and the receipt of instructions from myself. I decided to take W—— as my comrade and lieutenant during the proposed opera-

tions. I had soon ascertained the firmness of his
principles and the sincerity of his attachment to the
Ti-ping cause, and therefore gave him a document, somewhat similar to my own special commission, which I
had obtained from the Chung-wang for the purpose of
duly authorizing whomever I might choose as my deputy
and assistant. Major Moreno, who had held field rank
in several armies, I wished to place in supreme military
command of the legion (when raised), because his education as a soldier was complete, and it would have
been difficult, if not impossible, to find a man so
thoroughly qualified in China. Both W—— and Moreno were men of honour—far different from Gordon,
D'Aguibelle, Cook, and the other mercenaries hired by
the Manchoo—and willingly, as I did, tendered their
gratuitous services in the Ti-ping cause. This coincided
very agreeably with my intentions, and caused me to
reflect how superior would have been a force so organized
to the Imperialist legions constituted upon a basis of
blood-money! We had sufficient means to live; we would
not increase them by taking wages to kill our fellow-men,
even though the British Government had given an
example, by authorizing its naval and military officers
to fight in the ranks of a barbarous Asiatic despot, and
to take reward for so doing.

As the Imperialist steamer was under orders to
return to the front on the same day of her arrival at
Shanghae, I had but little time to make my plans. One
of the Canton men who had joined me was formerly employed on board our destined prize. I now sent him off
in a boat with the view to ascertain the strength of her
crew, whether steam was kept up ready for a start, how
many Europeans were on board, &c. In a short time he
returned with the favourable announcement that only
two foreign officers were in charge, the others having
gone ashore; also, that two of the quartermasters (Manilla
men) were absent, besides some of the Chinese soldiers.

My followers were only six in number—W—— and the five Cantonese. It was my only chance to seize the vessel. Yet success seemed doubtful; but I knew full well that the boldness of a sudden enterprise would prove more effective than numbers, and felt sure that a well-managed surprise would give us an easy victory. The people of the steamer being at Shanghae, in the very heart of the Manchoo power, surrounded and protected by their British and French allies, would, I imagined, be too much astounded at the sudden attack by Ti-ping partisans to offer much resistance.

Myself and comrade were soon ready for the attempt, our baggage being confined to a tooth-brush each, our revolvers, and a good-sized piece of soap; the Canton men took little besides their formidable short Chinese swords, and a supply of those huge double-barrelled pistols in which their countrymen delight.

Proceeding to one of the Shanghae wharves, I engaged a boat, embarked with my men, and in a moment we were proceeding as fast as possible towards the vessel of the enemy.

We started in broad daylight; in fact, but a short time after noon. About one o'clock we were close up to the steamer. Sculling against the ebb tide, our boat was slowly worked past the enemy, while, having observed all that could be seen from outside, I made arrangements to board. My plan was to drop alongside the steamer's bow, get on board with W——, and then engage the Europeans in conversation, until I decided upon the instant for our *coup de main*, which would be signalled to A-ling (who was to hold fast the boat and watch every movement) by a wave of my arm, who was then to rush on board with the other Cantonese. Myself, W——, and one man, were to seize and secure the two European officers; the other three, under A-ling's orders, were to overpower any resistance from the Chinese soldiers and crew, and then cut the vessel adrift; while their leader, who had been brought up as an engineer, and understood the duties of one, took charge of the engines and set them going ahead at full speed.

Three of our men now hid themselves behind the mat cover of the boat. When we got alongside, A-ling and another held fast to the steamer in such a position that they could observe the movements of myself and W—— in the after part of the vessel. Proceeding from bow to stern, and looking fore and aft the deck, we were able to notice that the crew on board consisted of twelve or fourteen soldiers, one Manilla man, six or eight Chinese— employed as firemen, &c.—and two Europeans. With my comrade I walked right up to the officers of the ship, and engaged in conversation with regard to my taking a passage to Quin-san with them. Their positions were respectively those of gunner and chief mate. They informed me that their trip to Shanghae was for the purpose of obtaining stores, and to deliver over to the Manchoo Governor several unfortunate Ti-ping chiefs, captured by them on the Ta-hoo Lake. This statement, given with a would-be air of conviction as to the glory and heroism of their achievement, made me quite determined to attempt the capture of the steamer at every risk, rather than lose a chance to prevent future acts of such cold-blooded atrocity. The flotilla, with which she had acted on the Ta-hoo, was commanded by one Marcartney, formerly surgeon of Her Majesty's 99th regiment, but who left his honourable profession to take service under Li, the Manchoo Governor of the province. This man, having made prisoners of the chiefs, set off in the steamer for Shanghae, where he quickly sought the presence of his Asiatic master, delivering up to him the miserable Ti-pings, who suffered merciless torture and a cruel death, while this noble-minded Englishman felt no compunction at becoming the recipient of Manchoo patronage. A more dastardly act than thus giving over vanquished enemies to certain death I never heard of, though it was the

ordinary practice of the Europeans in Imperialist pay
The case in question decided the fate of the steamer, and
made the Imps pay dear enough for the satisfaction of
torturing to death one or two helpless patriots.

The narrators had just finished the history of their
gallant exploit against unarmed boats, peaceable villages, and powerless captives, when I decided to
make my attempt. I stood close to the mate, while
W—— was ready at the side of the gunner; I had
just waved my arm to A-ling, and turned to seize
my man, when, fortunately casting a glance astern, I
observed two boats making for the steamer, and scarcely
fifty yards distant. Quickly giving A-ling the signal to
retreat, I managed to avoid giving any alarm, or even
to excite the least suspicion in the minds of our two
interlocutors, who believed that I intended to proceed up
country with them as correspondent for a certain paper.
The nearest boat contained seven Manilla men, including
two quartermasters belonging to the vessel, and their
friends; the other, the engineer, captain, and another
European, who was engaged to take command upon
reaching the lines before Soo-chow. It was, indeed,
fortunate that I happened to notice the approaching
boats before commencing operations; otherwise we would
certainly have succumbed to numbers within a few
minutes. When the captain arrived on board, I requested
a passage to Quin-san. This was arranged, and I then
took my departure.

Having ascertained that the steamer would not leave
until late at night, I fully determined to make another
effort to capture her for the Ti-pings. I found that it
was imperative, however, before making the attempt,
to have some addition to the number of my followers.
Besides the complement of four European officers, three
Manilla-men quartermasters, twenty soldiers, and eight or
nine other Chinese, it was expected that *General* Doctor
Marcartney, with an *aide-de-camp*, and the intended

future captain, would be present. Consequently, directly we reached the shore, W—— and myself proceeded to find a few Europeans whom we could engage for the service. Late in the evening we met at my house, and found that we could muster five recruits. The character of these men was far more than questionable; their social position was among the genus *rowdy*. However, we had not time to pick and choose; a reinforcement was essential to afford any prospect of a favourable issue to our enterprise; the *rowdies* were therefore engaged on the spot, simply to assist in the capture of an Imperialist vessel, for which service myself and lieutenant guaranteed to pay them well. We would not have had them in our young legion.

A VIEW ON THE JOURNEY TO SOO-CHOW, OF A PORTION OF COUNTRY NEAR THE CITY OF WU-SEE, LATELY DESOLATED BY IMPERIALISTS.
See p. 638.

CHAPTER XXIII.

Renewed Attempt.—Its Success.—Narrow Escape.—British Interference.
—How explained.—Its Failure.—The *Coup de Main* succeeds.—
Groundless Alarm.—Route to Soo-chow.—Its Difficulties.—Generous
Conduct.—Arrival at Wu-see.—Prize-Money.—Treachery.—Preparations for an Attack.—Manœuvring.—The Attack.—Warm Reception.
—The Enemy repulsed.—The Result.—Wu-see evacuated.—Return
to Shanghae.—Last Interview with the Chung-wang.—Manchoo
Cruelty.—Result of British Interference.—Evidence thereof.—Newspaper Extracts.—Further Extracts.—England's Policy.—Its Consequences.—Its Inconsistency.—Her Policy in Japan.—Religious
Character of the Ti-pings.—Their Christianity.

AS the steamer was expected to get under weigh about 1 a.m., I started with my men a little before midnight. Upon this occasion the very elements seemed to favour our design. The tide ran slack; the moon, after shrouding herself within a bank of silvery-edged clouds, retired below the horizon to rest; while even the never-setting stars were partially hidden by the volume of damp, misty vapour hanging over the surface of the river, and almost concealing our two small boats.

In little more than half an hour from the time we left the shore, we were right alongside our destined prize. With the exception of a sentry at each gangway, everything on board seemed silent and unprepared for an attack, although by the symptoms from the funnel and steampipe it was evident that the engines were in readiness. I decided to attempt cutting the vessel out immediately, as it seemed to me that her crew were probably turned in, and if so, not a moment should be lost in taking advantage of the opportunity, or they might be roused out to get under weigh, in which case we would hardly be able to effect the capture without loss of life.

Dividing my followers equally between the two boats, one being under my lieutenant's charge, and assigning to each man his duty in the attack, I gave the word to pull alongside, my own party to board on the starboard bow, the others on the port.

Another second and we were grappling at the sides of the steamer, and scrambling over her bulwarks, sword or pistol in hand. The Chinese sentinels on guard, and a Manilla-man who appeared on deck, were secured without either resistance or alarming those below. In fact, the Chinamen, directly they perceived the danger, seemed suddenly inspired with a strong determination to take no notice, but to be very diligent in marching up and down, and carefully employing themselves by intently gazing somewhere else. The calmness and attentive inattention with which they acted throughout the capture were really charming to behold. They betrayed neither surprise, fear, sympathy, *esprit de corps*, nor any other feeling. I then placed a guard over the hatches, set a party to slip the cable, and sent A-ling into the engine-room to get steam up; while, with four Europeans, I proceeded into the cabin and secured the officers. These comprised the intended captain, the mate, and the gunner, the others being still on shore. They submitted very quietly, gave up their arms, and were altogether too much confounded to attempt any resistance. Just as the vessel was entirely in our possession and I had given the order to go ahead full speed (the cable being slipped), the engineer came alongside in a *san-pan*, only to find himself a prisoner when he got on board. Directly the capture was accomplished, I produced the commission the Chung-wang had given for the purpose, and showed it to the senior officer of the steamer, informing him that we were Ti-ping partisans, and that we would endeavour to pass himself and brother captives from Soo-chow into Gordon's lines as prisoners of war.

Meanwhile, steam had been got up by A-ling, and we were carried along in the direction of the Ti-ping territory as fast as possible. During the capture, one of the Manilla quartermasters had jumped overboard and swam towards the shore. Fearing that this man would raise the alarm and bring a swarm of Impish Manchoos down upon us, I was compelled to lose no time in making good our escape, otherwise I might have managed to capture something more than the one steamer. A few days afterwards I was much vexed by ascertaining that I might have taken Marcartney prisoner, and with him a large sum of sycee destined to pay Gordon's mercenaries. It appeared, from the information given by the former officers of the steamer, when too late to take advantage of it, that the redoubtable *General* was to come off in a boat with the dollars and be picked up abreast of the Fu-tai's camp. If I had known this on the same night, I could easily have taken measures to effect his capture. Aggravated by the infamous manner in which Marcartney carried on hostilities against my friends, I would most assuredly have given him up to the Ti-pings, and he would have been justly punished for his cruelty to his unfortunate prisoners, if they had treated him by the strictest law of retaliation; but of this he would have been in little danger, the mad forbearance of the Ti-pings causing them to suicidally avoid the only means by which they might have saved themselves from slaughter by British means, viz., by proclaiming, and by *executing* the promise, that if any British help were given the Manchoo, either directly or indirectly, they would retaliate by destroying the silk and tea trade (totally in their power), and by generally making war upon British interests. As for the soundness of such policy upon the part of the revolutionists, it could not possibly have done them any injury, and it offered the only chance of arresting foreign hostility.

Some hours after the capture of the steamer, the Manilla-man, as I expected at the time, made his way to the

Fu-tai's camp and reported the circumstance. The Manchoo official had no sooner received the information than he sent off couriers to his very good servants and allies, the British authorities. Those devoted personages immediately made ready one of their national gunboats, and, placing a number of English soldiers on board, despatched her to overhaul and bring back the missing vessel to Shanghae.

Naturally enough my readers may be inclined to wonder what business the British officials had to interfere with the capture of an Imperialist craft by the Ti-pings, they must therefore have an explanation.

All the English admirals, generals, consuls, and others, who were fighting upon the side of the Manchoo, chose, with an amazing amount of injustice and arrogance, to assume that they and their disreputable allies were alone entitled to belligerent rights and privileges. Every act of their enemy was very indignantly branded as either atrociously piratical or a form of bloodthirsty brigandage. They alone were virtuous; they alone had any right to kill, burn, and otherwise destroy! In consequence of this very comfortable state of self-conceit, and in order to succour the dearly beloved Manchoo, some experimental warrior or statesman among the British officials, according to their enlightened *ex parte* diplomacy, did me the honour to designate my humble exploit a piratical outrage. This of course justified their praiseworthy efforts to capture the scoundrel who dared to differ from their immaculate selves, by presuming to prefer and assist the rebels instead of the Imperialists. Besides, is not the vile pirate an enemy of all mankind? And who would be so oblivious of merit as not to do them reverence when they caught him? Unfortunately for their visionary laurels, though fortunately for the pirate, they did not succeed in catching him.

Now, as even at the period referred to, the Ti-ping revolution included a population and a territory, the former at least equal in number, and the latter in extent, to the people and soil of England; and as they were not only recognised as a belligerent power, but as constituting the Government *de facto* throughout the large tract of country under their control, I cannot understand how the military service of such a Power, with an army of several hundred thousand men in the field, and an organized administration ruling their possessions, was termed piracy and brigandage.

I was not only duly commissioned by the Chung-wang, the proper Ti-ping authority, but also acted upon a special commission issued against the vessels of the enemy. If, therefore, the capture of the steamer could be termed an act of piracy, what should be the language used to express the raids and seizure of Ti-ping craft by Admiral Hope, Generals Staveley, Brown, Michel, &c.? when it is remembered that they performed such acts entirely without authority from their own Government or any one else. Some pirates might feel flattered by finding themselves in the same boat with such worthy people; but the author of this work begs most respectfully to decline the doubtful honour. There is another point connected with this employment of defamatory epithets. If I, holding authority direct from the Ti-ping Commander-in-Chief (whose acts were authorized by his king), were a pirate, then what can have been the *status* of Major Gordon, R.E., the commander of the Anglo-Manchoo contingent, who held no commission whatever from Imperial authority, but was simply employed by a *local* Chinese mandarin?

The British gunboat did not overtake my party, though, if she had been handled a little smarter, it would have been an easy matter, for we lost our way several times among the labyrinth of creeks in the interior. If it had not been prevented by the delay from taking wrong courses (thereby affording time for the seizure of the vessel to be made known to the enemy before Soo-chow), and from the fact that only one of the men I had engaged at Shanghae could be depended upon, I should have proceeded straight through the Imperialist lines and made an attempt to seize one of their two other steamers. However, I was obliged to be contented with my single prize. She mounted a capital pivot 32-pounder in the bow, a good 12-pounder howitzer in the stern, was well provided with the best description of ammunition, and she would probably prove very serviceable in the defence of Soo-chow.

In consequence of the impossibility of forcing a passage through the enemy's lines, it became necessary to follow some such route as that by which I had last reached Soo-chow, however difficult it might be to find a channel large enough to carry the steamer so great a distance.

After losing our course for the last time, and very nearly steaming into Gordon's head-quarters at Quin-san, we managed to reach the first Ti-ping position at San-le-jow. Directly we appeared, or rather, directly the funnel became visible above the dense growth of rush and bamboo lining the banks of the creek, the garrison of the fort rushed to arms and made ready to defend themselves against the supposed and dreaded enemy. The terror inspired by the appearance of the small steam-vessels acting with the Imperialist mercenaries was at all times excessive. From a distance the helpless Ti-pings were generally mowed down with perfect impunity, and heavy artillery carried destruction throughout their ranks, while the ships, white painted and low in the water, were almost invisible, and were able to maintain their advantage by retreating or advancing whenever it was desirable, at the same time retaining a position from which shrapnel, Moorsom, and other infernally destructive, though ingeniously contrived shell, could be thrown with deadly accuracy.

It was no wonder that as we suddenly hove in sight, with a volume of thick smoke puffing up from our high-pressure engines, the soldiers and civilians about San-le-jow were dreadfully alarmed. They were well aware that small mercy was ever shown by the "foreign brethren" in charge of the irresistible "hoo-lung paou-chwan," for, fighting or harmless, they were shot down whenever a gun could be brought to bear, and so long as the missiles could be made to reach them. The rowdy bravoes of the Imperialist flotilla being unacquainted with the principles of military honour, seemed to believe that their sole mission was to kill, burn, and destroy; as for extending mercy to those who were unable to resist their appliances of modern warfare, or treating the vanquished with magnanimity, they never entertained such ideas.

Fortunately for the people we came upon so suddenly, the steamer was under Ti-ping colours; therefore, their alarm presented only the most ludicrous character, unaccompanied by the tragic and heretofore inseparable consequences of such an event. From their isolated cottages the poor villagers rushed forth, carrying the most valued of their homely effects; men, women, and children ran frantically in the direction of the fort; some were laden with agricultural implements (for even these were often destroyed by the victorious Imperialists); others with household goods; while here and there a few noble labourers were observed trudging along with their aged fathers or mothers on their backs. Whenever the edge of a canal was reached, without a moment's hesitation, the fugitives would plunge right into the water, and give cause for merriment by the wild efforts they made to regain dry land, often rolling back, and floundering helplessly through the soft mud.

When I perceived the alarm our appearance had created, and that the soldiers were making ready to fire upon us with a few heavy gingalls mounted on their fort, I stopped our vessel's way and brought up alongside the bank, and then going ashore with A-ling, proceeded to the fort to satisfy the commandant as to our friendly character. When it was made known that we were in the Ti-ping service, the soldiers and people loudly professed their gratification. The chief was a bronzed and hardy veteran; and although his garrison did not muster nearly 100 men, he was quite determined to defend his post to the last, had we proved to be enemies. The answer he made when I asked him whether he would not have acted with discretion by retreating from the steamer if she had been still in Manchoo interest, closely resembled that given by a brave Ti-ping officer (who had charge of a most dangerous and exposed position near Ningpo) to a friend of mine, when the latter inquired why he did not abandon so precarious an outpost, which was nearly surrounded by the enemy; he replied, "Puh pa! laou Tien-ping tung shao" (No fear! an old Ti-ping soldier knows how to die).

Passing through San-le-jow, we soon reached the small town of Pimbong, barely twenty-five miles distant from Soo-chow, and also situated on the Grand Canal. At this place we were very kindly received by the chief, who, after seeing my commission, supplied me with provisions, coals, firewood, and other necessaries. Pimbong was almost the last Ti-ping position in the neighbourhood, as immediately beyond came the lines of the enemy besieging Soo-chow. Here our pilots ceased to be of service, and the chief sent on board a man well acquainted with the country, to guide us through the largest creeks. After trying every channel branching off from the Grand Canal, and finding them all too small for the passage of the steamer, we were compelled to proceed on to Kar-sing-foo, a city nearly twenty miles from Pimbong. Had the creeks we explored been available, we could have reached Soo-chow by a *détour* of not more than forty miles, but by going to Kar-sing the distance would be doubled at least.

After a short run down the splendid Grand Canal, we came to off the city, and sent messengers to apprise the governor of our arrival. In a little while that functionary, who proved to be the Yoong-wang, visited the steamer in great state; he met me with much friendliness, and declared himself delighted with the acquisition of the vessel so well known and dreaded. Two Europeans were with the chief; they had formerly belonged to the Franco-Manchoo contingent; and as my lieutenant had known them to be of good character—one had been a captain in the force—I expressed my wish that they should join me, and the Yoong-wang very kindly consented.

As time was precious for the success of my plans, we only remained a few hours at Kar-sing-foo, and then started away with a new pilot on board, who was instructed to take us to the largest creeks leading to the Ta-hoo Lake, which it would be necessary to cross in order to reach Soo-chow.

From Pimbong everywhere we traversed a most beautiful country; and although, from the rumours of approaching war, the influx of fugitives, and the scarcity of provisions, no little distress was prevalent, the people were far more happy, prosperous, and improved than Imperialists ever have been, or seem likely to be.

Directly we steamed away from Kar-sing our troubles began. Every creek we attempted to navigate proved either too small, or the bridges were too narrow and low for the steamer to pass them. After getting, perhaps, fifteen miles up a creek, and destroying several bridges by the way, the water would suddenly shallow to less than our draught, or the channel would narrow to less than our beam; of course, in such cases our only plan was to get back stern foremost and try some other canal. Fortunately the vessel was built of iron, so that her progress overland—for often we were obliged to pass a place not more than four feet deep, while the steamer drew five—did no further injury than bending or indenting her pliant sides.

At last, after spending a week exploring the principal

water communication of what seemed in every respect a free and Christian country, we approached the sea, and it was only when within fourteen miles of Hang-chow that we managed to find an available creek. Even to take advantage of it we were compelled to destroy many bridges; and, upon several occasions, clear the bottom of the channel, while the work of removing stakes and barriers was incessant. Had it not been for the willing assistance we received from the Ti-pings, we should never have been able to get through.

Eventually, after a passage no one would ever have believed the steamer could have effected against so many obstacles, we arrived at the great city of Hoo-chow-foo, situated just at the southern end of the Ta-hoo. At this place the commandant, Tow-wang, and the Luk-wang—whose nephew, the Mo-wang, was commandant of Soo-chow—came out and received us in state. Upon leaving them, after having dined with the chiefs in the city, I managed to reach the Ta-hoo after knocking down an obstructive bridge with a few Moorsom shells. Before proceeding to cross the lake, I obtained a dozen good men from the chiefs, and put the paddle-wheels (which had become much dilapidated during the passage of the creeks) in good repair; for I knew that if *General* Gordon, of the Manchoo mercenary service, had sufficient sense, he could easily intercept me with two, or even three, of the steamers attached to his force. However, fortunately for me, Gordon did not send his ships until too late; for had they overhauled their former consort, she would have fallen an easy prize, as I had not more than two or three Europeans and half a dozen Chinese on whom I could depend.

As I understood there were only two channels by which Soo-chow could be reached from the lake by a vessel drawing so much water as the steamer, and as one of these—*viâ* the Tung-shan hills and city of Wo-kong—was already in Impish hands, I adopted the only remaining course—a creek leading from the northern end of the Ta-hoo to the city of Wu-see; from whence, to Soo-chow, the Grand Canal afforded an easy passage.

While stopping at a small Ti-ping position on the west side of the lake, I was much pleased by witnessing the kind behaviour of the soldiers to a number of destitute country people, who had fled from the advance of the Imperialists down the Yang-tze-kiang towards Nankin. There were not more than 150 soldiers at the station, and from their *own rations*, which consisted solely of rice and dried fish, they charitably relieved more than 500 starving people. This is no idle assertion, for the whole of my confederates were present, and saw the distribution of rice. I went over the five gunboats belonging to the troops, and found that their stores of food were nearly exhausted. The chief told me that, when all was used, he would be obliged to abandon the place, and leave the unfortunate people to starve. I supplied him with a couple of bags of rice, and then bade him farewell; although I have never seen him since, I have not forgotten his praiseworthy conduct. Who has ever seen an Imperialist official do the like?

At length we found the creek leading to Wu-see, and on the same afternoon arrived at the city, greatly to the delight of the garrison, who were much harassed by a formidable flotilla operating against their lines of communication. Soon after our arrival, the commandant, Saou-wang, returned to the city with his army, having beaten the enemy after a sharp fight in the morning. The troops had marched upwards of forty miles to and from the battle-field, and directly they came to the creek encircling Wu-see, they threw down their arms on the bank, and plunged into the cooling water in dense masses, clothes and all; so that in a few minutes the surface was literally covered with them.

The Saou-wang having informed me that the Commander-in-Chief was encamped at a place named Ma-tang-chiao—on the shore of the Ta-hoo, and a place of strategic importance—equidistant from Wu-see and Soo-chow, I at once requested him to despatch messengers to inform his superior of my arrival. While awaiting their return, the commandant set a number of men to work pulling down a very heavy stone bridge, which it was necessary to remove before the steamer could be taken into the Grand Canal. At this city I saw upwards of 6,000 poor people, who were supported by the garrison. They had been driven from their homes by the progress of the Anglo-Manchoos in the neighbourhood, and were perfectly destitute. Every day one of the principal officers of the city came to superintend the distribution of rice, and the ravenous manner in which the people struggled for their food was something fearful to contemplate, especially when it was considered that such great misery was caused entirely by the unjustifiable intervention of my countrymen.

Upon this occasion I had not much time to notice the distress caused by the approach of the allied English and Manchoo devastators, messengers from the Chung-wang on the following morning bringing orders for me to proceed back into the Ta-hoo Lake, and take the steamer to Ma-tang-chiao. When I reached this place, the Chung-wang, attended by the Sz, Le, and several other Wangs, came on board, and appeared to be overjoyed with my successful enterprise and the appearance of the steamer. A-ling, the two Ti-ping officers, and the two Cantonese were instantly promoted; and the chiefs took off their own pearl ornaments to decorate them. The Chung-wang then took me ashore with him, and, upon reaching his head-quarters, confirmed my lieutenant's appointment, and declared that he would give 20,000 dollars prize-money for the capture of the steamer. This I considered amply sufficient for so small a service, and I determined to divide it equally among all who had assisted at the seizure—including the five rowdies who only came for money—besides giving a portion to some of the former crew, who had kept to their work and assisted me since the capture.

The encampment was formed around a large straggling village; and the people, like those of the neighbouring hamlets, appeared more happy, better fed, and less depressed than those of more distant parts of Ti-pingdom. This was always the result of the Chung-wang's presence in any locality, for he was not only the most able general, but also the most talented organizer and pacificator among the chiefs.

At Ma-tang-chiao the Chung-wang was concentrating an army of relief for Soo-chow; and, with the object of enabling the steamer to participate in the same movement, men were employed to remove several bridges and other obstructions on a creek by which she could reach the Grand Canal. This work was hardly commenced, when two or three fugitives, shortly followed by many others, from the suburbs of Soo-chow, arrived with the disastrous intelligence that the city was in the hands of the enemy. How it had fallen they could not say, further than by stating that it had not been captured by fighting, but by some treachery. The Chung-wang seemed much affected by the report, for Soo-chow was not only the most important and best fortified city, the most abundantly supplied and strongest garrisoned, but the commandant, Mo-wang, was his oldest and bravest brother in arms.

Orders were at once given to break camp and march upon Wu-see; and while the troops were so engaged, I returned with the steamer to the same city. On the following day the bad news became confirmed by the arrival of some hundreds of the garrison of Soo-chow. These men stated that the second in command, Nar-wang, with several other principal chiefs, had assassinated the commandant and then surrendered the city to the enemy. A great number of the Mo-wang's men were massacred by the followers of the other leaders, who commanded about 20,000 troops, while the Cantonese portion of the garrison

—some 5,000 strong, and unconnected with the treachery—were compelled to fight their way out of the city. These latter, having placed their wives and children in the centre, proceeded to force the west gate. Unable, however, to effect the narrow passage with their helpless families against the incessant attack by overwhelming numbers of Imperialist and renegade soldiery, they were driven to the horrible extreme of killing their own women and children to save them from the worse fate of degradation and torture, if captured by the enemy. Scarcely a third of the men succeeded in cutting their way through, and of these many were wounded, many were covered with the blood of their wives and little ones, while others had become raving maniacs.

The Chinese nature, although apparently so apathetic, is yet capable of the wildest frenzy of passion; in fact, no people have a more paradoxical and anomalous character. It is a well-known fact that Chinese non-combatants will commit wholesale suicide upon the approach of enemies; but few Europeans would credit the fearful acts which the Soo-chow fugitives were driven in desperation to commit, or the frantic excitement leading to such deeds, and to the insanity of many of the perpetrators. I shall never forget the terrible appearance of the madmen stained with the blood of their own dearest relatives, whom they had themselves killed. They rushed into Wu-see at an immense speed, passed the city, and came to the encampment outside, and then, yelling, shouting, and crying, threw themselves, in paroxysms of grief and frenzy, on the ground before the Chung-wang. Several attempted to drown themselves in a neighbouring creek; and one, a young chief, stabbed himself to death before he could be prevented. The unfortunate men were at last secured and taken into the city.

With the remnant of the Soo-chow garrison came seven Europeans. These men had been sent from the city to join my legion, by order of the Chung-wang, and having proceeded to Ma-tang-chiao, when they changed their route for Wu-see, they were overtaken by the fugitives, and came on with them. These seven men were not a portion of those whom I had sent from Shanghae; all the latter (with the exception of the brave Labourais, who was killed during a night attack on some stockades by the enemy only a few days previously) being within Soo-chow when that city was betrayed, and many of them there perishing. Three of the Europeans had straggled, and did not arrive for some days. Among the four who joined me were *Captain* Smith, and an engineer (for the steamer) who had hitherto been employed casting shell, guns, and executing other important work at Soo-chow.

As it was absolutely necessary for the increase and establishment of my legion that I should return to Shanghae, I wished to leave as soon as the Chung-wang reached Wu-see, particularly as both I and my lieutenant were in a very bad state of health, and urgently required medical assistance; but the Chung-wang having requested that I would join him in an attack upon the Imperialist force threatening Wu-see and Chang-chow-foo, I was obliged to defer leaving until after the battle. The enemy were intrenched in great strength within fifteen miles of Wu-see, and were assisted by a powerful flotilla of gunboats, which gave them entire command of the water communications of the city. It was to drive away or destroy this fleet that an attack was decided upon.

At last all obstructions in the way of enabling the steamer—now named the *Ti-ping*, and flying the Chung-wang's standard—to participate in the engagement were removed; and I joined the Commander-in-Chief's consultation held before commencing operations on the following morning. One thousand men, composing the *élite* of the Chung-wang's guards, and the first division of the Loyal and Faithful Auxiliary Legion, were placed under my orders, together with fifteen gunboats, which were to co-operate with the steamer. With this force I was ordered to attack the hostile flotilla, the Chung-wang himself disposing of his troops so as to prevent a junction between the enemy and their vessels. About midnight the army marched to take up its position, and at daylight I advanced with the steamer and gunboats, the men of my legion accompanying me in two divisions, one on each bank of the canal.

The morning was thick and foggy, so that we were enabled to take up a position within cannon-range of the enemy without either attracting their attention or discerning them ourselves. The place I chose for a halt until the fog cleared away was at a large stone bridge, parallel to the Grand Canal, up which we were proceeding, and over a creek leading direct into a small lake, about a mile and a half distant, on which the enemy's flotilla was stationed.

My plan of action was soon formed. I sent the gunboats in advance beyond the bridge, with orders to attack the enemy at the entrance of the lake, and then to retreat in confusion. By this manœuvre I hoped to draw the hostile gunboats into the creek, when I should be able to attack them with the steamer to an advantage. On the creek not more than a dozen boats could form abreast and work their guns, but on the lake the whole number, estimated at 60 to 70, would be able to open a concentrated fire on our advance; and one well-aimed shot could sink the lightly-built *Ti-ping*, or pierce her boilers.

Taking on board fifty picked men from the Cantonese musketeers of my legion, and making everything ready for action, I had the steamer moved close to the side of the bridge, where she lay perfectly concealed.

Towards noon the weather began to clear, and our small squadron immediately pulled forward and opened fire on their opponents. The Imperialists, encouraged by their great superiority of numbers, soon advanced into the creek and gave chase as our gunboats retreated. By the time that they had reached half-way to the bridge, however, the day became quite clear, and observing our troops spread out in line of battle, they gave up any further pursuit.

This was the moment for which I had been waiting. Sending forward my men on the shore at a run, I moved the steamer from her hidden position, passed under the bridge, and advanced upon the enemy at full speed, firing upon them with our 32-pounder, and warmly answered by their stern guns as they turned and pulled back to reach the lake, which they managed to do before we could close with them. As we approached the termination of the creek, we were saluted with a tremendous cannonade. The gunboats had formed in three divisions, one directly fronting the mouth of the creek, the others upon either flank, so that they were enabled to maintain a most powerful cross fire. I counted twenty-two vessels in the centre squadron, and twenty in each of the others. They were all fully manned with about 30 men in every boat, and each carried a bow-gun, from 6 to 18-pounder; a large swivel on either side, and a stern gun, a little smaller than that in the fore-part.

Of course, my land force could be of no assistance on the lake, all their use being to accompany the steamer on either side of a creek, and prevent the enemy's troops closing upon her in such an indefensible position. Our fifteen gunboats were armed with such inferior artillery that they were altogether unable to cope with the hostile vessels, every one of which carried good English guns supplied by the British at Shanghae. I therefore ordered them to remain in the creek, but to advance and take charge of any boats we might capture.

Directly we emerged from the creek, the enemy gallantly pulled towards us, decorated with innumerable flags, maintaining a very heavy fire, yelling terrifically, and deafening us with a tremendous beating of gongs and blowing of war-horns. Seeing that their only way of

NAVAL ENGAGEMENT AND CAPTURE OF IMPERIALIST GUNBOATS AT WU-SEE

retreat was by a creek in the rear of their starboard squadron, I immediately attacked the centre, because, if successful, we should not only succeed in capturing two-thirds of the flotilla, but would render them unable to fire upon the steamer through danger of injuring themselves. While steaming up to obtain this position—necessarily at slow speed, because the lake was very shallow—showers of grape, roundshot, and every species of Chinese rocket and missile, came rushing all around and about our heads. Fortunately the *mitraille* was fired too loosely, and the solid shot too badly aimed, to cause us much damage, while every discharge from our heavy gun, worked by *Captain* Smith, proved very effective among the mass of boats, men, and flags. In a short time the central squadron gave way, and the crews, pulling close to the shore, began to desert their vessels. The port squadron, in danger of being cut off, took to flight and became mingled with the centre. Meanwhile, the starboard division pulled up the creek in its rear, and took up a position, from which it maintained a sharp fire over the low land, nearly every shot passing close to the steamer or striking her. Several times I turned away from the discomfited vessels to follow their consorts up the creek, but on each occasion, with obstinate courage, the enemy rallied, remanned their guns, and stuck to them until our return to the attack drove them ashore again.

Thrice did the crews of the gunboats resume the conflict. On their last attempt to turn the fortune of the day, they actually advanced upon us, loading and firing as fast as they could, keeping up a fearful yelling and beating of gongs, and evincing every determination to board. Had they only possessed sufficient confidence to persist in this attempt, they might easily have succeeded in overpowering us by numbers and capturing the steamer. Fortunately, however, directly the heavy discharges from our pivot gun—double-shotted with grape and canister—and the incessant musketry fire from the small-arm men stationed on our upper deck began to take effect upon them, they gave way and retreated to the shore. After the last repulse, my squadron of gunboats having arrived on the scene of conflict, their crews took charge of the deserted vessels of the enemy and began to tow them away.

From their position on the creek, the starboard division of the Imperialist flotilla still maintained the action; so, abandoning the two others to our allies, we steamed after the still defiant squadron. In a few minutes a well-aimed shot from our 32-pounder sunk two of the gunboats, and eight others were captured. The remaining ten, after a short chase, were abandoned by their men, who escaped ashore, carrying with them, however, their small arms. At this moment I perceived that the creek was lined on either side by a cunningly-contrived breastwork, from behind which the gunboat *braves* began to fire heavily upon us. At the same time large columns of Imperialist troops became visible, as, by sheer force of numbers, they pressed back the Chung-wang's divisions, and threatened to occupy the bank of the creek by which I had advanced the steamer, and which formed the only line of retreat to Wu-see.

Before we could secure the last abandoned gunboats, a large number of musket-armed skirmishers were thrown into the intrenchments in our immediate vicinity. So heavy and effective became their volleys—every bullet striking some part of the steamer, riddling her light upper works through and through, and wounding many men, while we could neither reply with our heavy guns nor bring a rifle to bear upon the hidden foe—that we were compelled to save ourselves by precipitate flight, leaving the last captured vessels behind, and hurrying to the other creek at full speed, in order to avoid being intercepted by the advancing troops. Owing to the gallantry with which my land division held the enemy in check, we were able to effect our retreat, carrying off fifty-one gunboats as the substantial trophy of our victory, and capturing more than fifty of the Sung-wang's * flags.

Upon reaching the bridge we were warmly congratulated by the Chung-wang, who at once declared he would give 200 dols. prize-money for each gunboat, which promise he scrupulously fulfilled. As the enemy continued to advance in line of battle, orders were given for a general attack, and I was despatched with the steamer to the city of Chang-chow-foo, to join in the co-operating movements being executed therefrom. We were too late to participate in them, for, upon reaching some outworks, about twelve miles from the city, our orders were countermanded, the Imperialists being defeated at every point, and the stockades from which they had menaced the two cities being in the hands of the Ti-pings.

Our escape from the ambush into which we had fallen while pursuing the remnant of the Imperialist flotilla was something miraculous, for, although our casualties were only two Chinese killed, three Europeans slightly, my interpreter A-ling dangerously, and a dozen Chinese wounded, the steamer was pierced about her upperworks with countless bullets; so much so, indeed, that it was difficult to understand how every person on board had not been killed.

Some days after our victory, a large Imperial force advanced from Soo-chow and proceeded to invest Wu-see. Upon one occasion they advanced close up to the walls, but were driven back by the shell we threw among them from the steamer. As the city was rendered untenable by the loss of Soo-chow and other places, the Chung-wang decided to evacuate it and retire upon Chang-chow-foo. Before executing this arrangement the Commander-in-Chief, in his capacity of Vicegerent to the Ti-ping king, TIEN-WANG, commissioned me to promulgate among foreigners the objects of the revolution; the wishes and opinions of its leaders; the treatment they had received

* The late famous San-ko-lin-sin.

from England; and all subjects relative thereto upon which I might be able to write. This event has been the sole origin, besides my own feelings in the cause, of the present work—"Tai Ping Tien Kwoh."

My arrangements to return to Shanghae were soon made. *Captain* Smith, together with the Ke-wang (one of the Commander-in Chief's high officers), I left in command of my legion so far as it was organized, including the steamer and captured gunboats. My lieutenant, who was too ill to remain on duty, the five rowdies, A-ling and his two Cantonese friends, were to accompany me. Those who remained were given their prize-money, but I refused to receive the share for the others until we should reach the city of Kar-sing-foo, because this place was on the limit of the Ti-ping territory in the direction of Shanghae, and I felt confident that, if they had time, the rowdies would quarrel over their money, and, probably, injure one another. It will be seen that my anticipations were not groundless.

Thinking that the horrible Soo-chow treachery and massacre (the chiefs and their men who surrendered upon *General* Gordon's *guarantee of conditions* were put to death by the Manchoo colleague of the British officer) would surely occasion the British Government to withdraw its help from those whose sanguinary atrocities were not only dishonouring them by their participation as allies, but actually making them morally, if **not materially**, responsible; I set out for Shanghae under the impression that the Anglo-Manchoo alliance would cease, and the time prove favourable for advocating the Ti-ping cause and its claims upon all foreign, but especially British, sympathy.

Having taken leave of the noble Chung-wang and his son Maou-lin, I left Wu-see with an escort of fifteen gunboats; at the same time the city was evacuated, and the Commander-in-Chief started with his troops for Changchow-foo, carrying with him the four Europeans captured on board the steamer, whom he promised to retain as prisoners of mine until the return of myself or my lieutenant. It has since been reported that the bodies of these four men were found some time afterwards near Wu-see, and Major Gordon of the R. E., in his notorious capacity of uncommissioned general to Manchoo Governor Le, took upon himself to report that the Chung-wang had roasted them to death, his only authority being the testimony of a demented "old woman," who declared that "Cantonese rebels" had killed them! If the Ti-pings did kill the four prisoners, the act was not only the first instance in which they have retaliated upon foreigners,* but was also the result of Major Gordon's treacherous capture of Soo-chow, for I should have sent the men over to his lines as exchanged prisoners of war if I had reached that city. It is, however, believed by all in China who are acquainted with the facts of the case, that the men fell into the hands of the Imperialists, and were put to death by them; and this seems to me a very likely affair (if they have been killed, for it is by no means certain), because the rear of the forces that retreated from Wu-see were closely pursued by the troops of Le, Futai. But my strongest reason for believing that the Ti-pings had no hand in killing them, if murdered they were, is the fact that the Chung-wang was personally pledged (to me) to keep them unharmed and properly cared for; and even Major Gordon cannot state that this celebrated chief ever broke his word, or *sanctioned a violation of his guarantees by associates*. Moreover, I particularly gave the Chung-wang to understand that my future services would depend very much upon finding my prisoners safe and sound at my return; besides, he could not possibly

---

* Some people have thought that the four men were executed as a retaliation for the murder of the Wangs at Soo-chow, because, naturally enough, the Ti-pings considered the Europeans present were responsible for the atrocities. The four prisoners were members of Gordon's force, and it is just possible that they may have been put to death by some of the Soo-chow refugees.

have had any motive to injure them, and thereby lose what he expected might prove valuable aid; and certainly, to judge by the kind treatment they received within Wu-see, he had no intention of doing so.

At my last interview with the Chung-wang I shall never forget the speaking expression of his fine eyes, as I shook his hand for the last time and stepped back to take my final departure. His look seemed to express friendship and gratitude for what I had already done, doubt for the future, and a mutely pathetic request, imploring that I, too, would not desert him in his hour of need. This well-remembered glance created another bond between us which only death can obliterate, and which would alone have bound me to help the Chung-wang to the utmost of my ability. No wonder he seemed doubtful as to my future course, for the Ti-pings had never trusted a foreigner without being deceived, and they never experienced anything but insult or unprovoked injury from European officials!

From Wu-see to Kar-sing-foo, *viâ* the Ta-hoo Lake and Hoo-chow-foo, I was accompanied by the Shi-wang, a cousin of the Chung-wang, who had received instructions to facilitate my movements and make arrangements for my return, besides being commissioned to divert to the city of Hoo-chow the reinforcements on their way to Ma-tang-chiao. A few days after commencing our journey we fell in with a body of troops belonging to the Ting-wang's command at the provincial capital Hang-chow, who were proceeding to the appointed rendezvous; but the Shi-wang ordered them to Hoo-chow, where they afterwards proved very useful in maintaining communications with Nankin along the west shore of the Ta-hoo, *viâ* Chang-chow, Kin-tang, Li-yang, &c.

After the evacuation of Wu-see by the Ti-ping troops, the city, of course, fell into Imperialist hands; when the wretches, in their usual style, commenced a general massacre of the unfortunate inhabitants, it being estimated that 6,000, at least, were put to death, their crime being the fact that they were found in a city which had been held by rebels! The poor people who had been daily supplied with food from the Ti-ping granaries were now starved to death, for charity is a virtue unknown to Manchoo mandarins. I was at Wu-see for several weeks, and during that period I went over the country for miles in every direction, finding everywhere the same frightful results of British intervention—in the devastation of the country by the allies, and the starvation of the unfortunate Ti-ping country people. During my return to Shanghae, every place I saw exhibited more or less misery; a painful contrast to the prosperity universally prevailing only a few months before, when the power and rule of the Tien-wang was unshaken. Upon leaving the Ti-ping territory, or rather upon passing the few strong cities they still occupied in proximity to the frontier, the desolation of the country was perfectly appalling. Even throughout those portions of the silk districts still untouched by the enemy, everything was in a state of turmoil, inactivity, and distress. The mulberry-trees and the silkworms, which require constant care, were but partially tended; in many parts they were neglected altogether; so that these facts, coupled to the wholesale massacre of the people by the Imperialists, fully account for the great decrease of silk *since* the Ti-pings have been driven from the producing districts.

My readers have already been shown the prosperous condition of the country entirely under Ti-ping control during the years 1860-1-2-3. We will now notice for the last time the effect of British support of the barbarous Manchoo.

The change for the worse may be considered to have fairly commenced directly after the capture of the city of Quin-san by the Anglo-Manchoo forces. Since that event, entirely caused by British means, death and destruction have swept throughout the once free, Christian, and smiling land. I have wandered over mile after mile of the once happy Ti-ping districts (during the latter part of 1863 and beginning of 1864); I have passed through twenty and thirty villages in a day, and, horrible to relate, in almost every room of each house have found the unfortunate people starved, starving, or barely maintaining the embers of life by a fearful state of cannibalism, feeding on the dead bodies lying thick around them! I have seen this sight of unparalleled horror in large unwalled towns containing many hundred houses, and I frequently found as many as fifteen to twenty bodies in one dwelling, the great number being occasioned by refugees from places already occupied or threatened by Anglo-Imperialists. I have had the fearful consolation of resuscitating many of the miserable people for a short time by giving them all the rice I could obtain, though I was convinced it would only give them strength to undergo the pangs of starvation a second time. Some insensate patriots may accuse me of un-English feeling for my expressions against the policy of the *present* British ministry; but would not any Englishman feel and write strongly upon witnessing such scenes as those I am describing, and which have been solely caused by the wicked use of England's strength? I denounce the policy pursued against the Ti-pings as being not only egregiously stupid and suicidal in theory and practice, but absolutely iniquitous in every result. Nothing could work greater harm on living mankind.

From the few poor wretches I found able to speak, in most cases I gathered their expression of opinion "that it was through foreign soldiers coming to fight the Tienping (Ti-ping troops) that their distress had been occasioned." Some said that "they had come from places taken by the Kwan-ping (Imperialist troops), and reaching where I found them, could get nothing to eat, were unable to travel farther, and so had lain them down to die." Whenever I came to villages where the people were not yet reduced to the last stage of famine, mothers were offering their daughters to any one who would take them; but even this was unavailing! Although in other parts of China the young women would have been taken for evil purposes, in Ti-pingdom the laws strictly prohibited everything that was condemned as immoral, so they were left to starve if provisions were not supplied from better motives. These fearful scenes are so vividly impressed upon my memory that I am sorry I ever had the misfortune to witness them.

The desolating sword of Asiatic warfare has been ruthlessly carried into provinces for years in the most flourishing condition under Ti-ping rule. Hundreds of once happy villages have been obliterated from the face of the earth they once adorned, while the decaying skeletons of their industrious and inoffensive people are thickly scattered throughout the surrounding country, changing into a vast Golgotha and desert what would otherwise have remained an earthly paradise.

As many people would probably feel inclined to deny that the Anglo-Manchoo forces created the desolation I have described, because it has frequently been misrepresented by interested persons that the Ti-pings were the devastators, I have selected two or three statements which entirely corroborate my own.

The following narrative was given by a gentleman who has comparatively lately traversed the silk districts in search of mulberry-trees and silkworms, in order to estimate the probable extent of the next silk crop, and the causes of the present great fall-off. It appeared in the *Friend of China*, Shanghae paper, of January 13, 1865, from which I quote:—

"When Burgevine went to Nankin, that time the country between it and Soo-chow was a garden for loveliness. For eighteen *le* (Chinese miles) along the canal, on either side, the banks were lined with houses —the inhabitants busy as bees, and as thriving as they had reason to expect to be. With the reversion of Soo-chow to the Imperialists, these houses and numerous bridges disappeared. For the whole eighteen *le* there is not a roof—the country around, as far as the eye can reach, is a desert. The people have fled from the Imperialists as though they dreaded them like wolves and tigers; nor man, nor woman, nor child, nor beast of any description to be seen. Fowls, ducks, pigs, buffaloes—no such thing to be got for love or money.

"Twenty-seven *le* from Soo-chow brought me to Soo-za-qua, formerly a custom-house station, now the abode of part of the residue of Gordon's force. . . .

"The place is an oasis in the desert. For miles after leaving it, indeed, all the way thence to Wu-see, the same barren, weed-overgrown appearance meets the sight. Pheasants, partridges, and a wild deer now and then, gave me plenty of amusement for my fowling-piece. But the number of bleached skeletons, skulls, or partially decayed dead bodies, is awful to look at—to count them would be impossible—they literally cover the ground for miles. As for traffic in boats, there was none; trade is all gone. Wu-see is in ruins. Where they were going I could not make out, perhaps the boatmen themselves did not know beyond their next stage, but the number of soldiers passing up in boats was legion, the contrast between them in their fat, saucy appearance, and that of the meagre, starved-looking wretches in the streets, being very striking. Before reaching Wu-see I passed a camp of from 20,000 to 30,000 soldiers—impudent rascals, shouting after me, 'Yang-qui-tsze, Yang-qui-tsze' (Foreign devil),* till I was tired of hearing them; beckoning me to come on shore; waving spears and dashing them out to show what they would do if they could. They have evidently no love for Westerns, these Imperial Imps. . . .

"On to Chang-chow-foo, for 95 *le*, still the same howling desert, not a working soul to be seen. The depth and strength of the weeds now are prodigious. Alack, for my search for mulberry-trees! I could not see one. All are cut down, and if wood at all were seen, it was borne by hungry-looking people, propelled by soldiers who had impressed them into the wood-cutting line. It was for such a state of things as this, was it, that Gordon gave his talents? His reward would be a sorry heart (!), could he only view the misery he has made. They are perfectly rabid after firewood, these same Mandarin soldiers, and cut down green wood and everything they meet. I should say there must be from eight to twelve thousand men at Tan-yang, which I next got to—Loo-tszeur, a village between Chang-chow-foo and it, having disappeared to a brick; not a soul to be seen, though they have established a custom-house station about five *le* from it.

"Tan-yang, a small city on the left bank of the canal, is almost entirely deserted. Soldiers presenting here, as at the other places, the same fat, saucy

---

* My reader will contrast this with the treatment Europeans received when these districts were in Ti-ping possession.

appearance I before noticed, some of them wearing bangles, earrings, and jewels of value, while the people around are clotheless and miserable, and how the poor wretches live at all is a mystery. All that I saw them grubbing at was a species of porridge, consisting of the *husks* of paddy, a mess one would not give a horse. Oh, the skulls again! From Chang-chow-foo to Tan-yang the ground is literally white, like snow, with skulls and bones. The massacre of the unfortunate Taipings (inoffensive villagers, most likely) must have been awful! Between Chang-chow-foo and Wu-see stands a dilapidated pagoda, said to be 4,000 years old, and I went to look at it. What was my surprise to find it crammed with dead bodies, from which slices had been cut to eat as food! . . . I went on for 45 *li* beyond Tan-yang; the farther I went, the country getting worse and worse, if it were possible for there to be a difference when one description of 'bad' does for all, and I began to think that my search for a mulberry-tree, *in what, under the Taipings, was a splendid silk-producing country*, was useless, and I had better turn back."

Here we have the testimony of an impartial mercantile gentleman. Comment is needless. We will now turn to the evidence given by two of Gordon's own officers, men who were present during the operations against the Ti-pings, but who were ultimately honest enough to admit the truth. The following extracts are from a letter which appeared in the *Friend of China*, April 28, 1864:—

"TO THE EDITOR OF THE 'FRIEND OF CHINA.'

"SIR,—I read in the *North China Herald* a letter from Gordon's headquarters, in which the writer says that the slaughter among the rebels, after the capture of Hwa-soo, was terrible. Upwards of 9,000 were taken prisoners, and of these it was estimated 6,000 were killed or drowned, principally by the Imperialists. Further, that there is no doubt they would have killed ten times that number if they had the chance to do so. Now, Sir, I do hope there will be a stop put to such massacres, though I can but believe that the writer of that article must be, what they call in Australia, a *new chum*, for he cannot know much about the treachery of the Imps, or he would not dwell so much on it. Why, did not the Imperialists take rice, beans, wheat, and all other kinds of grain out of Wusee, even while those around were starving; and as the old people came up to the gate to go outside the city with their few catties of rice, were they not stopped and their food taken from them, while, if they spoke against it, they were bambooed? There was rice sufficient in Soo-chow and Wu-see to keep the poor in the districts around for many months; why, then, could not the Futai and other **Mandarins be made to relieve the poor in the** surrounding **country?**

"At Chang-chow, again, in place of bambooing the poor when begging for a few grains of that which was taken from them, why were they left to die outside by starvation? I saw this, for I was one of the officers engaged in the capture of Wu-see, **and other cities.** From Wu-see we advanced towards Chang-chow, where, at first, there were but few poor to be **seen.** After we had been there a short time, however, there was a great number of them. Why?—*Because the Imperialists had gained so much of the country, and the poor had been **robbed by** them.* As for the much-landed Gordon's troops, do they not **rob the** country people on the march? And if the disciplined troops do this with impunity, what can you think if the non-disciplined do it? I **have** seen beggars beheaded by these wretches in sheer wantonness.

"The *Herald's* **correspondent** writes within sight of the walls of Chang-chow, and says, the starvation and cannibalism which prevail are unrelieved by the fiends who have been the cause of so much misery! The writer of that article little thinks the Imperialists are the fiends, or he would not have written so. On the other hand, parties who have travelled in the rebel districts have seen the Taepings relieve their poor."

Besides the above letter, the following appears in the issue of the same paper on the **31st** of January, 1865:—

"TO THE EDITOR OF THE 'FRIEND OF CHINA.'

"Shanghae, 26th January, 1865.

"SIR,—I see you say in your 'apology' for rebels that the destruction of the city of Quin-san was caused by the Taepings on their evacuation of it. Such was not the case. The idol temples and official quarters were destroyed or ransacked by them; but the destruction of the dwelling-houses of the inhabitants was the work of the Imperialists. I was one of the first in the city after its evacuation by the Taepings, and what I now state I saw with my own eyes. Indeed, it was, as you have stated repeatedly, a practice with the Imperialists to burn all which the Taepings left. Why they did so I can hardly tell, further than that the men were encouraged to do it by their native officers.   "I am, dear Sir, yours truly,

"LATE OF GORDON'S FORCE.

"P.S.—Ching and Le* were the grand devastators, and have to be thanked for the bulk of the misery now so rampant all over the country."

As the Liberal Government has such a *penchant* for interfering in the internal affairs of other nations, why has

---

* Ching and Le were the principal Imperialist generals; they were acting in co-operation with Gordon.

it not devoted its meddlesome talents to killing some one either in Denmark, America, Italy, Poland, or Mexico? Cynical people may well say that the Premier and his colleagues dared not more than bluster in these cases; that in the centre of China, in Japan, Ashantee, New Zealand, &c., they became very brave and officious because they could be so with impunity, and that such disgraceful, unprofitable, and inconsistent, if not imbecile policy, is either the expiring flashes of their administration or the greatness of England.

Although it may be perfectly true that the Chancellor of the Exchequer and his *confrères* in office have saved the opium trade and the China indemnity (probably also their places in office, by covering the expenses of the last China war, which would otherwise have made a serious cause of opposition), at the immaterial responsibility of the destruction of a few millions of Chinese and the devastation of some districts of China three or four times the size of England, of what benefit has the meddling policy proved to general commercial or mercenary interests? The silk trade, the most valuable with China, has fallen off exactly one half at the present date,* since the due effect of driving the Ti-pings from their dominions has transpired. The interior, free and open under the revolutionists, who earnestly desired the friendship of Europeans, has now been closed to freedom of trade or travel by the very Mandarins who have been reinstated to tyrannize over regions their oppression had otherwise lost to them for ever; while the old hatred of foreigners, persistent determination to evade treaty obligations, and the haughty, exclusive policy of the Manchoo has been resumed, since the hypocritical pretence of adopting a more friendly line of conduct, in order to obtain foreign assistance, has become no longer necessary, by the recoil of the Ti-ping revolt before British arms. Besides this, having broken

* June 1865. See Appendix B.

the political power of the only movement in China which
afforded a prospect of improving, pacifying, or Christianizing that vast empire, England has been the means of
creating a general state of anarchy. The Ti-pings have
simply retreated to the interior and the sea-coast province
of Fu-keen, while in every other part of the empire the
people, no longer able to look upon the great revolution
as likely to overthrow the Manchoo, and being more than
ever oppressed by their foreign rulers, are not only driven
to discontent but open rebellion. Besides the Ti-ping
revolution, there are at the present time three or four
powerfully organized rebellions. The "Nien-fei," in the
north; the "Honan Filchers," towards the west; and the
so-called "Mohammedan rebels," in the central provinces.
Elsewhere, the innumerable local insurrections have settled
into a regular system of brigandism, because the discontented have no longer the opportunity or confidence to
join the diminished forces of Ti-pingdom. These circumstances, added to the fact that the Imperialist Mandarins
are now systematically enforcing at least five times the
treaty-legalized transit duties upon merchandise, are not
only greatly enhancing the price of foreign goods to the
natives, but, of course, considerably limiting their consumption. The only staple article of trade which has
not at present decreased in quantity is tea. Still the
price has become higher in China, and the non-diminution
of export is due to the fact that the Ti-pings evacuated
their former tea districts and captured the famous Vu-e,
or Bohea districts, which they held for some time, without
much fighting. It would be impossible to say that, since
the result of British hostilities against the revolutionists
has transpired, our commerce with China was ever in a
more stagnant, unprofitable, and generally unsatisfactory
condition. So much for the mercenary interests, to aid
which England has been unscrupulously dragged into a
clandestine and grossly criminal war!

Bad as the preceding effects of the foreign policy of

the Palmerston Government undoubtedly are, there is yet another and a far worse consequence to be noticed. Before adverting to the most serious fact it is as well to epitomize the political action which has created it. It has been fondly imagined and fatally supposed by the Liberal ministers themselves, that they, *par excellence*, are the enlightened men of England, the only framers of philanthropical and progressive measures; and, in fact, that their glorious and never-to-be-forgotten place-holding is a Government of "peace, retrenchment, and reform." The doctrine of non-intervention having even been especially professed, and having been carried so far as to make a certain noble lord sacrifice his publicly and officially declared determination that "Denmark should not stand alone" in the event of certain contingencies, by leaving her to stand alone when those contingencies did come to pass, and then framing another set of probabilities, about the chivalrous deeds he would initiate if the King of Denmark were to be made a prisoner. Doubtless the admirers of that noble lord—who once made the astounding and statesmanlike discovery that "all children are born innocent," especially those of his constituents, whose chubby "olive branches" were also discovered to be the best and most beautiful in England—considered their representative a marvellously proper man, and his bragging to fight and then retracting a very creditable proceeding, quite in accordance with the useful policy of non-intervention: yet, on the other hand, there are people who have the obstinacy to review this and similar affairs, and deduct therefrom, and observe the fact that in other parts of the world a very different policy has been enacted where it could be done with impunity, all of which affords sufficient evidence that the pretended adoption of a non-interfering policy is neither more nor less than an unprincipled truckling to strong powers, and an agressive bullying of the weak.

It is quite certain that, whether the rulers of China be Manchoo or Ti-ping, the vast industrial population would still produce tea, silk, and other commodities. Now, the professed motive for British intercourse with China is commercial—that is to say, to buy the above-mentioned articles, and sell the manufactures of the English markets—but not political; for meddlesome interference with the internal affairs of China would prove disadvantageous to both nations, and would certainly be well calculated to bring the Imperial authority into contempt, injure the Chinese organizations in an abortive attempt to substitute those for which they are not yet qualified, and simply foment the troubles already existing, by the natural consequences of injudicious and unnecessary meddling.

But the British ministers, who would justify their broken pledges in Europe by an appeal to the doctrine of non-intervention, act upon a very different system towards China and Japan. They seem to make it their business, not only to advance trade in the Celestial Empire, but to concern themselves with its private and political disturbances, to judge between the Ti-ping and Manchoo, and then to settle the affair by destroying the one and bullying the other.

In Japan they have attacked feudal chieftains as though no central Government existed in that country; and then, after degrading the Imperial authority in the eyes of the people, force has been used to compel the opening of ports to trade. Thus have British statesmen pursued the best course to increase the animosities already existing, to produce general anarchy, and to establish the violation of all principles of international law, which they are *compelled* to observe in Europe. The most convincing fact with regard to the folly of interfering in China, is, that *until* such idiotic, or rather wicked policy was commenced, the exports were largely on the increase, having risen from £9,014,310 in 1859, to £14,186,310 in 1863; while the consumption of British imports has decreased up to the same period — about which time the operations against the Ti-pings were exercising due effect—by more than half a million—£567,646. In 1863, the total value of British exports to China was £3,889,927—a sum less than the value of the exports to Brazil; yet for this comparatively paltry amount an enormous military expenditure has been maintained, whilst it is palpable, by the falling off of trade, that the policy has signally failed, and the number of persons who have perished through the mistake would make at least one life destroyed for every pound sterling.

We now come to the most serious point with regard to the war against the Ti-pings. It is well known, and has never been denied, that throughout the country, under their control, the Bible was circulated not only with freedom, but gratuitously, by the Government established at Nankin. Besides this *unparalleled* practice, the fact that they accepted the Word of God in its full integrity is also incontrovertible; and He has declared, "My Word shall not return unto me void." Furthermore, it is well known by all who have visited the Ti-pings in their cities and camps, that (so strict an interpretation have they placed upon the Commandments, &c.) they effectually prohibit not only the inveterate vices of the Chinese, and their heathen practices, but the evil indulgences which find full sway even in the most moral State of Europe. Their abolition of opium smoking; prostitution; the hitherto universal Chinese slave trade; the degraded Asiatic status of the women; the use of torture and bribery in courts of justice; the deformed small feet; the tail-wearing slave-badge of the men—these, and other facts proving their complete superiority to the hopelessly corrupt state of public and private life under the foreign rule of the Manchoo dynasty, we have already noticed. Let us ask, whence these great and glorious changes? Are they, as Lords Palmerston and Russell, and their correspondents upon anti-Ti-ping Chinese affairs, have repeatedly declared (when obliged to defend their un-English policy) the conduct of the Ti-pings to be, the natural acts of "bloodthirsty marauders," "locusts," "merciless brigands," "revolting impostors," "ferocious hordes of banditti," &c.? Or are they not rather the blessings bestowed by God upon people who, to the utmost of their power, and the sacrifice of their lives, have striven to follow His Word and Law? Man may change the public and outward forms of existence necessary for the body, but only God can alter the private and moral character necessary for the soul. There is a doctrine of original and natural sin; therefore it does appear presumptuous, if not profane, when people combine together against any vast movement in which the hand of God is visible—either in the supernatural or the presence of the Bible; especially as they believe that Divine interposition is necessary to convert and save the souls of all men, and as they have neither political nor national interest in the movement to even justify the worldly motives of their interference.

Present ministers[*] and their followers may possibly ridicule the idea, in order to justify their policy towards China, that whatever the Ti-pings might or might not have been—even setting apart the fact of their Christianity—if they have been killed for the sake of British commerce (especially the vile opium trade, which they prohibited), every bale of silk and chest of tea brought into this land bears with it an endless curse; and that these, together with every article of British manufacture forced upon China, are defiled with the blood of the victims who have been slaughtered to prosper, forsooth! "our commercial institutions!" Man cannot serve both God and Mammon. The efforts of the British Government to worship the latter have failed most signally; but even had they succeeded in creating the most stupendous

[*] Palmerston's Government.

trade the world ever contained, do they believe that a righteous and eternal God has not witnessed the *means*, and that He who notes the fall of a small sparrow hath not recorded the murder of every human being, during their unholy crusade against the unfortunate Ti-pings?

Throughout a vast extent of China the Bible became established; but now, through the assistance given by the British Government to the Manchoo, the people— even including the little lisping children—have been slaughtered, while the idols of Budha are re-erected, dominating for a season over the desecrated ashes of *our* Bible.

Nankin, the Ti-ping capital, has fallen, through British intervention, since my arrival in this country; the printing and circulation of the Holy Scriptures have therefore ceased, and the Ti-pings have become wanderers over the face of the earth they would otherwise have adorned. It is idle and unworthy to cavil at this dogma or that article of the Ti-ping creed: the revolutionists did their utmost to enter into the pale and brotherhood of Christendom. Truly and candidly speaking, the nation solely responsible for preventing so glorious a consummation, is—England.

CHAPTER XXIV.

Kar-sing-foo.—Christmas in Ti-pingdom.—Works of Art.—Dangerous Companions.—Narrow Escape.—Retribution.—Adieu to Ti-pingdom. —Mr. White's Case.—The Neutrality Ordnance.—Order of July 9th, 1864.—Intended Return to England.—Particulars of the Siege of Soo-chow.—Strength of the Garrison.—The Assault Described.— The Nar-wang's Treachery.—Its Cause.—Major Gordon's Report.— The *Friend of China*.—Gordon's Report Continued.—Narrative by an Eye-Witness.—The Soo-chow Tragedy.—Major Gordon.—His Conduct.—Gordon's Letter to Sir F. Bruce.—Analysis thereof.—Newspaper Extract.—Gordon's " Reasons" Refuted.—Analysis Continued. —Gordon's " Personal Consideration."—His Motives explained.— Newspaper Extracts.—Sir F. Bruce's Despatch.—Its Analysis.—Falsity of Gordon's Statements.—How Proved.—Extract from the *Times*.

UPON reaching the city of Kar-sing-foo, I was kindly received by the governor, Yoong-wang, who gave us all quarters in the Wei-wang's palace. This latter chief had gallantly assisted in defeating the Anglo-Manchoo forces on their first attack upon Tait-san; he had been promoted for his services, and was celebrated as a brave leader; yet, singular to relate, he had gone over to the enemy with the city (Haining), to which he had been appointed governor only a few days before my arrival.

Previous to the year 1860, treachery was a thing unknown among the Ti-pings. The baneful effect of British meddling had not been felt; they were successful, therefore the mercenary-minded did not find occasion to desert; neither was the number of chiefs so great as since the successes of 1860-61, nor the Tien-wang's appointment of them so imprudent. Latterly, however, the great extent of country and population included within the limits of Ti-pingdom rendered necessary the employment of a large number of civil and military officers; unfortunately, the king, having much secluded himself from the affairs of state to study religious matters, and being influenced by two or three of his non-military ministers, did not exercise sufficient care in selecting or controlling them. Thus, it came to pass that sometimes not only incompetent, but untrustworthy men were placed in high and important commands; and many of these new officials were neither animated by the patriotism, nor inspired with the religious fervour of the older chiefs. Self-aggrandizement was the motive of such men; and although some of them were brave soldiers, directly they found British hostility was making their cause a failing one, they did not scruple to change sides when they could obtain reward for doing so.

At Kar-sing-foo the Shi-wang left me, after having made arrangements for my return either to that city or Hoo-chow-foo (where I had left the engineer and another man from Soo-chow for the purpose of making shell, casting guns, &c.), and then proceeded on his way to other places, in order to collect men and money with which to rejoin the Chung-wang at Chang-chow-foo.

I found the country under the Yoong-wang's administration in a far better state than the desolate regions through which I had passed on my journey to his city, because the Imperialists and their allies had not yet attacked and ravaged the neighbourhood; although, before I started for Shanghae, they made their appearance.

Christmas Day I spent at Kar-sing-foo. The Ti-pings keep the festival two days before we do; and, if possible, venerate it still more. I made the Yoong-wang a present upon the occasion, and passed the day very happily at his palace, where a grand dinner was given to all the chiefs in the city, after special services had been held in the Heavenly Hall. My friend W—— was present with me, and we mutually declared that we had never enjoyed a better Christmas in our lives. Upon the 25th the Yoong-wang sent his own cooks, attendants, plate, &c., and spread a magnificent dinner at my quarters for all the European and Chinese followers I had in the city.

I found much to admire during my stay with the Yoong-wang. He was one of the best veteran Ti-ping leaders, and all his officers were stanch, trustworthy adherents of the cause. Of one Yu, who was a general of brigade, I became the particular friend, and dined with him nearly every day. This officer had charge of the artillery, and I gave him all the instruction I could in casting shell (which he had just commenced to do), making fusees, and sighting his guns. The organization within the city was so perfect that everything went like clockwork. Bars and bolts were not to be found; for thieves, beggars, or robbers were unknown in Kar-sing-foo. I felt a real happiness in living there, and was quite sorry when I took my departure. Here I found the most splendid building I have ever seen in China. It was a new palace, not quite finished, for the Ting-wang, governor-general of the province; and was a standing proof of the fact that the Ti-pings (had they been allowed to succeed by England) would have restored the arts of China, and especially the public works—all of which have fallen into decay since the era of the Manchoo. In general outline the palace resembled those I have already described as existing at Nankin, but every particle was far more beautiful and costly. Neither in China nor elsewhere have I ever seen such a magnificent work of complicated stone and wood carving. The gorgeous gilding and painting was, of course, in Chinese style; and though very effective and varied, too gaudy for European taste. The carved work was exquisite; I have stood for hours watching either the grotesque or the life-like representations. Many hundreds of sculptors, painters, and artisans were employed, at a very high rate of wages, upon the building; and I found that some of the former were the most celebrated professors of the two arts in China, and had been induced to come to Kar-sing from the most distant parts of the empire. From what I have seen of China, I do not believe such a building has been commenced for many hundred years.

At last the Imperialists came to overthrow all Ti-ping improvement, they having succeeded in capturing Pinbong, the nearest town, with the help of one Major Bailey and a powerful artillery corps, a few days before I left the city.

Previous to setting out for Shanghae, I gave the rowdies their share of prize-money; and although I fully expected that they might cut each other's throats over the coin, I hardly expected the attack they made upon myself and lieutenant, whereby our lives were placed in danger. It seemed that they were aware that we were taking funds to use at Shanghae; and to three of them the temptation to possess themselves of the same became irresistible. Upon receiving their prize-money, furnished with passes I obtained for them, they set forth from the city; but, on reaching the suburbs, the afore-mentioned trio made a halt for the purpose of planning our murder, and mustering up courage to commit the deed by indulging in a copious supply of that ardent spirit—*samshoo*. At length, having cunningly waited until the Yoong-wang had gone outside the city with nearly all his men, in the direction of Pinbong, they returned upon their murderous mission. Fortunately for myself and W——, they went in on the way for another dose of *samshoo*, which made one of them helplessly intoxicated, but the other two had become brave enough to proceed on their errand without him. After obtaining admittance at one of the city gates, they came straight to the Yoong-wang's palace, where we were engaged with an interpreter and one of the chief's secretaries making up a communication I wished to send to the Chung-wang.

A-ling, my own faithful interpreter and companion,

was quite incapacitated by the injury he had received at Wu-see. Although standing directly between him and the enemy's fire when he was struck, the ball passed me and inflicted a severe wound on his left shoulder, passing round the back and lodging on the right shoulder blade. The poor fellow was carried with me to Kar-sing-foo, and suffered much torture from the Chinese doctors, who treated him by thrusting long strips of twisted paper into the wound, and screwing them round until the ball was reached. At last, however, a better doctor was found in the person of the Yoong-wang's own medical attendant, who cut down to the ball and extracted it, much to the patient's relief. A-ling was not sufficiently recovered to accompany me to Shanghae; he therefore remained at Kar-sing-foo, and from that day to the present I have never seen him again, nor probably ever shall, for I believe he was killed when the city subsequently fell into Imperialist hands.

Directly our friends, the rowdies, came into the anteroom in which we were seated, they began to insult myself and lieutenant, knowing that the Yoong-wang was absent and could not arrest them, and that I could not do so either, as my few men were at the Wei-wang's palace in another part of the city. As they were no longer under my command, it was useless ordering them out of the place; I therefore sent an attendant to request the officer left in charge of the city to send a guard to remove them.

At this moment the most forward of the two suddenly drew a revolver and fired it at W——'s head, immediately afterwards turning towards me. Through the smoke I could not see whether my lieutenant had been killed or not; but before the scoundrel could shoot me, I had lodged a bullet in his carcase. Almost at the same instant I heard another shot fired—as it afterwards proved to be, by W——, and saw that my assailant was unable to discharge his revolver, though evidently tugging at the trigger. The other rowdy was now advancing; and as his companion still endeavoured to fire at me, I was compelled to again use my own revolver in self-defence. The would-be murderer now fell dead, while his cowardly friend ran up presenting his pistol by the barrel, and crying, "Don't shoot, don't shoot!"

I really did feel very much inclined to take vengeance upon the fellow, and my Cantonese (who now came up) would certainly have put him to death, had it not been for my lieutenant's request to leave him unharmed. As it was, the wretch seemed nearly frightened out of life, and it was singular how such a coward could have mustered up desperation enough to attempt murder; evidently, he depended upon the determination of his comrade; for, had he been at all resolute, we would assuredly have been killed. Upon examining the dead man's revolver, we found that although the powder had exploded, the bullet had never left the barrel, but had stuck just between it and the revolving chambers, thereby disabling the weapon, and probably saving our lives. We accounted for this singular circumstance by supposing the pistol must have been loaded a long time, and that the powder had consequently lost its strength.

Upon the Yoong-wang's return, I fully intended to give up the surviving ruffian to be dealt with according to the law. Again my brave lieutenant begged him off, blindly and suicidally, as it afterwards appeared, for ultimately he lost his own life through the treacherous act of the wretch he spared. The name of the man who was killed was Hart, an Englishman; his dastardly companion was an American named William Thompson.

I would here give a piece of advice to those who may have the misfortune to fall into the disreputable company of Yankee and cosmopolitan rowdies abroad. Act with quickness and decision, and you will defeat men who are mostly cowards at heart; but if you hesitate or endeavour to temporize, you are a dead man; for these murderous wretches will butcher a fellow-creature with less compunction than people generally feel at killing a fly. I have heard that the man Hart had murdered and robbed several Europeans in the silk districts, and I believe his Yankee confederate is now serving a long term of imprisonment for highway robbery. I engaged the five rowdies in the dark, and it has given me a caution against their *genus* that will never be forgotten.

The Yoong-wang having supplied me with a boat and guide, accompanied by W——, I bid adieu to Ti-pingdom and set out for the Imperialist territory and Shanghae. Between the outposts of the two belligerents I found a considerable tract of country entirely occupied by large bodies of banditti, who preyed alike upon Ti-ping or Imperialist. At one place we had a very narrow escape from falling into their hands, having to run the gauntlet of a large camp along the two banks of a narrow creek, which we successfully did amid a storm of bullets, not one, however, taking effect. These robbers were the wildest and most ferocious looking men I have ever seen, and it was said that they spared neither man, woman, nor child. Since my departure from China this sort of brigandage has become frequent in the country wrested from the Ti-pings.

At last we reached Shanghae, after running past all the Imperialist stations at night, when our small canoe-like boat was not easily discerned. We at once placed ourselves under medical attendance, and for a few days remained perfectly quiet. Within a week, however, I was grieved to hear that my lieutenant had been seized and thrown into prison *by the British Consul* for being in the service of the Ti-pings and having captured a Manchoo vessel, the ungrateful blackguard, Thompson, having given the information which led to his arrest.

Englishmen should be aware of the gross injustice exercised by their authorities in all affairs connected with the Ti-pings, and no more striking example is to be found than in the case of Mr. White, who was sentenced to three years' imprisonment by the Consular Court for doing upon the side of the Ti-pings exactly what Admiral Hope, Generals Staveley, Michael, and Brown, and Major Gordon, Captain Stack, Dr. Marcartney, &c., had done, and were doing, on the side of the Manchoo! He was actually condemned upon the ordinance of *neutrality* of Sir John Bowring, the said ordinance being instituted in 1855, at Hong-kong, to compel British subjects to observe neutrality towards *both* parties to the Chinese internecine war. This neutrality regulation had long been annulled by the acts of the above-mentioned gallant officers on behalf of the Manchoo, yet the Englishman who assisted the Ti-pings, and who was no more guilty of breaking the law than they were, was condemned by this broken and obsolete ordinance, and died (or rather, shall we say, was murdered; for confining a man dangerously ill in such a loathsome den was nothing else) a few days afterwards in his damp and comfortless dungeon! Is this British justice? How long have Englishmen understood "neutrality" to mean all help and military assistance to one belligerent, but open hostilities towards the other, and punishment of its allies? Had England remained neutral, or had she regularly declared war against the Ti-pings, there might be some grounds for prosecuting those who have assisted the latter; but as neither the one policy nor the other has been followed, it is no more right and just to punish those who have assisted the Ti-pings, than those who have assisted the Manchoo. The whole course of the hostilities against the Ti-pings was irregular and illegal, and certainly no one can deny that the British officers already referred to have committed a breach of neutrality quite as much as Mr. White did, even taking Sir John Bowring's ordinance as being in full force. The proof that this argument is correct may be gathered from the fact that when Colonel Sykes, M.P., and the Hon. Mr. Liddel, M.P., brought forward

Mr. White's case in the House of Commons, the Government, in order to protect its agents from prosecution, *then* passed an Order in Council* *condoning the offences against neutrality* of all those who had assisted the Imperialists, but not extending the same favour to those who had assisted the Ti-pings. A piece of more iniquitous and unfair legislature, or more opposed to English feeling, it would be impossible to find. Incredible as it may seem, the present state of the law by which British subjects are governed in China, viz., Sir John Bowring's ordinance of neutrality, is re-established, but *one half is declared null and void*, while the other is made executive by the Order in Council above mentioned, which acts both retrospectively and anticipatory! So that a law which can only exist, or be created, for application towards two belligerents, is here made *ex parte*, and exactly the reverse of what its denomination implies. The wording of this fraudulent document runs thus:—

" 1. Nothing in the said ordinance, made and passed on the 17th day January, 1855, shall extend or apply, or be deemed to have extended or to have been applicable, to any British subject, who, *at any time heretofore*, may have assisted, *or may hereafter assist*, the Government of the Emperor of China. . . . .

" 2. If any subject of Her Majesty . . . shall . . . levy war, or take part in any operations of war against the Emperor of China . . . such person shall be liable to the several penalties mentioned in the said ordinance of the 17th day of January, 1855."

It is thus perfectly evident that the ostensible neutrality ordinance is literally an alliance with one of the two belligerents. The style and title are maintained to satisfy and hoodwink the House of Commons, to deceive them into believing that the Government is pursuing a neutral policy in China, while the clauses tacked to the

---

* This Order in Council was passed on the 9th July, 1864. See "Copy of all Ordinances relating to Neutrality in China," issued in return to an address of the House of Commons, dated May 30, 1864. (Colonel Sykes' motion.)

old ordinance entirely change its every intention, and exclude the least particle of neutrality from its meaning.

If Lords Palmerston and Russell are so destitute of allies in Europe that they cannot restrain themselves from rushing into alliance with the Manchoo Emperor of China (who certainly does not reciprocate their extraordinary ebullition of feeling, and who would take infinite delight in making mincemeat of his officious friends and all their countrymen), why do they not proclaim the stupendous and ever-memorable fact openly? Why do they seek the most opposite and roundabout way of effecting their object by employing chicanery and double dealing to convert an ordinance of neutrality into an importunate treaty of alliance; instead of raising themselves from their slough of shuffling and fraudulent means, by repudiating the false ordinance and duly announcing the barbarous Manchoo despot as their very good ally? Surely the noble lords have not been deterred from giving to the world their wonderful act of statesmanship, by doubting that the contented British public would accept the affair as an agreeable compensation for their questionable European policy? Perhaps, however, it is as well that they have preserved a discreet reticence, because the Emperor of China is no party to the alliance they have thrust upon him, and is particularly liable to issue an edict for the extermination of all foreign devils, the noble lords included, at any moment that may appear auspicious.

The shameful Order in Council of July 9, 1864, is quite sufficient proof that the trial and condemnation of my unfortunate lieutenant was illegal; every British officer who committed a breach of neutrality by assisting the Imperialists was equally liable to prosecution. If the Cabinet Council had not, with oily complacency, justified the acts of their military subordinates in China *after* they were committed to the policy (in fact, when the operations resulting from their illegal intervention had terminated), and *after* Mr. White's death, the friends of the latter would undoubtedly have obtained heavy compensation.

Besides the fact that my medical adviser ordered a change of climate, directly I became aware of my lieutenant's fate I determined to take a trip to England.

Major Gordon, R.E., had retired with his whole force from active co-operation with the Imperialists since the Soo-chow treachery and massacre for which he was responsible. I therefore naturally concluded that he would not resume the position of tool to the sanguinary, faithless Mandarins, who had so completely dishonoured him. As a Christian, an Englishman, and a British officer, I did not think it possible he could himself wish to continue a participator in deeds of revolting barbarity, and I concluded that his Government would immediately recall him, and cease all active support of the blood-thirsty Manchoo. Although my latter supposition proved correct, the former was quite mistaken, as I found after my return to England. In consequence of these circumstances, and the fact that at Shanghae I was altogether unable to execute any of my projects for the service of the Ti-pings, I decided to abandon the sword for the pen, and to fulfil my instructions from the Ti-ping authorities by writing the present work, trusting that I should serve their cause by appealing to the sympathies of the British people, and hoping that foreign hostility would cease, in which case their ultimate success would be a certainty.

The emissaries of the Manchoo, and the hirelings of the slaves of the Manchoo, were not either intelligent or energetic enough to effect the capture of their humble servant, although they amused themselves by attempting to do so not only before but after his departure from China, by one of the overland mail steamers.

Having brought the history of the Ti-ping revolution and my own adventures down to this period, all that now remains to be noticed are the events which have transpired since I sailed away from the Chinese land. Before, however, proceeding with them, it will be necessary to return to the fall of Soo-chow, and resume our chronicle from the occurence of that tragedy.

There is but little doubt that the Ti-pings would have been able to hold their own against the enemy, even taking into consideration all the foreign support the latter received, had the betrayal of Soo-chow never taken place. Although Nankin, as the capital and seat of the Tien-wang's Government, occupied the first political place, Soo-chow, in consequence of the extraordinary measures taken to strengthen it, and its central situation in the Ti-ping dominions, became the principal military position. The capital, though surrounded by the highest and most massive walls in China, and defended by some commanding fortifications, was situated on the extreme verge of the Ti-ping territory, and was the most assailable point, while its resources were far inferior to those of Soo-chow. Moreover, directly the latter city became invested by the Anglo-Manchoo forces, a powerful army was moved within its spacious walls, while the Chung-wang, with his own division, co-operated from the outside. These troops constituted the only Ti-ping army in the field at that time, all the remainder of the forces being employed, according to a mistaken defensive policy, in garrisoning the numerous walled cities throughout their kingdom—tactics ordered by the Tien-wang in opposition to the wishes of the Commander-in-Chief, and which ultimately led to the destruction of the greater number of the garrisons in detail, and the loss not only of Nankin, but all the former possessions of Ti-ping-tien-kwo.

The siege of Soo-chow was prosecuted by an Imperialist army of from 50,000 to 70,000 men, including *General* Gordon's and other foreign contingents, altogether about 6,000 strong. At least 12,000 of the Imperial troops, under General Ching, were well armed with foreign muskets and rifles; they were partly disciplined, and constituted a very effective force, far superior to the usual class of Chinese soldiers. Attached both to the Anglo-Manchoo legions and ordinary troops, were many British officers, and, what was still more useful, a very large supply of every description of artillery. Three or four heavily armed and shallow steamers, together with a great fleet of Mandarin gun-boats, were possessed by the besiegers. Besides all this array of strength in a bad cause, several detachments of *British troops* were moved up from Shanghae, for the ostensible purpose of giving 'moral support' to the murderous intentions of the Manchoo, but, in reality, to afford succour in case the Ti-pings might defeat their assailants—a contingency far from improbable. The troops so fraudulently prostituted (fraudulent, because they were solely organized for the interests of the British taxpayer and not the Manchoo; prostituted, because yellow gold and mercenary motives caused their disgraceful employment) consisted of some companies of the Beloochee Regiment, sent to garrison Quin-san (about 14 miles from Soo-chow), and a force of H. M. 67th Regiment, Royal Artillery, and 22nd B. N. I., commanded by Captain Murray, R.A. Not only were these troops sent to participate in Manchoo atrocities, but the British General (Brown) in command actually took upon himself *to lend* the Imperialists every available piece of artillery on the station, as though the same were his private property and did not belong to the British nation, whose trust he was abusing.

To defend Soo-chow, the Ti-pings had a force of about 40,000 fighting men, including some 8,000 attached to the Chung-wang outside the city. About one third of these troops were the *élite* of the service, while all the others were brave and veteran soldiers. Besides Mo-wang, who was commandant of the city, four or five other Wangs were present; the principal among them was the Nar-wang, who commanded more than half the troops in garrison, his military power being greater than that of the commandant, although he was placed under the orders of the latter.

The Mo and Nar Wangs were the Commander-in-Chief's two principal and favourite generals. The former was a Kwang-si man, and had been the Chung-wang's companion in arms from the commencement of the revolution; the latter chief was a native of Hu-peh, and had joined the Ti-ping cause in the year 1854, since which he had been trained to military tactics by the Chung-wang. Both leaders were associated together in equal rank and command for nearly ten years, and it was always understood among the Ti-pings that they were not only bound together by the strongest ties of adopted brotherhood and friendship, but that they were equally attached to their renowned superior. Yet it will be seen that, in spite of the good influences and kindly associations by which the three were supposed to be governed, the Nar-wang was a man of evil nature, and small, treacherous mind.

After very severe fighting, *General* Gordon managed to effect the capture of all the stockades outside the walls of Soo-chow. This, however, was only accomplished after many a disastrous repulse, and a great loss of men and officers.

The following account of the last assaults upon the fortifications outside the East Gate, which were defended by a few pieces of artillery, is copied from "How the Taepings were driven out of the Provinces of Kiangnan and Che-kiang," and will be found to illustrate the bravery with which the garrison of Soo-chow struggled against irresistible odds:—

"On 27th November, after Major Gordon had all infantry (except 1st Regiment) and artillery assembled at Waiquedong, an order was issued that a night attack should be made on the Low-mun stockade, which formed the key to all other stockades on the east side of Soo-chow.

"White turbans were served out to all soldiers, so as to be able to distinguish them from the rebels, in case it should come to a hand-to-hand fight. About one o'clock Major Gordon himself, accompanied by Majors Howard and Williams, started with about two companies of men towards the stockade, leaving the remainder of the force behind already fallen in, so as to advance at a given signal. Everything seemed quiet, and in fact all thought the plan would succeed. After Gordon and his followers had been advancing close to the stockade, they found everything quiet, and no signs of the guards being aware of an attack. The remainder of the force, therefore, received orders to advance, while the advance guard had succeeded in climbing inside the breast-work. Scarcely were all troops up to the front and a portion of them crossing to reinforce Major Gordon, when the rebels began to direct a fire of grape, canister, and musketry on the force, which made every one shiver. The Quin-san artillery responded vigorously, and it was a fine spectacle to see fiery rockets and red-hot mortar shells going into the rebel works. But the rebels stood it gallantly, and did not retreat an inch. The whole line of stockade which the rebels held seemed one line of fire, and here Major Gordon perceived that Chinese are not fit to fight at night time, for all the begging and encouraging of the European officers could not make the troops try another attack; they seemed afraid of their own shadows. The only chance left therefore was to try and shell the rebels out of their position, and this was done till dawn of day, when Major Gordon, seeing the rebels still resisting desperately, and receiving thousands of reinforcements from the city, made good his retreat, leaving numbers of killed and wounded on the field. This was one of the most bloody fights the force encountered; and, judging by what the Quin-san force lost this night, the rebels must have lost tremendously. Still, the gallant fellows, encouraged by their brave chiefs, held their position manfully against a fire of about 20 guns, flying on them for about three hours. The loss of the Quin-san force was as follows:—Captains Wylie, 2nd Regt.; Christie, 4th Regt.; and Maule, 2nd Regt.; Lieut. King, 2nd Regt., killed. Major Kirkham severely wounded on the head; Lieut. Miok, 4th Regt., wounded in the shoulder; Major Tapp, wounded in the leg; and several more slightly, with about two hundred men killed and wounded. Major Gordon seeing this night attack frustrated, determined to pay the rebels off for it; and shortly after, on the 28th November, at night, all guns, about 46 in number, were brought in position within about 700 yards of this formidable stockade, and the infantry was to fall in near the guns at daylight on 29th of November, to make another attack. The rebels were quite prepared for it, for no sooner did they perceive all the artillery and infantry so near their works, than they hoisted their red flag as a sign that they meant to fight, and not give up this position so easy. Precisely at eight o'clock the signal rocket went up, and at once all guns sent forth their different missiles, some directing their fire on the Low-mun stockade, others directing their fire on the stockades lying to the right and left.

"The rebels seemed to preserve their ammunition, for but very little fire was encountered at first. The 8-inch mortars were playing havoc in the stockades, for every now and then houses, boats, etc., would be blown up in the air, under the cheers of the Imperialist soldiers, of whom thousands, under command of General Ching, were present, to support Gordon's force. Le Futai himself had taken up a place in rear, in one of the Imperial stockades, so as to witness the spectacle. About eleven o'clock the fire from both sides was furious, even the siege artillery had advanced within about one hundred yards of the rebel works, pouring forth grape at the rebels, who, however, inspirited by their noble leader, the Mo-wang, in person, stood it like European soldiers. The 5th Regiment, under Major Brennon, was now ordered up, to storm the stockade on the extreme right, near the Soo-chow creek, the most favourable point to cross the ditch; but although this brave regiment advanced with cheers, and some of the officers succeeded in crossing and trying to climb up the breast-works, the rebels defended this point desperately, and poured volley after volley of musketry into the ranks, so that after about ten minutes' struggle the 5th Regiment was obliged to retire, having lost several officers and men. This attack having failed, the bombardment was renewed with vigour, and orders given to the 3rd Regiment, under Major Morton, to go to the extreme left, to make feint of attack, so as to draw the attention of the rebels on that side. Gordon here succeeded beautifully, for scarcely had Morton and his regiment began to engage the rebels on the left, when the Mo-wang, of course anticipating a real attack on that place, ordered his best men to defend it. Scarcely, however, had the Mo-wang's men moved on, than Major Williams, of the 2nd Regiment, made a dash at the place where Brennon had met with defeat, and not waiting for bridges, but swimming the moat, followed by several officers and men, succeeded in getting inside the breast-work, which no sooner had the rebels perceived than the whole fled in confusion into the Low-mun evacuating all the stockades along the east side of the city, and leaving a good number killed and wounded on the field. The stockades were soon occupied by Imperial troops, and thus Gordon's force was within one hundred yards of the city wall. The Quin-san force, however, paid dearly for this victory, their loss being Lieutenant Jones (Artillery), Lieutenant Williams, 5th Regiment; Captain Aegar, 4th Regiment, killed. Captain Shaml'siffel lost both eyes; and several more officers slightly wounded, with about 100 or 150 soldiers killed and wounded. The ground around the stockades was as if it had been ploughed by the shell, and no doubt the rebels deserve credit for having defended the place so long against such enormous artillery."

Previous to the capture of the last outwork (the Low-mun stockade), and the day after the Anglo-Manchoos had experienced the severe defeat, in attempting to surprise the position at night, the Nar-wang secretly sent messengers into the besiegers' camp, and declared his wish to betray the city into their hands, requesting their co-operation to dispose of the Mo-wang, whose loyalty would be likely to defeat the proposed treachery.

The motive for this defection at a time when the Imperialist successes had come to a stand-still, and when Gordon himself doubted his ability to capture Soo-chow, seems to have been caused by jealousy the Nar-wang entertained against his old friend and companion, the commandant of the city. Besides this, it is probable that the previous treachery of the Americo-Ti-ping, or Burgevine, force had affected the leading traitor and his evilly disposed associates, by giving them the idea that they might arrange terms with the enemy, by which they would not only be able to obtain security for their lives and property (and retire from the now ceaseless hostilities, if not desperate straits, to which the Ti-ping cause was driven), but also receive substantial rewards from the Manchoo.

The Nar-wang's jealousy probably arose from the fact that the Mo-wang was placed over him, as governor of Soo-chow and its dependencies. That he entertained the most bitter animosity against his former friend and comrade is quite certain, for, in order to succeed with his treachery, he went to the dastardly extreme of assassinating him.

We have now to notice the death of the gallant and noble Mo-wang, the fall of Soo-chow into Manchoo hands, and the various events connected therewith. These cannot be more effectually described than in the words of Major Gordon, R. E., and in a review of his report by the *Friend of China*,—about the oldest and most independent paper in the foreign settlements in that country.

MAJOR GORDON'S REPORT. 711

"MEMO. (BY MAJOR GORDON, R.E.) ON THE EVENTS OCCURRING BETWEEN THE 29TH NOVEMBER AND 7TH DECEMBER, 1863." PUBLISHED IN THE "FRIEND OF CHINA," SATURDAY, 12TH DECEMBER, 1863.

"The morning after the failure of the attack by night on the Low-mun stockades, General Ching came to me, and informed me that Nar-wang, Ling-wang, Kong-wang, and Pe-wang, with thirty-five Tien-chwangs* and their followers, had opened negotiations with him for the coming over of their troops; that these men composed their quarter of the garrison, and had possession of four out of the six gates of Soo-chow, viz., She-mun, Tcha-mun, Tche-mun, and Low-mun; and that he had entertained their views, and had already seen Kong-wang. He said that they would have difficulty in disposing of Mo-wang, who was averse to a surrender; but that, if we resumed our attack on the Low-mun stockades, they would endeavour to shut him out of the city. *I consented to the defection with a good deal of pleasure,*† as I considered that, if the rebels fought, we should lose heavily.

"On the night of the 28th November, Chung-wang arrived in the city from Wusich, and was present at the combat of the 29th. His arrival made a change in the state of affairs, and the disaffected were unable to carry out their intention of closing the gates on Mo-wang. They, however, sent over three Tien-chwangs on the night of the 30th November, and proposed to remain neutral if we attacked the city, and would trust us not to touch their men or horses; their men to be distinguished by white turbans. These Tien-chwangs told us that Chung-wang, on his return to the city after his defeat, had proposed to vacate Nankin and Soo-chow, and for the whole Taeping force to go down to Kwang-si; and, in fact, give up the cause.‡ The Mo-wang was averse to this, and proposed to remain and fight it out. I have since learned that he was most anxious to see me, and I think to see what could be done. This I learnt from two Frenchmen who came out after his death, of whom more hereafter. The other Wangs did not meet the Chung-wang's views, as they intended coming over. Chung-wang then left the city, and proceeded to Wusich. General Ching came to me on the 1st December, and asked me if I would like to see Nar-wang. I said no, unless it was necessary, and told Ching at the same time that, if the Futai did not grant the Wangs sufficiently good terms as to induce them

---

* Tien-chwangs, colonels of regiments.

† Italics are by the Author.

‡ This the Chung-wang proposed, if the Tien-wang would authorise such policy. As for his having even thought of "giving up the cause," the assertion is equally false and absurd, which subsequent events have proved.

to come over, *I thought our attack on the city might be foiled,*[*] as we had lost heavily in officers and men on the attack of 27th and 29th November; and a little hitch with the bridge, which had to be seventy yards long, might cause a repulse. I told Ching on the same day that I could not see the necessity of my seeing Nar-wang. He, however, pressed it, and I consented to meet him at the north gate that evening. I accordingly went, and met Nar-wang in General Ching's boat. His first words were 'that he wanted to obtain help from me.' I answered that I was most happy to help him, and then I told him that this proposal to remain neutral would be of no avail, and that I could not accept it, as I should be only deceiving him and his chief if I did so, inasmuch as, if the city fell by assault, I could not, with an undisciplined force such as the one I command, restrain them from looting every one; and that, therefore, unless they could give a gate, it would be better for them to fight, or else vacate the city. I then told the Nar-wang what I thought of the Taeping prospects, and the little chance of success. I said that I wanted to make the Imperialists and rebels good friends (!); that, since the rise of the rebellion, the Imperialists had much changed; and did not dare, from fear of foreign Governments, to perpetrate cruelties as heretofore (?). He said he would see with General Ching what he could do about the city, and that he had no fear of Mo-wang knowing of his having seen me, or of Chung-wang either; that he had enough troops to keep both in check. I then left, and General Ching told me the next day that Nar-wang had decided to see the other Wangs, and to consult on the course of proceeding. The next day, the 3rd December, General Ching told me that Mo-wang had some idea of Nar-wang's negotiations, and wanted to decapitate him, but that Nar-wang was prepared. Nar-wang also sent out to tell General Ching that the other Wangs agreed to come over, that he personally wanted no command, but merely permission to retire to his home with his property; but that some of the other Wangs wanted to get commands of different sorts. He told me further that Nar-wang had some difficulty in seizing Mo-wang. On the morning of the 4th December, General Ching came to me, and told me that Nar-wang had determined and agreed with him to get Mo-wang on the wall of the city, and to throw him down and hand him over to us as a prisoner. I went to General Ching, and told him I must have Mo-wang given over to me; to which he acceded willingly, and in fact joyfully, as he had known him in former days. I then went to the Futai, who was out, but I saw a very high Civil Mandarin named Pow, who undertook to tell the Futai that Mo-wang must be my prisoner. I told him to tell the Futai that I would secure his not giving any more trouble to China. I had not come back five minutes before General Ching sent me over two Frenchmen, who had just come into

---

[*] Here we have Gordon's reasons for approving the treachery.

the lines. They told me that that afternoon, at 2 p.m., all the chiefs had been assembled in Mo-wang's palace, and after a dinner, they had offered up prayers and adjourned to the great court, and having put on their robes, crowns, &c., Mo-wang mounted his throne and began an address, in which he stated their difficulties, and expatiated on the fidelity of the Kwang-si and Canton men. The other Wangs answered him; the discussion got higher and higher, till Kong-wang got up and took off his robe. Mo-wang asked him what he was doing, when Kong-wang drew a dagger and stabbed Mo-wang in the neck.* The Mo-wang fell over the table in front of the throne, and the other Wangs seized him, and decapitated him in the entrance. They then mounted their horses and rode off to their troops; Mo-wang's head being sent to General Ching. Mo-wang's men and the other troops looted the palace. There was no fighting in the city till the morning of the 5th, when the Nar-wang's men had some trouble with the Cantonese, and drove them out of the city, killing some 50 or 60 of them. General Ching's men advanced, and with a small body, took charge of the Low-mun, my men being kept fallen in, as they were under stricter discipline than the Imperialist soldiers are. On the night of the 4th December the rebels all shaved their heads. I went to the Futai, and telling him that it would not do to let my men remain idle, proposed to him to march on Wusieh, if he would give the men compensataion of two months' pay, as they had received no reward since I had taken the command. He objected to it, and I told him if he could only promise, the matter could be settled well. He still objected, and I then told him I should leave *his service*,† and went myself to the city. The Imperialists had some men straying about, but not many. I went straight to Nar-wang's house, and saw him and all the Wangs. I asked him if all was right. He said that everything was satisfactory, and appeared quite secure. He had not seen Ching at the time. I went to Mo-wang's palace, and the body was where it had fallen. I then went out of the city, and arrived in time to see General Ching, who came to me on the part of the Futai to arrange matters. It was now 4 p.m. I told General Ching that I was helpless in the matter. The colonels of regiments and the officers had little authority over them unless they used the harshest means, which they would not do in this question. General Ching offered one month's pay, and the officers refused it. I told Ching that it was not my intention to accept anything; but that I felt that after the length of time the force had been fighting it was only right the men who wished to leave should have the means of doing so. Matters began to look bad, and I at last determined to make the men accept the one month's pay, which I did with difficulty, the men having made an attempt to march

---

* It was a follower of the Nar-wang who first attacked the Mo-wang.

† It will be seen that Gordon here admits he was not an Imperialist officer, but a *local* Mandarin's.

down on the Futai. I then, at the *Futai's request*,* gave orders for the march to Quin-san. Ching told me at this time that the Futai had written to Pekin, and said that he had extended mercy to the Wangs and the rebels. Next morning, after the troops had left, I started for the city, sending the two steamers to Wu-lung-chiao to meet me, as I expected to be able to retake the *Fire Fly* easily from information I had received from the letters in Mo-wang's house, and from some Europeans who were with Mo-wang, and who had escaped. I went to the Low-mun, and there learnt that Nar-wang and the other Wangs and chiefs were to come out and see the Futai at 12, noon, and that the city would then be given over. I thought I had better see Nar-wang before I went out, so I called at his palace, and took him aside and asked him if everything was all right, and if he wanted me to do anything. He said no; that everything was proper. I told him I was going to the Tai-hu; and he said, 'Why not wait? I am coming to see you.' I said it was important business, and that unless he particularly wished it, or thought it necessary, I would not stay. He said very good, and I left. He passed me on his way to the Low-mun very soon after on horseback, with all the Wangs, going, as I supposed, to the Futai. I went then to Mo-wang's palace, and then to the east, or Low-mun, to while away the time, till the steamers could get round from Wai-quai-dung to Wu-lung-chow. From the top of the Low-mun I saw a large crowd of people near Ching's stockades, and thought it was the ceremony of submission going on. A few minutes after, perhaps 12.30 p.m., a large body of Imperial soldiers came up, and passing the gate, rushed cheering into the city, as they generally do into vacated stockades. I thought little of it, more than expressing my disapprobation to some of them. They, however, went on pouring in and firing off their muskets in the air and yelling. Ching then came up,

---

* This sinister statement, when combined with the fact that Gordon soon afterwards returned to companionship and active co-operation with General Ching and the Futai, regardless of his responsibility for the Soo-chow treachery and massacre, certainly affords some ground for the belief that the whole tragedy was previously arranged; that Gordon retired only while compelled to do so by the unanimous expression of indignation among all Europeans (General Brown and other authorities included); and that his future course he originally intended to follow whenever the universal excitement became somewhat abated, and public attention less directed towards himself. Whether this conclusion be correct or otherwise, Major Gordon and his Manchoo friends alone can say; but in either case the Englishman fully deserves the imputation. His first conduct occasioned and made him *particeps* in the treachery; his last act condoned the atrocities at which he had pretended to be disgusted.

and looked rather pale. I asked him if the interview was over, and if it had been satisfactory. He said that Nar-wang had not been to the Futai at all. I said I had seen him going with the others. He said no; that he could not say for certain; but that he thought he had run away. I said I could not make out what for, as I had just seen Nar-wang, and he said everything was all right. I asked Ching if there was any trouble. He said that Nar-wang had demanded the command of 2,000 men, and of half the city of Soo-chow, the division to be a wall, and that the Futai had refused it, and also that he had let some of Chung-wang's men in. *The latter part I knew to be false, but, strange to say, I believed the former portion.* I asked him where Nar-wang could go to. He said that he would not go back to the rebels, but that he would go to some village and settle there. I thought the thing so strange that I asked Dr. Macartney, who was by me, to go to Nar-wang's house, and to see him, and tell him not to fear anything.* Ching then told me that his men alone would be allowed in, and that there would be no looting; and as I knew before that he had his men in good discipline, I had no fear, and therefore rode round the wall with him. He kept on firing vollies in the air, which I remonstrated at, and could not make out the object. He said it was merely to prevent Kwang-si men from doing anything to his men while they were taking possession of the city. I became uneasy about Nar-wang; and at the south, or Pou-mun, I left General Ching and rode off to Nar-wang's palace. I got there at dark, and found it had been gutted. I was then met by Nar-wang's uncle, who asked me to come to his house. Being only with my interpreter, I had no one to send for General Ching, or for my troops; but the entreaties of this Tien-chwang being so great I agreed to do so, and therefore went with Nar-wang's family to his house. When I got there his men were all fallen in, and the streets barricaded. I wanted to send my interpreter for assistance, but they would not let him go. I therefore remained till 2 a.m., keeping away the Imperial looting parties. At 2 a.m. I sent my interpreter and an Imperial soldier, who was with my horse, to get the steamers round to Wai-quai-dung to make the Futai answerable, and also sent for my body guard. After he had started, the man who went with him came back and said he had been beheaded by the Imperialists. I remained till 4 a.m., and then went out to send orders to the steamers myself. *I was taken by the Imperialists and detained an hour.* At last I got to the Low-mun, and sent the body guard to the Nar-wang's house, but it was too late, the Imperialists had entered and gutted it. I then went to the Low-mun, and met there General Ching, to whom I gave my opinion. He

---

* This statement is quite sufficient to make Gordon entirely responsible for every circumstance connected with the surrender of Soo-chow. He made all the assurances and guarantees, it appears, but never troubled himself to insure their observance, although he had complete power to do so.

was most anxious to excuse himself, but I did not listen to him. At this time I did not know that the Wangs had been beheaded. I then went down to Ching's stockades, and met Major Baily, commanding Ching's artillery there. He said that General Ching was very much put out; that the Futai had ordered him to execute the Wangs, and had given orders to the troops to enter the city, that he had lost face, &c. Baily then told me that he had Nar-wang's son, and brought him to me. I refused any communication with General Ching, Nar-wang's son came to my boat, and, pointing to the other side, said it was there that the Wangs had been executed. I went over, and recognised Kong-wang's, Nar-wang's, Sieh-wang's, and Sung-wang's heads, but the body of Nar-wang was not to be seen, having been buried. I took, at the son's request, Nar-wang's head. *The bodies had been cut down the chest, and the wounds on the head were most horrible, showing the brutality of the executioners.* I then was waiting for the steamers, as I had heard that there were some high persons still in custody, and I thought that I could frighten the Futai into giving them up. He, however, heard of my arrival, and went off to the city. *I left him a note telling him my opinion, and then moved off with the steamers to Quin-san.** I received, just before leaving, a letter from Futzu-quai, telling me that a chief had come over with 3,000 men to my officer in command; and that he, the officer in command, had received them. I sent orders to him to inform the chief of the treachery, and to let him go with his men and arms, if he liked, or else to bring his troops to Quin-san.

"This is a brief summary of the late events, *which will prove to the Imperial Government a most fatal blow.* I imagine that the Futai and General Ching arranged this matter, and know that it is viewed by the mass of Mandarins with disgust.

"Nar-wang's son tells me that Chung-wang was willing to come over; and that all the people in the silk districts are the same; but how to come they know not. Is not this a time for foreign governments to come forward and arrange the terms? The power is in this force, if the authority from Pekin is given to it to act under some *honest* Chinaman. What is now to be feared is that foreigners will join the rebels, and will thus cause the war to linger on to the extermination of the unfortunate people on

---

* Here is another extraordinary admission; for, though Gordon's honour was pledged to preserve the lives and property of the deceived traitors, he very coolly took himself off to Quin-san, without making the slightest exertion to save the unfortunate people who had trusted to his word as a British officer. Subsequent to this event hundreds and thousands of the betrayed garrison were cruelly put to death. Who is responsible for the massacre—the Manchoos, who followed their natural instincts and barbarous laws, or the British officer, who obtained the surrender, guaranteed the terms, and then quietly permitted the violation of his pledges?

whom the burden falls, and to the detriment of trade of every sort. That the rebels really do not possess the qualities of government cannot be doubted. They merely hold cities, and let the villages govern themselves. The head chief may know something of the Christian religion, but I will answer for it that nine-tenths of the rebels have no real ideas on the subject. It is sincerely to be hoped that the Government will interfere at this time.* "C. E. GORDON, Major Commanding.

"P.S. Prince F. de Wittgenstein was present at most of the above occurrences, and can vouch for the correctness of the same."

"'THE FRIEND OF CHINA,' SATURDAY, OCT. 12, 1863."

"We publish to-day a document which we consider one of the most remarkable that it has been our good or evil fortune to peruse for many a day. Emanating as it does from a man of Gordon's ability and position, we have been much more than disappointed. How we have been so, let our readers judge.

"The exact position of the major is, it would appear, that of Adjutant of Quin-san, though possessing less power than General Ching, whose faculty of lying seems to have the wonderful power (by attraction we suppose) of giving credence; though the major tells us that he knew the rogue *was* lying. We give the major's own words, 'the latter part I *knew* to be *false;* but, strange to say, I believed the former portion.'

"This General Ching, this cowardly liar, it was who voted as the right-hand man on all occasions concerning the conduct of negotiating with the rebels. The major tells us that the Taeping Wangs had opened negotiations with Ching for the surrender of at least four gates of the city. We suppose this was before the 29th of November. On the 4th of December we learn of Ching's being *joyful* at the prospect of the Mo-wang falling into the hands of Major Gordon, and on the same day we hear of his reception of the unhappy Wang's head.

"Ching next appears as Envoy of the Futai 'to arrange matters,' we suppose, for the surrender of the city. Here the major slips out of the 'matter' by declaring himself 'helpless,' and this, after he had assured the Nar-wang that he wanted to make the Imperialists and Taepings friends, and only wanted possession of 'a gate' to prevent looting everybody.

"Major Gordon does not tell us *why*, at the 'supreme' moment of the taking of Soo-chow, he was so anxious to get possession of the *Fire Fly.* We beg to call our readers' attention to the following statement:—'I

---

*This concluding paragraph is simply a tissue of mendacity and absurdity. Does the dishonoured officer intend to qualify the treacherous destruction of *his* prisoners, by introducing the totally irrelevant opinion that they have no Government, or "real ideas" of Christianity?

thought I had better see Nar-wang before I went out, so I called at his palace, and took him aside, and asked him if everything was all right, and if he wanted me to do anything. He said no; that everything was proper. I told him I was going to the Tai-hu; and he said, "*Why not* wait? I am coming to see you at the meeting of the Wangs," as he *supposed*, at the Futai's.' Why was Major Gordon absent? Why did he not make it his business to see that the assurances which he had given to the Nar-wang were carried out?

"The major tells us that he got 'uneasy' when he found that Nar-wang's palace had been gutted; however, his remaining till 4 o'clock next morning where he was (though why he did not go himself for his body-guard instead of sending his servant he has not told us) hardly seems to prove this assertion; but the affair of his steamers being of so great a consequence, he sends an assistant 'to send orders to them,' when he is taken and detained by the Imperialists for an hour. (General Ching was, of course, busy just at that moment, and Major Gordon's detention was most opportune.) The screaming farce of General Ching's losing face, and Major Gordon's refusal to have anything to do with him, here opportunely follows the tragedy—(one likes to laugh after the heavy business!). The idea of frightening the Futai is nicely got over. The latter gentleman ——*goes into the city*, where, of course, he *couldn't* be frightened! The major takes a steamer and goes off to Quin-san.

"*Leaving a note* for the Futai.

"Our readers have the major's letter before them, and they can judge for themselves whether our analysis be correct or not. Our own opinion is that the major—owing to his recent losses, fearing a repulse if the city of Soo-chow had then been attacked, and finding occasion of taking it himself by treachery, and yet desiring to shield himself from the infamy of such a transaction—would have acted precisely as he declares he *has* done.

"Though a considerable reader of history, our recollection does not supply a parallel to the infamous treachery practised upon the unsuspecting Taeping chiefs. The conduct of Pizarro, in Peru, was nothing in comparison. One Inca, and a room full of treasure, is a small affair when compared with the confiding Princes of Soo-chow. Now, we ask all right-minded men to take Major Gordon's statement to Nar-wang, which we quote literally:—'I said that I wanted to make the Imperialists and rebels good friends. That since the rise of the rebellion the Imperialists had been much changed; and did not dare, from fear of the foreign Governments, to perpetrate cruelties as heretofore.' And compare his account of the atrocities committed upon the Princes of Kong, Nar, Seih, and Sung.

"Our review of these facts is based upon Major Gordon's own statements; and if he does not find means of extrication, we have placed him upon a pinnacle of infamy whence he shall not readily descend. From the moment Major Gordon first became *particeps* in the affair of the surrender with General Ching (the very ideal of a Manchoo liar), he should have stood between the Manchoo butcher of a Futai and his confiding victims, and, as a true soldier (the soul of honour), yielding his life rather than have exposed himself to the execration of all society as a traitor of the deepest dye.

"Major Gordon will, no doubt, think us severe upon himself; but we assure him that what we have said is by no means meant as a personal attack. We are simply commenting upon his own statement of what has lately occurred at Soo-chow. It may possibly be true that he has been victimized by the liar, Ching, and the Futai. We are half inclined to think such to be the case, considering his simplicity in telling us, on the authority of the Nar-wang's son, that 'Chung-wang was willing to come over, and that all the people in the silk districts are the same.' He also tells us that the 'rebels do not possess the qualities of government.' That they actually allow 'villages to govern themselves;' and that while the 'head chief *may* know *something* of the Christian religion, nine-tenths of the rebels have no real ideas on the subject.'

"We are rather astonished at Major Gordon's information as to this point. We have been for many years in China. We have seen the way in which the cherished temples and idols of the Manchoos have been treated by the Taepings; and it is rather late in the day to tell us what rebel 'ideas' are on the subject of the Christian religion.

"In conclusion, Major Gordon hopes for the interference of the 'Government.' He means, of course, the *English* Government. If there were anything wanting to make Major Gordon contemptible in the eyes of all Europe and America, it was this last phrase. What! the English Government interfere to prop up the Manchoos after the statement of what Major Gordon says has occurred at Soo-chow! Major Gordon! We thought you not only an English officer in Chinese employ, but we considered you an honourable subject of our Sovereign, yet it seems you penned this sentence after the atrocious perfidy of Soo-chow—'It is sincerely to be hoped that the Government [English] will interfere at this time.'

"If he had not added this last sentence we could have pardoned Major Gordon everything. What! the Government of Englishmen to sustain a Government which, by Major Gordon's own showing, is so perfidious that we can make no possible comparison! There is no Englishman in this or any other part of the world who will not blush for Gordon, or the era in which it was found that an Englishman advocated assistance for a Government which has violated every treaty, and even the most sacred obligations recognised among men.

"As for ourselves, we are not military adventurers, and, perhaps, cannot understand how *any stratagem* may be fair 'in war as in love,' but we do hereby protest against a violation of a solemn word of honour given. Major Gordon must clear himself, or he will go down to posterity not only 'unhonoured and unsung,' but as a wretch who sold blood to General Ching and the present Futai of Kiang-nan.

"Major Gordon, in telling us that, or, in fact, asking the question, viz., 'Is this not the time for foreign Governments to come forward and arrange terms?' looks as though he fancied foreign Governments *could* entertain the idea of an honest Chinaman under authority from Pekin. But in spite of the testimony of the Prince Wittgenstein, or any other potentate, we are inclined to believe that unfortunate Taepingdom has little to learn from Manchoo morality, and still less from mercenary soldiers, whose honour is bought and sold!"

Some people may consider the article last quoted as too severe upon Gordon—perhaps they may change their opinion after perusing the following extracts from a narrative of a journey to Soo-chow, by the sub-editor of the *Friend of China*, soon after the great treachery. I prefer giving this authenticated description by an eye-witness, to narrating the facts myself, because I did not enter Soo-chow after its betrayal, and cannot, therefore, vouch for the subsequent massacre (and other disputed points) from my own personal observations, although otherwise I have the strongest proof that the reported atrocities were perpetrated:—

"TO SOO-CHOW AND BACK, VIA QUIN-SAN.

"After leaving Shanghae, our route (or creek) lay through a low, flat country, intersected by canals innumerable in all directions; the richest land in China, stretching away to the very horizon, unbroken to view, except by countless graves, commemorative arches, and heaps of ruins. The weather, though superb, seemed oppressive, from the utter abandonment of the country; not a soul was to be seen as far as the eye could reach, and the endless fields of neglected and fallow ground (once the garden of China) deepened that air of sadness which winter always seems to wear in the country. Though ashore the desolation is complete, not so on the water; Mandarin squeeze stations have sprung up in all directions.

"At Wong-doo we were actually stopped, and 400 cash demanded from our Louda. Our indignation getting the better of us, we did then and there write our protest against thievery upon the rogue's ribs; and in round, legible characters, too, we did all *we* could to teach *this* Manchoo robber that the higher the squeeze, the less commerce, and the less commerce will certainly produce less revenue. When will all Manchoos, Morrill tariff men, &c., learn this lesson?

"There were, besides, a few wretches fishing by means of cormorants (so often described that I will say nothing about it), making up the sum total of population. At last, Quin-san pagoda became visible; and after a short run over the country (our boat following), we reached the city.

"Of course, we went to see the 'lion' of the place. He seemed to be in a consumedly bad humour; but, nevertheless, granted us passes for Soo-chow. Dropping metaphor, Major Gordon impressed us as a very young man (say thirty) *without* an 'old head on his shoulders.' We suppose coolness is a quality which he constantly displays on the field; he certainly displayed it in his own house when we called upon him.

"On the 18th December, after a run of fifteen miles from Quin-san, we reached the stockades outside the city of Soo-chow. They had evidently been the scene of a fierce encounter. Innumerable shot (solid) in their interiors told the tale of carnage; and numerous unburied corpses were lying about in all directions, in spite of the number which had been disposed of in the creeks. As we drank our tea that evening, we studiously avoided any remark on *this* subject. Four or five miles more brought us to the lofty walls of Soo-chow. Inside the gate (Lo-mun) an immense stone wall and water-gate (as protecting the outer bastion) will ever stand a monument of Taeping energy. Of course, our first move was to see the 'lion' of Soo-chow, the *in*-famous Futai. The palace of this magnate (the former Ya-mun of the Chung-wang) really 'impressed' us as something worthy of the 'Mings,' in which style it is erected.

"We have visited hundreds of such structures, but the Soo-chow pagoda is certainly the finest we have ever seen. In ascending we counted 220 steps, and judged the height to be from 150 to 170 feet from base to summit. It is nine stories high (as usual, an odd number); but when we reached the top, the view there presented well repaid our trouble. The vast city lay at our feet—the Venice of China—intersected with hundreds of canals, pagodas, and temples (in the tent-like style of the Chinese), relieving the otherwise monotonous view of infinite tiled roofs.

"In many places the city was obscured by the burning of houses, set on fire by the Imperialist soldiers.

"On the 19th December, having sent our cards before us, we called upon General Ching. While waiting for his appearance, we had time to examine a magnificent English clock (looted from Mo-wang's palace), which formed the main ornament of the 'reception-hall.'

"Over the dial was a fountain of water (in glass), and under it a pastoral scene, with moving figures of impossible shepherds and shepherdesses, worthy of Arcadia—all moved by the mechanical contrivances provided in the clock itself. At last Ching entered, and at first took us for a second edition of General Brown, for he immediately entered upon a defence of Le Futai. After telling him who we really were, he suddenly became so reserved that we beat a polite retreat (for the fate of the Taeping-wangs had by no means faded from our memory).

"As it was still noon, we determined on a visit to the residence of Chung-wang's secretary in the neighbourhood.

"On our arrival we found that the house had not only been looted, but that the valuable furniture it contained had been literally smashed to atoms by the Imperialist soldiery.

"In the rear we discovered a large hall, over the entrance of which a rebel tablet still remained—'Teen-foo-dong'—'Hall of the Heavenly Father.' But what really astonished us was to find on the walls a complete set of elegant lithograph engravings, which Roman Catholics are accustomed to call the 'stations,' a series of pictures representing the sad journey of Jesus from the house of Pilate to His place of execution.

"One of the pictures we became possessed of, and we shall ever keep it as the most precious *souvenir* of our trip to Soo-chow; for we think that the affecting story of Jesus' passion and death was *appreciated* by these *Missionary-forsaken* patriots.

"It certainly shows that a high Taeping official loved to contemplate the various scenes of that awful tragedy (for principle's sake) over which the world, till the end of time, shall weep the bitter tears of violated right and triumphant wrong.

"*20th Dec.*—The day being fine, we determined to have a look at the steamers *Feilong* and *Sycee.* A smart walk to the Padi-cho gate brought us to the 'fifty-two arched bridge,' where we saw the heavy artillery just outside.

"We looked with regret upon those splendid 'peace-makers,' that *they* should have been *loaned* to the butcher of Soo-chow—that *they* should be the property of the British Government—were thoughts upon which we need make no comment.

"Captain Baily in charge, and very creditably too! His hospitality is the last pleasant impression we had of Soo-chow, if we omit the feeling of relief we experienced when once outside of its walls on our way to Shanghae.

"*21st Dec.*—On learning (to our surprise) that the *locale* of the 'execution ground' was neither more nor less than the court-yard of the '*Shing-s-tah,*' 'twin pagodas,' where the unhappy rebels had paid with the forfeit of their lives for trusting in the word of honour of their unprincipled assailants, we determined on a trip thither. On our arrival, we examined several most ancient tablets of stone, whence we gathered that these pagodas were erected long anterior to the Ming dynasty (*i.e.* reign of Tai Ching, dynasty of Sung); but we will not detain our readers with antiquarian trifles. On entering the court-yard (about half an acre) we found the ground *soaked* with HUMAN BLOOD! the creek forming its drain was still (after twenty days of slaughter) reddish with blood, as the officers of Dr. Macartney's force can testify. The ground for three feet deep stunk with blood (and the best blood of China); though the weather, except at noonday, did not favour the corruption of animal particles, Soo-chow being situated in lat. 31° 23′ 25″ N., and long. 120° 25′ E.; consequently of rather a warm climate even in winter.

"Our Chinese informants told us that 30,000 rebels had been led to these shambles, and executed. We had proofs enough to know that the number was enormous; we have it on authority of an European *eye-witness* that this creek was so full of decapitated rebels that the Mandarins employed boatmen to clean it, by pushing the bodies with boat-hooks outside of the city into the principal stream.

"We quitted the 'execution ground' (travellers will know it by the 'twin towers'), faint at these horrible proofs of *human* butchery which had met our view, and overcome with emotion. Was it for *this* that Englishmen fought? Was it for this that English guns had been loaned by the representatives of the British people? Was it for *this* that the 'first nation of the world' and the two *Scotchmen*, Gordon and Dr. Macartney, had fought?

"Let the spirit of Robert Bruce forbid it! Let the noble sons of Scotia contemn it; and all Christendom, in the name of . . . . liberty, protest against the unspeakable perfidy, the horrible treachery, and brutal butchery of Soo-chow!

"*22nd Dec.*—Though the experiences of yesterday made us long to leave Soo-chow, we determined to visit the ruins of Mo-wang's palace; though completely burned, it had evidently covered an immense area of several acres; huge bronzes half melted obstructed the passage, and only a solitary drum stood sentinel at the entrance.

"It was with a melancholy satisfaction that we gazed at the wreck of his palace.

"Among so many traitors (his brother Wangs) he had been *true* to his flag. HE knew what Manchoo honour meant, and his death by the hands of Taeping traitors is his eulogium. If his spirit *can* visit this world of ours, we must rejoice that the Manchoos have not profited (even in money) by his destruction.

"If the infamous barbarity of the Futai *can* be excused; if his atrocious violation of justice and right can be pardoned; if there is any possible Jesuitical ground of justification for his immeasurable atrocities, it is this—he betrayed the betrayers of their own cause: he was a traitor to traitors, and has broken faith with the recreant Wangs.

"Depressed in spirit, we hurried from the ruins of Mo-wang's palace to our boat, and instantly gave orders to our crew to get under weigh for Shanghae.

"Hardly had we quitted the gate, when a letter was placed in our hands by a trusty agent from Chung-wang, dated Kia-ching-foo; what were our feelings in perusing it and finding these words:—' You foreigners are like the Manchoos; you have no honour! you have deceived us!' We, as a foreigner, felt all the bitterness herein contained. We, a personal friend of his, blushed for our nationality in being compared to perfidious Manchoos!

"We candidly avow it, if we thought that the sword was really stronger than the pen, we would have girded it on, and be one more 'witness' to the glorious cause of liberty! We should like to prove to the Taepings that European nations are not *all* unprincipled liars, devoid of every virtue recognised by men, and that sacred volume which teaches a morality of which one would think they were ignorant. So much for our trip to Soo-choo and back. "S. E. F. O. C."

The dreadful Soo-chow tragedy may be considered the terminating point of that unrighteous period of British policy commencing with the organization of the Anglo-Manchoo flotilla; the hiring out of Major Gordon and other officers; and the making of those infamous Orders in Council authorizing military and naval support of the Manchoo, while it has since been declared that an ordinance of neutrality was in force all the time! That the terrible result of their policy would have so far influenced the supposed Christian and civilized principles of those members of Lord Palmerston's Government who originated it, as to make them admit their mistake with worthy humility, and seek to rectify the wrong already done by an essay towards the much easier path of right, is very doubtful. However, the spirit of Englishmen could no longer be restrained, and the Government were driven to rescind their former Orders in Council (placing the forces of England at the evil disposal of the Manchoo) by the unanimous voice of the Parliamentary representatives of the people.

Englishmen may thus flatter themselves that they have repudiated the atrocities which they had occasioned; but the very fact that their mistaken policy entirely caused such deplorable results, makes them morally responsible for the same. Still the national complicity *may* be glossed over. The participation of the agents on the spot, and especially the principal, Gordon, cannot, by any stretch of imagination, be excused.

If Major Gordon had resigned his employment in the service of the local servant of the Manchoo Government, he might, by thus immediately forsaking his brother generals when he became involved in their deeds of blood and treachery, have saved his honour from suspicion and his name from everlasting infamy. If he had possessed the least particle of self-respect, humanity, or Christian feeling, he could not possibly have followed any other course. Incredible as the fact must ever seem to right-minded Englishmen, Major Gordon, after craftily passing two months at Quin-san, still in command of the Anglo-Manchoo contingent, and still receiving his pay from his employer, resumed active service with those sanguinary monsters and consummate betrayers, General Ching and the Futai Le.

Men judge by actions, but despise words. Gordon has *said* that his disgust was something stupendous at the revolting barbarities perpetrated by his friends; yet the sentiment did not make him refuse their pay, neither did it prevent his return to participate in fresh atrocities within two months, nor shock him sufficiently to stay his early reconciliation with the blood-stained wretches who had smeared him with the same unfading and polluting mark. Of course, before returning to active service, the British officer induced his Manchoo master to indite a cunningly worded Chinese despatch, setting forth that he was not actually concerned in the massacre of the confiding Soo-chow victims. Naturally enough, to retain the services of Major Gordon (and the consequent assistance of the British Government), without which they would still have been powerless before the Ti-pings, the Manchoos, through Futai Le, verbosely declared all that was required. Shortly afterwards, besides resuming his employment, the major responded by writing an official letter, in which he forgot his former disgust, and had the singular audacity not only to exonerate the Futai from blame for his unparalleled atrocities, but to request Sir F. Bruce not to make any further complaint about the same *—events that had seriously stained the honour of Great Britain, and which only the most prompt and unqualified repudiation, together with entire cessation of further countenance and help to the Manchoo, could either erase from her scutcheon, or clear her policy from the imputation of complicity.

Unfortunately for the reputation of Major Gordon, since his elevation to the position of General of Futai Le's Anglo mercenaries, he had been too much accustomed to intrigue and encouragement of treachery to have felt a proper indignation at the Soo-chow affair; and it is possible he might have had some knowledge of the planned perfidy before it was put into execution, and so was not sufficiently horrified to throw up his 1,200 taels (£400) per month. Gordon's behaviour in the treachery of the Burgevine-Ti-ping legion is one specimen, and a very strong one too, of the conduct referred to. He induced the Europeans who went over to him to desert the Ti-ping cause by his promises of office, bribes, and safe conduct to Shanghae for such as were tired of fighting. Some mistaken individuals have ascribed this proceeding to the humane disposition of the man who condoned the ruthless massacre of his paroled prisoners, who assisted as a principal agent in the vast destruction of life and desolation of country during the unjustifiable British hostilities against the Ti-pings, and who never put himself to the trouble of saving the lives of those he assisted to vanquish. It must be a rather lax code of military honour which could reflect any *credit* on Gordon for rewarding many of the traitors (mostly low

---

* See Inclosure 1 in No. 9, "Return to an Address of the Honourable House of Commons," dated July 1, 1864:—for "Copies of Communications which have passed between Sir F. Bruce and Colonel Gordon."

American rowdies), by bestowing upon them various commands in his own force; and he—supposed to be an English officer and gentleman—with open arms receiving them as his messmates and brother officers: even less creditable is the fact that he obtained pecuniary reward for those whom he did not make his *friends*.

The letter written to Sir F. Bruce by Gordon as a justification for his fresh alliance with the Futai Le, appears in the Parliamentary Papers, as noticed by the foot-note on the preceding page. This document is so important, as showing the character of Gordon's connection with the Imperialists, that I quote it in full, and then subject it to a close analysis.

"INCLOSURE 1 in No. 9.
"*Major Gordon, R.E., to Sir F. Bruce.*
"Soo-chow, February 6, 1864.

" My dear Sir Frederick Bruce,—

Par. 1.—" *In consequence of the danger which will arise by my delaying inaction with the force any longer in a state of uncertainty, I have arranged with the Footae* to issue a proclamation (which he will send to you), clearing me of any participation in the late execution of the Wangs, and have determined to act immediately."

Par. 2.—" The reasons which actuate me are as follows :—*I know of a certainty that Burgevine meditates a return to the rebels; that there are upwards of 300 Europeans ready to join them, of no character; and that the Footae will not accept another British officer if I leave the service*, and therefore the Government may have some foreigner put in, or else the force put under men of Ward's and Burgevine's stamp, of whose action at times we should never feel certain."

Par. 3.—" *I am aware that I am open to very grave censure for the course I am about to pursue;* but in the absence of advice, *and knowing as I do that the Peking authorities will support the Footae in what he has done, I have made up my mind to run the risk.* If I followed my own desire I should leave now, as I have escaped unscathed and been wonderfully successful. *But the rabble, called the Quin-san force, is a dangerous body,* and it will be my duty to see that it is dissolved as quietly as possible, and that, while in course of dissolution, it should serve to benefit the Imperial Government."

Par. 4.—" *I do not apprehend the rebellion will last six months longer if I take the field. It may take six years if I leave,* and the Government does *not support the Imperialists.* I propose to cut through the heart of the rebellion, and to divide it into two parts by the capture of Ye-sing and Liyang."

Par. 5.—"If the course I am about to pursue meets your approbation, I shall be glad to hear; but, if not, shall expect to be well rebuked. However, *I know that I am not actuated by personal considerations, but merely as I think will be most conducive to the interests of our Government.*

"The Footae does not want the force to move against Nankin I imagine, as Tseng-kwo-fan has the wish to capture it himself."

Par. 6.—"*The Footae, if he is to be believed, has some extenuating circumstances in his favour, for his action;* and although I feel deeply on the subject, I think that we can scarcely expect the same discernment that we should from an European governor.

"This letter will relieve you from any responsibility on this matter, and thanking you very much for your kind letter, which I will answer shortly, I am, &c.,

(Signed) "C. G. GORDON."

Par. 7.—"P.S. *If you would let the matter drop,* and make me responsible for my action in the matter, *I think it would be more conducive to our good relations with the Pekin Government than pressing them to punish or degrade the Footae.*

"C. G. G."

NOTE.—The parts of the letter in italics are those subjected to review.

Analysis of Major Gordon's Letter.

Par. 1. Now, with regard to this first premise, what right had Major Gordon to make a prospect of danger to the Imperialists a pretext to resume *friendship* and *alliance* with the faithless and barbarous wretches who had already implicated him in their revolting atrocities? Major Gordon's duty as a British officer, specially executing the policy of his Government, and leaving it responsible for his conduct, was simple and palpable. To avoid the deathless guilt of participation in the Soo-chow treachery and massacre, he should have repudiated both. What course did he pursue? He wrote and talked a great deal about disgust, indignation, horror, &c., but never took any *action* to fulfil his otherwise worthless protestations. By the only part we find he really performed and did not merely talk, it appears that he actually had the unparalleled audacity, folly, or knavishness, to *arrange* terms with the Futai, although any intercourse, arrangement, or communication whatever, upon a friendly basis constituted a direct condonation and approval of the atrocities which would have made an unqualified separation from *all* interests and future connection imperative to any man of honour, humanity, or Christian principle.

Par. 2. The assertion that Gordon *knew for a certainty* that Burgevine intended to rejoin the Ti-pings, is best controverted by the following extract from the *Friend of China*, Shanghae newspaper (issue of September 29, 1864), which, being one of the principal organs among a population of Europeans and Americans, scarcely numbering 2,000 souls, may be credited for being well informed upon affairs in their midst; moreover, the editor was personally acquainted with Burgevine, and was aware, equally with myself, that he entertained no enthusiasm for the Ti-ping cause.

The article referred to states :—

"As for Gordon's assertion to Sir F. Bruce that he knew for a certainty Burgevine meditated a return to the rebels, and that upwards of 300 Europeans—[This estimate is supremely absurd. During the whole time Burgevine was with the Ti-pings, and when everything seemed to favour his enterprise, he could never obtain more than one-third of 300 Europeans]—of no character, intended to join him. This being written in February last, we know for a greater certainty that, at that time, neither did Burgevine meditate anything of the kind, nor were there thirty—the tenth of 300—Europeans in this quarter available for any such game. And though Gordon may have been under an impression that he was writing truth when he made this assertion, his common sense might have told him the thing was as improbable as it has eventually proved incorrect. We say he *may* have been under an impression that he was writing truth. We may not refrain, however, from saying we doubt it. Why, Gordon knew as well as we did that the rebels never sought the assistance of foreigners, did not care to see them in their ranks, and were always jealous of them. Gordon knew right well, moreover, that when Burgevine left Soo-chow he left the rebel service for ever; that he was sick and disgusted with it; and if ever he meditated anything afterwards, it was operation rather as an independent buccaneer than as a Ti-ping general. The assertion—yarn, wilful lie, or whatever it shall be called—did very well, however, in the place it was intended for, viz. Pekin, a place so far away from the scene of action, that there was no possibility of contravening it at the time."

Besides the facts—incontrovertible to those acquainted with the case—in the above refutation of Gordon's "reasons" for his fresh blood-alliance with that cold-blooded murderer, the Futai, another strong argument may be proved against his veracity:—

1. We may be quite sure that the Ti-pings would never have accepted a second time the services of the man who had once betrayed them. From my own knowledge of the opinions entertained by the Chung-wang, I am quite assured on this point. 2. Then with respect to the probable action of Burgevine himself. Having deserted the Ti-ping cause before Soo-chow had fallen, and while its prospects were in vastly more favourable condition than at the period of Gordon's statement, he would, consequently, never be disposed to join when its circumstances had become desperate. 3. As for the "300 of no character," mercenaries would certainly not espouse a failing movement, which, in fact, had become still more "unprofitable" than when the Burgevine-Ti-ping legionaries ran away because, even at that time, they found no sufficient inducement to remain. These propositions cannot fail to damage the "reasons" given by Gordon, because they show that all common sense and reason points to an exactly opposite conclusion. Thus we find that logic reverses Gordon's "reasons," while facts entirely prove the falseness of his statements. The principal argument is the fact that Burgevine *did not* join the Ti-ping, and the mythical "300" were never more heard about.

Par. 3. This paragraph of Gordon's letter seems to contain about the most severe condemnation of his "reasons" that it would be possible to imagine. He states that "he is open to very grave censure for the course he was about to pursue," and that, "knowing the Pekin authorities will support the Futai in what he has done," he had made up his mind to "run the risk;" that is to say, he knew that the Manchoo Government would approve the treachery and massacre in which the Futai had involved him; yet such was his obliquity of principle that he actually used as a reason to resume the sanguinary alliance the very fact which should have made his separation from the Manchoo still more imperative.

With regard to the ungenerous, if not treacherous, manner in which Gordon, behind their backs, termed his comrades "the rabble," it is well noticed in the quotation from the *Hong-Kong Daily Press*, at the end of this analysis.

Par. 4. This section of the letter exhibits a very pretty ebullition of overweening self-conceit. If the writer takes the field again, the rebellion cannot last "six months;" without that mighty warrior's hostility, it would last "six years." Well, Bombastes did take the field, but the "rebellion" still flourishes. It will be seen that the blower of his own trumpet modestly puffs his value at only twelve times that of any other officer who might conduct the operations against the Ti-ping.

Par. 5. Concerning this protestation of disinterested motives—"I know that I am not actuated by personal considerations"—I beg to refer my readers to the concluding paragraph of the analysis, when they will find that this statement is no less questionable than others by the same author. With regard to Gordon's excessive care of the "interests of our Government," and his declaration (in paragraph 2 of the letter), "that the Futai will not accept another British officer if I leave the service," the article in the *Friend of China*, already quoted, continues from where we left off:—" And just as likely to be true was the statement that the Futai would not accept another *British* officer if he, Gordon, left the Chinese service. How did Gordon learn that fact, or that story? What can there be in *British* officers that they should be so repugnant to the Deputy Viceroy? What Gordon really meant was :—If I leave, 'the Government' will not find such a faithful tool in any one else as they have found in me."

Par. 6. In this part of the precious letter it is shamelessly declared that "the Futai has extenuating circumstances in his favour" for breaking faith and cruelly butchering the defenceless prisoners at Soo-chow, who solely surrendered upon the terms guaranteed by Gordon himself.

Par. 7. This postscript makes a fitting conclusion to the bad principle and illogical reasoning of the letter we have reviewed. Gordon has the audacity to request that the " matter"—affecting not only his own character, for that is immaterial, but the honour of the British army and the fair fame of England herself—may be "let drop," and to opine that "good relations" should be maintained with the Pekin Government, by no longer expressing any indignation at the immeasurable disgrace reflected upon England by the revolting barbarities perpetrated by her very good Manchoo allies, through the aid, and in the actual presence, of British officers.

Before concluding the analysis of Gordon's apology for resuming active operations with the Futai, it is necessary to make a few further observations. In the first place, it is quite impossible to deduce a sufficient cause from the three "reasons" by which he declares himself to have been actuated (paragraph No. 2). Even suppose we admit the allegations that Burgevine meditated a return to the rebels; that 300 Europeans were ready to join him; and that the Futai would not have accepted another *British* officer, to what conclusion do they lead us? Simply, that *if* these suppositions became realized, the event might prove disastrous to the Manchoo. Now, as Gordon chose to make this his excuse for comfortably passing over the Soo-chow affair, and resuming active service, it is perfectly clear that (whether he intends to convey this meaning or not) he pursued such conduct in the interest of his Imperialist friends; and this reduces the three "reasons" into a plea of duty to the Manchoo. Moreover, from the independent action claimed throughout the letter, the writer does not attempt to justify himself by any pretence of duty to his own Government. British officers, and, indeed, all their countrymen, may well feel astonished and disgusted at the extraordinary reasoning of Gordon, who, though merely the hired mercenary of a *local* Mandarin (Le Futai), and being totally without *status* in the Imperialist service,* made his duty to the Manchoo, forsooth, a reason for condoning the atrocities in which they had already involved him, and justifying his future participation in deeds equally abhorrent to every civilized and Christian sentiment.

We now come to the question as to the worth of this plea of duty. Either Gordon was the servant of the Manchoo Government or the British Government. When the English Commons compelled ministers to revoke the Order in Council authorizing the employment of British officers by the Manchoo, and to recall all so employed, *in consequence of the Soo-chow massacre*, Gordon, eventually, was withdrawn from service with the Futai. Now this proves that he was *bonâ fide* the servant of the British Government, and not only destroys his implied plea of duty to the Government of China, but virtually disclaims any countenance or indorsement of his act in joining the Futai and resuming active operations subsequent to the Soo-chow tragedy. Thus it is palpable beyond any manner

---

* See "Our Interests in China," by H. Lay, C.B., late Inspector-General of Chinese Customs, pp. 37—41. This *exposé* of British policy in China fully proves, together with Blue Book information, that Gordon never held any commission from the Emperor of China; that neither did he hold any commission from the local authorities, but, by serving without, was in reality a "filibuster."

of doubt that the course Gordon pursued was *entirely* according to "personal considerations;" was at his own responsibility; and was neither in consonance with duty to his own Government nor that of the Manchoo.

There are but three other motives which might be held to account for Gordon's conduct. The first would be, duty to his God—but this never has been attributed to him, and it would be gross blasphemy to do so; the second, philanthropy, has been professed both by himself and friends; the third, which is pecuniary, has been more frequently ascribed to him. The philanthropical motive will be controverted shortly when we come to a case in which it is attributed to him. With one exception (the *China Mail*), the whole European press of China lamented Gordon's connection with the Futai at Soo-chow; still more indignant were the channels of public opinion when they found that he quietly ignored the treacherous massacre by remaining at his post; and then rumours were not wanting with regard to the mercenary motives believed by many people to be the real cause of his return to active service. Major Gordon has not only brought himself into evil repute, but also the service of which he is so questionable a specimen. Take, for instance, the following extract from the *Friend of China* (issue February 20, 1864):—"If it be true that Major Gordon has again coalesced with Le Futai, he must not blame us if we judge of his motives according to the old maxim, 'actions speak louder than words.' It would seem that his late rejection of rewards from the hand of Kung was simply because of its having been too little for his acceptance, not too vile. His retirement to Quin-san was a safe dodge to quiet public opinion in regard to the Soo-chow massacre . . . We hope that he has stipulated for tens of lacs of rupees. Why should a soldier of fortune not make a fortune? When the major returns to Scotland, will any of his 'canny' countrymen ask impertinent questions as to the source of the 'siller'? To be sure, military men who wear Queen Victoria's uniform may hem and haw, cough and look doubtful; but we assure the major that if one British officer can sell his sword, the others have no right to complain about the price . . . Dollars cover every defect, and a wealthy soldier can afford to buy the respect which he cannot exact. Let the trade of murder flourish, as it always has done, and may Major Gordon fully enjoy all the wealth that the Manchoos can give, and that mental satisfaction which faithful servitude never fails to bring to those of integrity! Is not faithfulness bought and sold in 'Vanity Fair,' and should that not be looked for in the conduct of a—British soldier?"

If this article were to be literally intended, it would probably indicate the principles of Gordon. It appears very unfair to judge him by the code of honour, civilized morality, and Christian doctrine, when he does not seem either to appreciate such restraints or conform to them; therefore it is possible that the press has been too severe when condemning acts that, in this case, may, perhaps, be rather virtuous than otherwise.

We now bring the analysis of Gordon's "reasons" to a close by the following extract from the *Hong-kong Daily Press* (October, 1864), which refers to paragraphs 2, 3, and 5 of the letter, and finishes by making a direct accusation of mercenary motives for his coalescence with the Futai:—

"We believe it is well known that had Gordon left, Macartney would have succeeded. Certain it is that Macartney was an applicant for the post when Gordon was nominated, and as he had subsequently completely won the Futai's confidence, there can be little doubt about the matter.

"It will be seen, therefore, that Gordon's pretexts are shallow subterfuges, which will not stand the test of truth for one moment. He admits he is open to grave censure, but he says, 'knowing as I do that the Pekin authorities will support the Futai in what he has done, I have made up my mind to run the risk.' That is a nice process of reasoning, certainly!

"He then turns round on his comrades—calls them a dangerous rabble, 'which he will make it his duty to see dissolved as quietly as possible, and that while in course of dissolution it should serve to benefit the Imperial Government.'

"Apart from Gordon's unprincipled conduct with respect to the perfidy of the Futai, and to the murder of the Wangs—conduct which must heap disgrace on his name, and for ever prevent him from looking an honest man in the face again—we doubt whether, in the whole page of history, a parallel is to be found of a victorious fortunate commander turning on his comrades in the disgraceful, and we will add treacherous, manner in which Gordon turns on the Quin-san force in the letter before us. Let the reader remember the number of times Gordon had led the Quin-san force to victory—how splendidly they behaved in the campaign which Gordon was about to lead them through when he thus treacherously denounced them! Whatever they were, they had made him what he was; and bad as they might have been, we doubt whether any one of them ever departed more directly from the code of honour laid down by himself than Gordon did in rejoining the Futai, or even whether any one of them so far betrayed his comrades as Gordon does in the letter before us.

"A letter from Sir F. Bruce to Earl Russell, dated Pekin, 21st March, encloses a letter from Mr. Hart, the Inspector of Customs, to Sir Frederic, communicating the important fact that, at the interview which Colonel Gordon had had with the Futai at Soo-chow, about the beginning of February, he, Mr. Hart, acted as interpreter between the two. The ostensible reason for Mr. Hart thus acting was to enable the Futai to exculpate himself, which, according to Mr. Hart, he most completely did. Why did not Gordon mention this important circumstance in his letter to Sir Frederic advising His Excellency that he had again taken the field?* How came it that Mr. Acting-Consul Markham in his letter to Sir Frederic announcing the reconciliation, was silent on the point? How came it that General Brown was either ignorant of, or suppressed the fact? How did the fact come to be kept so secret from the public? Not a whisper nor a hint of Mr. Hart's presence is to be detected in the despatches of these officers, let alone the complete vindication of the Futai which that gentleman avers was effected at the interview?

"The answer is plain. Mr. Hart is a man of good repute, of high standing, and is a true and faithful servant. The Mandarins have great faith in him, and his word goes a long way. If they sent him to Gordon with an offer of 50,000 *taels*, the colonel might be assured not only that the money would be placed to his credit in any bank in London he might name, but that the transaction would be kept an inviolable secret.

"There, reader, you have the clue to Gordon's sacrifice of principle, and Mr. Hart's visit to Soo-chow."

---

* It will be seen that Gordon's letter is dated from Soo-chow.

Before narrating the events subsequent to Gordon's return to active operations, and bringing the history of the Ti-ping revolution down to a close, it is necessary to review a despatch written by Sir F. Bruce, the British Minister in China. The document constitutes the only authority, or rather the only official approval, Gordon ever received for rejoining the Futai. It is necessary to notice the same, because, as it was an entirely conditional approval, and the conditions were *never* observed, it naturally became null and void. It is, therefore, our duty to prove these facts, and thereby elucidate what might otherwise be held to remove the responsibility from Gordon, and, in fact, justify his conduct. The following despatch is the one in question, and it will be seen that it is the reply to Gordon's letter:—

"Pekin, March 12, 1864.

"Sir,—I have received your letter of the 6th of February, stating the reasons that have led to your continuing operations in concert with the Governor of Kiang-soo. I informed the Chinese Government that I did not feel called upon to interfere with the course you have taken, *but that my acquiescence was founded on the passage in their despatch to me, which states*, that in any future operations in which a foreign officer is concerned the rules of warfare as practised among foreign nations are to be observed, and that I should enclose you the extract of that despatch for your guidance, and as containing the arrangements agreed upon for the future. [1.]

"I have received the strongest assurance that it will be strictly adhered to, and that the Governor Le is to be instructed to that effect. I need not impress upon you how essential it is that there should be no repetition of the occurrence at Soo-chow.

"I fully appreciate the motives that led you, after the correspondence that has taken place, to resume operations at once, and to expose yourself thereby to hostile criticism. You might have limited yourself to a statement of the reasons which rendered the step expedient, and have thrown upon others the onus of decision before committing yourself to any action.

"But you appear to have felt, as commander of a Chinese force, and as the only person thoroughly acquainted with its composition and with the dangers to which this force, if indiscreetly handled, might give rise, that the decision must be based on your representations, and you therefore assumed its responsibility.

"This honourable and manly conduct on your part entitles you to a frank expression of my opinion on the subject.

"I think it due to you to state that my concurrence in the step you have taken is founded in no small measure on my knowledge of the high motives that have guided you while in command of the Chinese force, *of the disinterested conduct you have observed in pecuniary questions*, and of the *influence in favour of humanity you exercised in rescuing Burgevine and his misguided associates from Soo-chow.* [2.]

"I am aware of the perseverance with which, in the face of serious obstacles and much discouragement, you have steadily pursued the *pacification of the province of Kiang-soo*. In relieving it from being the battle-field of the insurrection, and in restoring to its suffering inhabitants the enjoyment of their homes and the uninterrupted exercise of their industry, you may console yourself with the assurance that you are rendering a service to true humanity as well as to great material interest. [3.]

"It would be a serious calamity and addition to our embarrassments in China were you compelled to leave your work incomplete, and were a sudden dissolution or dispersion of the Chinese force to lead to the recurrence of that state of danger and anxiety from which, during the last two years, Shanghae has suffered.

"Her Majesty's Government cannot be expected to garrison Shanghae indefinitely, and tranquillity cannot be relied on until a civil administration suited to Chinese ideas and habits is firmly established in the province, and until the disorderly and brigand elements which form the force of the Taeping insurrection are either put down or so thoroughly repelled from its frontiers as to leave that unfortunate province in peace.

"To the force under your command we must look for that result, and to its efficiency and discipline your presence is indispensable. In a body so composed a state of inactivity is full of danger, and I approve your not awaiting the result of the inquiry into the Futai's proceedings at Soo-chow, *provided you take care that your efforts in favour of humanity are not in future defeated by the Chinese authorities.** [4.]

"I am, Sir, your obedient Servant,

"FREDERIC W. A. BRUCE.

"Major Gordon, R.E., &c."

[1.] Now, here we have the *condition* upon which Sir F. Bruce agreed to Gordon's action. Let us see how the condition has been observed. If my readers will take the

---

* Italics by the Author.

trouble to turn back to the preceding chapter, they will find that the capture of Hwa-soo and Wu-see (as corroborated by the letter dated "April 28, 1864," from one of Gordon's own officers) was followed with a complete violation of Sir F. Bruce's conditional "acquiescence" by the wholesale massacre of the unfortunate Ti-pings. Furthermore, the following chapter will prove that at every city captured by Gordon and the Imperialists "the rules of warfare as practised among foreign nations" were *not* observed, nor even pretended to be fulfilled according to the terms of the condition upon which Gordon's action was approved: the principal cases referred to will be found to be the capture of Kar-sing-foo, Hwa-soo, Chang-chow-foo, and Nankin.

[2.] The preceding quotation from the *Hong-kong Daily Press*, and the description of Burgevine's hegira in Chapter XXII., sadly differ from Sir F. Bruce's "pecuniary" and "influence in favour of humanity" theories formed at Pekin upon evidence supplied by Gordon himself. Burgevine had actually *left* Soo-chow before Gordon interfered.

[3.] Readers of this history will at once perceive the falseness of these statements, Major Gordon having, in fact, not only *prevented* the "pacification of the province of Kiang-soo" by the Ti-pings, but *made* it "the battle-field of insurrection" by his "steadily pursued" *invasions* of the otherwise peaceful and settled Ti-ping territories. As for the hypocritical cant about "a service to true humanity," &c., I need only refer to the narrative of the journey to Soo-chow by the sub-editor of the *Friend of China*; the travels of the silk-merchant through the *pacified* country; the letters from two of Gordon's own officers, &c.

[4 and 1.] Combining the first and last paragraphs selected from the precious letter for review, we will briefly notice the facts proving in what manner Gordon fulfilled the proviso of Sir F. Bruce—" I approve your not awaiting the result of the inquiry into the Futai's proceedings at Soo-chow, PROVIDED you take care that *your efforts in favour of humanity* are not in future defeated by the Chinese authorities." In Chapter XXIII., the letter from one of Gordon's officers contains the following statement relative to the capture of the village of Hwa-soo, subsequent to the reconciliation between the official Manchoo murderer and the British bravo, and also subsequent to the establishment of the conditions by Sir F. Bruce's despatch :—" The slaughter among the rebels *after* the capture of Hwa-soo was terrible. Upwards of 9,000 were *taken prisoners*, and of *these* it was estimated 6,000 were killed or drowned, principally by the Imperialists." Now, Gordon himself commanded on this occasion, but he did not " take care " that " the rules of warfare as practised among foreign nations should be observed." This distinct violation of the British Minister's conditional sanction is alone sufficient to illustrate the fact that his *protégé's* conduct was contrary to his wish or intention, and, also, to withdraw his stipulated justification. Moreover, we shall find that, at every succeeding capture of a Ti-ping city the same barbarities were perpetrated, and the same indifference to his superior's instructions exhibited by Gordon, who stuck to his dear Imperialist friends with extraordinary devotion and tenacity, considering their sanguinary deeds and treacherous nature.

The *Shanghae Recorder* (a paper supporting the policy of the British Government in China, and their very good Manchoo allies), in its issue of March 31, 1864, thus narrates the capture of Kar-sing-foo by the Imperialist General Ching and Major Baily, one of Gordon's subordinates :—" As we expected, the usual horrible and revolting cruelty was exercised, after the *surrender* of Kar-sing-foo, by Ching's troops. On entering the city they encountered no resistance, when the unfortunates (*all non-combatants*) found remaining were laden with loot, obliged to carry it out to the Imperial lines, and forthwith beheaded, as payment in full! Truly it is the cold-blooded butcheries which disgrace the Imperialist cause, and deaden every feeling except unmitigated disgust at their mode of warfare." The city had been evacuated by the troops.

The *China Mail* (describing the capture of the city of Chang-chow-foo) by Gordon's Anglo-Manchoo force and an army of his Imperial friends, in its issue of May 30, 1864, states :—" The two breaches were carried in a rush, and quarter was given *to only a few hundred men* who had offered to surrender some weeks before." The families of the garrison and the other inhabitants of this large city numbered many thousand; but all, excepting the "few hundred men," were cruelly butchered in cold blood during several days.

The *Times*, in its issue of September 28, 1864, in a leading article upon the fall of Nankin, states:—" What the cost of human life has been on this occasion we cannot yet calculate. It is plain that no mercy was extended, and although the treacherous deeds at Soo-chow must have acted as a warning to the European officers, the account of the European eyewitnesses makes it evident that the carnage was very great." According to my own private advices, the *Friend of China* and other journals, the Ti-ping capital was evacuated; therefore, the unfortunates butchered by the Imperialists were, probably, the sick, wounded, and poor inhabitants who were unable to fly, or had not sufficient inducement to do so.

With regard to Gordon's "influence in favour of humanity," can any man of ordinary mind understand these results as philanthropical: viz., the slaughter of thousands in the field; the cold-blooded massacre of thousands of helpless prisoners; and the death of even hundreds of thousands by starvation; the destruction of Christianity and free circulation of the Bible, as practised among the Ti-pings; and the re-establishment of Buddhism? Those who ascribe philanthropical motives to

Gordon must entertain curious ideas as to the love of mankind, when they illustrate it by ravaging Ti-pingdom with fire and sword!

Having now terminated the narrative of Gordon's reconciliation with the Futai, the next chapter will describe the subsequent events.

CHAPTER XXV.

Operations Resumed.—Attack on Kin-tang—The Battle of the Brickbats.
—Ti-ping Success.—Active Operations.—Manœuvring.—Hang-chow
Invested.—Fall of Kar-sing-foo.— Gordon's Proceedings.— Chang-
chow-foo.—Narrative of the Siege.—Fall of Chang-chow.— The Foo-
wang.—Manchoo Cruelty.—Debate on the Chinese War.—Lord
Palmerston's Policy.—Its Errors.—Mr. Cobden's Policy.—Mr. Layard.
—His Inaccuracy.—Extracts from the Debate.—Result of Lord
Palmerston's Policy.—Fall of Nankin.—" Imperialist " Account.—
The Chung-wang's Capture.— Other Reports. — Digest of Events.—
The Chung-wang.—His Position in Nankin.—Events in the City.—
Newspaper Reports.—Doubts as to the Chung-wang's Fate.—The
Retreat from Nankin.—Newspaper Extracts.—The Shi-wang's Pro-
clamations.—Lee Shai-Yin's Address.

LATE in the month of February, 1864, the Futai's *General*, Gordon, resumed operations against the Ti-pings. Upon this occasion it appears that he acted entirely on his own responsibility, neither under the orders of his hitherto controller, General Brown (commanding H.B. Majesty's forces at Shanghae), nor the Futai. Consequently, the campaign to be noticed partook more strongly of filibustering than any of the preceding raids already described.

The first movement the Anglo-Manchoo force made was directed against the walled city of Yih-sing, on the western shore of the Ta-hoo Lake, and about forty miles south-west of Wu-see. After a short engagement, the usual result of such operations occurred. The garrison, unable to resist the overwhelming artillery employed by Gordon, an arm newly replenished from the British arsenal at Shanghae before taking the field, was driven from the city with much loss; those who managed to escape retreating to Li-yang, the nearest walled town. Soon, however, they were followed up to this place, but the commandant having received orders to retire to another city, it was evacuated upon the appearance of the disciplined troops and their irresistible guns.

The appearance of the country lately wrested from the Ti-pings is given as follows by one of Gordon's own officers (who was present during all operations) in his notes, "How the Taepings were driven out of the provinces of Kiangnan and Chekiang." Describing the march to Yih-sing, he states :—

"Some commissariat boats also went astray, causing the infantry a few days' hunger, as scarcely any food could be obtained, the country being all deserted and devastated. Seemingly it had not been cultivated easily *after the Taepings lost possession.* Hundreds of dead bodies were strewn along the roads, people who died from starvation; and even the few who were yet alive, watched one of their comrades dying, so as to obtain some food off his dead body." *

Sleep calmly and sweetly, ye China-rebel-subduing English politicians, and speak authoritatively as to the benefit of your intervention in the Chinese civil war, after reading this testimony from the hand of one of your mercenary tools! Is there a man so ill-"liberal" as to consider Lord Palmerston and colleagues are responsible for the results of their policy of interference towards the outlandish Chinamen? What do the starving Chinamen above mentioned say?

Their easy successes seem to have made the victorious enemy too confident in their own prowess, and less cautious than heretofore. Leaving a garrison at Li-yang, and also a considerable portion of his artillery, Gordon next advanced upon Kin-tang, a small city to the north-west. Elated by his former triumphs, and believing that his appearance alone would cause the submission of all

* See *Friend of China*, July 11, 1865.

Ti-ping cities in the district, and place their long-haired people under the barber's razor, Gordon expected no resistance at Kin-tang, and was induced to think that the place would open its gates to receive him as a sort of "conquering hero" whenever he might choose to enter. It will be seen that he became the victim of misplaced confidence.

Although, since my departure from China, and since the Ti-pings have been driven far inland, all information has been received from Chinese sources—false, exaggerated, and figurative—it seems pretty certain that the Chung-wang, after parting with me at Wu-see, placed the Shi and Foo Wangs in charge of the military position, while he proceeded to Nankin in order to confer with his king, the Tien-wang. Chang-chow-foo became the headquarters of the Foo-wang, and it so happened that Kin-tang was similarly occupied by the Shi-wang (a general second only to the Commander-in-Chief in talent and capability), when Gordon arrived before its walls. Both cities were situated on the southern road from Nankin, and their retention was absolutely necessary to maintain either the communications of the capital, or insure the retreat of the garrison, should they be obliged to abandon their charge. In consequence of this the Chung-wang divided about 10,000 of the best Ti-ping troops between his two lieutenants for the express purpose of holding Kin-tang and Chang-chow, while another force was organized to co-operate in the field.

The two Wangs had concentrated all their strength at Chang-chow when intelligence of Gordon's advance upon Kin-tang reached them. The Shi-wang, with a division of several thousand men, by forced marches, managed to throw himself into the city just before the enemy appeared.

When the Anglo-Manchoo contingent arrived under the walls on the 20th of March, they summoned the place to surrender, but no reply was made, for the battlements were silent and deserted, neither soldier nor spear, nor sign of living occupation being visible. The gates were all fast closed, and although Gordon had been looking forward to enter peaceably, and when he had arrived could see neither trace of man nor prospect of opposition, something there must have been ominous and suspicious in the stillness reigning over the city, for he preferred battering the walls down to knocking at the gates and demanding admission. The heavy guns were moved up to within a few hundred yards; the boats, containing supplies, followed them by the creeks; and batteries were soon thrown up, still amidst the same profound and mysterious silence upon the part of the garrison. During the bombardment all the noise was on one side; nor flag, nor face, nor living thing could be observed about the encompassed battlements. After several hours' constant firing, a large and practicable breach was effected, and the 1st regiment of Anglo-Chinese ordered to storm the silent ramparts. The enemy came forward with a loud cheer, bearing with them bamboo bridges to throw across the moat, while the stormers were closely supported by portions of the 2nd and 5th regiments, who were allowed to enter the city ditch in their boats and cross unopposed. The short space between the moat and the foot of the breach was soon passed, and the storming column began to ascend. At this moment the hitherto invisible garrison appeared and broke their previous silence in a manner fatal to the assailants. Manning every available position, they threw such incessant showers of brickbats that the Imperialists, despite the gallant behaviour of their foreign officers, were unable to advance. The Ti-pings then rushed into the breach, and charging with their spears, drove them back in confusion. Three times the enemy turned to renew the struggle, but on each occasion were hurled back with loss, being quite unable to cope with the Ti-ping soldiers in a hand-to-hand combat. The breach was now played upon by the artillery, and the defenders driven back with great loss of life from the canister, grape, and shell. Gordon then ordered his Adjutant-General, Kirkham, to bring up fresh companies of the 2nd and 5th regiments, and himself to lead them forward to a second assault. Scarcely, however, had he given the order, when a jingall ball reached him at his almost secure distance and wounded him in the leg. *Colonel* Kirkham, with great bravery, led his men into the deadly breach, but when half-way up, fell severely wounded. Still, with courage worthy of a better cause, his men followed their officers only to be again charged by the valiant garrison and completely routed after a desperate conflict at close quarters. Again the murderous artillery swept away the defenders of the breach, and *Major* Brown, Gordon's *aide-de-camp*, leading forward fresh columns, made a last desperate attempt to storm the yawning chasm. Again the disciplined Chinese and their foreign officers rushed upon the blood-stained ruins; but with dauntless and undiminished courage the Ti-pings again met them—spear to bayonet and firelock, and man to man. After a terrible struggle the assailants were finally driven off, and retreated upon Li-yang, with *Major* Brown and all their commanding officers *hors-de-combat*. This action has been called " the Battle of the Brickbats," such missiles being the principal means of defence used by the garrison.

The attack upon Kin-tang was the most severely contested action that the Anglo-Manchoo troops had ever fought. Their defeat is to be attributed to the fact that they were not assisted by an overwhelming park of artillery, which usually did all the fighting. If the Imperialists had not been supplied with British guns, men, and munitions of war, *ad libitum*, the Ti-pings would have been quite able to manage the disciplined legions. Gordon, in this assault, lost fourteen European officers and nearly one-seventh of the men engaged. The destruction amongst the defenders of Kin-tang must have been equally severe, not less than 600 having fallen.

At this period the Ti-pings seem to have made a desperate effort to defeat the overwhelming numbers of the enemy encircling them on every quarter. At Nankin, Chang-chow-foo, and Kin-tang they managed to defeat the Imperialist forces almost on the same day at each place. The garrison of the capital having sallied forth in strength, defeated a portion of the great beleaguering army under Tseng-kwo-fan (Imperialist Commissioner and Governor-General of the two Kiang provinces) with much slaughter. Upon reaching Li-yang, after narrowly escaping being surrounded by the troops pursuing from Kin-tang, Gordon received intelligence the same evening that the garrison of Chang-chow had sallied out, completely routing the large investing force commanded by the Futai's brother, and following up the success by moving between Soo-chow and Shanghae, thereby threatening not only to recapture all the country lately wrested from Ti-ping rule, but isolate his division and more than counteract its operations by a powerful diversion upon Shanghae or Soo-chow.

Leaving a strong detachment to garrison Li-yang, Gordon at once proceeded with the remainder of his force, and all the artillery, to operate against the Ti-pings from Chang-chow. On the 29th of March he came upon them at Hwa-soo, in the neighbourhood of the city of Chang-zu, about 35 miles north-east of Soo-chow. On the morning of the 30th, finding that the Ti-pings did not number more than 3,000, he ordered about 1,500 infantry to attack them, while he followed in the boats with the artillery, to give assistance if required. Again, as at Kin-tang, the Royal Engineer was completely outgeneralled. The Foo and Shi Wangs were both consummate strategists, and at irregular warfare, when artillery was not employed against them, would easily have foiled Major Gordon.

The Ti-pings continually gave way as the disciplined troops advanced; but they were manœuvred so as to draw their pursuers into a position from which for a time they were themselves invisible, while a masked breastwork, ingeniously stretched across the end of the slight hollow, helped to conceal them. Barely had the retreating forces disappeared behind their slight intrenchment and the inequalities of the ground, when they were doubled back upon each flank so as to almost completely envelop the enemy. The Ti-pings were allowed to execute their manœuvre thus easily through the incautious advance of their antagonists, for the latter halted in the very hollow to which they had been enticed, directly they lost sight of those whom they were pursuing. When next the Imperialists saw their opponents, it was in the form of a serried line, surrounding them upon every side except a small space in their rear, and charging them on front and both flanks. After a feeble resistance, during which they lost seven English officers and more than 200 men, the ranks of Gordon's force were broken, and the whole mercenary contingent fled from the field with precipitation.

According to the published accounts of this engagement, the Ti-pings were commanded by the Foo-wang, "numbered about 3,000," and were "badly armed." It will thus be seen that, without artillery being brought to bear against them, they were quite able to cope hand to hand with the disciplined troops, officered by foreigners and well armed with musket and bayonet as the latter were, although poorly equipped with a small supply of jingalls, a few bad European firearms, and a majority of bamboo spears.

During the spring of the year 1864, the Ti-pings struggled with deperate bravery against the odds opposed to them; and for some time it seemed very doubtful whether they would succeed or not. While Gordon and the Imperialist troops were being defeated in the northern districts of the Ti-ping territory, the Franco-Manchoo contingent and co-operating forces were meeting a similar fate in the south. Late in February the Imperialists besieging Hang-chow, the provincial capital of Che-kiang, were totally defeated by a sortie of the whole garrison. About the same time another large army was routed by a Ti-ping force in the neighbourhood of Fo-yang, a city not far from Hang-chow. Having recovered from their former repulse and obtained fresh supplies of British mercenaries and munitions of war, the Mandarins again proceeded to invest the provincial capital. On the 2nd of March the Franco-Chinese, commanded by *Generals* D'Aiguebelle and Schodelana, attacked the above city, and after several hours' hard fighting, succeeded in capturing three forts on the south side; only, however, to be driven out by a desperate charge the Ti-pings made during the afternoon, with a loss of fourteen Europeans and more than a hundred men. On the 29th of the same month, the besiegers recommenced active operations. Supported by a strong body of Imperialists, the Franco-Chinese attacked and carried the outworks of the city a second time, the garrisons retiring within the walls after some hard fighting. The next day fire was opened upon the city from numerous siege artillery, and a practicable breach was soon effected. Again the Franco-Chinese, or more correctly speaking, Manchoos, led the assault, but met with such gallant resistance that they were driven back to their supports in confusion. Twice they bravely rallied, and twice they endeavoured to storm the breach, rendered impregnable by the brave hearts and ready hands defending it, and each time they were repulsed with great slaughter. At the close of the day the assault was given up, after a heavy loss of life, and a vast expenditure of British shot and shell without other result.

Although Hang-chow could not be wrested from the Ti-pings by force of arms, a few days later it fell from external influences, having been rendered untenable through the capture of Kar-sing-foo by the enemy, whereby its supplies and lines of communication were cut off.

About the same time that Gordon commenced his raid upon Yih-sing, Li-yang, and Kin-tang, Manchoo General Ching proceeded with a large army and an auxiliary force composed of detachments from the English contingent, to beleaguer the city of Kar-sing-foo, situated about midway between Soo-chow and Hang-chow, on the Grand Canal. Ching was the bravest native general engaged against the Ti-pings; he was a renegade from their cause, and we all know that such people make the most bitter enemies. He had already been defeated before the city, shortly after I had left it on my last return to Shanghae. Gordon's subordinate, *Colonel* Bailey, had charge of the large siege train accompanying the army, and in a few hours after establishing his batteries, managed to effectively breach the walls of the doomed city. On rushed Ching's men and their allies, but their efforts were useless, for every assault failed; and Ching himself received a wound which, more than a month later, proved mortal. Some few days subsequent to this repulse, large reinforcements were received by the enemy, fresh breaches were made, and the small but devoted garrison was compelled to evacuate the place at night, having lost their gallant commander, Yoong-wang, and nearly two-thirds of their number. When the Imperialists at last entered, they put to the sword all the unfortunate non-combatants who had not fled the city,* sparing neither man, woman, nor child, during their cruel butchery of the unoffending inhabitants. Does Colonel Gordon, R.E., call this "observing the rules of warfare as practised among foreign nations," according to the proviso of Sir F. Bruce? Does Sir F. Bruce, after the massacres at Wu-see, Kar-sing, &c., still term Gordon's conduct "a service in favour of humanity"?

* See the account from *Shanghae Recorder*, at the end of the preceding chapter.

After the loss of Kar-sing, Hang-chow was also evacuated, and the two garrisons retreated to the large city of Hoo-chow-foo. The fortune of war now set strongly against the Christian patriots. With a few memorable exceptions, they were everywhere defeated, through the British influence so cruelly brought to bear against them, for which they were always unprepared, and equally unable to resist.

Having retired to Quin-san (the head-quarters of the Anglo-Manchoo contingent), after his defeat at Hwa-soo, Gordon was shortly joined by an Imperialist army of 15,000 men. A body of troops, commanded by officers of H.B. Majesty's 67th regiment, was also moved from Shanghae to support them. The Imperialists and the whole disciplined force, together with the latter's large park of artillery, now took the field again and moved upon the Foo-wang's position. The Ti-pings were still lightly intrenched at the village of Hwa-soo; they had been strongly reinforced by the Shi-wang, but were considerably hampered by a large number of country people who had fled from the enemy.

On the 11th of April the Imperialists commenced their attack, but, warned by former defeats, they entirely depended upon their artillery, to which the Ti-pings had not a single gun to reply with. The over-matched defenders were at last shelled out of their open breastworks with great slaughter, and being outflanked by the disciplined and undisciplined enemy, were much cut up during their retreat, while a great number were made prisoners and savagely put to death, as described in Chapter XXIII. by the letter of an officer present, under the eyes of *General* Gordon. The loss of the Ti-pings on this occasion was very heavy. Although the Shi and Foo Wangs succeeded in cutting their way through the enemy with their best troops, at least 8,000 unfortunates, principally country people, were killed.

Following up his success, Gordon pursued the retreating force to Chang-chow-foo. Meanwhile troops were being concentrated upon the same point from every quarter, so that within a few days the city was surrounded by an immense Imperialist army, which was estimated to exceed 100,000 men. The Shi-wang having proceeded to Kin-tang, the garrison commanded by the Foo-wang cannot have consisted of more than 7,000 to 8,000 effective soldiers, but at least 10,000 civilians, including all persons of any standing in the Chang-chow district, and who were Ti-ping subjects, or held civil office under the Tien-wang's Government, had sought refuge within the city walls, carrying with them their movable property and their families, whereby the number of non-combatants was more than doubled.

Three times already had the Imperialists been completely routed before the city, and the siege raised by the gallant resistance of the garrison, although on two occasions the enemy were assisted by detachments of foreign artillery and disciplined troops. After much hard fighting the defenders were driven from all their outworks and strictly confined to the city walls, when the besiegers at once proceeded to effect several breaches. The following account of the subsequent efforts of Gordon and the Futai to storm the place is partly transcribed from the narrative of an officer engaged, and which was published in the *Shanghae Recorder* of May 2, 1864.

The Ti-pings having been driven from all their stockades and intrenchments to the west of the city, and these being occupied by a strong force of Imperial troops, Gordon moved round opposite the south-east angle, and commenced forming his siege batteries, while the Imperialists placed their guns on his left, facing the south of the city. A combined attack was arranged for the 27th of April, but as the Imperialist batteries were ready on the 24th, and the troops who had so often been defeated were eager to storm, and averse to relinquish their hope of taking the city, the Futai gave orders to open fire, and

3 c

by three o'clock in the afternoon a capital breach was effected. The advance was sounded and the stormers pushed on steadily to the city ditch, but were there thrown into confusion by some defect in the bridges. At last, however, they scrambled across, and advancing through the stakes got to the foot of the breach, where they maintained themselves for a considerable time; but the defenders, notwithstanding a most destructive covering fire from the Imperialist guns and from a battery of Gordon's enfilading the *terre plein*, manned the breach and wall with great courage, regardless of life, and compelled the assailants to fall back with heavy loss. This ended the first day's assault.

Gordon's guns having been put in position during the night, and a pontoon bridge laid down over the city ditch (the garrison was too weak to prevent the same by a sortie, and had not a single cannon to oppose its construction), at daybreak he opened fire, while the Imperialists' batteries did the same to knock away the barricades thrown up in their breach. Bang, bang, went the heavy guns, as quickly followed by the boom of bursting shell tearing up ponderous masses of the wall, and burying beneath them many of the defenders, while the smaller guns laid along the parapet right and left operated with deadly effect wherever the garrison appeared, or opened fire with their jingalls or musketry. By half-past twelve o'clock the new breach was rendered practicable, and the signal was given to the Imperialists to storm at the old one. On rushed the 4th Regiment of Anglo-Manchoo mercenaries, bravely led by *Colonel* Howard, and forward came the Ti-pings to the breach, determined and daring, to be mowed down in heaps by the terrible covering fire of the artillery; but no sooner down than their place was filled by their followers rushing with unabated courage to the defence. In the words of the officer whose narrative we are making contribute to this history:—The edge of the city ditch was gained, and over went the 4th Regiment's colours, accompanied by Colonel Howard, Captain Cane (R.A.), and Lieutenant Stackpole, and up the breach through a shower of missiles and fire-balls. Then came that deadly pause, the colours waving on the breach, defended by a few brave men. The defenders and assailants hesitated. They stood at bay for a moment. The "celestial" nature shrank from the dread conflict hand to hand. The officers attempted to break the spell: they pushed their men, they pulled them, they beat them with their swords, but in vain. The Ti-pings, fighting for life, sooner recovered their presence of mind, and every man discharged his missile on the heads of the assailants. The colours and their defenders were pushed off the wall down the breach, and had to retire over the bridge on their column. A murderous fire was poured from every loop-hole, men were falling fast, yet the attacking force stood its ground, but hesitated to advance to where it would have been comparatively safe, being too low for the aim of the besieged. The retire was now sounded, and the stormers fell back to cover.

The Ti-pings suffered terribly from the superior arms of their assailants, and now that they had succeeded in repulsing them a second time, they were swept from the shattered walls by the artillery, which still continued to fire on them. At half-past two o'clock in the afternoon the enemy were ready at both points of attack for a simultaneous movement. Up went their signal rockets, a yell burst from the ranks of Gordon's force, which was taken up and carried along the Imperialist lines, and on came both storming parties at a rapid pace. The 3rd Regiment of the English contingent now made the assault, and their colours were borne up the breach by Captain Winstanley (H.M.'s 67th Regiment), and other officers rallying around them and fighting hand to hand with the defenders. The Imperialists crossed their bridges, crowded at the foot of the other breach, and waved their flags about, but hesitated to mount it. With their bamboo spears, and undiminished courage, the brave garrison rushed to meet their well-armed enemy, while all who possessed firearms plied them diligently from the walls, and others kept up an incessant volley of brickbats from the heaps piled ready for use around the rampart, and which formed a principal means of defence. Still Gordon's troops maintained their position on the walls, and, if possible, began to increase the extent of their lodgment, whilst the Ti-pings were falling fast from the musketry of the enemy, which they had but small means to answer. At this critical moment the Foo-wang headed a last desperate charge in person. Leading forward all his unwounded men, this gallant chief inspired them with fresh ardour, while the efforts of the assailants began to flag. As one present stated: The contest every moment became more close, and was prolonged for at least twenty minutes. At length the stormers were driven from the ground they had gained, and hurled to the bottom of the breach. Several times they struggled to mount again, but every attempt was futile. The rear ranks of the enemy being under the fire from the wall, lost heavily in killed and wounded, while the front ranks, so desperately opposed, could not advance. The order to retire was now given, and the assaulting forces were withdrawn to cover, while their artillery again swept the breach with canister, shell, and grape, inflicting fearful havoc among the dauntless garrison of Chang-chow. During all this time the Imperialists had hurried on column after column to assault by their own breach, but none were able to effect a lodgment within the well-defended walls of the city. Every attack was repulsed with great slaughter upon both sides, and at last the bravest of the late General Ching's— he had died from the effects of a wound in the head received at Kar-sing—Mandarins advanced with his men, but though he passed the sticking point and got his colours partly into the breach, yet he too was brought to a stand and obliged to retire. The assault was now abandoned, and the besiegers carried off their killed and wounded, including 27 European officers, 400 of the English contingent, and about 1,500 Imperialists.

Although the Ti-pings were victorious, and had succeeded in defeating every attack upon the city, their triumph was only purchased by an awful sacrifice of life. When the stormers mounted the wall a fearful sight was before them. "Far as the eye could see, heaps upon heaps lay dead and mangled." During the different assaults at least one half the garrison were placed *hors-de-combat*, principally by the murderous fire of the enemy's artillery, which they were totally unable to countervail, having none to reply with. Chang-chow being completely surrounded by the vast Imperialist army, its fall, either by famine or the sword, was certain.

Having established fresh batteries at a different part of the city, on the 11th of May the enemy succeeded in capturing it. Upon this occasion two immense breaches were made, while the incessant artillery fire, and the overwhelming rush of the enormously superior assailing force over the wide-spread ruins of the wall, quickly overpowered the last gallant resistance offered by the remnant of the garrison. A comparison of the casualties of the English contingent at each attack affords the best proof that the terrible results of the first had almost exterminated the defenders. At the first attack the contingent lost 27 officers and 400 men; at the second, only 2 killed and 5 wounded! When the Imperialists poured through the two fresh breaches, the best and bravest of the remaining Ti-ping soldiers sacrificed themselves in the futile effort to repulse them, while their comrades, although fighting desperately to the last, were driven from the walls, and then through the streets of the city, still disputing the ground step by step. At last the few survivors were brought to bay in the commandant's palace. Throughout all the fighting the brave Foo-wang had been foremost in leading and encouraging his troops, and now, still unwounded, with several officers and a score or two of men, he made a last desperate stand in his own house. One by one his few followers—unable to conquer, but determined to die with their faces to the foe and their hands raised to the last in defence of their noble cause—fell around him, and then for a moment he fought alone against a host of assailants. Still he was not killed, for a price was fixed upon his capture alive. At length this dauntless chief, whose acquaintance I have valued, and whose elegist I am proud though grieved to have become, was overpowered by numbers and beaten to the ground, though not until many an enemy had fallen under his heavy sword. Even when disarmed and helpless in the grasp of the foe, he still struggled against a fate that would never have befallen him but for the unexpected, irresistible, and unrighteous military interference of England. One report of the capture of Chang-chow (*China Mail*, May 30) states:—"The chief (Foo-wang) of those who were in command of the city, fought in his palace to the last, and required ten men to bind his hands and secure him; and, when brought into the presence of the Futai, refused submission or to pay any respect to him, saying, 'Ah! were it not for the aid of the disciplined troops (under Gordon) he defied all the Futai's hosts to take the city from him.'" If the British army, arsenals, and navy had been thrown open to supply the young and vigorous revolution, instead of *wasting* their help upon the corrupt and hopeless Manchoo, how great would the success and future results have been! With all the British assistance the Imperialists have barely been able to drive the Ti-pings from their cities and possessions in the provinces of Che-kiang and Kiang-nan, much less to suppress the great Christian and patriotic movement, or insure its final extinguishment.

The Foo-wang was cruelly put to death by his merciless captors. "The two breaches were carried in a rush, and quarter was given *to only a few hundred men*;" so says the report above quoted from. How many days the triumphant Mandarins were engaged butchering the unfortunate inhabitants does not transpire; but, with the exception of the small number mentioned, the whole 12,000, besides the garrison, with their families, were massacred. Two years' provisions were found in the city, and this being stored in the Ti-ping granaries, was the entire produce of the district, and was the sole means destined to support the people during the ensuing season. The whole supply was seized by the Imperialists; and though previous to their success much misery had been caused by the general effect of the war, after their capture of the departmental city the entire department was starved; such being the usual result of Manchoo re-establishment in any locality, and particularly so at Chang-chow-foo, as proved by the letter of the first English-contingent officer in Chapter XXIII.

We have now noticed four authenticated instances (the captures of Wu-see, Kar-sing-foo, Hwa-soo, and Chang-chow-foo), subsequent to Gordon's return to service, when the conditions upon which Sir F. Bruce gave his approval to that officer's action were violated by the wholesale massacre of the vanquished and prisoners. We may, therefore, while expressing boundless disgust at Colonel Gordon's persistent continuance in the Futai's service after each and every one of these atrocities, fairly presume that the astounding assertion as to his influence in favour of humanity—in spite of the eulogy by Mr. Montgomery Martin at a late "China dinner" in London, wherein he stated that the officer in question had done more *for* the "civil cause" in China than all the bishops, merchants, and military put together—is not only negatived, but quite reversed.

Soon after the capture of Chang-chow-foo, Colonel Gordon was compelled to withdraw from active military operations by the Order in Council, prohibiting further aid to the Manchoo. He managed, however, to continue acting contrary to the ordinance, by organizing camps of instruction and proceeding to Nankin in person, there to advise the besieging forces commanded by Tseng-kwo-fan.

About the time the events noticed in this chapter were taking place in China, in England the energetic opposition of such men as Lord Naas, Colonel Sykes, Hon. Mr. Liddell, Mr. White, Messrs. Bright, Cobden, &c., from their places in the House of Commons, drew attention to the subject, and will ever stand as a memorable protest against the criminal policy of the Government.

During the second debate of the session on "British relations with China" (May 20, 1864), Mr. Baxter, M.P., very happily termed the policy of the Government "not a comedy of errors, but a tragedy of errors." Lord Palmerston, in this case, defended his policy by a very extraordinary argument, which it is singular that his opponents did not use to his confusion. Coming out as the advocate of intervention in foreign affairs, he stated, as a justification of his war against the Ti-pings:—

"We have interfered in other countries, and with great benefit to those countries. . . . We interfered in the case of Greece, and established the independence of the Greek state. We interfered in the affairs of Belgium, and established it as an independent state. We interfered in the case of Portugal, and enabled the people of that country to obtain a free and parliamentary constitution. (Hear, hear.) We interfered in the affairs of Spain with equal success, and a similar result. . . . We interfered in a great measure in those events which led to the Crimean war. . . . We interfered in the affairs of China; and why? Because our treaty rights *were* endangered, and our national interests *were* at stake."

Now, the noble Premier here cites a number of precedent cases; unfortunately, however, for his argument and acumen, on each occasion referred to, England, as worthily became her, interfered in the cause of an oppressed people; whereas, in the present case, he had been the active originator of an intervention diametrically the very opposite—a military interference *against* the oppressed natives of China, who were striving to liberate *and Christianize* their unfortunate country. If Lord Palmerston had interfered in the spirit of the cases which came so glibly to his voluble tongue, he would have interfered to support the Ti-pings—not to slaughter them.

After striving to justify his policy by precedents which should have entirely reversed it, Lord Palmerston was equally unhappy in his faulty explanation of the reasons "why" he interfered in China. As the Hon. Mr. Liddell, M.P., well said in his speech after the Premier, "The noble Viscount said that the Government interfered because the treaty rights were in danger. He wanted to know in what single instance had our treaty rights or our trade been in danger? He had asked that question before, and he now repeated it. (Hear, hear.) He wished to know any instance in which either the property or the life of a British subject had been placed in danger?"

Every member of the British Parliament, who questioned the China policy of the Government, has asked the same question. It has never been answered, because there is really not a single fact on which to base an answer. Colonel Sykes, M.P., has frequently defied and challenged the Government to cite one act ever committed by the Ti-pings prejudicial to British interests, and they have been quite unable to do so; for none are upon record.

Those who have been interested enough to wade through the compiled portion of this work will, no doubt, at once perceive the truthlessness of Lord Palmerston's charge against the Ti-pings, viz., that they endangered the treaty rights and national interests of England. No particle of truth mingles with the unfounded charge; no tittle of proof has ever been produced to justify the undeclared hostilities perpetrated against a friendly people which were consequent on it.

Besides this, the venerable Premier was no less unfortunate with each proposition he chose to base his arguments upon. To prove the cruelty of the Ti-pings, he stated:—

"A steamer, called the *Firefly*, was carried off, and four or five men, who were upon the vessel, were roasted to death.

"Colonel Sykes.—'By whom?'

"Lord Palmerston.—'The Taepings.'

"Colonel Sykes.—'No, no!'"

Now, by the above extract from the *Standard's* report of the debate, we find that the Prime Minister's vivid imagination positively roasted the men whose fate has never yet been ascertained even in China. They are referred to in Chapter XXIV. of this work, but whether they are living or dead, and, if dead, how they were killed, are questions which have never yet been satisfactorily answered; and, from the mystery in which the fate of the unfortunate men is involved, probably never will be.

Again, in a feeble effort to vaunt the duration and existence of the Manchoo dynasty, and, consequently, to make it appear that the Ti-pings were not striving to expel a foreign rule of comparatively modern establishment (which has never been entirely acknowledged nor submitted to, which has always been rebelled against, and which is still foreign to and hated by the Chinese), but, on the contrary, were simply rebels against an ancient and legitimate throne, Lord Palmerston made another very singular and important *mistake*. He tried to be satirical in commenting upon the excellent speech made by Mr. Baxter, M.P., who brought on the debate, by stating:—

"My hon. friend says he has studied the Blue Books, but I apprehend that he has not equally studied the history of China. He talks of the Imperial dynasty as having been recently established over a conquered country; and, if I am not misinformed, I think it has existed for nearly 500 years."

Well, the noble Premier was misinformed, and very much so, too. The Manchoo Tartars invaded China A.D.

1644; they had not established themselves as its masters before the year 1683. It was, doubtless, very funny and gratifying to chaff a troublesome member out of countenance, but still there must be some people who expect the Chief Minister of the British Government to be pretty accurate in the statements he makes from his place in the House of Parliament.

We will now notice a few incidents of the next, and last, debate on China; when the late Mr. Cobden, on the evening of May 31, 1864, rose to move in the House of Commons:—

"That, in the opinion of this House, the policy of non-intervention, by force of arms, in the internal political affairs of foreign countries, which we profess to observe in our relations with the states of Europe and America, should be observed in our intercourse with the Empire of China."

Mr. Cobden, after making a truly magnificent and exhaustive speech, was replied to by Mr. Layard, the Under Secretary of State for Foreign Affairs. Out of the many distinguished Members who followed, only one, Mr. Gregson, supported the policy of the Government; and he, by faintest praise and three minutes' unmeaning talk, proved but a poor champion, if he did not make a worse case for his superiors.

At the termination of the debate, Mr. Cobden withdrew his motion because Lord Palmerston distinctly avowed the failure and abandonment of his policy of intervention in China, and declared his intention to preserve an entirely neutral, defensive attitude in future.

The faithlessness and falsehood induced by the evil course adopted by the British Government in persistently endeavouring to carry out Lord Palmerston's pertinacious, crotchety, unrighteous policy to force British trade upon China (which involved the necessity of crushing the Imperial power, and then that of the Ti-ping revolution which would have succeeded it, so that, in fact, the British Government could dictate its whims without fear of refusal or opposition) were singularly exemplified during the debate referred to.

We have seen that in the preceding debate Lord Palmerston plainly and frankly declared:—

"We interfered in the affairs of China: and why?"

Now, Mr. Layard, when replying to Mr. Cobden's speech, stated:—

"Her Majesty's Government had been accused of supporting the Chinese" (Manchoo) "government against the Taipings. [Cries of hear, hear.] He had pointed out that such was not the case."—He then qualified this sentence by saying,—"Beyond our preventing the Taepings entering the treaty ports FOR THE PURPOSE OF DESTROYING THEM, a course which we were compelled to take."

First, Mr. Layard denies the interference declared by Lord Palmerston, and then he admits it, attempting to justify the policy by the sweeping assertion in capitals. Now, if the ministers were "compelled" to prevent the Ti-pings entering the treaty ports, how is it that they were allowed to capture and occupy the treaty port of Ningpo? And now, to impugn Mr. Layard's veracity, if the Ti-pings endeavoured to enter the treaty ports " FOR THE PURPOSE OF DESTROYING THEM," how is it that they held the city of Ningpo for many months and did not destroy the least particle of property within its walls?

Mr. Layard's fault is a common one, only in an uncommon position. He knew that the policy of the Government was wrong, he knew that he was wrong himself, and besides occupying the pugnacious position of buffer or breakwater to the Foreign Office, he did not like to admit it. Poor Mr. Layard's situation must be an unpleasant one sometimes. He has unpleasant work to do. Undoubtedly he has an irritable temper and a sharp tongue, but it is rather unfortunate that he has a bad memory. After stating that her Majesty's Government had not been interfering, "such was not the case," be-

yond preventing the destruction of the treaty ports,
and affirming, "the hon. gentleman the member for
Montrose (Mr. Baxter), the other evening, after condemning the policy of the Government, concluded by
expressing a wish, that the Government would continue
to defend the treaty ports and protect British interests in
China. *That was what the Government had been doing all
along.*" After thus expressing himself, Mr. Layard
declared, "His hon. friend had really condemned a state
of things in China *which no longer existed.*" That is to
say, Mr. Layard firstly stated that the hostilities waged
against the Ti-pings were only to protect British interests;
in fact, simply a defensive policy; and, secondly, he stated
that such policy "no longer existed!" Therefore, the
natural deduction is that the British Government ceased
to protect British interests at the treaty ports; such, however, was not and is not the case. The change that took
place was the abandonment of the policy "of supporting the
Chinese (Manchoo) Government against the Taepings,"
and the cessation of further aggressive military and naval
operations against them. This was satisfactorily proved
by the Premier's speech, who sadly contradicted his subordinate's defensive theory, as the following extracts from
it will show :—

"Now, it is almost unnecessary, I think, for them" (the members who
had spoken against his policy) "to have expressed their opinion with
regard to the expedition of Captain Osborn, and the employment of Major
Gordon and others, because we have stated on former occasions that those
Orders in Council under which those officers *were employed*" (by the Manchoo Government; how about Mr. Layard's "such was not the case"?)
"have been revoked. . . . Therefore that policy is at an end." (Now
the following is a plain avowal of what Mr. Cobden brought his motion
against.) "I think that we were perfectly justified in the steps we took,
because it is evident that the more *we* can contribute to the *internal classi-
fication* of China, the more the trade, which everybody agrees is the main
and principal object of our going to China, the more that trade would
flourish. . . .

"If, by allowing a British subject *to enter into the service of the Emperor* of China,* we have been the means of strengthening the hands of the Chinese Government, and enabling them to put down in any degree or diminish the scope of that rebellion, I say we should have been rendering not only a service to China, but promoting those objects to which alone our intercourse with China ought to be confined.† Those measures have failed, and I am sorry for it."

After this expression of opinion it is by no means surprising to find the Premier declaring a little further on, in the same speech: "I say it is the duty of this country to endeavour by *all the means* in her power to extend her commerce." Under *these* circumstances it is not difficult to account for the intervention in China, and while Englishmen, who have any respect for the principles of right and justice, may regret their late lamented statesman did not say, "by all the" righteous or legitimate "means in her power," they cannot fail to feel gratified that "those measures have failed," even though the originator of the measures, their late popular and jaunty minister, was "sorry for it."

Those measures have failed! it is true. They have failed miserably; they have failed to work good, but not to do harm. England has derived no benefit from them, China has received much evil. The schemes to Anglicise the Chinese army, navy, and civil service have failed; the efforts to extinguish rebellion against the Manchoo allies of the British Government (after the last war had rendered them quite powerless and docile *for the time being*) have likewise signally failed, for rebellion is more rife than ever: but "those measures" have been famously successful in causing an enormous sacrifice of life, in injuring the cause of Christianity and civilization, and obstructing its progress in China for the present.

The failure of Lord Palmerston's policy came all too

---

* Referring to Colonel Gordon, Captain Osborn, R.N., and their subordinates.

† Meaning the noble occupation of buying and selling; and that, too, at the point of the bayonet.

late for rectifying the evil already perpetrated. Within two months of his public announcement that the measures of his administration had failed, Nankin, the capital and the political strength of the Ti-pings, fell into the hands of the Imperialists. Assisted, as we have described, by the powerful, though underhanded, British alliance, the Manchoo forces were enabled to capture or isolate every city beyond the capital. When Chang-chow-foo was taken by the Englishman Gordon, the neighbouring cities of Tan-yang, Kin-tang, &c., became untenable, and were consequently evacuated by their garrisons. Under command of Le-shih-seen, the Shi-wang (the Chung-wang's cousin, sometimes figuratively referred to as his "brother"), were also the troops from Hang-chow (capital of Chekiang), Kar-sing-foo, Yih-shing, Li-yang, and many smaller places. Between these forces and Nankin the vast army commanded by the Imperialist Le-Futai now intervened, but their communication with the great city of Hoo-chow-foo, at the south of the Ta-hoo lake, and strongly garrisoned by several wangs, was still intact.

Unable to advance against the superior forces of the enemy, much less to reach Nankin and endeavour to rescue it from the besieging army of Imperialists under Tseng-kwo-fan, at least 80,000 to 100,000 strong, the Shi-wang commenced what seems to have been a preconcerted retreat to the south. This occurred during the month of June.

Shortly afterwards, on the 19th of July, 1864, Nankin reverted to Manchoo authority. Thus the city which had been the capital of the great Ti-ping revolution and the head-quarters of its Government during more than eleven years, and which throughout that period had defied the strongest efforts of the rulers of the greatest and most populous empire in the world, succumbed at last through the unjustifiable hostilities and crotchety, bullying, meddlesomeness of the British Government or some of its members.

Again, soon after this overwhelming disaster, the Ti-ping forces at Hoo-chow-foo, after soundly beating their immediate adversaries, evacuated that city, and followed in the rear of the Shi-wang's army, if they did not join it during the nearly simultaneous retrograde movement. During the months of May, June, July, and August, 1864, the remnants of Ti-pingdom continued retreating to the southern provinces.

We must now consider for a moment the loss of Nankin. Of the two other events—the retreat of the Shi-wang's army and the retreat from Hoo-chow—it is needless to say much, as these fugitives are well known to be safe, and at present advantageously disputing the enemy in the south of China.

The only records of the fall of the Ti-ping capital are those of Imperialist origin, and the lying proclivities of the whole body of Manchoo officials are too well known to need comment.

The following particulars are condensed from the Mandarin reports.; they cannot be depended upon except to a very limited extent, and are, therefore, succeeded by a version I have deduced from almost every source of European information in China, comprising the Shanghae and Hong-kong press, and intelligence gathered for me by friends on the spot. Besides this, I have carefully traced the progress of events since the fall of Nankin till the present moment, and have found my former experience of much value in disentangling contradictory and confused statements.

The Imperialist accounts of the capture of Nankin are to the following effect:—

On the 17th of August news reached the besieging army that the Tien-wang had committed suicide by swallowing gold-leaf. The Imperialists now pushed on their works more rapidly than before, and on the 19th of the same month, having run an enormous mine under the north-east gate, they fired it, and completely destroyed a portion of the wall, about one hundred and twenty feet in length. It is also reported that 68,000 pounds of powder were used in the explosion.

The Imperialists stated that they lost 5,000 killed and wounded in the breach, but, as the *North China Market Report* observed, "for this assertion there is not the slightest foundation, as on the day following the assault there remained no trace of a struggle." In similar style they declared that their losses while storming the Tien-wang's palace were immense, but, as the European journals say, "This assertion is in like manner utterly false. The gate must have been forced with little or no difficulty, or quietly given up, and the very citadel of Taepingdom was in the hands of the enemy."

Now, after having poisoned the Ti-ping king with gold leaf, the enemy very curiously burned him to death.

Immediately after the capture of Nankin, Mr. Adkins, H.M. Consul at Chin-kiang, proceeded to the city on board M.M.S. *Slaney*, in order, as he expresses himself in his despatch to Earl Russell on the subject, "to congratulate the Chinese (Manchoo) Commander-in-Chief on the auspicious termination of his two years' siege." Well, the commander, or some of his followers, told the officious Mr. Adkins that when they made good their entrance into the city, "they found that the palace of the Tien-wang *had been burnt to the ground.*"

What about the "immense loss" of the other version, in which they do such heroic deeds to capture the palace?

Mr. Adkins goes on to say "that the impostor (?) and his immediate attendants lie buried in its ruins."

The victors also reported that they captured the Chung-wang a few days later, and also the Kan-wang when they entered the city, finding him in the Tien-wang's palace. Chung-wang, they say, managed to leave the city with a number of followers, but was captured three days later by a body of cavalry sent in pursuit: this was the account given to Mr. Adkins. Another Imperialist version states that the Ti-ping Commander-in-Chief was captured by *some villagers* a few miles from the city, through having given up his own white horse (celebrated for great strength and fleetness) to his young prince, the Tien-wang's son, and having compelled him to mount it and escape when he saw that at least a portion of his party must be captured. Certainly this seems very characteristic of the Chung-wang's brave, loyal, and generous nature, but then it is the only incident in the whole narrative which bears the appearance of truth and probability. Besides the above two stories of his capture, when the enemy obtained possession of Hoo-chow-foo, they reported that they had caught the Chung-wang *there*, and from that place a head, stated to be the great rebel general's, was sent over the country as a warning to the people.

As for the story of the Kan-wang's capture, there are several contradictory and apparently authentic statements: one by a certain Patrick Nellis, who personally saw the chief and talked with him at Hoo-chow (subsequent to the fall of Nankin), where it seems that he proceeded with an escort to communicate the loss or abandonment of the capital, and concert measures for the evacuation of Hoo-chow-foo as well.*

Besides the above reports, others were promulgated by the Mandarins, in which they defeated different Ti-ping armies *en route* for the south, killing thousands and tens of thousands of rebels and capturing many chiefs, among them the Shi-wang, who, singularly enough, still managed to be in command of the Ti-pings near Amoy, until within the last few months, when he retired to join other leaders farther inland. Confessions were produced which professed to be written by the penitent rebel leaders in their dungeons, while awaiting their turn to be disembowelled,

* *Times*, January 12, 1865. *China Overland Trade Report*, 30th November, 1864.

or "cut into a thousand pieces"—a pleasing prospect, of course likely to make the destined victims suddenly feel inspired with love and respect for the benevolent Manchoos, whom they had so vigorously opposed all their lives! Among these seemingly fabricated confessions only one is worthy of any attention, and that is a lengthy composition, entitled, "The autographic deposition of Chung-wang, the faithful king, at his trial after the capture of Nankin." Were it not for the known mendacity of the Mandarins, and their particular addiction to forging documents of this sort in order to lessen the prestige of the revolution by representing its principal leaders as in their merciless power, there would be little doubt but that the one in question was genuine. In 1852, previous to the capture of Nankin by the Ti-pings, the Imperial authorities concocted an article they named the "Confession of Tien-teh," pretending that it was the deposition of the leader of the rebellion, whom they falsely declared was their prisoner. It is quite probable that the "Chung-wang's deposition" is of similar truthlessness, and was made up by some prisoner of note (who may have been pardoned in consequence), and the cunning writers attached to the Governor-General of the two Kiang, Tseng-kwo-fan. Still it must be admitted that many portions of the alleged deposition bear not only the impress of truth (in so far as historical events, data, &c., are concerned), but expressions closely resembling the well known sentiments of the great Ti-ping general; so that if, as we trust, he was not the author, some one pretty intimately acquainted with him must have been. However, some facts tending to support the theory (for there is no direct proof in any case except the Shi-wang's movements subsequent to the fall of Nankin) of the Chung-wang's escape, will be given in the course of our narrative.

Having noticed the Imperialist reports, it is now necessary to give the following digest of the events referred to, and which may be depended upon as the only possible version to be derived from the existing and attainable sources of information:—

It is known that when the Chung-wang became convinced England was determined to persist in prosecuting hostilities against his people, and likewise felt their inability to cope with the foreign power, he at once decided upon the best military movement under the circumstances—namely, an entire abandonment of all accessible possessions, and a retreat into the interior, where British hostility could not reach them, and where no Manchoo forces could either prevent their operations, restrain their consequent reinforcement, or impede their future progress.

Before parting with the Chung-wang, I was myself present at several councils when the above plan was discussed, and unanimously agreed to by every chief present. But one impediment prevented the Commander-in-Chief from acting with his usual brilliancy of conception and wonderfully successful rapidity of execution; it was the Tien-wang, who refused even to listen to any proposal to abandon his capital.

Different people will view this ruinous obstinacy of the Ti-ping king in various ways. Some will look upon it as sheer, downright folly; others, as the useless, fanatical sacrifice of a bigot; while some may consider that that great, heroic, noble-minded man, having once established the capital of his dominions and the centre of his religio-political movement at Nankin, did right and gloriously in meeting death rather than turning backwards on the grand path. If we ascribe to the Tien-wang motives partaking equally of the three traits—nobleness, fanaticism, and rashness—we shall probably be pretty near the truth.

At all events, the Tien-wang passionately refused to entertain the only plan by which the existence of the Ti-ping power, and the perpetuation of his dynasty, seemed possible. All the court officers, cabinet ministers, and other high authorities of Nankin, were blindly subservient to the will of their king, and equally infatuated with his religious and temporal command. Besides, many of those about him were of the Hung family, and, being nearly related to their chief, not only followed implicitly his wishes, but jealously formed themselves into a clique about him, to the prejudice and exclusion of other more capable and independent officers. All the fighting Wangs were outside the capital, and incessantly engaged with the enemy; few troops were in garrison, while many thousands of helpless non-combatants daily diminished the stores of the failing granaries; and if the multitudinous besieging army, encamped and fortified all round the devoted city, had been animated with the slightest particle of courage or military spirit, they might easily have captured it many months before it eventually fell through starvation, or was evacuated by the troops.

The Chung-wang, after his separation from myself at Wu-see, proceeded direct to Nankin *viâ* Chang-chow-foo. His only object was to save the king and his own family (living with his aged mother, whom he loved with excessive filial tenderness), by inducing them to leave the untenable city. He, alone, proposed the unpalatable manœuvre to the Tien-wang, whose severe displeasure he had already incurred, being punished in various ways—by deprivation of titles, refusal of audience, accusation of disloyalty, &c. How the time (December, 1863, to 19th July, 1864) was passed, from the arrival of the Chung-wang to the fall of the capital, unless the professed " autographic deposition " be true, or the garrison really abandoned the city and escaped, will probably never be known to history. Either, as the "deposition" states, the whole city petitioned against the departure of the renowned commander, or he personally elected to remain, rather than desert his king in the hour of death and darkness, even though such calamity might have been avoided but for the fatal perverseness of the monarch; perhaps both causes operated to confine him to useless inactivity within the walls of the doomed city—inevitably doomed, and encircled by the numberless siege works of the enemy as with a band of impenetrable steel.

How the poor people, fated by the passive stubbornness of their rulers, must have gathered together round their great warrior, as men will rally about a tower of strength; how the unnumbered thousands of helpless non-combatants must have rejoiced at the presence of him whose very name was an army, a bulwark to his people, and a terror to the enemy; how bitterly must the brave, energetic soldier have grieved and chafed at the unnecessarily-incurred annihilation, and growing horrors of the siege, which should have been avoided; but, alas! how could one great man, without means, save a people, a sacred cause, and a city invested by 100,000 savage foemen?

Loyalty and filial duty brought the "faithful prince" to Nankin; the same motives bound him there to await destruction, when his presence in the field—at the head of his own army, left under command of his cousin, the Shi-wang—would have proved invaluable, and would surely have placed the Ti-pings in a much better position than they occupied at the close of the year 1863.

Nankin fell at last. All that is *positively* known by Europeans—apart from false, garbled, and exaggerated Mandarin sources—may be summed up in few words:—Frightful privations were endured before the enemy took possession; and when the city was entered by Mr. Consul Adkins, and other gentlemen, the streets and houses were literally blocked up with the bodies of the dead, by far the greater portion having the appearance of death from starvation; and many being very far advanced in decomposition, proved that, long before the Imperialists found courage enough to blow an opening through the undefended walls, the unfortunate people had succumbed to famine faster than the living could bury the dead—in fact, it was evident that no such effort could have been successful from the numbers who had daily perished.

Mr. Adkins, in his despatch to Earl Russell, places the number of people slaughtered by the Imperialists on their entry at 10,000; but other visitors state as many as 30,000, which is probably nearer the truth.

It is also certain that many chiefs with their followers left Nankin in safety. A successor to the Mo-wang, assassinated at Soo-chow, having afterwards appeared at Hong-kong; the Yu and Hsieh Wangs (the latter being one of the Tien-wang's brothers, and always attached to the court) being heard of in Kiang-si at the head of an army; while the following extract from the narrative of one Patrick Nellis, already referred to, and which was made on affidavit before the British Consul at Shanghae, seems to prove that the Ti-ping prime minister escaped from Nankin, and such being the case, undoubtedly there are strong grounds to believe the military leaders did likewise. In the evidence sworn to, Nellis, after describing an engagement with the Imperialists, states:—

"On our return to Hoo-chow-foo, Kang-wang arrived from Nankin with an escort. Great ceremonies were shown at his reception; he did not look as if he had suffered any hardship. . . ."

In speaking of the evacuation of the city, Nellis makes the following statement:—

"Kan-wang spoke to me in English very slowly. He asked me what I was. I said, 'an Englishman.' He said he had never met a good foreigner, and asked me if I would go with him to Kiang-si. I said I should be very glad if Tow-wang (Commandant of Hoo-chow) would let me."

This conversation took place more than a month after the fall of Nankin, and a few days before the abandonment of Hoo-chow-foo on the 28th August, 1864. Upon the strength of such facts the *Friend of China* has steadily maintained that Nankin was abandoned by all but the poorest civilians when the Imperialists made their breach and marched through without opposition.

Another circumstance damaging to the veracity of the Imperialist reports, is a statement (contained in one of the Mandarin's inspired " confessions,") purporting to be that of the Tien-wang's son (the heir to the throne). The young prince is made to state that his father "succumbed to sickness on the 24th of May, 1864;" but of this all-important event the "Chung-wang's deposition" makes no mention. Here is an inconsistency which at once proves either one or both the "confessions" false; because, if the Tien-wang had really died, the Chung-wang would have been at liberty to carry out his own views and abandon Nankin; whereas his professed "deposition" states that, to the day the city fell, he was unable to do so in consequence of the Tien-wang's opposition.

The *Friend of China* also states that a Mr. Butler, of Shanghae, actually witnessed the withdrawal of the garrison. Moreover, adding together the few spared by the enemy, those slain and those destroyed by famine, we should even then scarcely have the number of destitute people—labourers, coolies, and friendless non-combatants—who were relieved by the Chung-wang alone during the early part of the year 1864, when he kept a list of about 80,000 dependent upon his resources and charity. In 1863 rations were daily issued to upwards of 400,000 people. At the period now referred to, when the Chung-wang shut himself up in the beleaguered city, the population, inclusive, was certainly not less than a fifth of a million, and, probably, far exceeded that number; therefore, even supposing that one-half (which is a large estimate) perished, were slain, or made prisoners, during and at the termination of the siege, how can we account for the 100,000 remaining, unless we believe that they had previously managed to effect their retreat from the city?

In the *Friend of China*, August 16, 1864, appears the following:—

"We are still assured by parties who have means of knowing, that our first story of the evacuation of Nankin by its soldiery, before the Imperialists sprung their mine and rushed in, was the correct story; all those 30,000 massacred individuals told of by the *Recorder* (but *not* mentioned at the Asiatic Society with the "flushing of a pheasant") being inoffensive men, women, and children.

"The Chung-wang, it is said, is not dead. He is at Hoo-chow-foo, while the Tien-wang is still in the body."

The strongest support of the Imperialist statement of the death of the Tien-wang, and the capture and subsequent execution of the Chung-wang, is the fact that, since the fall of Nankin, nothing whatever has been heard of them elsewhere. On the other hand, however, it was supposed that one or the other was commanding the forces in the interior, acting in Fu-keen in concert with the Shi-wang when he occupied the city of Chang-chow, near Amoy, from October, 1864, to May, 1865: and what seems to lend force to this supposition is that he appeared to be acting under the orders of some superior farther inland; the only chiefs of higher rank being the King and his son, the Chung, Kan, I (several years absent in Sz-chuen), and Si Wangs—the latter being a young man (son of the original Western King) attached to the court at Nankin, and totally without authority in military affairs. Upon the whole, it is quite possible that the Ti-ping King, his son and heir, Prime Minister, and General-in-Chief, may have met with the fate ascribed to them by the enemy; still there is no positive proof, and there are good grounds for supposing that some, if not all, are yet living and directing the Ti-ping movements.

The siege of Hoo-chow-foo by the Imperialists was merely nominal, for, up to the abandonment of that city by the Ti-pings, they were never allowed within range of its walls, and were compelled to act almost entirely on the defensive, so repeated and vigorous were the attacks by the garrison and a corps of observation they had encamped outside the place on a neighbouring range of hills. Only a few days before the evacuation took place, the garrison succeeded in capturing a number of Imperialist stockades, several hundred gun-boats, and three or four thousand men, besides inflicting heavy loss in killed and wounded; the Franco-Manchoo disciplined auxiliaries alone losing 6 officers and 800 men. Very soon after this victory, the evacuation was effected with consummate skill, the enemy not discovering that the Ti-pings had flown until the day after. The number of troops forming the garrison and encampment was very considerable, 50,000 being the lowest estimate;* their line of retreat was either through the province of Fu-keen or Kiang-si, and their destination is even yet unknown, none of the chiefs from Hoo-chow having been recognised anywhere since. It is, however, pretty certain that they acted in concert with the forces led by the Shi-wang, though keeping an inland position, while the latter advanced to the sea-board at Amoy.

The *Friend of China*, Sept. 8, 1864, under the heading,— "Another of the parties despatched by us a short time ago, to learn the real state of affairs about Hoo-chow-foo, has just returned,"—reports as follows:—

"The Chung-wang was in command up to the last. . . . Hoo-chow was evacuated. . . . Three days afterwards—we repeat—three days afterwards, Le Futai gallantly marched into the city with a thundering noise; and then what did he? The gates were closed, and then commenced a general sack, and the usual massacre of innocent individuals. . . . A laughable story is told of the *second* capture of the Chung-wang here, at Hoo-chow; his head—the veritable caput—with loud clamour of gongs, being sent round to all the villages, that people might behold the head of the arch traitor! Our reporter, wicked sceptic! loudly declares that the head *said to be* the Chung-wang's, truly sat on the shoulders, a week ago, of a man whose highest grade in life was that of a coolie!"

---

* The *Times*, October 26, 1864, in its China intelligence (under date, "Shanghae, September 4"), describing the evacuation of Hoo-chow, makes the following statement, which is a further proof of the total or partial escape of the Nankin garrison:—"The rebel force had been so greatly swollen by fugitives *from Nankin* and other places, that it constituted quite a formidable army."

In the month of October, 1864, the residents of Amoy were suddenly surprised to hear that a body of Ti-pings, about 10,000 strong, had surprised and captured the city of Chang-chow, barely twenty miles inland, and situated on a river emptying itself into the sea at the Treaty Port.

From this reappearance of the Ti-pings close to a Treaty Port, we are enabled again to obtain some authentic records—many Europeans, including the British Consul, having visited them at Chang-chow. One English gentleman wrote the following account (which may be relied on as authentic) of his experiences to the *Daily Press*, and the same was reproduced in *The Overland China Trade Report*, 1st January, 1865 :—

"A VISIT TO CHANG-CHOW.
"*To the Editor of the 'Daily Press,' Hong-kong.*

"Sir,—As you appear desirous to obtain information regarding the insurgents in this neighbourhood, I take leave to furnish you with the following result of my personal observations, which were derived in the course of a visit amongst them.

"The city and suburbs of Chang-chow are still occupied by the Taeping insurgents. About three-fifths of the whole city is burnt, and in the ruins may be seen the dead bodies of the late inhabitants, uninjured except by fire; not a wound could I see on any, which plainly shows, and as the rebels themselves affirm, that the inhabitants set fire to their dwellings themselves, and perished in them; having previously drugged themselves with opium rather than fall into the hands of the insurgents.

"Those portions of the city unburnt are occupied by the rebels, but there are many streets of Hongs, the doors of which are sealed up, uninhabited, and apparently full of merchandise. The rebels appear to be very numerous; I should estimate them at about 12,000; but they affirm themselves that they number 15,000. There are a great number of boys and youths among them, but I saw no women. They are much sunburnt, thin, and haggard in their appearance, and evidently have undergone much hardship before they took this city. I was told by many of them that they underwent extreme privations during their retreat from the north; that food of any kind, at many places, could not be obtained, on account of the country people being extremely hostile, and destroying everything as soon as they heard that the rebels were nearing them. That at several small towns on the borders of the Provinces of Che-kiang and

Fokien human flesh was used for food; and that a peasant's body was retailed out at 80 cash per catty by the fortunate rebel who had killed him!

"The chief in command at Chan-chow is Tszle-wang,* brother to Chung-wang. He was at Ningpo during its occupation by the insurgents in 1862, and he commanded in the defence of that city when he was attacked and driven out by the British naval force, under Captain Dew. But he says he bears no animosity towards the British on account of it, as he is aware that Captain Dew was subsidized by the Chinese Government to retake Ningpo from the rebels. He professes the profoundest respect for the British nation for their bravery and power; and what he most ardently wishes is to be on friendly terms with her; and all that he requests is for her to act fairly up to her *professed neutrality* to both contending parties. He says that, should they not succeed in conquering the Imperialists, he would be most happy to see the country under British rule. He promised he would not venture nearer to Amoy than Chang-chow (which is about twenty miles distant), provided the Mandarins at Chau-bay, a town situated on the river, about half way between Amoy and Chau-chow, did not blockade the river, and cut off all native trade and communication with them. That, in case they did, he should be compelled to take Chau-bay. That he should on no account attack Amoy, as he did not wish to have any rupture with foreigners. That he was very sorry the trade of Amoy suffered on account of their occupation of Chau-chow. That he would be only too happy to open trade reciprocally with foreigners; and that he would grant them every privilege and protection. That he was willing to trade with them for any description of European goods and native produce in return. Opium was not interdicted. He has made a law to protect all native farmers and tradespeople, and this has been already felt by the country people who have opened a day market in one of the main streets of the south suburb; and, from daylight to dark, until the gates are shut, every description of native 'Chow-chow' is to be obtained. Tszle-wang told me that the establishing of this market, though doing a great deal of good to both parties, had led to many executions of both rebels and country people—the former on account of taking goods and not paying for them, and natives found in the city setting fire to houses and plundering; who, when caught, are taken before a rebel Mandarin, and, if found guilty, executed; as no rebel, under penalty of death, can take the life of any person, except in action. The rebels appear to be well armed with rifles, revolvers, and muskets. The Imperial soldiers in this respect are not to be compared to them, as their arms consist entirely of

---

* The writer of the letter has evidently made a confusion of the name, Le, and title, Shi, of the chief, for the following proclamations prove him to be the Shi or Shee Wang.

native matchlocks, gingalls, and spears, and not one in ten has even a matchlock; and they are a wretched lot of ragged rabble. On the other side, the rebels are very neatly dressed, more cleanly, and are drilled after European tactics. There are some Europeans amongst them, but I had no communication with them. They have entirely routed the Imperialists in every engagement they have had with them; and on the 2nd instant they came down on the Imperial lines 2,500 strong, the Imperial troops numbering 11,000; who have advanced to within about five miles of the city, to endeavour to protect the farmers, to gather in the standing crops of rice, which are in great abundance for many miles around the city, and which the rebels have gathered in and secured. The Imperials were encamped on both sides of the Rim, but their greatest force was on the right bank, behind a rugged hill, the inner extremity of which was crossed at right angles by a valley, which could have been easily protected by throwing up a few earthworks and mounting a few guns in them. Their weak point they could not see; and the rebels, taking advantage of the hilly ground in the neighbourhood to advance under cover during daylight, and, coming down the valley at dark, entered the Imperial camp about eleven p.m., without any warning being given. The Imperials were completely panic-struck; and having no retreat but by river, rushed to their boats in such numbers that many of them were swamped, and hundreds of soldiers drowned. Many of them ran and hid themselves wherever they could, and among the latter was the chief Mandarin in command. They offered little or no resistance; and the rebels, after killing 1,000 and taking 450 prisoners, destroying the camp equipage, returned to the city at daylight. Tszle-wang told me that his plan of campaign would be next to take the large and populous town of Tong-wah, and from thence march upon the district city of Chin-chew in the spring. That the amount of the whole rebel force in the province of Fokien under his command fell little short of 50,000 men; and hoping to increase it to 80,000 after the capture of Chin-chew, he should then endeavour to open communication with the British authorities, and arrange to take Foo-chow-foo.

"Tszle-wang appears to be a man of considerable calibre. He appears, for a Chinaman, to be well up in foreign politics, and conversant on many subjects that you generally find the Chinese most ignorant on. He is affable and engaging in his manner, and appears to treat those about him with kindness. He is thirty-one years of age; short, stout, and well-made; his face is much sunburnt, and complexion, say dark; any person might think he was of Malay origin, as he has both the features and colour of a Malay. That he is some strategist and has considerable military tact must be acknowledged by the manner he took the city of Chang-chow, before a rumour was even circulated of the rebels being anywhere near the place, or intending to capture it; and from the defeats the Imperial force has sustained in every engagement they have had with him, although in numerical strength the Imperial force has always been 3 or 4 to 1. I should like to pay another visit to the insurgents, but all foreigners are interdicted from visiting them, both by the Consuls and Mandarin authorities; in fact, we are now not even allowed to enter the river, which is only a mile and a half, and nearly twenty miles from Chang-chow, on the usual shooting excursions, wild fowl being very plentiful in the river, and which is our only amusement at this season of the year. The whole foreign community feel this to be very hard indeed, and consider it to be very arbitrary on the part of the Consul, as this place is extremely dull—no amusements whatever, our only recreation being in a picnic or shooting excursion up the river—but Mr. Pedder tries to make himself as unpopular as he possibly can, and he has told the Mandarins that they can arrest any foreigner they can find on the river under any circumstances whatever, and the Mandarins have threatened to decapitate any boatmen who may hire their boats to or take foreigners up the river. I also hear that the British Consul some few days ago issued a *warrant* to search the private dwelling of an English resident here for arms and munitions of war; and, if any were found, to bring him prisoner to the Consulate; but, happily, his suspicions were wrongly placed, as they found nothing of the kind in the gentleman's house whatever. Has a British Consul authority to search a gentleman's private dwelling whenever he may please, and set spies to watch the movements of a person to please the Chinese Mandarins? Really this is cringing or holding the candle to the Celestials, and taking away the liberty of the subject entirely; and if it goes any further, I cannot say how it may end.

"Your obedient servant,

"Amoy, 14th December, 1864." "VERITAS."

In a subsequent letter, describing another visit to Chang-chow, the same writer states:—

"The rebel campaign is about to be carried on with vigour in this quarter; of the 30,000 men collected in Chang-chow, not one-fifth are required to garrison the city. I heard from Tszle-wang myself that he should immediately detach 7,000, under Tsi-wang, to assist in the capture of Tong-san, and another force would be despatched simultaneously to attack Tong-wak and Chin-chew. The rebels (Ti-pings) are in possession of six cities in this part of the province of Fu-keen, and within a few days' march. *The rebels told me that Tien-wang's son was at one of the cities.*"

The violation of the Queen's Order in Council (commanding neutrality to be observed after the Soo-chow massacre) by the British Consuls in China, is well shown by the previous letter of "Veritas." Besides the partisan acts therein complained of, six or seven English steamers were hired to the Mandarins at Shanghae to carry Imperialist troops to Amoy. They did so, and were well paid for the affair; but is this neutrality? Moreover, every kind of war material was freely supplied to them, and British officers were allowed to command some of the Imperialist troops (*Colonel* Kirkham, formerly with Gordon, and one *Captain* Macdonald being particularly noticed), while all supplies for, or communication with, the Ti-pings were forbidden and attempted to be cut off; but, notwithstanding, munitions of war, and some Europeans (including *Colonel* Rhode, Gordon's late Adjutant-General, and *Colonel* Williams, who had commanded one of the Anglo-Manchoo regiments) managed to reach the revolutionists.

Shortly after the capture of Chang-chew, the Shi-wang issued the following proclamations :—

"NOTIFICATION FROM THE TAIPING CHIEF AT CHANG-CHOW.

"Notification from His Royal Highness Lee, Shee-king and Protector General, ordering the people to submit willingly and to continue their occupations.

"Whereas agriculture is the chief of the occupations of mankind, upon which people necessarily subsist, and whereas, since I rule this city I have always informed the people everywhere that they may continue their duties and occupations as usual—be it therefore known that those who submit to this government are called good people. Strict orders have been given to my officers and soldiers not to make any disturbance among the inhabitants, which orders you must have heard.

"But how is it that at present the fields are left uncultivated and all agricultural business seems to be entirely neglected? The plantations of sugar-cane are nearly ready for harvest, but will spoil if not cut, and the grains and paddy are nearly rotten, the reason of which we cannot comprehend. Probably the raising of arms is the cause of it, of which the people stand in awe, consequently they moved to their countries; or is the cause that at the time of fighting they are afraid that they may be implicated, that on this account they fled to other places? But the benevolent and just army will not destroy the good people; while they exterminate the wicked, they will not punish the innocent.

"Now two villages on the south and north have already submitted, they are settled as usual. You people should be diligent at all times in trade and agriculture.

"Further, in the four villages of that place, the sugar-canes may be converted into sugar and the grains be collected: if you do not immediately return and resume your occupations, then how will the people get their subsistence? Furthermore, the people who fled away have not paid their taxes due, being thus ignorant of the plan of seeking peace.

"I treat others with great liberality, and therefore again and again issue these notifications, intimating to you that all those who have fled away may quietly return to cut the sugar-canes and collect the grains, and those who have not paid their taxes must, with submissive mind, come and pay their taxes. You must not cherish any doubt or hesitation, nor have a different heart, otherwise you will too late repent what you have done. I protect the people as children, and look upon them as wounded; therefore, for more than a month since I have taken possession of the place, I have never allowed a single soldier or officer to go to any village to give trouble. Now all the regulations have been arranged and the laws rectified, and strict orders have also repeatedly been given to the army thus treating you people bountifully and kindly. When the superior is so affectionate, you inferiors should readily come and pay tributes.

"After this notification has been issued, if those who have not paid their taxes and still insist on their obstinacy by disregarding it, troops will be raised to punish them in order to warn those who are perverse and stubborn, without lenity. Every one of you must obey this command and not disappoint me of my affection to you.

"LEE-SHAI-YIN,

"Shee-king, and Protector General of the Celestial Dynasty.

"Taiping Celestial Kingdom, 14th year, 19th moon, 30th day."
—*Daily Press.*

"ADDRESS FROM THE TAIPING CHIEF AT CHANG-CHOW TO THE TREATY POWERS.

"His Royal Highness Lee-Shai-yin, Shee-king and Imperial Protector General of the Celestial Dynasty, to their Excellencies the Plenipotentiaries of England, France, United States, and the people of their respective countries.

"Since creation our Chinese Empire was first governed by Shinnung, then by the Emperors Yaw and Shun, who afterwards resigned their throne. Again the Emperors Tang and Mo attained to their throne by force of arms; then Dynasties Chun, Han, Ngai, and Tsiun transmitted their thrones to their respective posterity, and were succeeded by the Dynasties Tang, Sung, Yune, and Ming. It would be a matter of considerable difficulty, when referring to the distant generations, to repeat them all, but as a nation it had hitherto been in amity with all your various nations, no distinct border having been marked out. I was born late, and have not had the fortune to view these good prospects, and to enjoy the administration of the benevolent Government, but I have examined maps of the world, and studied the histories, and I am happy to possess a thorough knowledge of them, and the contents of which are as before me. For a man to guard a place, the watchword is to remember the fact that when the lips are cut off, the teeth will be endangered. To be in amity with adjacent countries, and for one to keep intercourse with neighbouring countries, it is essential not to forget the maxim of one large nation serving another small one. Of the history of China in counting back from the Dynasties of Ming and Yune, there have been innumerable successive revolutions of kingdoms who invariably paid tributes and presented precious stones to each other when due, and who never encroached upon other's territory. But the Tartars were of a different species, remarkable for their ravenous disposition, and for this reason, the central kingdom with the eastern provinces, in order to prevent their invasion, built the great wall. Unfortunately, during the latter part of the Ming Dynasty they were allowed to invade the interior, we became their victim, and have since been disgraced by them for these two centuries or more. Who then with common sense and natural patriotism would not strike his breast and weep? Even your various nations, in a practical point of view, are countries and in relation as lip to teeth, would not fail, I think, to hate them.

"Long had it been designed to raise the just standard, but in consequence of their being few in China who would support the movement, the design had for a time to be abandoned. Happily our Heavenly Father the Almighty God did not desert the descendants of Han (China), and hated the Tartars, and sent down my Lord who settled at Kinling* as a basis of operations for more than ten years, and during that period exterminated thousands and ten thousands of Tartars. My Lord had always been in friendship with the heroes and enterprising men of your various nations who carried on their respective trades as usual. Further, the provinces of Kwang, Cheh, Yu, and others have been opened, and the ministers and people of various nations have travelled and rambled, and trade has been carried on uninterruptedly as usual. Is this not excellent? In obedience to my Lord's command I have been ordered to extirpate and root out the Tartars. Recently I attacked and took Chang-chow, where I encamped my soldiers. Whilst there I was glad to hear that you were close by, and I would ere this have sent a despatch to you, but various difficulties were thrown in the way. I now write this and tell the people of Tai-po-tsz of Cha-chow to present it for your perusal, earnestly hoping

* This must mean Nankin.

that after reading, you will consider the importance of lip-lost-and-teeth-endangered phrase, and perceive the advantage of a large nation serving a small one; that you will support our just movement by combining together to put an end to the Tsing Dynasty, in order that the people may live in happiness, and your various natives enjoy peace. The doctrine of our Heavenly Father, the Almighty God, and of Jesus Christ, teaches us that He is merciful, saving us, answering to prayers and unselfish—all mankind should look to future and believe in Christianity.

"Therefore, more than ten years before my Lord's accession to the throne, he believed in Christianity, as his conduct would show.

"He also received the Rev. Mr. Roberts, who preached the Gospel to the Chinese who believed and praised with him to God. We have welcomed your doctors, who cured many Chinese, and healed their diseases. We all feel grateful for their merciful kindness, and are under obligation for their favours. From this you will see that your nations and our Chinese in a universal point of view are as one. But the Tartars believe in Buddhism, despise Christianity, and turn a dead ear to its doctrine. It may be argued that belief or disbelief rests with them, and they will afterwards reap the fruit of their conduct. Well, why then do they persecute Christian converts so that their lives are in jeopardy? Therefore my Lord reluctantly took up arms, raised an army, and coped with them. This has been going on for these more than ten years, and through the mercy of our Heavenly Father, the Almighty God, and Jesus Christ, and through the assistance of your various nations, my Lord has taken many cities and provinces, and killed many Tsing devils. Still to conquer and subdue an empire of eighteen provinces, combined with a strong army of Mongols and Chinese, who have ample munitions of war and provisions, must be extremely difficult.

"Let us learn from the ancients as well as the moderns that to lead an army to battle it is indispensable to have reinforcements; and to establish a kingdom it is essential to get assistance from the neighbouring countries. Your various nations and China are at present like lip to teeth, and similar to a large country serving a small one. Let me ask you that before my Lord settled at Kiang-nan, could you get admittance into the interior? Now you can ride from east to west and from north to south, and the provinces of Hupeh and Ngan-hoin have been opened to trade. If your various nations do not ally with me to exterminate the Tsing Dynasty, and in case our force being unable to cope with the Tartars, as we are deficient in naval power, we shall be conquered, then the result of lip-lost and teeth-endangered will soon follow. Therefore it is desirable that your various nations should embrace this opportunity as presented.

"If, on the other hand, your various nations, relying on the omnipotence of our Heavenly Father and Jesus Christ, and acting upon the doctrine of Christianity, will come to terms with us for destroying the Tsing Dynasty, if you command your naval armies and attack those places near the water, and whatever cities, districts, ports, and passes you will have taken and conquered by your force, you will be at liberty without the least hinderance on my part to keep them, and whatever treasures and food found therein, you will be at liberty to appropriate them. And so I will attack on land, and whatever cities, districts, and passes I conquer, and whatever treasures and food I find, I will divide, giving one half to you, and all the distant cities, ports, and marts will be surrendered to you.

"Thus having your naval armies, we can cross the ocean and bestride the rivers without obstacle or hinderance. Our army, I must confess, in its beginning is weak, and food is not plentiful; and unless your various nations lend a hand to assist me, the Tartars will be more ravenous and their ferociousness will be greater, *and if once our army is subdued, they will as a matter of course come upon your various nations,* when, it is clear, you will be precluded from trading and travelling in the provinces of Kiang, Kwang, Cheh, and Yu. I earnestly pray that you will despatch your soldiers and co-operate with me to exterminate the evil posterities, and that we all may obtain advantages. Hoping you will comply with my views is my earnest prayer.

"The statements I have made, though they are vulgar, I undertake to swear before heaven that I will keep them. Let us write in benevolence to accomplish our undertakings, then we shall make peace with each other, trade with each other from generation to generation, and enjoy together universal peace. Is this not the best plan? The city of Chang has been and is a rich place, at present both the soldiers and inhabitants are happy, trade is flourishing, and treasures are plentiful. I also earnestly request that you will convey merchandise and vessels containing all kinds of foreign cargo, and the caps, powder, &c., which will be sold immediately here. You have no occasion to fear that some of my men will take them without paying for them. I will make up the damages should they do so, and surely I will not break my promise!

"On the day of this epistle reaching you, you will favour me with a reply.

"With my best compliments to your gentlemen of your various nations,
"I am your obedient servant,
"LEE-SHAI-YIN,

"Shee-king, and Imperial Protector General of the Celestial Dynasty
"Taiping Celestial Kingdom, 14th year, 10th moon, 1st day."
—*Daily Press.*

CHAPTER XXVI.

Results of British Policy.—Its Effect on Trade.—The Inspectorate System. —The Tien-tsin Treaty.—Present State of China.—Rebellion in the Ascendant.—Proposed Remedy.—The Mandarin Policy.—The Extradition Treaty.—The Mo-wang's Case.—Its Injustice.—Its Illegality. —Burgevine's Case.—Our Treatment by the Manchoos.—Russia's Policy in China.—Contrasted with that of England.—Russian Progress.—Statistics.—Acquisition of Territory by Russia.—Her Approach to British India.—Russia's Advantages.—Her Future Policy.—"Peking and the Pekingese."—Its Author's Misstatements, —Misquotations.—Examples thereof.—"Chinese Miscellanies."—Tiping Movements.—The Future of the Ti-pings Doubtful—Latest Movements.—The Kan-wang.—Nien-fie Victories.—Future Prospects.—Finis.

SINCE Whig Ministers took it into their heads to become Manchoo Mandarins, the result may soon be told.

The wars have all been undertaken for the purpose either of forcing trade—principally, if not wholly, that in opium—upon the Chinese, or else to chastise that people for endeavouring to put their own laws against opium smuggling into force, from the time of the *fracas* with Commissioner Lin to the lorcha *Arrow* pretext for the last war.

The results of the late British policy in China are summed up generally in the following sectional review:—

1. As for the vaunted treaty of Tien-tsin, *forced* from unwilling Manchoos by the results of the "*Arrow* war," it has greatly restricted trade along the coast of China, closed ports (such as Wan-chew, Tai-chew, Lam-quan, Hoc-kau, Chin-chew, &c.), which were virtually open to foreign trade, and by confining commerce to a few Treaty

Ports, played exactly into the hands of the anti-foreign Mandarins. Upon this subject a capital article appears, from an old resident of many years' standing in China, in the *Overland Trade Report*, September 11, 1865, which, as the editor says, " contains the most able exposition of the defects of the treaty of Tien-tsin, of the pernicious results of the foreign inspectorate, and of the crusade carried on against foreign shipping visiting non-treaty ports, that we ever read." The article is long, but some of its salient points are to the following effect : Until the signing of the treaty of Tien-tsin, the whole coast-line, from Canton to Woo-sung, with all its intermediate ports, was virtually open to foreign trade ! Foreign vessels of all nations were allowed and even encouraged by the local authorities to enter any port they chose, and were permitted to trade in any article, either native or foreign, without hindrance or molestation, provided they paid the lawful duties.

The disadvantages to which British (and all foreign) trade is subjected by the treaty of Tien-tsin, and the establishment of the foreign inspectorate of Chinese Customs, are these :—

1st. To pay nearly double as much duty on both imports and exports as native vessels or junks are charged.

2nd. Heavy tonnage dues are enforced, consisting of 4 mace or 4·10 of a tael (6s. 8d.) per ton, every four months, instead of every six months as previous to the war; junks paying no tonnage dues!

3rd. Interdicted from carrying or trading in *salt*, one of the principal articles of trade in all parts of China and Formosa. Likewise saltpetre, sulphur, alum, and some other articles of general commerce, on pain of confiscation of vessel. Junks allowed to carry or trade in any article either native or foreign !

4th. Interdicted from entering any port on the coast of China, except those specified "open port" by the treaty, on pain of *confiscation* of vessels and cargo. Junks free to enter any port or harbour either in China or foreign countries. What a contrast of advantages and disadvantages! Whereas, before the concoction of the Tientsin treaty, foreign vessels enjoyed equal privileges with native craft, they have since been placed at a discount by the execution of the retrogressive measures of that treaty so inimical to British interests. No doubt the astute Manchoo statesmen who acted for China during the negotiations gained many advantages over the representatives of England. They succeeded in obtaining terms which restricted trade, and limited foreign intercourse to a few ports; their latest act has been to follow this up (now that the dread of the Ti-ping is over and the Ta-ku forts in their hands again) by interdicting the employment of foreign vessels to carry goods on Chinese account even between treaty ports!

2. The foreign inspectorate of Chinese Maritime Customs was a scheme effected by officials of Lord Elgin's embassy to China; its aim was to make sure of the indemnity by placing Englishmen in charge of the Imperial revenue, and to enable the squeezed Government to suppress rebellion by handing it over the remainder. Beautifully has the Pekin Cabinet responded by taking advantage of every opportunity to limit the rights of Englishmen, and resuming step by step its habits of repellance and exclusiveness!

A very significant event has lately taken place, being the elevation of Tseng-kwo-fan, leader of the anti-foreign party, and sometime besieger of Nankin, to a position of unprecedented magnitude. This Mandarin has been appointed to the absolute civil and military control of all the officials and troops, whether Tartar or Chinese, in the three provinces of Chili, Shangtung, and Honan. Speaking of this appointment, the *China Overland Trade Report*, 12th August, 1865, states:—

"Lest it may be hoped by some that Tseng-kwo-fan is a man adapted to the times, and likely to carry into effect salutary reforms, it should be mentioned that he is the quintessence of a Mandarin in the full acceptation of the term—corrupt and venal to a degree, and perfectly indifferent to the welfare of the country or the people. His anti-foreign tendencies form the leading feature of his political creed, and there is good reason to suppose that Prince Kung fully agrees with him. . . . The influence he obtains in the empire will be irresistible, and must insure success in whatever line of policy he may feel inclined to pursue."

Tseng-kwo-fan's rank is that of Commander-in-Chief and General Viceroy of the empire.

The inspectorate system has placed a set of cosmopolitan mercenaries in a position not only to govern but to prey upon the whole foreign trade with China. They are ever upon the *qui vive* to seize and confiscate the merchandise of their own countrymen, and have caused the effectual closing of every port on the coast of China, except those opened by treaty. Property that may be unprotected by every legal right, or may be placed (through the owner's ignorance of inspectorate forms) in such a position as to incur some of the vexatious penalties attaching to every infraction of rules almost daily issued by the European Commissioners of Customs, or their Mandarin colleagues, *ad libitum*, is eagerly pounced upon and appropriated. In fact, it may safely be said that, instead of benefiting foreigners and their trade, the scheme acts directly against their interests; that it places a number of European and American adventurers in a position to assist the Mandarins in taking every advantage of each flaw in the treaty, while at the same time constituting a capital shield behind which the still repulsive Manchoos can execute their anti-foreign plotting in safety.

3. The hostilities against the Ti-pings were caused through the unrighteous policy established by the treaty of Tien-tsin, the foreign inspectorate of Customs, the extortion of indemnity for the war, and the protection of the vile opium trade. This policy has been a great success, in so far as arresting and beating backward

the only portion of the multitudinous Chinese whose progress afforded a prospect of change for the better. It has, with still greater iniquity, warred against and prevented the spread of Christianity; destroyed many thousands and tens of thousands of those who professed that faith, and has stopped the circulation and printing of the Bible in its full integrity by the Ti-ping Government, besides having caused the re-establishment of idolatry on the ashes of the destroyed Book, and the wholesale slaughter of those who only begged for our friendship and instruction. Through the wicked intervention of England, the former territory of the Ti-pings has been wrested from them, and the bleached bones of the victims mark the country thick and close for hundreds of miles. The starvation, the horrors, have been fully described; and now it is reported from China that many of the solitudes created where once happy villages of Ti-pings were found, have become infested with beasts of prey—wolves, panthers, and tigers.

As for having effected the slightest improvement in British relations with China, made the Manchoo authorities less unfriendly and illiberal, or rendered the least service to the general welfare of humanity, the past policy of the British Government has proved a lamentable failure.

By unjustifiable meddling, England has thrown China into a state of general anarchy. The cruelty and excessive corruption of the Manchoo officials throughout the country have always been sufficiently great to cause local insurrections and different regular systems of rebellion; but it was only to the great Ti-ping revolution (which proved its power so superior to that of the Imperial Government as to threaten the rapid extermination of the latter, and compel the assistance of England to save it) that people could look for success, and eventual pacification of the empire. Well, these urgently required results have been prevented by the policy in question.

Unable to depend upon the success of the Ti-ping movement, the disaffected Chinese have joined other rebellions, and at this day there are many desolating the country. In the north, a great amalgamation of the Yellow River rebels (an old organization, sometimes under allegiance to the Ti-ping king) or Nien-fie, with a force of Ti-pings, and a large body of Mohammedan rebels, has taken place. The army of this league is estimated at over 300,000 men; in the summer of 1865 they defeated the Tartar Generalissimo (of Pekin campaign memory) San-ko-lin-sin, who was afterwards killed by some country people with whom he sought a refuge—thus showing the state of feeling amongst the population. The northern rebels then seriously menaced Pekin itself, and at one time it was reported that they had captured the city; lately they seem to have moved more to the westward—probably to effect a junction with other revolutionists; but it is quite certain that the Imperialists are unable to subdue them.

Besides the league, there are two other formidable rebellions raging in the north of China—the Mohammedan rebels, who defy the power of the Government in Shen-si, Shan-se, Kan-su, and other parts of the empire. To the south of these come the "Honan filchers," a horde of more than 100,000 banditti, who maintain, as they have done for years, an independent existence in the Honan Province. Away to the west, the large Tartar province of E-li, four times as large as Great Britain, has been wrested from the Imperialists by a rising of Mahommedans.

Along the western boundary general anarchy prevails: it would almost seem that as Russia advances into central Asia, the Mohammedans were moving towards China.

In the great province of Sze-chuan, the Ti-pings under Shih-ta-kae, the I-wang, or his successor, are still in power. At Hankow (treaty port) in Hu-peh, and at Kew-kiang in Kiang-si, the Imperialist troops lately revolted and set up the standard of rebellion. In Ngan-whui serious disturbances have arisen. Farther south, in Kwei-chow, Yun-nan, and Kwang-si, the Miau-tze, or independent mountaineers, are steadily increasing in strength; in fact, every **province of China** is more or less the scene of formidable revolution or **local revolt.**

The Ti-pings, in strong force, under the Shi-wang and other leaders, are **making rapid progress on the borders of** the provinces of **Kwang-tung, Kiang-si, and Fu-keen, and** the Imperialist **troops seem totally unable to interfere** with them.

Referring to the distracted state of China, the *Overland China Mail,* June 29, 1865, truly states that "there must be something in the conduct of the Imperial Government, and of the local Mandarins, which provokes a strong feeling of resentment against their authority in all parts of the empire." Singularly **enough,** the same journal has always opposed the revolutionists who tried to alter a Government the people hate.

The *Times,* in its Chinese intelligence of June 21, 1865, referring to the **successes of** the Nien-fie League, states:—

"So far as we can at present see, the Nien-fie insurrection is likely to prove quite as formidable as was that of the Taepings. Their leaders have substantial wrongs to avenge, and the people themselves have been subjected to so many hardships at the hands of the local Mandarins that the slightest spark is sufficient to set the whole north of China in a blaze of rebellion."

Those who have advocated interfering against such a movement as that of the Ti-pings, and supporting such a dynasty as that of the Manchoos, **must have very curious reasons** to plead for a justification—they have generally admitted the necessity for a change of government, and then amused themselves by **resisting** the change when offered.

The **only policy which could have benefited China** would have been, either an energetic protectorate esta-

blished by England, and maintained with energy until the evil Government had been thoroughly and radically reformed in every branch; or, what would have been far better, the Chinese should have been left to themselves and allowed to choose their own rulers. If England had simply preserved her honour and remained neutral, China would have had a native, progressionist, and powerful Government at the present day. That huge empire has lasted more than 2,000 years, and the only deterioration its constitution has suffered has been caused by the Tartar conquest. The resources of China are as great, the capacities of her people as vigorous, and the elements of her ancient civilization as durable as ever: once let the incubus of Manchoo maladministration be removed, that vast and intelligent people will rapidly establish a native Government which will inaugurate an era of progression and improvement. For some time the usurping dynasty has been tottering towards its fall; England would have done well to have avoided supporting the decayed and hopelessly corrupt fabric. She has served a dying despotism, too far gone to feel even gratitude for her assistance, and has repelled a young successor who wished ardently to become of the same brotherhood as herself!

4. By her aggressive, meddling policy, England has alarmed the naturally suspicious and treacherous Manchoos. Making them feel towards the "outer barbarians" the passion of fear as well as hate, has, of course, only tended to make them more exclusive and repellant than ever. Every mail from China brings successive proof of the fact. Those who receive advices from the East cannot fail to notice such passages as the following:—

The *Overland China Trade Report*, in its issue September 11, 1865, states:—

"Each succeeding mail takes some instance of Mandarin repellance towards foreigners. There can be no doubt that this feeling is the policy decided on by the Pekin Cabinet. . As bearing upon this point, reference is called to a notification . . issued by the Shanghae authorities, forbidding Chinese to hire foreign vessels . . . The hand of Tseng-kwo-fan, the leader of the anti-foreign party, becoming visible in the present foreign policy pursued."

The article then proceeds to notice the fact that the Mandarin policy of preventing the employment of foreign shipping, and encouraging that of native craft, simply tends to increase piracy by providing prey; and is further reprehensible because the Mandarins will not assist to suppress an evil which, were it not for the presence of British men-of-war, would destroy their entire maritime commerce. Mr. Hart, the Inspector General of Customs, endeavoured to induce the Imperial Government to allow Chinese to own vessels constructed after the foreign mode, but the hatred of foreign innovation, however beneficial, prevailed, and the authorities refused the much-desired boon.

Another instance of Manchoo repellance is the withdrawal of the concession formerly granted to foreign vessels to visit the ports of the Island of Formosa.

And again: the port of Wan-chew was open to foreign trade before the treaty of Tien-tsin, and became a place of much importance. Why it was not included in the list of open ports it is difficult to understand. The foreign representatives and merchants lately endeavoured to obtain the concession of having it opened to foreign trade, and for a time were encouraged by Prince Kung to believe that their request would be complied with. But since Tseng-kwo-fan has come to the front, the concession is rejected, and the idea abandoned.

The notification referred to as prohibiting the employment of foreign vessels was issued by Lin, Imperial Commissioner, and acting Viceroy of Kiang-su, in which province Shanghae is situated. It seems to have proved very effectual, and very injurious to British shipping interest.

The last mail from China brought the *Overland Trade Report*, dated "Hong-kong, October 15, 1865." It contains these lines:—"The repellance and anti-foreign tendencies of the Mandarins are becoming more broadly marked as each month advances."

The *North China Market Report* states "that the Chinese are rapidly learning to disregard the most important of the treaty stipulations." In fact, all sources of information are unanimous as to the hostile feelings of the Manchoo Government England has done so much to bolster up.

Just six months have elapsed since the Colonial Government of Hong-kong perverted its powers by giving up an unfortunate refugee from Nankin to the sanguinary Imperialist Mandarins. After noticing the facts of the case, we will observe how the Manchoos responded to the officious and unwarrantable efforts of the Hong-kong rulers to execute the exterritoriality clause of the notorious treaty of Tien-tsin, the twenty-first article of which stipulates that, "if *criminal* subjects of China shall take refuge in Hong-kong, or on board of British ships there, they shall, upon due requisition by the Chinese authorities, be searched for; and, *on proof of their guilt*, be delivered up."

Acting upon the above clause, the Canton Mandarins, in the month of April, 1865, demanded from the Colonial Government the rendition of a certain Chinaman residing at the latter place, on the plea of his having been a pirate. The man demanded had been residing in Hong-kong since September, 1864, and the following facts transpired during the inquiry instituted. He had been a Ti-ping chief, known as the Mo-wang (probably a successor to the rank of the assassinated Commandant of Soo-chow); and, upon the evacuation of Nankin, had escaped and made his way to Hong-kong, with a considerable sum of money. As this became known to members of some secret societies established amongst the Chinese there, he was subjected to much extortion from people who threatened to denounce him to the Mandarins as a rebel unless he satisfied their demands. At last the persecution drove him to seek legal advice from some English lawyer, who told him that he was perfectly safe on British soil. Consequently, he defied his persecutors; and they, doubtless, to obtain reward from the Mandarins, fulfilled their threats. The principal Manchoo official at Canton, who was certain of promotion should he succeed in catching a rebel of such rank, forthwith demanded his rendition *as a pirate*.

The man was seized and tried before the magistrates' court, where the above evidence was obtained. The proof of his piracy (although consisting of the testimony of only *one* Chinese witness, *sent down specially by the Mandarins*) was considered sufficient; and, notwithstanding the protest of the counsel retained for the prisoner, the magistrate, under the direction of the law officers of the Crown, made out the requisite order for his rendition.

The valuable account from which the facts of this case are taken * states:—

"On this being communicated to the Mo-wang, he made up his mind to commit suicide, if possible, by jumping overboard on his passage to Canton, knowing, as he did too well, the horrid fate that there awaited him. When *handed over* to the Chinese officials, he begged to be released from the handcuffs; but one of our civil officials (the man's name should be made public), not in the police, would not permit this; and he was therefore conveyed to Canton in the manacles of the Hong-kong police. On his arrival there he was taken to prison, the next day brought before the Mandarin, where he refused to plead, acknowledging himself a Ti-ping chief: he was taken back to prison, and the next day was executed in the way reserved for *political offenders*, viz., he was tied to a cross, his cheeks then sliced off, then the insides of his arms, thighs, &c., and finally disembowelled while yet alive. This put beyond a doubt the real cause of the demand for this man, and the real offence for which he was wanted."

Now, in this cruel case of rendition the Government of Hong-kong committed an act repugnant alike to humanity and the Christian principles of their countrymen, and which was not only entirely illegal, but grossly unjust.

* Published in the *Daily News*, August 8, 1865.

The Mo-wang was demanded and given up as a pirate. The only evidence against him was given by *one* Chinaman, and tended to prove that the chief had once stopped a Chinese vessel, on board of which was the witness, endeavouring to run past the Ti-ping Custom House established at Nankin. The junk was confiscated by the Ti-ping authorities. Here we have the main point of the case. This was the only act charged against the Mo-wang. The only question is whether it was piracy. The Colonial authorities, true to the Mandarin-worshipping-and-Ti-ping-destroying policy, answered in the affirmative. Let us examine their decision.

First. The Ti-pings had been recognised as belligerants; and, moreover, as an established power, by repeated acts upon the part of representatives of Great Britain (and other countries); how then could the seizure of a vessel of the enemy by the Mo-wang—a regularly commissioned officer of the Ti-ping Government—be construed into an act of piracy? Why, the United States of America would have stronger (though none the less unreasonable) grounds to demand from England the rendition of every ex-Confederate officer, as a pirate, who might be found within her jurisdiction! The decision of the Hong-kong authorities is clearly against the rights of the case and the law by which it was tried. But what conclusively proves this is the fact that the Mandarins demanded the Mo-wang as a pirate, but executed him as a *political offender*, and nothing else.

Thus, it cannot fail to be seen that the unfortunate victim was not a pirate—the Hong-kong Solons gave him up as one.

Secondly. The extradition treaty with China specially declares "*criminal*" offenders as those who may be given up, upon "*proof* of guilt." The Mo-wang was not a criminal, therefore the Hong-kong authorities violated the law by giving him up as such.

Thirdly. The treaty of Tien-tsin was not the law of

Hong-kong, therefore the authorities had no legal right to render up even a criminal subject of China—how much less the innocent Mo-wang! As the Hong-kong *China Overland Trade Report*, May 30, 1865, truly states, in reviewing this atrocious affair:—" It would appear that the local authorities have not only read the treaty erroneously, but that they have no power whatever to meddle in the matter, no ordinance ever having been passed to enable them to take cognizance of offences under the Tien-tsin treaty. . . .

"The case of the St. Alban's raiders has elicited the fact that a treaty is not a statute, and cannot be adopted by a court of law without a statutory enactment. The Ashburton treaty was not the law of Canada, because the Government had neglected to legalize it by statute. So the Tien-tsin treaty is not the law in Hong-kong, because no ordinance has been passed to legalize it."

The above three objections to the rendition of the Mo-wang pretty strongly prove that his death was a judicial murder by those who unlawfully gave him up to so frightful a doom. Another example of British malversation in China, and a further instance of persecution of the Ti-pings!

It might at least have been expected when British officials exceeded their authority and so misapplied the exterritoriality clause of the treaty in order to oblige the Mandarins, that the latter would have responded. We will observe how they did so.

Within *one month* of the rendition of the Mo-wang, the Imperialists in the neighbourhood of Amoy captured the mercenary soldier, Burgevine (already noticed in these pages), an Englishman named Green, and a British East Indian subject, whilst endeavouring to join the Ti-pings at Chang-chew. These men had committed no crime, and were caught *before* having committed any political offence (any previous episode of Burgevine's life constituting another case, which did not concern the

Englishman, Green). Even if they had succeeded in joining the revolutionists, and had afterwards been caught levying war against the Imperialists, their only offence would have been a political one, viz., breach of neutrality, punishable by deportation from China or three months' imprisonment.

The American Consul at Amoy, hearing of the seizure, demanded, as in this case he had a perfect right to do, the rendition of Burgevine, according to the terms of the exterritoriality clause of the treaty. The Mandarins refused to fulfil their obligations and give up the men. They carried them into the interior and murdered them by heavily ironing, and then drowning them, afterwards pretending that the three unfortunate prisoners had met their death by the capsize of a boat in which they were being conveyed across a river!

Thus we see that immediately after a Chinese *political* offender was illegally given up to the Manchoo Government by the authorities of Hong-kong, the Mandarins deliberately violated the exterritoriality stipulations of the treaty, by refusing to give up the three men whom they had seized before offence, on suspicion only, and by cruelly putting them to death.

The last mail from China brings intelligence of the murder of three Europeans at the treaty port of Chin-kiang. Two (Messrs. Filleul and Pickernel) were Englishmen, and old friends of mine; the third, a Mr. Lewis, was an American. These men were set upon by Imperialist soldiers in the dead of the night, while sleeping, and cruelly murdered, without having given any offence, although another European had struck a Chinaman on the previous day. The murderers belonged to a disciplined contingent, commanded by a Mandarin named Kwo, a force which had been raised, officered, and equipped by British means!

Besides the continual violation of the exterritoriality clause of the treaty, the Manchoos have lately displayed their growing disregard for their obligations and their increasing repugnance to foreigners in a variety of illiberal measures. To those which we have already noticed may be added the late blunt refusal of the Pekin Cabinet to allow the construction of a proposed Russian line of telegraph from Siberia to that city.

Another very serious blow to British and Chinese interests has been the fruitless mission of Sir M. Stephenson. The Manchoo Government has pointedly refused to grant permission for the introduction or construction of railways, and the local authorities have obstructively prevented the formation of proposed experimental lines at Canton, and between Shanghae and Woo-sung, a distance of about fourteen miles.

There is another case in point, which effectually proves the thorough impracticability of the Manchoos. A few months ago an enterprising Shanghae merchant, Mr. E. A. Reynolds, was public-spirited enough to erect a line of telegraph from Shanghae to the sea-coast. He made all arrangements, compensated various native landowners, and erected his posts, only to find them all chopped down again one fine morning. The Mandarins, when appealed to, insulted the British Consul, and refused to allow the erection of the telegraph, the alleged reason being that it interfered with Fung-shui—the spirit of geomancy, the air, or something else.

Shortly before the above outrage, the Mandarins showed their gratitude for the assistance England had given them, by closing the whole of the silk districts and interior to steam communication or transit by foreigners, the same having been free and open under the rule of the Ti-pings, who encouraged the employment of steamers.

Many other instances of Manchoo repugnance and hostility could be mentioned, but those noticed are sufficient for all purposes, and so we will close our review of *some* of the results of British policy in China.

After having examined the conduct of England, it may not be out of place to follow with a short sketch of Russian policy, which is daily becoming so closely connected with China, whilst the frontier of the great Muscovite Power is rapidly extending towards the Chinese and Indian empires in one direction, is peacefully established against Chinese territory in another, and is gradually annexing to herself vast portions of Chinese territory in the north.

Although the Manchoos have always been hostile to British intercourse, "there is a system of European policy which they can and do appreciate," as the *Standard*, August 28, 1865, well said. The substance of the article referred to so thoroughly expresses what I would say, that I cannot refrain from using it:—

The Manchoos comprehend the spirit of Russia, and dwell at peace with that empire on her borders. Instead of a great wall, they are divided from their powerful neighbour by a wooden paling, and there has not been a shot fired between Russia and China, contiguous though they are, during the last fifty years. But what has been the course pursued by Russia with regard to that which is loosely and inaccurately termed the Ti-ping revolt? One of complete neutrality. We, however, from the coast, hoisted our flag in the war. We have taken an active and open part, declared against a tremendous national movement, and been virtually beaten off the Chinese soil and waters. Looking for results, it is impossible to find any, except that our name is hated by millions of people who desired to live and trade upon friendly terms with us. Our representative diplomacy at Pekin is a nullity, and there is every chance that, a change of dynasties intervening, we shall have to undo our Manchoo statesmanship, and comply with a very different set of political necessities in the East. Your Chinese are very intelligent fatalists; they rarely quarrel with facts; they are convinced, it may be, of the English fighting quality; but they can feel little respect for our wisdom when they see us standing in a baffled attitude between both their great parties, blundering and bewildered, with an enormous trade to foster, with prodigious future interests to foresee, and yet with a diplomacy which means neither peace nor war, which binds us to no intelligible line of conduct, and which has brought us to a condition wherein, through any accident, whether of Imperial or insurrectionary success, we may be called upon to defend our rights by force of arms.

It is a fact no less singular than true, that the Russians, in contradistinction to all other Europeans, show a strong tendency to amalgamate with the higher races of Asia. In consequence of this, her rapid progress on the continent referred to partakes of the nature of absorption and not of conquest. The policy of Russia seems inseparable from continual increase of her already vast dominions. In every direction her frontier is determinately advanced, while thousands of strange people are submitting to her sway. In Europe she uses force to obtain any desirable locality; and although it is true that occasionally some obstinate or patriotic chief of Central Asia may dispute her advance, such obstructions would seem to form the exception to the general progress she is enabled to make rather by conciliation and clever seizure than by force of arms.

If people have the audacity to use their eyes, and the unparalleled hardihood to discover the extraordinary increase of the Russian empire, there is a clique of venerable wiseacres who always think to annihilate them by the crushing denunciation, Russophobia! Now, these old gentlemen—it is presumed that they are rather decrepit—may call the knowledge of modern geography and the continual increase of Russia whatever gives them a little innocent amusement; but all the calling in the world cannot alter the fact.

There are two questions which particularly concern

England: is she content to halt on the forward path of nations, while Russia, by reclaiming the people of Asia, bids fair to rival her in every duty assumed by great civilized Powers? Is the meeting of the frontier lines of Russia and India, which, according to the regular increase of the Russian possessions in Central Asia, might be calculated almost to the day, likely to prove disastrous to British empire in the latter country?

Other European Powers can afford to look on without being interested, for only England has so precious a jewel as Hindoostan. The first question may be passed over as merely bearing upon the advancement of abstract principles, or the propagation of Christian doctrine, philanthropy, and civilization; but the second is very different, relating as it does exclusively to the material and commercial interests of Great Britain. Before explaining how these may be affected by the future movements of Russia, or describing the present position of that Power in Central Asia, it will not be out of place to give a short sketch of Russian progress.

At page 410, vol. ii., "MacGregor's Commercial Statistics," the following interesting calculations are given:—

"Russia contained—

At the accession of Peter I. in	1689	... 15,000,000	inhabitants.
At the accession of Catherine II. in	1762	... 25,000,000	,,
At her death in	1796	... 36,000,000	,,
At the death of Alexander	1825	... 58,000,000	,,

"Her acquisitions from Sweden are greater than what remains of that kingdom.

"Her acquisitions from Poland are nearly equal to the Austrian empire.

"Her acquisitions from Turkey in Europe are of greater extent than the Prussian dominions, exclusive of the Rhenish provinces.

"Her acquisitions from Turkey in Asia are nearly equal in dimensions to the whole of the smaller states of Germany.

"Her acquisitions from Persia are equal in extent to England.

"Her acquisitions in Tartary have an area not inferior to that of Turkey in Europe, Greece, Italy, and Spain."

The valuable work quoted from was published in the year 1844. It proceeds to state :—

"The acquisitions she has made within the last sixty-four years are equal in extent and importance to the whole empire she had in Europe before that time.

"The Russian frontier has been advanced towards—

Berlin, Dresden, Munich, Vienna, and Paris ... about	700 miles.
Constantinople ... ... „	500 „
Stockholm ... ... „	630 „
Teheran ... ... „	1,000 „

"It is to be borne in mind that the Russian tariff *of exclusion* has been extended to all those acquisitions where formerly British merchandise was freely sent."

To the above may be added the Russian acquisitions in North America, which are nearly five times the extent of the British Isles.

Her acquisitions from the Chinese empire, the river Amoor territory in Manchuria, are about equal in dimensions to England.

Her acquisitions from independent Tartary since 1844 are more than four times greater in extent than the British Isles. The advance of the Russian frontier from Orenburg to Samarkand is about 800 miles.

Every mail from India brings intelligence of further Russian progress or conquest. The position at which we have placed her is within 200 miles of Cabul, and 400 of Jellalabad and Cashmere. Nothing but the mountains of Cashmere and Cabul separate the Russians from British India. Foiled and driven back by the results of the Crimean war, Russia changed her line of aggression from facing directly through Turkey, Persia, and so to Hindoostan ; but, by concentrating her forces upon and crushing poor Circassia (which might have been protected with almost more reason than Turkey was), she opened a direct passage to Persia upon the west of the Caspian Sea, whilst at the same time other legions were carrying her frontier line at a quick march through

Tartary to the eastward. The command of the Bosphorus would have made the Black Sea a Russian lake, and the only assailable flank of a march into Persia would have been protected against the great naval Powers. That position has been *par force* abandoned, but Russia has succeeded in obtaining another almost equally good. By her extraordinary efforts against Circassia she has at length managed to obtain the long-coveted Caucasian Mountains. These, in the hands of a comparatively small force, constitute an effectual barrier to any foreign offensive movement against her operations on, and to the eastward of, the Caspian Sea. Thus it is palpable that no European Power could in Europe, upon equal terms, or with a chance of success, oppose her designs on the southern and eastern portions of Asia. Meanwhile she is steadily possessing herself of the territory yet independent on the frontiers of India and Thibet. During the last few years she has successfully absorbed Khiva, the territors of the Kirghiz and Kalpak Tartars, the provinces of Turkestan, and the principal points of Kokan. The great cities of Tashkend and Samarkand are in Russian hands, and the last mail from India (December, 1865) announces that war has commenced between them and Bokhara — the last independent kingdom of Tartary. There is an old Muscovite prediction, which declares: "When the Russians shall have conquered Samarkand, and shall have returned to the cradle of their Tartar ancestors, there shall be but one rule in Asia, and the Mongols and Tartars united shall brave the whole world." Certainly this prophecy is in progress; it remains to be seen whether it will be accomplished.

The last telegrams report that the Russians are within six miles of Bokhara, the capital of the country of that name, and that many thousands of workmen are engaged constructing their military roads through that kingdom. And where are these roads leading? In a direct line for the nearest portion of British India! Perhaps the Russians only wish to build summer-houses on the northern slopes of the mountains of Cashmere, though it is strange military roads and large bodies of troops are required for such a purpose. Perhaps they wish to get on the other side of these mountains,—time will show.

Such is the present (December, 1865) position of Russia in Asia ;. but already there are signs indicative of a much farther progress. Already the people a little beyond her advancing frontier are in turmoil and confusion. Kashgar, Yarkend, and other portions of eastern Thibet, together with Cabul, being in anarchy, and waiting for the arrival of the pacificating, absorbing invader, whilst the great Mongolian province of I-li has thrown off its allegiance to the Emperor of China. Already the next nations are breaking up like fallow earth before the resistless ploughshare.

The *Bombay Mail* of December 13th states :—

"Many reports are current of commotions in the Affghan states and along the Punjaub frontier. . . . The internal commotions in Cabul continue. . . . An envoy from Kotan has arrived at Cashmere. . . . The object of his visit is said to be to offer the Empress of India the allegiance of Kotan, in return for an assurance of protection from the Russians. . . . The inhabitants of Soket, in the hills north of Jullunder, lately made an attack on Mundi. . . The country near Yarkand is reported to be in a state of insurrection. It is conjectured that this manifestation of revolt is an indication of *some greater power having instigated it*, having for its object the creation of universal revolt, and thus breaking the influence of China in these parts.

"An affray recently took place between the sepoys of the Jeypore Rajah and the Rajah of Khetra, in which several lives were lost. Government have called upon the former chief for explanations.

"Advices from the north-western frontier indicate the necessity for being more than ever on the alert against the increasing raids by various sects. Letters recently received report that the Wahabee Moulvies at Sittana have been purchasing the favour of the Akhoond of Swat, who was to stir up the tribes to a united effort against the British.

"It is reported from Peshawur that the Afreedies are very restless, and inclined to give trouble. This tribe occupies the hills all along the western side of the Peshawur Valley, and their territory interposes between the Peshawur and Kohat districts. They can muster some 20,000 fighting men, all of them as good soldiers as can be found on the frontier."

It is quite plain to those who have studied the question, that Russian progress towards India and China is seriously affecting the material and commercial interests of Great Britain. For some years the Russians have successfully competed with British merchants in China. Although their trade has been carried on through a vast extent of territory, still the import of Russian woollen and other manufactured goods, *viâ* Irkoutsk, Kiachta, and Mongolia, has been sufficient to suit and satisfy the market of Western, Northern, and Central China, besides Mongolia and Thibet. Every day increases this commerce, and makes it less expensive. Russia brings into the contest with England (whether it be commercial or military) overwhelming natural advantages. She is rapidly extending her railway and telegraphic lines throughout her Asiatic dominions; and these, besides serving to introduce the sciences, arts, and mechanical inventions of modern civilization, are being constructed for the conveyance of armies to the utmost limits of her empire. It is quite possible that, by the time the Russian frontier joins that of India, railway communication will be extended to the same point, and afford the opportunity of conveying large bodies of troops. Russia undoubtedly has a great future in Asia, and it is difficult to see how England can ultimately avoid yielding before the natural advantages that will be brought into the field against her—for that they will be so employed one cannot doubt; unless, indeed, there be some charm by which British interests are made sacred to her rival, and certainly the Russians are not likely to prefer a barren steppe of Tartary to a rich slice of India. As for the principle of the thing, the less said about that the better. Considering the manner in which England obtained her dominions in Hindoostan, the Russians have quite as much right to take them, if they can; and why should we flatter ourselves that they will not try when they become our neighbours, when we see them indiscriminately seizing all territories which lie in their way?

It may be that we should rather rejoice at the position Russia is taking up against India and China; it may be that, even should the result prove injurious to us, it will not be felt till something like the lapse of another century; but these are grave questions, and it is quite within the bounds of probability that another few months may find us either defending our Indian possessions, or crushing internal dissension created by Russian intrigue amongst our coloured subjects.

It is scarcely to be expected (except in the event of European war) that Russia will make any direct attack upon British India, but the very contrast of her method of conquest with ours will create disaffection amongst the excitable, fanatical, treacherous natives. Why this result should ensue is explained by the well-known fact that (probably from the admixture of Tartar blood) the Russians can amalgamate with Asiatics, while the English cannot. Englishmen may flatter themselves that British rule is adored in India, but all the flattery in the world cannot obliterate the remembrance of the terrible mutiny, which, considering the numbers that joined it who were not sepoys, might more appropriately be termed a rebellion. Unless we have thoroughly established our rule in the hearts of the people, we may be sure that the vicinity of Russian dependencies will cause trouble, because Asiatics will become Russianized far sooner than we can Anglicise them, and Russian influences are already at work in Affghanistan, if not also in Cashmere—whence disturbances were lately reported. In conclusion, on this subject, it may fairly be said that Russia is performing a great work, no doubt to the benefit of thousands of uncivilized nomades, and that her course is very likely to lead her into collision with British India. England cannot stop her if she would; but England *might have had* a powerful friend and ally in the shape of a great Asiatic Power if she had not destroyed the Ti-pings who would have established it. By the wilful, unjustifiable, short-sighted policy of her Government, England has lost the glorious opportunity of helping to establish a vast Christian empire in Asia—a course the more impolitic because its reverse would not only have tended to raise a balance against the incessant encroachment of Russia in the East, but to create a strong friendly Power on the frontier of her own Indian possessions.

One object for which the author has steadily laboured, and which has had no small share in causing the production of this work, is to counteract the gross amount of ignorant prejudice which has been excited against the Tipings through the medium of false reports in England. Persons either individually implicated, or credulous enough to believe the interested statements of those who have been concerned in slaughtering the Ti-pings, have been gratified at the diffusion of their opinions by sundry publications, journals, and magazines—patriotic, very, no doubt, but nevertheless either unscrupulous or gullible.

Just to prove the utter worthlessness of the reports referred to, the following statements are selected from two new books ("Peking and the Pekingese," by Dr. Rennie; "Chinese Miscellanies," by Sir J. F. Davis); whilst it is also unhesitatingly affirmed that every similar effusion, having for its basis defamation of the Ti-pings, is equally untrustworthy, and as easily, if not more so, refuted.

In the Dedication of the former of the two works to Sir F. Bruce, Dr. Rennie has sufficient power of imagination to term that official's vacillating and inane diplomacy—

"A policy auguring so *favourably** [1] for the future of China."

---

* The italics are ours.

With a further combination of inaccuracy, adulation, and prejudice, Dr. Rennie proceeds to state:—

"And which, *having been mainly conducive to the extinction of the Taeping rebellion*, [2] has already been attended with results of the highest importance to the *cause of humanity*." [3]

[1] It is for those who peruse this work, and all who have other opportunities than such as Dr. Rennie gives to enlighten them, to judge whether the "policy" in question has proved "*favourable*" or the reverse.

[2] As for the second passage, if Dr. Rennie means that the shuffling, spiritless, and vacillating conduct of Sir F. Bruce, marked by total want of energy and impartiality, conduced to a certain result, by means of having established no policy or principle of statesmanship whatever, he is right; but if he means that his patron advocated, advised, or countenanced the massacre of Ti-pings, he is labouring under some extraordinary delusion, and the words of him he tries to praise, but clearly misrepresents, prove it. Not only has the weather-vane of the political fancies of Sir F. Bruce never been blown to within many points of recommending direct intervention, but on the other hand he has *violently* deprecated any such operation, as may be seen by referring to page 280, Chapter X., and many other parts of this work. The finishing blow, however, is given to Dr. Rennie's illusory though amusing panegyric, and his unfortunate premises are proved to be without foundation; by the well-known fact that the "extinction of the Taeping rebellion" has neither taken place, nor even seems likely to be, as appears by a telegram in the London papers (November 24, 1865), viz.:—

"Shanghae, October 9, 1865. The Taepings are reported to be again appearing in large bodies."

[3] With regard to Dr. Rennie's rodomontade about "*the cause of humanity*," as the Ti-pings are not yet *exterminated*, it is simply unmeaning; and all that can be

said in its favour is, that it is correctly copied from the Blue Book (see p. 738, Chap. XXIV.).

At the 89th page of "Peking and the Pekingese," Dr. Rennie endorses the following misrepresentations:—

> "The Taepings who, Mr. Parkes states, endeavour to copy the most objectionable traits in the Imperialist character (?), in addition to which a sort of 'High life below stairs' farce is enacted, embracing the most absurd assumptions of dignity, with general licentiousness, blasphemy, and obscenity. . . ."

Then Dr. Rennie's ire becomes aroused at the thought of such wickedness, and the consciousness of moral rectitude filling him with a strange *cacoethes scribendi*, he abuses the Ti-ping Wang very cruelly, by declaring:—

> "This lunatic monarch (for such he would really seem to be) is waited on only by women, no males being allowed to approach him; bigamy (?), with general immorality, is said to be the prevailing institution of the Court of Nankin."

Now the above statement is no less incorrect than absurd. The Tien-wang regularly held council with his ministers and chiefs. The insertion of the word "bigamy" suggests motives on the part of the writer, who, we may suppose, means polygamy. He not only forgets to blame his Imperialist friends for conforming to *the same custom of China*, but he must be ignorant of the fact that "bigamy" means the crime of marrying more than one woman *only* in countries where the civil law makes such connection illegal. Not satisfied with thus abusing those he had never seen, Dr. Rennie proceeds to *mis*quote from Blue Books. He says, at the same page:—

> "The following rhapsody has lately appeared, in the form of a proclamation, from the Teen-wang."

He then quotes a decree, issued on the 7th of March, 1861, to establish certain regulations in the civil department of the Ti-ping Government,—a translation of the same being given at page 44 (Inclosure 6, in Number 11) of the Blue Book on China, presented to the British Parliament, " in pursuance of their address, dated April 8, 1862."

The clause which either Dr. Rennie or his authority has altered, in the original and official translation, is as follows :—

> "Thus, in addition to the perfect regulations, we have added six more, making nine altogether. Do not go and turn your backs on the Father, Brother, myself, and my son, who illuminate all places, benevolently harmonizing them for a myriad myriad generations. . . ."

The words " Father—Brother" are, in the Chinese text, *raised* the usual number of spaces above " myself and my son," which at once properly represents the Divinity. Any unprejudiced mind would certainly understand the sentence as meaning that—" the Father, Brother, Myself, and my Son," in our respective spheres, benevolently harmonize all things. Dr. Rennie, however, tries to prove the blasphemous nature of the Ti-pings in the following manner :—At page 90, first volume of his work, he misquotes the clause of the proclamation referred to in this way :—

> "Now do not in the least turn away your back upon Ya-ko-chum and Yan (?)—God, Christ, myself, and son—who illuminate all places AS ONE BODY POLITIC, benevolently harmonizing them for ten thousand times ten thousand generations."

Where does Dr. Rennie get the interpolation from ? It is a totally un-Chinese expression, but a favourite term *with English diplomatists*. It appears a clever attempt to alter the sense of the proclamation, and brand the Ti-pings with the crime of blasphemy. There are other cases in which the author of " Peking and the Pekingese" goes out of his way to endorse second-hand opinions inimical to the Ti-pings; but as he does not attempt to corroborate them by any mention of his own experience, it is unnecessary to further notice such valueless statements; the misquotation exposed above, not only evidences how little reliance is to be placed on the clique of Ti-ping maligners, but forms a fitting conclusion to our acquaintance with a book which would have been more valuable had the author refrained from aspersing a political cause of which he knows literally nothing.

The misrepresentation contained in "Chinese Miscellanies," though merely consisting of one sentence and a foot-note, is important and worthy of contradiction, because it is promulgated by Sir J. F. Davis. Speaking, in the preface, of the Governments of China and Japan, he states:—

"With all their faults they are, in their integral characteristics, better than the *mock* Christian* Taepings of China. . . ."

As for the mockery of Christianity, perhaps the readers of "Ti-ping Tien Kwoh" may agree with its author in believing that it has been altogether upon the part of those who, like Sir J. Davis, have scoffed at, abused, and ridiculed the faith of the Ti-pings. Many millions of men do not establish a great revolution, and sacrifice their lives for a *mock* purpose, whatever Sir J. Davis may think to the contrary. If "it has been *plain from the first*" that the Ti-pings were no more like Christians than Mahomet was like a Jew, will the clever discoverer kindly explain the meaning of the statements of the Bishop of Victoria, Revs. Edkins, John, Medhurst, Muirhead, &c., referred to and quoted in this work?

All that now remains to be noticed are the movements of the Ti-pings since capturing the city of Chang-chew, near Amoy, their present circumstances and position.

After holding a large portion of the province of Fu-keen for about eight months, on the 16th of May, 1865,

---

* "It has been plain from the first, that they were no more like Christians than Mahomet was like a Jew" (p. iv).

the Ti-pings evacuated the city of Chang-chew, and moved off to the westward.

This proceeding took both Europeans and Imperialists completely by surprise; for, up to the day before the Shi-wang left Chang-chew, his outposts were five miles from the city, and the Manchoo forces had not ventured to attack them for a long time. The place was also strongly fortified and well-provisioned—so much so, indeed, that large stores of grain, &c., were left behind,—while the country to the west and south was entirely under the control of the Ti-pings.

The explanation of the Shi-wang's sudden movement is due to the fact that eleven days afterwards he joined his forces with Hung-jin, the Kan-wang, at a distance of eighty or ninety miles inland.

Of course, as usual, frightful accounts of Ti-ping atrocities on the march were concocted to harrow the feelings of those simple enough to believe them. It is fortunate that trustworthy evidence exists to prove that the Ti-pings have not yet become the "horde of banditti" England's policy has worked so hard to make them. The Rev. W. McGregor, English Presbyterian Missionary at Amoy (about fourteen miles from Chang-chew), in a letter dated 10th April, 1865, declares that, whilst conquering neighbouring parts of the province by expeditions issuing from Chang-chew,* "the Ti-pings had been guilty of no wanton destruction of property or slaughter of the people." Again, in another letter, dated 26th May, 1865, after the revolutionists had retreated inland, he states:—

"Of course many stories are being put in circulation about the cruelties of the Taepings when in possession of Chang-chew; but it must be remembered that these come from Mandarin sources, and thence through the foreign custom-house pass into circulation in the foreign community, while

* Published in *The English Presbyterian Messenger*, July 1st and August 1, 1865.

a little investigation often shows them to be quite unfounded. For example, it was reported that the Taepings left Chang-chew a perfect shamble, having massacred all the people that were of no use to take with them, and in corroboration of this some of the foreign community were taken up, and shown the city burning in several places, with numbers of dead bodies lying about; but it has to be kept in mind that, before this the Mandarin troops had been some days in the city, and the remembrance of Soo-chow ought to teach Englishmen, at least, how these days would be spent. The Chinese have a technical term for a proclamation issued ordering soldiers to desist from *indiscriminate* slaughter and plunder, and I casually got the information from my teacher (who has the means of getting all news circulating in the Yamens), that Chang-chew was in the hands of the Imperialists four or five days before this proclamation was issued. The fact is, that, immediately on the Taepings leaving, the people whom they left (they took a large number with them as baggage-bearers, &c.), endeavoured to escape from it as fast as possible; and we have information from some who have escaped that, before the departure of the rebels no slaughter took place. How the Imperialists have acted in Chang-chew and the surrounding villages will be apparent from the single fact that, since they entered the city, the soldiers have been selling women at four dollars each. No evidence has yet been produced that the Taepings have been guilty of such atrocities as are implied in this statement. A short time ago, in consequence of some disturbances in the Tung-an region, a body of soldiers were detached from the Mandarin force, near Chang-chew, who by their own account burnt over twenty villages and massacred over 2,000 women and children, without meeting with any resistance. They ultimately returned, in consequence of the villagers, farther north, forming a combination for mutual protection, and threatening to join the rebels. We have not heard of an instance of the Taepings acting in such a manner."

It is impossible to tell, at present, whether the Ti-pings may become a scourge to their country, or whether they will again rise into power and importance, and occupy their old position. But the fact must be carefully recorded that, in event of the former deplorable contingency, it is British interference which has made them what they are, and that it must be regarded as the original and responsible cause of all that is or may be objectionable. It is now placed beyond doubt that the Kan-wang is at the head of a great body of Ti-pings, although it is equally certain that other divisions not under his command exist in various directions; but, so long as he remains in authority, there need be little fear as to the deterioration of the movement. One fact in connection with the retreat from Chang-chow speaks volumes. It seems that when some missionaries visited the place immediately after the Ti-pings had fled, they made the interesting discovery described by Dr. Carnegie (medical missionary) in the following words:—

* "Only some two or three of the Christians have been heard of. . . . A native preacher is amongst the missing. An interesting fact, however, remains to be told in connection with the rebels, and it is this:—That whilst they gutted the heathen temples and utterly demolished the many hundreds of idols with which these temples were stored, they respected the Christian places of worship, and in one of the chapels, where there is a scroll bearing these words, 'The pure religion of Jesus,' some of them added underneath, 'MAY IT SPREAD OVER THE WHOLE EARTH!'"

As Colonel Sykes, M.P., truly observes in a letter upon the above subject, published in the *Star*, December 28th, 1865:—

"These two testimonies, standing unscathed in a desolated city, will fall gratingly upon the memories of those who, with British bayonets and British shot and shell, in violation of good faith and in violation of a commanded neutrality, have aided a Government, which has been characterized for its constant perfidy and cruelty, to defeat a national party, in which, as we see, was not only a germ of Christianity, of probable development into a rich harvest, but which party also constantly had manifested a desire to cultivate friendly relations with foreigners, with a view to the introduction of Western science and art, as contra-distinguished from the Imperial Government, which stupidly and doggedly opposes itself to every proposition for the establishment of railways, telegraphs, the steam navigation of internal waters, and other useful objects."

Since the evacuation of Chang-chow, but little information has been received regarding the movements and whereabouts of the Ti-pings. From the depositions of

* See p. 13, "Occasional Paper," No. 10, dated July, 1865, issued with the Tenth Annual Report of the China Mission at Amoy and Swatow, 1864-5.

two foreigners (Mansfield and Baffey), it has been ascertained that the Kan-wang is in supreme command, nothing whatever being heard of the Tien or Chung Wangs. Besides the force from Chang-chew, and the main body with which it effected a junction, another division seems to have arrived from the city of Kia-ying-chow, in the province of Kiang-si, but it is not stated under what leader. The concentration of these troops was probably caused by the orders of the Kan-wang, who, it would seem, has since led them northward into Kiang-si. Whither they are marching is as yet unknown. It is quite possible that their intention is to join the Nien-fie in the northern provinces, who have again defeated the Imperialists under Tseng-kwo-fan, and seem to be moving in every direction in overwhelming numbers, while one body is especially reported as making a diversion to the south-west.

The men, Mansfield and Baffey, were present at the junction of the Ti-ping forces. The latter, in his deposition, states: "The Kan-wang is about 35 years of age. He is the principal rebel-chief at the present moment. . . . When I left, the rebels were talking of retreating towards Kiang-si. They have great confidence in the Kan-wang. The latter is an exceedingly clever man, very fond of European ideas, but very distrustful of foreigners"—as well he may be.

Between the Nien-fie league in the north and the Ti-pings in the south, it seems very probable the Manchoo dynasty will ultimately be overthrown. If the Imperialist forces are concentrated in the north, in all other quarters insurrection breaks out, and the Ti-pings rapidly increase their strength and conquests; and so, upon the other hand, when they move against the Ti-pings in the south, the Nien-fie, Mohamedan rebels, &c., gain numberless adherents, and capture city after city with impunity. Every mail brings some dim tidings of disaster to the Tartar cause England has been so wantonly led to support. It is extraordinary that while internal dangers are rapidly increasing, the Manchoos should be fulfilling their anti-foreign intentions when foreign help alone can save them. A late number of the *China Overland Trade Report*, dated Hong-kong, 31st December, 1865, states:—

> "Since the late evacuation of the Taku forts much labour and outlay have been expended in strengthening the fortifications; in fact, it is said that when the plan adopted shall be carried out, these forts will be impregnable except to iron-clads. The proceeding is significant when taken in connection with the anti-foreign policy known to be cherished."

Intelligence from China, bearing date February 1st, 1866, announces a Ti-ping victory in the province of Fu-keen, the Imperialists losing their leader, Kwo-sun-liang. The Ti-pings have also re-captured the important city of Kia-ying-chow, which had been evacuated by the third division of the army, at present combined under the Kan-wang's command, before the junction was effected.

At the same time further victorious progress of the Nien-fie is reported, and a large rebel force (supposed to be of that movement) has appeared within 30 miles of Hankow, the great commercial city and treaty port situated some 700 miles up the river Yang-tze-kiang. It would thus seem that a considerable division of the Nien-fie army has been detached on a rapid march to the south-west; at the same time the Ti-pings have moved to the north-west, and captured Kia-ying-chow, so that it is plain, if each force continues its advance, they will shortly meet, which is very likely their intention.

What the consequences will be if the Ti-pings are fortunate and wise enough to effect a junction with the Nien-fie can scarcely admit of a doubt. Without foreign assistance the Imperialists are unable to cope with either of the great rebellions, how much less would they be able to resist the two combined! It only requires such an amalgamation of the two great parties in opposition to the Manchoo rule to cause the native population to rise *en masse*. Each mail brings tidings of fresh outbreaks in every part of the distracted empire, and it is ominous for the present dynasty that the literary class, the highest in China, are beginning to raise and lead local insurrection, as was the case in December, 1865, at the town of Chin-shan, only 65 miles from Shanghae, a part of the country just pacified by British swords!

"The unfortunate have always been deserted and betrayed," and how much more by those who have guiltily made them unfortunate in the first place! It is therefore easy to understand the nature of the hostility which has been excited in England against the Ti-pings—against the only section of the people of China whom righteous men can look to as affording a prospect of forwarding the true interests and improvement of that vast and beautiful and incalculably rich country.

It is bad to go to war at all; it is highly criminal to make war upon an unoffending neighbour; and it is enormous guilt to use hostilities for the purpose of subduing a free and happy people because they *might* interfere with our profits; but in what words can the double crime of waging war upon mercenary grounds against the cause of liberty and Christianity be expressed? Yet such, unfortunately, is the course which England has pursued by taking part against the Ti-pings.

It is true there is yet some hope that the policy of the Cabinet of her late lamented statesman, Lord Palmerston, may prove a failure. The Chinese Christian patriots have still a chance of successfully defending themselves, and they have strong hope, for their chiefs have repeatedly said, "The Mings took a hundred years to found their dynasty, and possibly so may we, but most assuredly, sooner or later, we shall expel the Tartars and succeed, for the Heavenly Father is with us, and who can triumph against Him?"

Let Englishmen therefore trust that their rulers will in future observe the neutrality they have once more professed, and not again wage an unrighteous war without even declaring it, and in violation of their official pledges. All men whose minds have a spark of philanthropy, civilization, or Christian faith, will wish their Chinese brothers God speed.

Let us trust that, phœnix-like, the Ti-pings may rise from the ashes of their former glory and yet succeed in their great religio-political movement, that they may again print and widely circulate the Holy Bible, which, throughout all their former territory, British bayonets and Manchoo torches have for a time destroyed, and that England will not have to answer for the sin of crushing the first Christian movement in modern Asia, and the last apparent opportunity of Christianizing and liberating China.

While looking forward hopefully to the future of the Ti-pings, because the cause of liberty is theirs, and the cause of the Gospel is theirs also, let it be remembered (as applying to the former phase) that a great man has said:—

> "For freedom's battle once begun,
> Bequeathed by bleeding sire to son,
> Though baffled oft, is ever won."

And let it be remembered (as applying to the latter phase) that the Ti-ping movement was originated through acceptation of the Gospel, and that to comfort those who are persecuted for Its sake, it is therein declared:—

> "We are troubled on every side, yet not distressed; we are perplexed, but not in despair.
> "Persecuted, but not forsaken; cast down, but not destroyed."

APPENDIX A.

RELIGIOUS PUBLICATIONS WRITTEN BY THE TIEN-WANG HUNG-SIU-TSHUEN, AND USED BY THE TI-PINGS.

DECALOGUE.

THE TEN CELESTIAL COMMANDS WHICH ARE TO BE CONSTANTLY OBSERVED.

THE FIRST COMMAND.

THOU SHALT HONOUR AND WORSHIP THE GREAT GOD.

Remark.—The great God is the universal Father of all men, in every nation under heaven. Every man is produced and nourished by him; every man is also protected by him: every man ought, therefore, morning and evening, to honour and worship him, with acknowledgments of his goodness. It is a common saying, that Heaven produces, nourishes, and protects men. Also, that being provided with food we must not deceive Heaven. Therefore, whoever does not worship the great God breaks the commands of Heaven.

The Hymn says:—

Imperial Heaven, the Supreme God is the true Spirit (God);
Worship him every morning and evening, and you will be taken up;
You ought deeply to consider the ten celestial commands,
And not by your foolishness obscure the right principles of nature.

THE SECOND COMMAND.

THOU SHALT NOT WORSHIP CORRUPT SPIRITS (GODS).

Remark.—The great God says, Thou shalt have no other spirits (gods) beside me. Therefore all besides the great God are corrupt spirits (gods), deceiving and destroying mankind; they must on no account be worshipped: whoever worships the whole class of corrupt spirits (gods) offends against the commands of Heaven.

The Hymn says:—

Corrupt devils very easily delude the souls of men.
If you perversely believe in them, you will at last go down to hell.
We exhort you all, brave people, to awake from your lethargy,
And early make your peace with your exalted Heavenly Father.

THE THIRD COMMAND.

THOU SHALT NOT TAKE THE NAME OF THE GREAT GOD IN VAIN.

Remark.—The name of the great God is Jehovah, which men must not take in vain. Whoever takes God's name in vain, and rails against Heaven, offends against this command.

The Hymn says:—

Our exalted Heavenly Father is infinitely honourable;
Those who disobey and profane his name, seldom come to a good end.
If unacquainted with the true doctrine, you should be on your guard,
For those who wantonly blaspheme involve themselves in endless crime.

THE FOURTH COMMAND.

ON THE SEVENTH DAY, THE DAY OF WORSHIP, YOU SHOULD PRAISE THE GREAT GOD FOR HIS GOODNESS.

Remark.—In the beginning the great God made heaven and earth, land and sea, men and things, in six days; and having finished his works on the seventh day, he called it the day of rest (or Sabbath): therefore all the men of the world, who enjoy the blessing of the great God, should on every seventh day especially reverence and worship the great God, and praise him for his goodness.

The Hymn says:—

All the happiness enjoyed in the world comes from Heaven;
It is therefore reasonable that men should give thanks and sing;
At the daily morning and evening meal there should be thanksgiving,
But on the seventh day, the worship should be more intense.

APPENDIX.   825

THE FIFTH COMMAND.

THOU SHALT HONOUR THY FATHER AND THY MOTHER, THAT THY DAYS MAY BE PROLONGED.

Remark.—Whoever disobeys his parents breaks this command.

The Hymn says:—

History records that Shun honoured his parents to the end of his days,
Causing them to experience the intensest pleasure and delight:
August Heaven will abundantly reward all who act thus,
And do not disappoint the expectation of the authors of their being.

THE SIXTH COMMAND.

THOU SHALT NOT KILL OR INJURE MEN.

Remark.—He who kills another kills himself, and he who injures another injures himself. Whoever does either of these breaks the above command.

The Hymn says:—

The whole world is one family, and all men are brethren,
How can they be permitted to kill and destroy one another?
The outward form and the inward principle are both conferred by Heaven:
Allow every one, then, to enjoy the ease and comfort which he desires.

THE SEVENTH COMMAND.

THOU SHALT NOT COMMIT ADULTERY OR ANYTHING UNCLEAN.

Remark.—All the men in the world are brethren, and all the women in the world are sisters. Among the sons and daughters of the celestial hall the males are on one side and the females on the other, and are not allowed to intermix. Should either men or women practise lewdness they are considered outcasts, as having offended against one of the chief commands of Heaven. The casting of amorous glances, the harbouring of lustful imaginations, the smoking of foreign tobacco (opium), or the singing of libidinous songs must all be considered as breaches of this command.

The Hymn says:—

Lust and lewdness constitute the chief transgression,
Those who practise it become outcasts, and are the objects of pity.
If you wish to enjoy the substantial happiness of heaven,
It is necessary to deny yourself and earnestly cultivate virtue.

THE EIGHTH COMMAND.

THOU SHALT NOT ROB OR STEAL.

Remark.—Riches and poverty are determined by the great God; but whosoever robs or plunders the property of others transgresses this command.

The Hymn says:—

Rest contented with your station, however poor, and do not steal.
Robbery and violence are low and abandoned practices.
Those who injure others really injure themselves.
Let the noble-minded among you immediately reform.

THE NINTH COMMAND.

THOU SHALT NOT UTTER FALSEHOOD.

Remark.—All those who tell lies, and indulge in devilish deceits, with every kind of coarse and abandoned talk, offend against this command.

The Hymn says:—

Lying discourse and unfounded stories must all be abandoned.
Deceitful and wicked words are offences against Heaven.
Much talk will, in the end, bring evil on the speakers.
It is then much better to be cautious, and regulate one's own mind.

THE TENTH COMMAND.

THOU SHALT NOT CONCEIVE A COVETOUS DESIRE.

Remark.—When a man looks upon the beauty of another's wife and daughters with covetous desires, or when he regards the elegance of another man's possessions with covetous desires, or when he engages in gambling, he offends against this command.

The Hymn says:—

In your daily conduct do not harbour covetous desires.
When involved in the sea of lust the consequences are very serious.
The above injunctions were handed down on Mount Sinai;
And to this day the celestial commands retain all their force.

"NOTE.—The expression 'corrupt spirits' in the remarks upon the second commandment, rendered by the translator 'gods,' refers probably to the numerous malevolent spirits whom all uneducated Chinese believe to have power over all things noxious to the human race. The gods of thunder, lightning, wind, &c., are the principal of these, but there are also hundreds of inferior spirits whom poor householders believe to be abroad at night, with power, if they so will, to spread pestilence, disaster, and fire, and who consequently receive daily and nightly offerings of prayer and incense from the timid and trembling poor, who dread the exercise of their malevolence."—(*The Taepings in China.*)

THE TRIMETRICAL CLASSIC.

EACH LINE IN THE ORIGINAL CONTAINING THREE WORDS, AND EACH VERSE FOUR LINES.

The Great God
Made heaven and earth,
Both land and sea,
And all things therein.

In six days
He made the whole;
Man, the lord of all,
Was endowed with glory and honour.

Every seventh day worship,
In acknowledgment of Heaven's favour;
Let all under Heaven
Keep their hearts in reverence.

It is said that in former times
A foreign nation was commanded
To honour God;
The nation's name was Israel.

Their twelve tribes
Removed into Egypt;
Where God favoured them,
And their posterity increased.

Then a king arose
Into whose heart the devil entered;
He envied their prosperity,
And inflicted pain and misery.

Ordering the daughters to be preserved,
But not allowing the sons to live;
Their bondage was severe
And very difficult to bear.

The Great God
Viewed them with pity,
And commanded Moses
To return to his family.

He commanded Aaron
To go and meet Moses;
When both addressed the king,
And wrought divers miracles.

The king hardened his heart
And would not let them go;
Wherefore God was angry
And sent lice and locusts.

He also sent flies,
Together with frogs,
Which entered their palaces
And crept into their ovens.

When the king still refused,
The river was turned into blood!
And the water became bitter
Throughout all Egypt.

God sent boils and blains,
With pestilence and murrain;
He also sent hail,
Which was very grievous.

The king still refusing,
He slew their first-born;
When the King of Egypt
Had no resource,

But let them go
Out of his land;
The Great God
Upheld and sustained them.

By day in a cloud,
By night in a pillar of fire;
The Great God
Himself saved them.

The king hardened his heart,
And led his armies in pursuit;
But God was angry
And displayed his majesty.

Arrived at the Red Sea,
The waters were spread abroad;
The people of Israel
Were very much afraid.

The pursuers overtook them,
But God stayed their course;
He himself fought for them,
And the people had no trouble.

He caused the Red Sea
With its waters to divide;
To stand up as a wall,
That they might pass between.

The people of Israel
Marched with a steady step
As though on dry ground,
And thus saved their lives.

The pursuers attempting to cross,
Their wheels were taken off,
When the waters closed upon them,
And they were all drowned.

The Great God
Displayed his power,
And the people of Israel
Were all preserved.

When they came to the desert
They had nothing to eat;
But the Great God
Bade them not be afraid.

He sent down manna,
For each man a pint;
It was as sweet as honey,
And satisfied their appetites.

The people lusted much,
And wished to eat flesh,
When quails were sent
By the millions of bushels.

At the Mount Sinai
Miracles were displayed,
And Moses was commanded
To make tables of stone.

The Great God
Gave his celestial commands,

Amounting to ten precepts,
The breach of which would not be forgiven.

He himself wrote them,
And gave them to Moses;
The celestial law
Cannot be altered.

In after ages
It was sometimes disobeyed,
Through the devil's temptations
When men fell into misery.

But the Great God,
Out of pity to mankind,
Sent his first-born Son
To come down into the world.

His name is Jesus,
The Lord and Saviour of men,
Who redeems them from sin
By the endurance of extreme misery.

Upon the cross
They nailed his body,
Where he shed his precious blood
To save all mankind.

Three days after his death
He rose from the dead,
And during forty days
He discoursed on heavenly things.

When he was about to ascend,
He commanded his disciples
To communicate his gospel
And proclaim his revealed will.

Those who believe will be saved
And ascend to heaven;
But those who do not believe
Will be the first to be condemned.

Throughout the whole world
There is only one God,
The Great Lord and Ruler
Without a second.

The Chinese in early ages
Were regarded by God;
Together with the foreign states
They walked in one way.

From the time of Pwan-koo,*
Down to the three dynasties,†
They honoured God,
As history records.

---

* Pwan-koo, the first man, was, according to Chinese mythology, the offspring of Chaos, and the creator of the earth, sun, moon, and stars.
† The period of the three dynasties began B.C. 2207, and ended B.C. 217.

APPENDIX.

T'hang of the Shang dynasty,*
And Wan of the Chow,†
Honoured God
With the intensest feeling.

The inscription on T'hang's bathing-tub
Inculcated daily renovation of mind;
And God commanded him
To assume the government of the empire.

Wan was very respectful
And intelligently served God;
So that the people who submitted to him
Were two out of every three.

When Tsin obtained the empire ‡
He was infatuated with the genii,
And the nation has been deluded by the devil
For the last two thousand years.

Suen and Woo of the Han dynasty§
Both followed this bad example,
So that the mad rebellion increased
In imitation of Tsin's misrule.

When Woo arrived at old age,
He repented of his folly,
And lamented that from his youth up
He had always followed the wrong road.

Ming of the Han dynasty ‖
Welcomed the institutions of Buddha,
And set up temples and monasteries
To the great injury of the country.

But Hwang of the Sung dynasty
Was still more mad and infatuated,
For he changed the name of Shang-te (God)
Into that of Yuh-hwang (the pearly emperor).¶

But the Great God
Is the supreme Lord
Over all the world,
The Great Father in heaven.

His name is most honourable,
To be handed down through distant ages;

Who was this Hwuy,
That he dared to alter it?

It was meet that this same Hwuy
Should be taken by the Tartars,
And together with his son
Perish in the northern desert.

From Hwuy of the Sung dynasty
Up to the present day,
For these seven hundred years
Men have sunk deeper and deeper in error.

With the doctrine of God
They have not been acquainted,
While the king of Hades
Has deluded them to the utmost.

The Great God displays
Liberality deep as the sea;
But the devil has injured man
In a most outrageous manner.

God is therefore displeased
And has sent his Son **
With orders to come down into the world
Having first studied the classics.

In the Ting-yeu year (1837)
He was received up into Heaven,
Where the affairs of Heaven
Were clearly pointed out to him.

The great God
Personally instructed him,
Gave him odes and documents,
And communicated to him the true doctrine.

God also gave him a seal,
And conferred upon him a sword
Connected with authority
And majesty irresistible.

He bade him, together with the elder brother,
Namely Jesus,
To drive away impish fiends
With the co-operation of angels.

---

* B.C. 1766.
† B.C. 1121. Both these emperors (T'hang and Wan) are stated by Du Halde to have worshipped Heaven.
‡ B.C. 247.
§ B.C. 74—A.D. 25.
‖ A.D. 58. The emperor Ming, having heard that the true religion was to be found in the west, despatched (A.D. 66) ambassadors into Northern India, who, finding the majority of the people in that region to be worshippers of Fo, brought back with them several Bonzes in order to spread the faith; and thus Buddhism was introduced into China.
¶ This emperor (Hwuy) was a firm believer in the superstitions of the Taouists. A.D. 1101—1126.
** Hung-siu-tsuen.

There was one who looked on with envy,
Namely, the king of Hades,
Who displayed much maliguity
And acted like a devilish serpent.

But the great God,
With a high hand,
Instructed his Son
To subdue this fiend,

And having conquered him,
To show him no favour;
And in spite of his envious eye
He damped all his courage.

Having overcome the fiend,
He returned to Heaven,
Where the great God
Gave him great authority.

The celestial mother was kind
And exceedingly gracious,
Beautiful and noble in the extreme,
Far beyond all compare.

The celestial elder brother's wife
Was virtuous and very considerate,
Constantly exhorting the elder brother
To do things deliberately.

The great God,
Out of love to mankind,
Again commissioned his Son
To come down into the world.

And when he sent him down,
He charged him not to be afraid;
I am with you, said he,
To superintend everything.

In the Mow-shin year (1848)
The Son was troubled and distressed,
When the great God
Appeared on his behalf.

Bringing Jesus with him,
They both came down into the world,
Where he instructed his Son
How to sustain the weight of government.

God has set up his Son
To endure for ever,
To defeat corrupt machinations
And to display majesty and authority.

Also to judge the world,
To divide the righteous from the wicked,
And consign them to the misery of hell,
Or bestow on them the joys of heaven.

Heaven manages everything,
Heaven sustains the whole;
Let all beneath the sky
Come and acknowledge the new monarch.

Little children,
Worship God,
Keep his commandments,
And do not disobey.

Let your minds be refined,
And be not depraved,
The great God
Constantly surveys you.

You must refine yourselves well,
And not be depraved;
Vice willingly practised
Is the first step to misery.

To insure a good end,
You must make a good beginning;
An error of a hair's breadth
May lead to a discrepancy of a thousand li.

Be careful about little things,
And watch the minute springs of action:
The great God
Is not to be deceived.

Little children,
Arouse your energies:
The laws of high heaven
Admit not of infraction.

Upon the good blessings descend,
And miseries on the wicked;
Those who obey Heaven are preserved,
And those who disobey perish.

The great God
Is a spiritual Father;
All things whatever
Depend on him.

The great God
Is the Father of our spirits:
Those who devoutly serve him
Will obtain blessings.

Those who obey the fathers of their flesh
Will enjoy longevity;
Those who requite their parents
Will certainly obtain happiness.

Do not practise lewdness,
Nor any uncleanness;
Do not tell lies,
Do not kill and slay.

Do not steal,
Do not covet:
The great God
Will strictly carry out his laws.

Those who obey Heaven's commands
Will enjoy celestial happiness;
Those who are grateful for divine favours
Will receive divine support.

Heaven blesses the good
And curses the bad:
Little children!
Maintain correct conduct.

The correct are men,
The corrupt are imps:
Little children!
Seek to avoid disgrace.

God loves the upright,
And he hates the vicious:
Little children!
Be careful to avoid error.

The great God
Sees everything;
If you wish to enjoy happiness,
Refine and correct yourselves.

ODE FOR YOUTH.

EACH LINE IN THE ORIGINAL CONTAINING FIVE WORDS,
AND EACH VERSE FOUR LINES.

ON THE WORSHIP OF GOD.

Let the true Spirit, the great God,
Be honoured and adored by all nations;
Let all the inhabitants of the world
Unite in his worship, morning and evening.

Above and below, look where you may,
All things are imbued with the Divine favour.
At the beginning, in six days,
All things were created, perfect and complete.

Whether circumcised or uncircumcised,
Who is not produced by God?
Reverently praise the Divine favour
And you will obtain eternal glory.

ON REVERENCE FOR JESUS.

Jesus, his first-born Son,
Was in former times sent by God:
He willingly gave his life to redeem us from sin;
Of a truth his merits are pre-eminent.

His cross was hard to bear;
The sorrowing clouds obscured the sun.
The adorable Son, the honoured of heaven,
Died for you, the children of men.

After his resurrection he ascended to heaven;
Resplendent in glory, he wields authority supreme.
In him we know that we may trust
To secure salvation and ascend to Heaven.

ON THE HONOUR DUE TO PARENTS.

As grain is stored against a day of need,
So men bring up children to tend their old age;
A filial son begets filial children,—
The recompense here is truly wonderful.

Do you ask how this our body
Is to attain to length of years?
Keep the fifth command, we say,
And honour and emolument will descend upon you.

ON THE COURT.

The imperial court is an awe-inspiring spot,
Let those about it dread celestial majesty;
Life and death emanate from Heaven's son,
Let every officer avoid disobedience.

ON THE DUTIES OF THE SOVEREIGN.

When one man presides over the government,
All nations become settled and tranquillized:
When the sovereign grasps the sceptre of power,
Calumny and corruption sink and disappear.

ON THE DUTIES OF MINISTERS.

When the prince is upright, ministers are true;
When the sovereign is intelligent, ministers will be honest.
E and Chow are models worthy of imitation:
They acted uprightly and aided the government.

ON THE DUTIES OF FAMILIES.

The members of one family being intimately related,
They should live in joy and harmony;
When the feeling of concord unites the whole,
Blessings will descend upon them from above.

ON THE DUTIES OF A FATHER.

When the main beam is straight, the joists will be regular;
When a father is strict, his duty will be fulfilled:
Let him not provoke his children to wrath,
And a delightful harmony will pervade the dwelling.

ON THE DUTIES OF A MOTHER.

Ye mothers, beware of partiality,
But tenderly instruct your children in virtue;
When you are a fit example to your daughters,
The happy feeling will reach to the clouds.

ON THE DUTIES OF SONS.

Sons, be patterns to your wives;
Consider obedience to parents the chief duty;
Do not listen to the tattle of women,
And you will not be estranged from your own flesh.

ON THE DUTIES OF DAUGHTERS-IN-LAW.

Ye that are espoused into other families,
Be gentle and yielding, and your duty is fulfilled;
Do not quarrel with your sisters-in-law,
And thereby vex the old father and mother.

ON THE DUTIES OF ELDER BROTHERS.

Elder brothers, instruct your juniors;
Remember well your common parentage;
Should they commit a trifling fault,
Bear with it and treat them indulgently.

ON THE DUTIES OF YOUNGER BROTHERS.

Disparity in years is ordered by Heaven;
Duty to seniors consists in respect.
When younger brothers obey Heaven's dictates,
Happiness and honour will be their portion.

ON THE DUTIES OF ELDER SISTERS.

Elder sisters, instruct your younger sisters,
Study improvement and fit yourselves for Heaven.
Should you occasionally visit your former homes,
Get the little ones around you and tell them what is right.

ON THE DUTIES OF YOUNGER SISTERS.

Girls, obey your elder brothers and sisters,
Be obliging and avoid arrogance,
Carefully give yourselves to self-improvement,
And mind and keep the Ten Commandments.

ON THE DUTIES OF HUSBANDS.

Unbending firmness is natural to the man,
Love for a wife should be qualified by prudence;
And should the lioness roar,
Let not terror fill the mind.

ON THE DUTIES OF WIVES.

Women, be obedient to your three male relatives,
And do not disobey your lords:
When hens crow in the morning,
Sorrow may be expected in the family.

ON THE DUTIES OF ELDER BROTHERS' WIVES.

What is the duty of an elder brother's wife,
And what her most appropriate deportment?
Let her cheerfully harmonize with younger brothers' wives,
And she will never do amiss.

ON THE DUTIES OF YOUNGER BROTHERS' WIVES.

Younger brothers' wives should respect their elder brothers' wives,
In humility honouring their elder brothers;
In all things yielding to their senior sisters-in-law,
Which will result in harmony superior to music.

ON THE DUTIES OF THE MALE SEX.

Let every man have his own partner
And maintain the duties of the human relations
Firm and unbending; his duties lie from home,
But he should avoid such things as cause suspicion.

ON THE DUTIES OF THE FEMALE SEX.

The duty of woman is to maintain chastity;
She should shun proximity to the other sex;
Sober and decorous, she should keep at home:
Thus she can secure happiness and felicity

ON CONTRACTING MARRIAGES.

Marriages are the result of some relation in a former state
The disposal of which rests with Heaven.
When contracted, affection should flow in a continued stream,
And the association should be uninterrupted.

ON MANAGING THE HEART.

For the purpose of controlling the whole body,
God has given to man an intelligent mind;
When the heart is correct, it becomes the true regulator
To which the senses and members are all obedient.

ON MANAGING THE EYES.

The various corruptions first delude the eye;
But if the eye be correct, all evil will be avoided:
Let the pupil of the eye be sternly fixed,
And the light of the body will shine up to heaven.

ON MANAGING THE EAR.

Whatever sounds assail my ear,
Let me listen to all in silence :
Deaf to the entrance of evil,
Pervious to good, in order to be eminently intelligent.

ON MANAGING THE MOUTH.

The tongue is a prolific source of strife,
And a multitude of words leads to mischief;
Let me not be defiled by lying and corrupt discourse,
Careful and cautious, let reason be my guide.

ON MANAGING THE HAND.

To cut off the hand whereby we are dragged to evil
Appears a determination worthy of high praise;
The duty of the hand is to manifest respect,
But for improper objects move not a finger.

ON MANAGING THE FEET.

Let the feet walk in the path of rectitude,
And ever follow it, without treading awry;
For the countless by-paths of life
Lead only to mischief in the end.

THE WAY TO GET TO HEAVEN.

Honour and disgrace come from a man's self;
But men should exert themselves
To keep the Ten Commandments,
And they will enjoy bliss in Heaven.

APPENDIX B.

EXPORT OF TEA AND SILK FROM CHINA,

Showing the State of the Trade before, during, and after the Occupation of the producing Districts by the Ti-pings.

[From the following Figures the Effect of their Presence upon Commerce may be judged.]

TOTAL EXPORTS during the Five Years immediately preceding the Outbreak of the Ti-ping Revolution.

DATE OF EXPORT.	TEA.	RAW SILK.
	Pounds.	Bales.
Year .... 1845—1846	57,580,000	18,600
,, ... 1846—1847	53,360,000	19,000
,, ... 1847—1848	47,690,000	21,377
,, ... 1848—1849	47,240,000	17,228
,, ... 1849—1850	53,960,000	16,134

Remarks.—These returns are quoted by Col. Sykes, M.P., in his pamphlet on "The Progress of Trade with China, 1833—1860," and are copied from the *Friend of China*, which journal, then established at Canton, published a tabular form, showing the total exports (exclusive of Ningpo) from all Treaty Ports, 1843 to 1858.

TOTAL EXPORTS during the First Three Years of the Revolution, while the Ti-pings were steadily progressing northward.

DATE OF EXPORT.	TEA.	RAW SILK.
	Pounds.	Bales.
Year .... 1850—1851	64,020,000	22,143
,, ... 1851—1852	65,130,000	23,040
,, ... 1852—1853	72,900,000	25,571

Remarks.—It will be seen that the progress of the rebellion did not interfere with trade, which continued steadily increasing.

TOTAL EXPORTS from date of Capture of Nankin, and many producing Districts, by the Ti-pings, to 1859.

DATE OF EXPORT.	TEA.	RAW SILK.
	Pounds.	Bales.
Year .... 1853—1854	77,210,000	61,984
,, ... 1854—1855	86,500,000	51,486
,, ... 1855—1856	91,930,000	50,489
,, ... 1856—1857	61,460,000	74,215
,, ... 1857—1858	76,740,000	60,736

Remarks.—It will be seen that the exports, although to a certain extent coming from, or passing through, Ti-ping territory, continued regularly increasing, especially in the case of the silk trade.

TOTAL EXPORTS during the Two Years preceding the Capture, of the entire Silk, and about half of the Tea, Districts.

Date of Export.	Tea.	Raw Silk.
	Pounds.	Bales.
Year .... 1858—1859	65,789,792	81,136
„ .... 1859—1860	85,938,493	69,137

Remarks.—These returns are carefully copied from the bi-monthly issues of *The China Overland Trade Report.*

TOTAL EXPORTS during the entire Occupation of the Silk Districts.

Date of Export.	Tea.	Raw Silk.
	Pounds.	Bales.
Year .... 1860—1861	87,220,754	88,754
„ .... 1861—1862	107,351,649	73,322
„ .... 1862—1863	118,692,138	83,264

Remarks.—The Ti-pings captured Soo-chow, the capital of the silk districts (and shortly after the *whole* of that valuable country), in the month of May, 1860. It will be seen that, instead of injuring the silk trade, at the termination of the next business year—season 1860-61, commencing June 1, 1860, and ending 31st May, 1861—they had *increased* it to 88,754 bales, the greatest number ever exported from China in one year; to 73,322, season 1861-62; and 83,264, season 1862-63; whilst the export of tea, mostly from regions in their possession, was raised from 66,000,000 pounds in 1860, to 119,000,000 in 1863! These figures cover the period of entire occupation of the silk districts by the Ti-pings, and their occupation of the tea districts of Fy-chow, Taeping-hien, and others in the provinces of Ngan-whui, Che-kiang, Kiang-si, and Kiang-su, and extend to the end of May, 1863.

TOTAL EXPORTS *since* the Ti-pings have been driven from the Silk Districts.

Date of Export.	Tea.	Raw Silk.
	Pounds.	Bales.
Year .... 1863—1864	119,689,238	46,863
„ .... 1864—1865	121,236,870	41,128

Remarks.—These returns prove, better than any history or argument, who were the devastators of the former Ti-ping territory. While the revolutionists held and governed the valuable silk districts, that article was produced and exported in larger quantities than had ever been known before. After the British had made the producing districts the theatre of the war, and finally succeeded in driving the Ti-pings out, the supply of silk at once fell to half the export during the Ti-ping dominion, and the second year after to still less.

APPENDIX C.

MEMORANDUM OF TI-PINGS KILLED DURING THE BRITISH HOSTILITIES AGAINST THEM.

Where Killed.	Date.	By what Force.	Number Killed.	British, or Allied, Casualties.
Before Shanghae, while striving to peaceably negotiate.	August, 1860	British and French	300	Nil.
Near the city of Soong-kong (twenty miles from Shanghae).	December, 1861	Ward's disciplined Contingent	2,000	100 killed and wounded.
At the capture of the village Ka-o-kiau	21st February, 1862	British and French	150	1 killed by a stray shot.
During the capture of stockades at Ming-hong	1st March, 1862	Ditto	1,300	Nil.
At capture of Wong-ka-dza stockades	4th April, 1862	Ditto	600	1 killed, 1 wounded.
Capture of the village of Lo-ka-kong	5th April, 1862	Admiral Hope's and Ward's forces.	500	Nil.
At the village of Che-poo	17th April, 1862	British, French, and Ward's forces.	900	Nil.
At the capture of the city of Kah-ding	1st May, 1862	Allied British, French, and Imperialists.	3,500	5 or 6 wounded.
At the capture of the city of Tsing-poo	12th May, 1862	Ditto	2,500	2 killed, 10 wounded. French admiral killed, 16 men wounded.
At the capture of the village of Na-jaor	17th May, 1862	British and French	500	5 wounded.
At the capture of the town of Cao-lin	20th May, 1862	Ditto	3,000	1 killed, 4 wounded.
During an engagement near Kah-ding	31st May, 1862	British naval & military forces	500	1 killed, 4 wounded.
Upon the expulsion of the Ti-pings from Ningpo.	10th May, 1862	British, French, and piratical flotilla.	150	3 killed, 23 wounded.
During the recapture of Kah-ding, Tsing-poo, Cho-lin, Chee-poo, &c., by the Ti-pings.	June, July, & August, 1862.	British, French, and Imperialists.	5,000	About 100, all told.
During the operations in the Ningpo district, leading to the capture of Tse-kie, Yu-yaou, Fung-wha, Shou-sing, and other cities.	August, 1862, to the end of 1863.	Force under Capt. R. Dew, R.N., Anglo-Manchoo, Franco-Manchoo, and Imperialist troops.	20,000	About 2,000 or 3,000.
At the second capture of Kah-ding	24th October, 1862	British, French, and Imperialists.	1,500	4 killed, 20 wounded.

APPENDIX.

Event	Date	Forces engaged	Numbers	Casualties
Engagement during Ti-ping attempt to recapture Kah-ding.	November, 1862	British, Ward's force, and Imperialists.	3,000	5 killed, 15 wounded.
During the repulse of the attack on Tait-san.	14th February, 1863	Anglo-Manchoo Contingent and Imperial troops.	1,000	2,500 killed & wounded.
Capture of Fu-shan village, and relief of Chang-zu	6th April, 1863	Filibuster General Gordon's force.	1,200	2 killed, 3 wounded.
Capture of the city of Tait-san.	2nd May, 1863	British, Gordon's, and Imperial forces.	2,000	200 *hors de combat*.
Massacre of Ti-pings during their evacuation of the city of Quin-san.	30th May, 1863	The Anglo-Manchoo disciplined and foreign-officered Contingent, and an Imperialist army.	3,000	Gordon's force, 2 killed and 5 drowned : Imperialist loss, about 300.
During the retreat of the Chung-wang's army from the northern provinces; caused by the British hostilities in the neighbourhood of Shanghae and Ningpo.	June, 1863	Died of starvation, made prisoners, and executed by Imperialists, and killed in action.	40,000	Loss of Imperialist troops, 2,000 to 3,000.
At the capture of Wo-kong city	29th July, 1863	Anglo-Manchoo Contingent and Imperialists.	150	1 killed, 15 wounded.
Engagements at Kah-poo.	5th, 6th, & 7th Aug. 1863.	Ditto.	1,000	50 to 100.
Engagements in the neighbourhood of Wo-kong	October, 1863	English, French, and other disciplined 'mutin-gout', assisted by a large Imperialist army.	3,500	About 200.
Engagements before Soo-chow, and capture of stockades outside the city.	September, October, November, and December.		6,000	About 2,000.
The Soo-chow massacre upon capture of the city.	3rd December, and subsequent days.	Imperialists.	30,000 Estimated by both Impts. & T.-pings at this No.	Nil.
Engagements around Wu-see and Chang-chow-fu.	November & December	Ditto	4,000	5,000.
Upon occupation of Wu-see (civilians put to death)	12th December	Contingents and Imperialists	6,000	Nil.
Capture of Yih-sing	2nd or 4th March, 1864	English Contingent	500	About a dozen casualties.
Defeat of Gordon's force before Kin-tang	20th March, 1864	Ditto	600	About 150.
Defeat of Gordon's force at Hwa-soo	30th March, 1864	Ditto	100	About 207.
Assaults upon Hang-chow (capital of Che-kiang), capture of Fo-yang, and other cities in the same district.	Jan., Feb., and Mar. 2nd, and 29th; April and May, 1864.	English & French Contingents, and several large Imperialist armies.	5,000	Loss of Contingents, 600 ; Imperialists, 3,000.
Massacre of non-combatants after capture of Kar-sing-foo.	End of March, 1864.	Imperialists and detachments of English Contingent.	7,000	Loss of Imperialists and detachment under Col. Bailey during the siege, 1,000.

MEMORANDUM OF TI-PINGS KILLED DURING THE BRITISH HOSTILITIES AGAINST THEM—continued.

Where Killed.	Date.	By what Forces.	Number Killed.	British, or Allied, Casualties.
Defeat of Ti-pings, and massacre of prisoners, at the village of Hwa-soo.	11th April, 1861	Imperialists and English Contingent under Gordon.	8,000	Loss of Allies, 100.
Repulse of Imperialist assaults upon Chang-chow-foo	24th and 25th April, 1864.	Ditto	3,500	427 of Contingent, 1,500 Imperialists.
Capture of Chang-chow, massacre of garrison and inhabitants.	11th May, 1864	Ditto	About 20,000	7 of Contingent, 300 Imperialists.
During the capture of Tan-yang, Kin-tang, Ly-heong, and all other Ti-ping towns, besides the districts in which they are situated, subsequent to the fall of Chang-chow-foo.	May to September, 1864.	Principally Imperialists, assisted by all foreign Contingents except Gordon's.	About 10,000	2,000 or 3,000.
During the siege of Nankin about 70,000 people perished from famine within its walls.	Ditto	Imperialists advised by Gordon, assisted by French officers.	70,000	Nil.
Killed during the siege	Ditto	Ditto	10,000	5,000 to 10,000.
Massacred after the capture of the city	18th & 19th July, and subsequent days.	.. ..	30,000	Very small.
Killed during the siege and fall of Hoo-chow-foo	January to September, 1864.	Imperialists and French Contingents.	15,000	9,000 to 10,000.
A rough estimate of the number of people killed during all the actions not recorded, captures of villages, skirmishes, &c., which were innumerable.	August, 1860, to September, 1864.	Imperialists, English, & French.	50,000	Much less.
To the above may be added *at least* 2,000,000 to 3,000,000 people who perished from the terrible famine occasioned, during the years 1863 and 4, by the allied operations, whilst the Ti-pings were being driven from their territories, and the whole country so utterly desolated as to be covered with the bodies of the starved and dying.	.. ..	.. ..	2,500,000	
TOTAL NUMBER OF TI-PINGS KILLED AND DESTROYED BY THE BRITISH INTERVENTION	.. ..	.. ..	2,872,550	

COX AND WYMAN,
ORIENTAL, CLASSICAL, AND GENERAL PRINTERS,
GREAT QUEEN STREET, LONDON, W.C.

www.ingramcontent.com/pod-product-compliance
Lightning Source LLC
Chambersburg PA
CBHW032139010526
44111CB00035B/616